Pe[...]
B<small>EHIND</small> B<small>AMBOO</small>

Rohan Rivett (1917–1977) was born in Melbourne. He was the son of the distinguished scientist David Rivett and a grandson of Alfred Deakin. He studied at the Universities of Melbourne and Oxford before joining the *Argus* newspaper in 1939 as a journalist. He was a war correspondent in Singapore when it fell to the Japanese in 1942, and survived as a prisoner-of-war for more than three years; *Behind Bamboo* (1946) documents his Second World War experiences. Rivett returned to journalism after the war and later became a director of News Limited and a director of the International Press Institute, Zurich (1961–1964). He published several non-fiction books and a biography of his father.

Sir Edward Dunlop, AC, CMG, OBE, KCSJ, MS, FRCS, FRACS, FACS, LLD (Hon.), DSc. Punjabi (Hon.), was born in 1907 near Shepparton in rural Victoria. 'Weary', as he is known, graduated in medicine and surgery just before the outbreak of the Second World War. He served with the AIF in the Middle East, Europe and the Pacific during the war. Captured in Java by the Japanese in 1942, he survived more than three and a half years in some of the most notorious Japanese prison camps; his devotion to his men and his inspirational leadership are legendary. Since his return to Melbourne in 1945 Sir Edward has continued to practise as a surgeon and has been actively involved in community service in Australia and abroad. He was knighted in 1969. *The War Diaries of Weary Dunlop*, his exceptional account of prison-camp life, was published in 1986.

AUSTRALIAN WAR CLASSICS
PRESENTED BY E. E. (WEARY) DUNLOP

BEHIND
BAMBOO

ROHAN D. RIVETT

PENGUIN BOOKS

Penguin Books Australia Ltd
487 Maroondah Highway, PO Box 257
Ringwood, Victoria 3134, Australia
Penguin Books Ltd
Harmondsworth, Middlesex, England
Viking Penguin, A Division of Penguin Books USA Inc.
375 Hudson Street, New York, New York 10014, USA
Penguin Books Canada Limited
10 Alcorn Avenue, Toronto, Ontario, Canada M4V 1 E4
Penguin Books (NZ) Ltd
182-190 Wairau Road, Auckland 10, New Zealand

First published in Australia by Angus & Robertson 1946
Reprinted 1947
New edition published 1950
Reprinted 1952, 1965
New edition published by Rigby 1973
This edition published by Penguin Books Australia Ltd 1991

10 9 8 7 6 5 4 3 2

Produced by Viking O'Neil
56 Claremont Street, South Yarra, Victoria 3141, Australia
A Division of Penguin Books Australia Ltd

Cover design by Jan Schmoeger
Printed in Australia by The Book Printer, Maryborough, Vic.

National Library of Australia
Cataloguing-in-Publication data

Rivett, Rohan, 1917-1977.
   Behind bamboo.

   ISBN 0 14 014925 2.

   1. World War, 1939-1945 – Prisoners and prisons, Japanese.
   2. World War,
   1939-1945 – Personal narratives, Australian. 3. Prisoners of
   war – Australia.
   I. Title. (Series: Australian war classics).
940.547252092

FOREWORD

I feel deeply honoured to be asked to contribute an introduction to what I regard as the classic account of prisoner-of-war life in the Japanese camps in Java, Singapore, Malaya, Thailand and Burma during the Second World War. I still cherish an autographed copy of the original 1946 edition. I have little doubt that the experiences Rohan Rivett describes so vividly in this book contributed to his early death. He is, however, one of whom it could be said, 'In a short time he accomplished a long time'.

Rivett possessed singular erudition and gifts of communication, allied to a sparkling mind and a lively sense of adventure. His release from the second AIF, late in 1941, was arranged to allow him to deploy those gifts as news editor of the Malayan Broadcasting Association. Characteristically, he volunteered to maintain radio broadcasts during the tragic days that followed the fall of Singapore.

Rivett's considerable experience as a journalist and his access to the high command equipped him to collect and store a wide range of invaluable records of captivity, which he maintained throughout his period of incarceration with a high sense of mission. The meticulous diary entries that salt the book have a stark immediacy and authenticity. I am well aware of the formidable difficulties and personal risks that were involved in maintaining such records at that time, difficulties and risks that were shared by prisoners who operated ingenious wireless sets.

The opening section of *Behind Bamboo* describes Rivett's escape from Singapore on a patrol boat, his arduous seven-day crossing of Banka (now Bangka) Island and the subsequent hazardous journey by rowing-boat some 700 kilometres down the coast of Sumatra to his final capture in western Java. Rivett's writing has the gripping sense of adventure found in the books of Defoe, Ballantyne and Stevenson that enthralled me as a boy.

After the high-spirited, personal adventure of the early chapters, the book becomes a meticulous, horrifying day-to-day record of appalling events in the 'hellships' and camps, where sickness, starvation and death were rife, and of the savagely driven, near-naked and emaciated wrecks who built the Burma–Thailand railway and performed other Herculean tasks. Some of the prisoners in the camps were executed for trying to escape or other reasons – a fate which they met with stolid bravery. Since the Japanese refused to mark prisoner-of-war camps, grievous casualties were also incurred when Allied planes bombed their own men.

Rivett's account depicts the grim humour, indestructible spirit, resourcefulness and mateship of the Australians working from the Burma end of the railway into Thailand. It testifies to the nobility of the many men who, in the last extremity of hunger, fatigue and illness, took upon themselves the burdens of others. Rivett himself suffered extreme attrition and was often covered with festering sores, yet he was always willing to give beyond the call of duty.

There is a sad line of Virgil, 'Time removes everything, even the memory'. The skin of civilisation remains perilously thin. It would be appropriate for the present generation, and for the generations of men and women yet unborn, to read this unvarnished tale of horror and of the triumph of the human spirit over adversity. The tens of thousands of men delivered to the Japanese were the victims of an ineptitude, selfish preoccupation and neglect that allowed events to drift until they assumed hideous proportions. The men's bitter confusion was increased by the contempt of a merciless foe who despised prisoners. Nevertheless, naked suffering stimulated them to rise to the very heights of the human spirit.

Rohan Rivett's whole life was characterised by scholarship, patriotism, articulate expression and, above all, generous action – the hallmarks of a brave, chivalrous and distinguished Australian. Perhaps hindsight might have added something to his judgements on the events of his times, but his immediate record is of immense value. Australia has been the poorer for the premature loss of his keen mind and inspired pen. *Behind Bamboo* will long remain an enduring memorial to one whose gallantry and usefulness equalled his distinction.

E. E. Dunlop

Wherein I spake of most disastrous chances,
Of moving accidents by flood and field,
Of hair-breadth 'scapes i' the imminent deadly breach,
Of being taken by the insolent foe
And sold to slavery, of my redemption thence
And portance in my travel's history;
— Othello, Act i, sc. 3

CONTENTS

FOREWORD TO THE 1945 EDITION

THIS book is the fulfilment of a pledge.

The great onrush of the Japanese hordes at the outbreak of the Pacific war submerged Southern Asia and the islands which stud the sea between Asia and Australia. In those lands, thousands of men, who strove in vain to dam the flood, were overwhelmed, slain or carried into captivity.

Yet it was these men who delayed the Japanese drive southwards. It was they who won for Australia the precious weeks and months which enabled her, with the aid of the United States, to transform this country into a mighty base from which, at length, were launched those operations which ended in the occupation of Japan.

An ominous silence descended over those engulfed by the Japanese flood. Overnight free men were delivered into bondage. Soldiers, sailors and airmen were reduced to a state below that of the coolie. The captor, scorning all international agreements, including those to which he had put his signature, now revealed the naked beast beneath the thin civilized veneer which he had so recently assumed. Every humiliation was imposed upon the captives to degrade them in the eyes of the local Asiatic populations.

With suffering and with bitterness a lesson was brought home to us: "In barbarous times, superior moral virtues — physical strength, courage, skill, discipline — were required for seizure of a supremacy; and in the hard evolution of mankind the best fitted stocks came to the fore. But no such guarantee exists today. There is no reason why a base, degenerate, immoral race should not make an enemy, far above them in quality, the prostrate subject of their caprice or tyranny."

Those words were written ten years before our capture by one seeking to arouse his countrymen to the paramount importance of the latest weapons and devices in modern war. The lesson was not heeded until after the writer, Winston Churchill, became Prime Minister of Great Britain. Japan's captives were among those who paid the price for that neglect.

For three and a half years we were cut off from the world we knew; our families and friends could learn little or nothing about our fate. Over sixty thousand of us, including twelve thousand Australians, were carried off into the jungles of Burma and Siam. Of these, many thousands will never return to their homes.

Some have come home permanently disabled or prematurely aged. No one of us has emerged quite unscathed. Our values, our aims, and even some of our beliefs, have changed. Yet, in a hard school, we have all learned lessons which must influence and assist us for the rest of our lives.

In many odd places throughout our captivity — on long marches, in the holds of hellships, in native jails and in bamboo-and-attap huts amidst the jungles — fellow prisoners, Australian, English and American, said: "You've got to write a book about all this. We're counting on you."

In the Burma jungle camps I resolved to write our story if I had the luck to come through. My pledge was made to four friends who did not live to see its fulfilment. So this book is dedicated to them and to all those fellow prisoners who rest for ever in jungle graves.

At the request of representatives of the British Ministry of Information, I was released from the A.I.F. at the end of 1941 to go to Singapore as News Editor, and subsequently War Correspondent, of the Malaya Broadcasting Corporation which was to be built up to become the Allied Daventry of the Far East. Shortly after the outbreak of the Pacific war, I flew to Singapore.

I have not attempted here to tell any part of the story of the Malayan campaign. The first part of this book is limited to an account of our attempt to escape from the Japanese net.

Thereafter, this is a story of one man's experiences in the Japanese prison camps. It does not purport to be the complete story. Doubtless things will have been omitted which others would have included. Yet if it brings home to our people some understanding of the Japanese mentality and if it gives some picture of our days and nights, our laughs and sorrows, our hopes and our fears, it will not entirely have failed.

Compared with many, I was fortunate along the railway. The full burden rested on the shoulders of those men who toiled day and night in the mud and rain. In paying tribute to their splendour, one has not forgotten the seamy side of our existence. In such a struggle for survival, there were, inevitably, selfishness, racketeering, meanness and injustice. Yet these things were small compared with the unbeatable courage and optimism and the sterling loyalty to comrades with which the vast majority faced starvation, disease and persecution.

Australians of the 8th Division, of the 7th Division units captured in Java, of the R.A.A.F. and the R.A.N. wrote a saga of Australian pluck and comradeship across the jungles of Burma and Siam. It is that story which I have sought to tell for those at home, on whose behalf these men were sacrificed.

Although this is a personal record, it is not merely one man's book. Many officers and men have helped in assembling its material. The notes and diaries on which it is based have been guarded and hidden with the assistance of loyal friends. At various times, materials for this book have reposed in the roofs of attap huts, in the bottoms of tins and bamboo containers, under the ground, in the framework of my bed and inside bandages strapped around my thighs and waist. The risk attached to "running" my papers through over a hundred searches lent excitement to even the dreariest and most sordid periods of our captivity. I hope that in the pages that follow my comrades will find some justification for their kindness and generous help.

Where I have drawn on my diary, I have edited it as little as possible, but have altered many nicknames and abbreviations in order to give a man's full name and unit or home town for purposes of identification. For odd errors in names and details, which may have crept into the text, despite all checks, I must plead as excuse the desire to complete the record as soon as possible.

My thanks are due especially to Staff-Sergeant Bev Browne, of Launceston, for aid in concealing some of my papers; to Captain Ron Winning and Lieutenant Peter Rossiter, of Melbourne, for their assistance when a part of my own records was lost; and to "Flip" Relf (2/4 Aust. A. Tk. Regt.), himself a P.O.W., for his excellent drawings.

Certain incidents and comments in this book have already appeared in part or in similar form in the *Argus*, Melbourne; News Chronicle, London; *Statesman*, Calcutta; the *Advertiser*, Adelaide; the *Telegraph*, Brisbane; *West Australian*, Perth; *Examiner*, Launceston; *A.B.C. Weekly* and the *Australasian*.

To Professor Walter Murdoch and to my father I am indebted for their review and criticisms. For the typing of the M.S. I must thank Mrs E. Lough of Upwey. My chief debt for success in finishing this book in the time available is due to my wife who assisted in ways too numerous to detail.

Sunningdale,   R.D.R.
   Upper Ferntree Gully,
      Victoria   *17 November 1945*

PART ONE

ESCAPE FROM ILLUSION ISLE

CHAPTER I

LAST HOURS IN SINGAPORE

Happy the man, and happy he alone,
He, who can call today his own:
He who, secure within, can say,
Tomorrow do thy worst, for I have lived today.
—DRYDEN, translation of Horace.

I GULPED in a deep breath and as the red light flashed on behind the microphone I said very carefully, "Attention everybody! Here is the communiqué just issued by Malaya Command: 'Last night after a heavy bombardment, enemy forces succeeded in crossing . . .'" and then I went on to read out the announcement which told the world that Britain's Eastern fortress had been violated and that the Japanese had landed on Singapore Island.

It was 8.28 a.m. on Monday, 9 February 1942, in Singapore. When I had finished, I took another deep breath and then repeated the statement. On the last word the technicians switched us over just in time to let Malaya hear the B.B.C. announcer in London say: "This is London calling." After about four minutes of news came the words: "We have just received the following announcement from Singapore", and London repeated to the world the communiqué that had been released from Fort Canning only eight minutes earlier.

All night our flat at the top of the Cathay Building had reverberated to the roar of gunfire from the other side of the island. I had been at my desk in the news room of the Malaya Broadcasting Corporation before 7 o'clock, but it had proved impossible then to get any official word of what was going on a few miles away.

Finally my chief, Mr R. H. Scott, a member of the War

Council and Director of Information and Publicity in Malaya, said that he was hopeful that Malaya Command would release a communiqué within a few minutes. I pointed out the urgency of getting it on the air before the B.B.C. news bulletin at 8.30, Singapore time. At exactly 8.26 the phone on my desk trilled and Scott dictated the communiqué. Ignoring the protests of my typist and the tambis, I bolted out of the room, raced up four flights of stairs, burst into the control room, barked: "Cut this ——— woman, and give me the mike!" at the technicians, and pushed open the door of the studio. A startled woman conducting the Tiny Tots' Breakfast Session rose like a rocketting pheasant from the chair in front of the microphone and I slid into it, gasped for air, and then let fly.

This business of combining the functions of news director, news writer, tambi and announcer was only an exaggerated version of what had been going on since 31 January, when I took over control of all news bulletins and commentaries put on the air from Singapore. The bulk of the M.B.C. staff was evacuated to Java on that day and a skeleton staff remained to carry on. In the news room where there had been a surging horde of some eighty news writers, typists, translators, monitors and tambis, H. D. Johns and I were left alone with a small fraction of the Asiatic staff. Nevertheless, we had been turning out seven news bulletins and two fifteen-minute talks or commentaries each day; and Henry Stokes of the Australian Broadcasting Commission was kind enough to write: "R. got down to it in Australian fashion and, working fifteen hours a day and more, did the work of the several men handling the same work before him."

Life was indeed hectic, but far more fun than it had ever been. I suppose we made dozens of mistakes. Indeed, I remember allowing a female member of the staff to put on the air "A Woman's View of Singapore Today" which a colleague justly described as "the world's worst talk ever broadcast". But there wasn't time to think twice about any decision, because when I wasn't dictating news bulletins or talks or trying to handle awkward brushes with army or air force

H.Q., or the censorship I was scouring round the island in my car trying to collect air-raid stories first hand.

The rest of the skeleton staff was marvellous and, realizing that the news room was the key centre of all broadcasting activities from Singapore, Mr Eric Davis, the brilliant chairman of the M.B.C., put himself at my disposal and said he'd do any job whatsoever that would help us through the crisis until the main staff managed to feed us with bulletins from Batavia. However, although they started to do this after seven days, their news was so patchy and out-of-date as far as Singapore was concerned that we carried on with our own bulletins.

At night at eight o'clock or at ten-fifteen—and sometimes at both—I went on the air with "Singapore News Talk" and "Singapore News Letter" on both medium and short wave. These talks were under the pseudonym of Terry Goulburn—a combination of my wife's maiden name and a good Australian one—since we were not allowed to broadcast under our own names. I never quite fathomed the reason for this restriction, but if it was to protect us in case we fell into the hands of the Japs, I probably owe my life to it.

As the unfortunate Singapore papers were absolutely starved of news of the progress of the Malayan campaign, these radio talks, which had a semi-official flavour and occasionally a little extra information, were plastered across the front pages of the morning papers. I am afraid that some of them were a shade melodramatic and flamboyant, but that was the mood of the moment and it was the mood we were trying to foster in view of the ordeal which the city was about to face.

One or two extracts from newspaper versions of these talks, mailed home before all communication was cut, may be interesting as an illustration of the mood of many soldiers and civilians in Singapore at the beginning of February. One, dated 2 February under a banner headline "This Is Our Greatest Hour", ran:

The Siege of Singapore has begun in deadly earnest. Japanese megalomania—the insane ambition of a group of ruthless military egotists—has brought this beastliness on the peoples of Asia and the Pacific. For five years these maniacs have been on the rampage through China, slaying, ravaging and destroying . . .

They have now reached the south of this peninsula. Today, we, the inhabitants of Singapore, stand full in the track of the advancing horde and so today it has become our turn to make history.

From Northern Norway to the southernmost point of Australia, from the snows of Russia to the pampas country of South America, the eyes of all peoples are on us tonight. . . . To us is given the opportunity to link ourselves in the world's story to peoples whose names will echo and re-echo down the corridors of history through all recorded time. . . . peace-loving, simple folk, who have been called upon to face the fury of Fascist terrorism in all its vileness. . . .

We of this island are now one with the people of Madrid who for month after month defied overwhelming odds with a heroism that lit a torch throughout the world. We join the fellowship of the garrison of the Westerplatte. . . . Today it is given to us to measure ourselves against the people of the little island of Malta where raid has followed raid in endless succession for twenty long months. . . .

We stand in the world spotlight, and the hopes and prayers of four-fifths of the people of this earth are with us in this hour. . . .

Bombs are no respecters of persons. They are just as likely to shatter the millionaire's palatial mansion as they are to fall on the tenement of the coolie he employs. The danger is common and equal for all. . . . It is true that today we are all in the front line, but the troops and the airmen are carrying the brunt of the conflict. We should never let them down.

The scythe of Fascist aggression has come a full sweep. . . . Now it has sliced across Southern Asia into Malaya until the blade is only a few score miles from Singapore. We stand in the path of the swinging stroke. . . .

This is our greatest moment. In after years we may well look back on it with pride as our supreme hour.

And, in fact, in the long years that followed in the Japanese prison camps, many of us did feel exactly that.

In another talk was a sentence which gratifyingly ran round Singapore like a catchy line from a popular song, "Singapore's maxim today: 'A war bird in our sky is worth fifty in America's.'" In my diary I noted: "This has caused more confusion among the local brass-hats than a bushel of Japs, but it has been chalked up as the saving feature of what I thought was a very humdrum talk."

These sections from a personal diary which got home to my family among the last mail to reach Australia from Singapore suggest something of the atmosphere of these days:

. . . I've seen more in the past month than in any twelve months of my life before—sights the horror of which beggars description and jokes of a Gargantuan standard—the sort of enormous jests that the Dealer only hands out to mortals when death is hanging over the game. There are so many things seen or heard which I cannot yet put down and may never put down. . . .

Let's set down the sights of one pair of eyes; at least here's a list of those that can be chronicled and which strike me at this moment. . . . Many men, in fact every living being on a boat, killed in an instant by a tremendous explosion apparently caused by a mine within half a mile of the shore as we stood watching the vessel from the veranda of the Cathay—something the tragedy of which only eats into you slowly. . . . Bombs, bombs, everywhere, bombs whistling down diagonally with an unmistakable scream, bombs bursting on streets, on shops, on houses, on military targets—eighty major raids in twenty-four days in this fair town. . . . A silent city glimmering in the gorgeous full moonlight waiting for the inevitable drone of bombers, as we saw it last night—so fair, so death-ridden, like a mad nightmare of blended beauty and horror defying description. . . . Comic things like the sight of the chief of British Information east of Cairo diving at a ditch and missing it—painfully—because of the appalling crash just behind him of—lightning! . . . One's own ludicrously inconsistent reactions, sitting wrapped up in a book, completely controlled, with bombs exploding all round, and then, less than twenty-four hours later fairly leaving one's seat because of the same lightning crash. Complete calm in the face of appalling horror and then a shaking through all one's system at missing an unseen four-inch step in the blackout. . . .

Here you see human souls in the raw. Here the mask is lifted for all time. . . . Today in Singapore there is only one colour line, the line between the yellow and the non-yellow, and it has nothing to do with race. It has nothing to do with being scared—we're all scared stiff half a dozen times a day. But the yellow line runs between those who go under and think only of escape and those who carry on. . . . I've come in the space of a week to rely on men I detested, and to despise men I wanted to like: in most cases intuition has proved right in sifting the trumps from the rubbish, but sometimes intuition has been false.

On several days we have had more casualties here than Coventry or London at the height of the blitz. No one who survives the siege of Singapore will ever be the same again. Most of us will be more ruthless or cynical or cruel or religious or melancholy or ribald for the rest of our lives. Because no matter how old or how young you may be this thing that is happening to us will change you. . . .

Norm [Norman Carter of the M.B.C. who flew over from Australia with me and who was sharing my flat] and I, the more we think of the position, feel that this situation is that one you strike only once in your life when you really are at the centre of all things. This is the time when you're weighed in the scales. If you live to see it through you have something behind you which establishes you better than all the dollars in the world. If you don't get through, you go out doing your job, which is the best way anyone can go out any time. . . .

Today I've got a chance—it may well be my last chance of any kind. On me falls the whole burden of keeping Radio Singapore on the air with news for the troops and for the million odd souls now huddled on this little island. . . . Eight of us carry on the whole show formerly carried by eighty. There will be assistance, but we are the skeleton to keep the thing running and, thank God, the news is the kernel and guts of everything, and it is my responsibility.

Declaratio fidei in modestate et veritate: (1) I hate bombs. (2) I'm scared out of my seven wits frequently and I'm good and uneasy for much of the time in between. (3) I vary between exaltation and profound depression—only really bad once.(4) I honestly and beyond all question would not rather be anywhere else: in fact, I'd hate to be anywhere else. "One crowded hour of glorious strife" [my misquotation] is certainly worth any number of ages of the other thing. . . .

A cameo—Jack Shepherd's room, eleven floors above the street, last night, above the city bathed in silver moonlight awaiting the bombers. Eight or nine of us in the darkness singing the songs of our childhood; the songs of America, England, Scotland, Ireland, Australia, to the accompaniment of Shepherd's concertina—singing for nearly two hours perhaps a hundred songs from "Tipperary" to "Way Down Upon the Swanee" from "Waltzing Matilda", to "Drink To Me Only", from "Clementine" to "Loch Lomond". . . .

Tues. 3 Feb. Well here is one man's day—my yesterday. It's not copyright, in fact anybody can have it free gratis and for nothing; it's what's termed "My Day", by Eleanor Roosevelt, only Eleanor would never have lived so long if she'd had a day like it. [Then follows a description of the day from 7 a.m. until 11 p.m.] In all honesty it must be admitted that my last two commentaries have been p.b. awful, but I'm not seriously worried 'cos you can't keep churning out decent stuff day in and day out when you're organizing the production of about fifty-five minutes straight news daily, writing two talks, having repeated conferences—important, confidential and trivial—and handling the problems of a staff of about thirty Asiatics, all of whom at this juncture in this island's story have more personal worries, grouches, problems and fears than a dog has—well, you know what a dog has. . . . These fourteen-hour days are a wonderful antidote to Jap attempts to break your morale, but you sometimes wonder how you'll ever tolerate life at a normal tempo again after the fierce exhilaration of always being about seven jumps behind where you ought to be and with an air-raid overhead. . . .

The whole tempo and atmosphere on Singapore Island changed drastically after the night of 8 February, when the

Japanese gained and maintained a footing on the island. Next morning, two hours after the broadcast announcing the landing, I was on my way with five other correspondents— among the last of a rapidly dwindling band which had numbered more than a hundred a fortnight before—to the field headquarters of the Australian G.O.C., Major-General Gordon Bennett.

As the house was being sought by Japanese bombers, and as it had been shelled on the previous day, we had to leave the car half a mile away and go up along the road, under the shelter of the bushes, in single file. Finally, we were all gathered in the presence of the red-haired Australian commander about whom so much controversy has raged. As usual, General Bennett was blunt and perfectly frank and anxious to disabuse the world of the false ideas about Singapore's security still promulgated through blind censorship and propaganda. He indicated that there was no possibility of preventing the Japs from reinforcing their bridgehead or from extending it each night along the northern shore of the island. After all the lies and absurdities handed out to correspondents from official channels, the Australian general told us the plain unvarnished facts and left us to draw our own conclusions. We were so sick of being given statements which everyone in Singapore and, above all, the Japanese enemy knew to be transparently false, that this interview was a refreshing draught of sanity in the midst of a flood of phantasmagoria from Alice's Wonderland.

All that afternoon we, the censorship, Malaya Command, and Gordon Bennett, fought a four-cornered fight as to how much of his statement could be published. The general stood by all his guns and said that it was far too late for anything but the truth. The wiser of the military and censorship authorities stood with him, but masses of red tape and traditional prejudice had to be trampled on before the following limited account could be released:—

I interviewed Major-General Gordon Bennett at Australian field head-quarters yesterday morning. Describing the Japanese landing on the previous night, he said that there had been considerable enemy shelling of our forward positions during the morning and afternoon. Japanese aircraft were constantly overhead reconnoitring our forward positions and gunposts. Firing grew heavier as evening approached, and a tremendous artillery duel developed at nightfall between guns on both sides of Johore Strait.

Japanese gunners, aided by aerial observations, destroyed some of our searchlights and forward posts, and it soon became evident that enemy troops were crossing the strait in force. On one occasion our lights revealed that many craft, of all types, were crossing the narrow strip of water.

A landing was effected only against a storm of fire from heavy guns and machine-gun posts. A series of fierce fights occurred round our forward posts, some of which successfully withdrew to a stronger line. Our guns must have taken heavy toll of the enemy.

My dispatch which, by permission of the Information authorities, was one of a series going to the Australian press, continued:

Singapore vibrated with continuous artillery fire throughout last night although the fire was never as heavy as during the hours before midnight on Sunday. . . . Even the sporadic shelling of the city has ceased temporarily. . . . The night was one of full tropical beauty, and it lent Nature's sublimely ironical smile to the human struggle. Meanwhile to thousands of British, Australian and Indian troops it was a hellish night of mortar and machine-gun fire.

On return from Australian Field H.Q., I was called to give an account of the general's views to the daily confidential conference of department heads in the Cathay. Sir George Sansom, chief of the Ministry of Economic Warfare, Mr R. H. Scott, chief of Information, Mr Eric Davis, chairman of the M.B.C., and other executives, received the blunt tidings with a mixture of resignation and dogged determination. Then we all went on with our respective jobs.

It would take many chapters to tell the full story of the next forty-eight hours. At intervals the city resounded to the roar of bursting shells from the Japanese long-range guns across Johore Strait and now and then the Jap bombers would scatter their pattern of death over the harbour or the city.

The evacuation of women, civilians, and certain selected key personnel of the services continued in the confused and disorganized fashion of preceding weeks, except that the disorganization was rather worse than before. Hundreds of private cars, abandoned by their owners, choked the approaches to the wharves. Japanese snipers were already active in some parts of the city and, on the night of the ninth, a bullet whistled past the head of Norman Carter as he stepped out on to the balcony of our flat for a moment at sunset.

Chinese morale throughout the city was on the whole very high, although there was nothing for the densely packed Asiatic population to do but sit in their homes and pray that the bombs and shells would fall somewhere else. Throughout this week the death toll ran into thousands daily.

Sporadically we saw a Hurricane or a Buffalo in the sky; but for the most part the hundreds of Japanese planes had the air above Singapore to themselves, and made full use of the privilege.

The story of the fighting on the island must be told in another place. It demands and will receive a book unto itself. As in the death struggles of all great cities overthrown in the course of war, there were countless instances of heroism, loyalty and self-sacrifice, just as there were instances of cowardice, desertion and selfishness. For one more time in the world's most terrible war the gigantic pageant of a great modern city's destruction had begun to unfold itself. The day was darkened by the dense pall of smoke from huge conflagrations all over the island; the night was made bright by soaring pillars of flame leaping hundreds of feet into the air. The whole unforgettable scene stood out against an orchestral accompaniment of heavy guns, bomb explosions and mortar and machine-gun fire.

By the Tuesday morning most of us in close touch with the situation knew beyond all hope that the end was a matter of days. That afternoon a fellow correspondent told me that General Bennett had told Ian Fitchett, official Australian war correspondent, to get out and that the last of the correspondents were already down at the docks or were leaving immediately. The end must come in three or four days and those who didn't get away were doomed to rot in Jap concentration camps, probably for years. He wanted me to leave with him. I said I had undertaken to carry on and that I was staying as long as we could transmit.

We were determined in the M.B.C. that we would stay on the air to the bitter end, but events on the Tuesday night moved so rapidly that, at dawn on Wednesday, the Thompson Road studios were under Japanese machine-gun and mortar fire and it seemed likely that the enemy would be in physical possession of the building by nightfall.

I was sitting at my desk in the news room at half past eight on the morning of Wednesday the eleventh when the phone rang and I heard Mr Davis's voice, hoarse with emotion, saying that he had been told by the military that we must close down at 11 o'clock since the transmitting plant had become untenable. It was a bitter blow, no less heavy because it was not unexpected.

Most members of the staff were already down in the basement of the Cathay awaiting transport to the docks. In the next hour the last of us received orders that we were to be evacuated to Java immediately to carry on from there. I heard that Mr Davis was staying alone, so rang and asked to be allowed to stay with him. He said some very nice things, but added that there was nothing more to be done and that he expected to get on a ship himself that afternoon. I had the satisfaction of seeing him on a ship that drew out of harbour just ahead of ours as twilight was falling. The Malaya Broadcasting Corporation was the very life-blood of Eric Davis, who had built it up from the humblest beginnings. His friends say he was a heartbroken man in the succeeding days. Although he reached Java with most other members of the skeleton staff, he would not leave that country and at the time of writing his fate is still uncertain.

CHAPTER II

FIERY LEAVE-TAKING

The flames and horrors of this fatal night;
The foes already have possessed the wall,
Troy nods from high and totters to her fall. . . .
Thus when a flood of fire by wind is borne
Crackling it rolls, and mows the standing corn. . . .
The palace of Deiphobus ascends
In smoky flames, and catches on his friends.
Ucalegon burns next; the seas are bright
With splendour not their own, and shine with Trojan light.
                                                    —*The Aeneid*

NORMAN and I arrived at the wharves about noon. The Japs gave us a warm welcome by dropping a packet all round the wharf and on the square leading to it. There was a bit of blast as we dived with more haste than dignity behind some piled sandbags, but no member of the party was injured. Ten minutes later a number of us put off in a motorboat tender and set out across the harbour towards the medley of shipping anchored at intervals all over Keppel Harbour. Eighteen Jap bombers chose this moment to sprinkle their cargo over the harbour, but no ship was hit except a small sampan about two hundred yards from us, which was set alight by a bomb splinter and blazed furiously for an hour or two before it sank.

Our motorboat drew up alongside a squat, ugly looking vessel of about 2500 tons which we afterwards learned was the *Siang Wo*, a Yangtze riverboat, used by the navy since the outbreak of war as a coastal patrol and anti-submarine craft. After the women on the tender had been placed aboard, married men were called for, so Norman and I threw in our lot with the *Siang Wo*. It was a fateful decision. Other members of the staff got on another boat and have never been heard of since. The majority went aboard a gaudily camouflaged gunboat and reached Java safely. But most of the shipping which lay around us off Singapore that afternoon was at the bottom of the ocean in or around Banka Strait inside the next seven days.

At this late hour the chances of getting through were slim indeed. I thought the odds against us about three to one. But this was too optimistic.

Getting on this boat I was separated from Johnny (H. D. Johns), the only other European member of the news room staff who had stayed on after the end of January. Bill Knox, war correspondent of the Sydney *Truth* and *Mirror* said to me thirty-six hours before the end that I was killing myself trying to do the jobs of nine men. He forgot that I had Johnny to help me, and he was worth a whole platoon. How Johnny, Norm and I met again is another story told later in this book.

Twenty minutes after boarding the *Siang Wo*, the ship's alarm bells clanged hysterically, and most of the two hundred odd naval officers, soldiers, and civilians aboard were herded below, although only some thirty could jam into the small shelter prepared on the lower deck. The rest of us crowded around as close to protecting sandbags as we could get. After about three minutes someone on deck yelled out: "Look out below!" and we heard the shrill scream of a bomb. Norman and I dived flat on our faces amidst a tangle of heads and boots, and a second later with a terrific bang a bomb went off close to the ship's waterline. Shrapnel tore through the hold, smashing itself against bulkheads, but the ship, after a lurching heave, settled back again.

Two minutes later the crew discovered that a large hole had been blown in the port side, about thirty feet from where we had been standing. For the next hour Norman and I, with other volunteers, shovelled sand and mixed concrete, passed down bags to block the hole and repair the damage.

There were three more raids in the next two hours and more shrapnel came aboard, but the most serious damage done was the bursting of the pipes in the officers' bathroom on deck. A gang of us met this emergency with a chain bucket system and at the end of the afternoon, apart from shrapnel scars, the ship was no worse off for these attacks.

There was much speculation and irritation among the passengers because we had to sit through the last seven hours of daylight acting as a kind of Aunt Sally for the Jap bomber pilots. They failed to realize that, once we were clear of the harbour ack-ack batteries, there was nothing to prevent the enemy from pressing his attacks home. The *Siang Wo's* sole armament consisted of a four-inch naval gun in the bows and a machine-gun on the stern. The naval gun was of very little use against aircraft, as it could not be elevated above forty-five degrees and had no ack-ack shells, so that only by the miracle of a direct hit could it bring down a plane. There was also a Bren-gun somewhere on deck; but it jammed early in the afternoon and was of no use to us subsequently.

About six o'clock a gunboat, camouflaged like a zebra's nightmare with grey, green and black, moved out of the harbour across our bows and we waved to Aubrey Herbert, M.B.C. programme director, and others on her deck. As twilight descended rapidly, we began to move slowly out of the harbour, but the coming of night did not bring darkness, because of the immense conflagrations all around us.

The tremendous pall of smoke which had overhung the entire island for the past few days had spread seawards and now stretched as far as one could see from horizon to horizon. Much of it was oil smoke from dumps on the island, reinforced by the gigantic soot-like clouds pouring from Pulau Bukom, where immense reserves of high octane fuel for planes were now being destroyed. Neither the Naval Base nor the dumps on the island, which had been set on fire either by our own sabotage or by enemy action, had provided anything comparable to the blaze on Pulau Bukom. It was calculated that it must burn for fourteen days before the vast tanks were destroyed. On this night of 11-12 February there were moments when the flames towered to a height of 600 feet, lighting up the harbour and the vessels in it as boldly as a hundred searchlights.

One could not help reflecting how often in the world's history a doomed city must have provided a similar display of awe-inspiring pyrotechnics. Here were horror and beauty, panic and heroism, tragedy and immense spectacle similar to those made immortal in the lines of Virgil and Homer describing the destruction of Troy three thousand years ago.

We crept slowly through the minefields and then anchored only a few miles outside the harbour. We lay here with many ships around us right through the precious hours of darkness.

I leant over the rail, listening to two of the survivors of H.M.S. *Repulse* telling the story of the last hours of *Repulse* and *Prince of Wales* a little farther up the Malayan coast, two months before. That had been the prelude to the piece to which the present pageant of destruction provided the climax in the grandest and most terrible tradition of the ancient drama.

Silhouetted by the surrounding fires, watching the labour and planning of many years and the fruit of millions of pounds of expenditure disappearing into clouds of smoke before one's eyes, one would indeed have needed to be mineral or vegetable to remain unmoved. Here was being enacted the last scene of one more major human tragedy, its very splendour underlining the magnitude and bitterness of our own defeat.

A few miles away across the island, thousands of Allied troops were making their last hopeless stand before the inevitable capitulation. No Australian could suppress feelings of bitterness and disgust at the thought of the difference between the impregnable fortress depicted for, and believed in by, the people of Australia, and the virtually defenceless island on which our troops with their British and Indian fellow-soldiers were now making a last stand. The fact that our own ship and the ships around us carried women, the last of whom should have been evacuated at latest at the beginning of January, deepened the general feeling that here there had been bungling on an appalling scale.

I dozed for a couple of hours on the deck and then got up to watch the first hint of dawn seeking to break through the haze which reduced vision to less than a hundred yards, even an hour later. In the silence of that grey and ominous dawn, I watched a lean British cruiser (I believe it was H.M.S. *Durban*) round up the seventeen ships which had left Singapore that night. Presently, one by one, they disappeared southwards into the haze. We were the last but one to move.

I learned later that *Durban* kept close to the fastest and biggest ship, one of the Empress boats, carrying a number of R.A.F., R.A.A.F. and naval personnel. These vessels were bombed throughout the day by waves of Japanese aircraft but, except for one hit on *Durban's* turret, they came through unscathed and reached Batavia within thirty-six hours. At least they diverted the attention of the Japanese bombers from smaller fry like ourselves during the whole of Thursday, 12 February.

Our vessel had a maximum speed of eleven knots at the best of times. Now, with an emergency fire crew and with the hole in her side, she nearly shook herself to pieces when asked to do more than eight. She soon proved to be the lame duck of the seventeen, and by eleven o'clock that morning, when we lay up in deep water within a few yards of two tiny, thickly vegetated atolls, all the others had disappeared over the horizon. One could not help feeling that whatever the merits of *Siang Wo* on the Yangtze, she was not the ideal vehicle for a desperate attempt to get from Singapore to Java at this particular moment in the world's history.

We had several alerts while hiding up between these islands, and then early in the afternoon we set off again. Planes, unquestionably hostile, were sighted once or twice; but they had other fish to fry. So darkness came down once more as we were labouring along, not yet half-way to the entrance to Banka Strait and not a quarter of the way to Batavia.

As some of us tried to doss down for the night on the main deck, comic relief was provided by a buxom red-haired charmer whom we shall call Ginger. Ginger had spent a sleepless night on the deck planks the night before and had announced in the morning that she had no intention of repeating the experiment. At nightfall she came round, highly supercharged with gin, to inform us that a beautiful bunk in a beautiful cabin had been procured for Ginger for the night. Just as we were settling down on deck Ginger emerged once more, *en deshabille*, saying that she could not find her silk nightie, and was not going to bed without it. A long and blasphemous search followed, during which our little party stoutly denied all knowledge of the missing garment. Finally, Ginger was led away, still protesting tearfully. I thought no more about it until daybreak when I started to unwrap the odd pieces of blanket, canvas and coats in which I lay. Then I discovered Ginger's nightie swathed decoratively around my feet!

It was Margaret Robinson, one of the seventeen women on the *Siang Wo*, and the last of the Cathay female staff to be evacuated, who said suddenly, just as we were all settling down for the night: "Do you realize what tomorrow is? It's Friday the 13th!"

I was not then superstitious to the smallest degree, but I must admit that I had an uneasy presentiment that Thursday had been too good to be true.

CHAPTER III

FRIDAY THE THIRTEENTH

Hold Infinity in the palm of your hand,
And Eternity in an hour.
—WILLIAM BLAKE

FRIDAY, 13 February 1942, dawned blue and cloudless, the morning sun making the sea a dazzling blend of sapphire and ultra-marine. The alarm bells jangled fiercely at ten minutes to eight, just as Carruthers, an M.B.C. announcer, Norman and I were trying to organize some biscuits, sardines and tea for breakfast. We decided not to try to get down to the shelter towards the stern, and went and lay in the companion-way between the officers' cabins below the bridge.

Planes droned to and fro overhead for five minutes and then two came down in an unmistakable dive. The four-inch having fired once when the planes were well down on the horizon, with no other effect than the shattering of glass in the wardroom and the scaring of most people out of their senses, our ack-ack barrage now consisted of sporadic rifle fire from a dozen .303 on deck and the brave chatter of the Lewis at the stern. Above it now came the familiar whine of bombs. There were four explosions and the ship heeled violently to port. From the deck above, someone yelled, "O.K.! All missed!"

Two minutes later the droning overhead changed into the roar of diving planes and again the whistle of bombs. This time there were only two and they both fell badly astern. Then the planes made off.

On deck we found that some more of the wardroom windows had been broken by blast and there were new shrapnel marks on the hull and bulwarks. I climbed up into the sandbagged gun-deck where the crew of the four-inch were sitting bemoaning the fact that as soon as the planes got over the ship they were helpless, because their gun could not be elevated sufficiently. They were loud in praise of the Old Man, who was manoeuvring the ship like a wizard each time the planes dived at him. Estimates of the height from which the bombs had been released varied between 1500 and 500 feet. "If only we had a Bofors!" we sighed in unison.

The rest of the morning was not exactly peaceful for anybody. At intervals of about ten minutes someone would yell "More planes!" or "There are four more heading in!" and then the alarm bells would peremptorily drive everyone below decks again. On three occasions planes circled over us for a while and then went off without dropping bombs.

I got very sick of climbing up and down the companion-way and when the bells jangled once again I decided to sit tight on deck with a plateful of exceedingly cold and uninteresting salmon kedgeree which was 99.9 per cent rice and the rest rather high salmon. Someone said there were eight bombers coming in, but I was ravenously hungry and went on eating. Then the gun crew sighted other planes to the east and the four-inch went off again. It was always a far bigger shock to the nervous system than the bombs, for you had plenty of warning when they were coming down. With more of the wardroom windows cascading down around the deck, I decided that discretion was the better part and clambered down the companion-way to join Norman Carruthers and his wife, and Margaret Robinson, who were lying in the gangway below the bridge. I had given one of the girls my tin hat, which had been an inseparable companion for the past month, and consequently had that peculiar sense of nakedness and vulnerability about the head which is a typical obsession in such circumstances.

I just had time to fling myself flat as the bombs went off. This time there were a couple of sticks of them and they tossed the ship about like a cork in a bucket. Someone on deck cried, "Great Christ! There's sixteen of the b——s coming in!" This did not conduce to any great cheerfulness, but the girls were marvellous and, except for one woman who cried hysterically for hours, they took it like Trojans.

The four-inch boomed off again, the sixteen planes went over and on to some other objective, and then two more dived at us in rapid succession but dropped all their bombs to starboard. Then we clambered on deck again and I went in search of my abandoned kedgeree. It was still there all right, but beside it on the middle of the blanket where I had been sitting, was a large piece of shrapnel which had smashed against the bulkhead exactly where my spine had been about thirty seconds earlier. After that, I decided that there would be no more nonsense about sitting up on deck to have a look.

Some fatuous Naval Reserve Officer in the wardroom, where several of them were sitting making a large hole in our very limited whisky supply, kept asserting, whenever planes were sighted, that this time they were definitely "ours". According to him the sixteen, which had actually been the usual Japanese Army 97 medium bombers, were British Hurricanes. I doubted whether all the whisky in Singapore, where there had been 35,000 cases in one dump near the godowns, would be sufficient to give me a similar happy illusion.

I went off and had another cigarette with the gun crew, a grand lot of chaps who were enjoying it immensely, since they had a grandstand view and were perfectly safe from anything except a direct hit behind their rampart of sandbags.

We reckoned that the odds on our being hit very soon must now be getting rather steep, for with our tortoise-like speed we were an excellent target despite all the skipper's manoeuvring, and we had nothing in the way of gunfire with which to stop the Japs from coming down to the masthead to ram home their attacks.

About noon four planes were sighted coming in from the east, probably from the bases which the Japanese had established in Borneo. As we reached our gangway between the cabins, we heard a bibulous voice outside declaring, "It's all right: they're Dutch this time!" These should be added to the list of famous last words, because the whistle of bombs followed instantly. Once again we heeled violently to starboard and all the bombs fell to port.

Between that moment and the time when we were actually hit was by my watch two hours and five minutes. But clock time had nothing whatever to do with the period during which we lay face downwards on the coir matting of the gangway, lifebelts flung over our arms, listening with the five senses given us by God and several faculties acquired during the past hours to the droning, roaring and whistling of circling and diving planes and descending bombs. We soon lost count of the number of times they came at us. Occasional remarks flung down at us from the officers on the bridge indicated that there were sometimes four, sometimes eight and sometimes more planes overhead almost continuously during this period, which may have been 125 minutes elsewhere but was more like 125 years on our chugging, rattling old tub.

We all knew that there was no reason why the attack should not go on until darkness came at seven o'clock, but the minute hands of our watches remained utterly immune to our pleading glances. Again our friend in the wardroom assured everybody that two more planes, just sighted on the horizon, were Hurricanes coming in to deal with our persecutors; but this time he provoked only an outburst of profanity, because nerves had become a little too strained.

Finally, about half past two, there was a yell from the deck synchronizing with the scream of bombs, and then a terrific explosion which made the ship shudder from stem to stern. She seemed to lose way immediately, while a deafening noise of escaping steam came from the burst pipes. Several of us hurriedly scrambled on deck, but there was only confusion until someone managed to assure the bulk of the passengers, huddled down in the aft hold in and around the shelter, that the ship was in no immediate danger of sinking.

Norman and I soon discovered that she had been hit aft. The bomb had burst either right on the very stern or on the waterline just above the rudder, blowing the Lewis-gun post to smithereens, smashing the steering-gear and slightly damaging some deck gear near the stern. We made our way there and joined forces with several members of the crew who were trying to do something about the steering-gear. In the meantime, the vessel had begun to describe a series of circles about 300 yards in diameter, in the most pathetic fashion.

We were just off the northern tip of Banka Island and could see the Muntok lighthouse, which marks the entry to Banka Strait.

I know very little of what went on on deck during the next two hours because we were making Herculean attempts to get the emergency steering-wheel into action. Norman Carter had served his apprenticeship on the *Worcester* in the days of Edward VII and it stood him in good stead now, for the ship's officers were too busy on deck to take charge of operations, and Norman directed the show.

After a good deal of profanity and the loss of some temper and much sweat we managed to get the rudder answering to the emergency steering-wheel in the stern and the ship ceased to go round and round inanely like a decapitated hen.

Thanks to some merciful dispensation of providence, the enemy bombers had apparently decided that we were helpless and that they had better targets elsewhere because, after being hit, we remained unmolested. However, I subsequently learned in Batavia that, from half past two onwards, the Japanese concentrated on seven ships of our convoy which were then just at the other end of Banka Strait. Captain Daniels, a British M.O., told me that from the deck of the smallest of these vessels he watched the Jap bombers sink or set on fire each of the other six ships within the space of an hour. It was impossible for his own ship to make any attempt to pick up the survivors struggling in the water, and in his belief very few, if any, from these six ships would have had a chance of getting ashore. His own vessel got through only because most of the bombers had used up their cargoes.

On the *Siang Wo* it had been decided to try to get the women off to Batavia on a small trader's boat which was lying just off shore near Muntok. About five o'clock the seventeen women, including Mrs Leong, the wife of my Chinese typist, were put off in one of the ship's boats.

But the trader's boat developed engine trouble and finally only two women—Mrs Robinson and Mrs Marsden—left for Batavia in a tiny R.A.F. yacht, which was the only other boat available. The other women were put ashore that night.

The captain of the *Siang Wo*, after consultation with the ship's officers, and with the two senior lieutenant-commanders among the Naval Reserve evacuees, decided that the ship was too crippled to have any chance of reaching Batavia, and therefore resolved to beach her on the Banka coast. Already two or three smaller ships lay high and dry, not far from the lighthouse, where they had been beached, as a result of earlier attacks.

We therefore ran inshore until the keel grated on the bottom as we came to rest a few hundred yards from the Muntok jetty. The captain, having gone ashore and conferred with the Dutch resident, who was practically the sole remaining Dutchman in Muntok, reported that the Japanese had been expected hourly for the past week and that there had been a general exodus towards Java. As a result of this, and of sabotage by the local natives, there was not a single navigable boat to be had at Muntok for love, money or murder.

On being told of the situation by the ship's chief officer, I went up to the captain's cabin and suggested to him that, since I had authority for sending receiver-paid cables from any part of the world to Melbourne, I might send word of our plight to my paper for relay to Navy Department, Melbourne, in the hope that a destroyer or M.T.B. could be sent out from Batavia to pick us up. The captain favoured the idea at first and I was about to leave the vessel to go ashore when one of the Naval Reserve commanders said that such action would be breaking the imposed ban on the use of wireless. Whether, in fact, in these circumstances "wireless silence" should have been kept, only the naval authorities can determine, but we did feel that some effort of this kind should have been made to get the women away to Batavia immediately.

Authority was now handed over to the senior officer among the naval evacuees, and he determined that everybody should stay on the ship until nightfall. This seemed an unnecessary folly for, however vulnerable we had been before, we were ten times more so now, stuck fast on a sand-bar with not even our Lewis-gun in the stern to protect us. The Lewis-gun and the Malay operating it had been the only major casualties caused by the explosion at the stern of the ship.

Really, we were amazingly lucky to be still alive. A piece of shrapnel from the bomb had lodged within two inches of one of the depth charges we carried in the stern. Had it been detonated every soul on the vessel would have been instantly blown to smithereens.

Most of us were so exhausted by the strain of six and a half hours of almost continuous bombing that we did not worry much during the last period of daylight in what might, in other circumstances, have been a very grim vigil. We ransacked what remained of the ship's stores, but even then did not get a square meal.

Finally, after dark, by the light of a couple of hurricane lamps, carefully shielded, we trooped down the gangway into two large barges which had been brought out from the shore. The less said about the evacuation of the ship the better. The Naval Reserve officer in charge was exceedingly drunk and particularly rude throughout the evacuation. At the end he kept us waiting at the ship's side for ten minutes while he detailed a rating to search for his gear which he had mislaid. When we got to the jetty, he capped an ignominious performance by kicking the baggage belonging to some of the women into the water in a fit of rage. None of this luggage was recovered.

After some delay ashore, all officers and civilians, together with the fifteen women who had not got away to Batavia, proceeded to the Muntok Hotel, while the ratings and troops on board went to the Y.M.C.A. hall in another part of the town. The Eurasian proprietor of the hotel had never seen such an invasion in the island's history and declared that he had no food or accommodation to cope with it. However, beds were found for all the women, while fourteen of us shared one bedroom, four in the double bed.

So ended what must have been one of the loveliest days of that season, for there had not been a cloud in the sky from dawn until dark. Unfortunately, we had had few chances of appreciating it. I felt as Macbeth felt: "So foul and fair a day I have not seen."

CHAPTER IV

INTO THE BANKA JUNGLE

The untented Kosmos my abode,
I pass, a wilful stranger;
My mistress still the open road
And the bright eyes of danger.
—R. L. S.

THE next day, Saturday the fourteenth, was enlivened by a series of attacks by Jap fighters and bombers on the Muntok area. Discovering that Muntok boasted only one gun of any kind, they conducted some of these at tree-top level which, in the state of nerves to which some of the party had been reduced, was scarcely helpful. Norman and I spent most of the morning and afternoon first in the slit-trench behind the hotel and then out in the jungle, in the intervals of trying to find out what was being done to get boats. The Japanese had a wonderful time bombing the abandoned *Siang Wo*, but although they scored a very large number of near misses, she remained as unhittable as ever. They also dropped a few bombs on buildings in the centre of the town and on the aerodrome but, although they came down very low looking for us, they apparently failed to spot the hotel which was partially hidden by tall trees.

The hotel proprietor was convinced that local Japanese agents had informed the enemy by radio of our presence, and he was expecting to see his hotel go up in smoke at any moment. I am afraid that, in the light of what we discovered about his food supplies after he had kept us starving all day, some of us would not have been unduly upset if his fears had been fulfilled.

Towards evening, Norman and I walked across the square,

or public gardens, in the middle of the town to the resident's house. He was out on his veranda burning the last of his official papers, and gloomily informed us that there was not a boat left along the whole of the Banka coast and that the Japanese were arriving before midnight. The last of his fellow Dutchmen had motored off that morning, but he had orders to stay and hand over to the Japanese when they arrived. He offered no solution to our problem about getting the women away, but asked us what we thought the Japanese would do to him. As he was such a Cheer-up Society and as I thought the whole business of his remaining very fishy, I expressed the opinion that they would certainly shoot him.

Norman and I went back to our bedroom where a conference was proceeding among certain members of the party who were getting restless at the attitude of the Naval Reserve commander, who seemed incapable of action of any kind. We got a few hours' sleep and then I woke up to hear somebody whispering feverishly out in the main hall, and the first words I could distinguish were, "They're pulling in towards the jetty now. They'll be here in the next two hours—thousands of 'em!" One had no doubt who "they" were. It was now about 3 a.m. I pulled on some clothes and joined the conference in the hallway. The sentries who had been posted down at the jetty said that a large number of ships had entered Banka Strait from the north-east just before midnight. Cruisers and destroyers were recognizable among them. After much shouting and signalling, both from the shore and from the ships, many boats were lowered, and when the last sentry left the wharf some hundreds of soldiers were already only a few hundred yards from the shore.

Commander Vickers, who had now taken charge, decided that all the women should be sent forthwith to the Dutch hospital, where they would be with the nursing sisters and under the Red Cross. Those who had husbands among the party were escorted by them. The commander then issued orders to all officers to jettison their revolvers and prepare to surrender at the hotel. So arms and ammunition were thrown out into the jungle and the forty-odd officers stood by to surrender.

Nothing happened during one of the least cheerful hours I ever remember.

In the meantime some of us had been carefully conning an old map of the island, of pre-Great War vintage, which hung as joint adornment of the hotel lounge with the famous poster of a Balinese beauty which has brought so much tourist revenue to the Dutch East Indies. Just as day was breaking, several of us told Commander Vickers that we thought it our duty to attempt to escape, and asked permission to make a break for it. The commander said hastily that we were mad, since we knew nothing of the swamps and mountains of the island and would certainly get picked up by a Japanese patrol and shot out of hand. If we stayed and surrendered formally in the hotel we might be taken prisoner.

However, when further representations were made, the commander changed his mind and said we could do as we liked, although in his opinion it was sheer suicide. At this critical moment, the hotel proprietor had a change of heart, or heard the whisperings of conscience, and suddenly opened up a pantry stocked with tinned foodstuffs of every kind. We were so hungry that we spent the next ten minutes eating soup, condensed milk, potted meat, fish paste and jam straight out of the tins with a spoon.

Then, just as we were departing, there was an alarm from the picket on the veranda and someone said, "It's no good, it's too late!" But it turned out that the occasion for the alarm was only the passing of a native soldier pedalling flat out on his bicycle. Without more ado, we went out of the back of the hotel and plunged straight into the tangled mass of banana and date palms and mango-trees. Before we had gone 200 yards we were hailed from the rear and joined by the chief officer and second officer of the *Siang Wo*—Kinnear and Marr.

So, finally, there were seven of us—three officers of the Malaya Naval Reserve, Kinnear, Marr, Norman Carter and myself. We little knew, as we set off together, that we were embarking on an Odyssey of which even Ulysses would not have been contemptuous. It was about half past six on the morning of Sunday, 15 February. As we climbed a knoll, keeping as far as possible in the shadow of the trees, someone said, "Do you think they're still fighting in Singapore?"; and I said, "They may be but I doubt if they'll be still fighting tonight." It was only a month later that I learned how accurate this had been.

After going for a little over an hour we stopped to take stock of our assets. We found that between us we had thirteen small tins—mostly sample size—of foodstuffs, one pound tin of cocoa and roughly 300 cigarettes. We had an impossible amount of clothing, much of it white naval uniform, totally unsuitable for an attempt to evade Japanese patrols in the jungle. Thanks to the unfortunate order regarding revolvers, we had nothing more lethal than a jack knife between the seven of us. We stripped ourselves of everything except one change of clothing and a few personal possessions and set off again, climbing up the shoulder of the first of a series of steep, thickly-wooded ridges.

Half-way up we heard the chatter of machine-gun fire and, from an outcrop of rock, saw a couple of Allied bombers, which I subsequently learned were Lockheed Hudsons of No. 1 R.A.A.F. Squadron, making a hit and run raid on the Japanese flotilla of cruisers, destroyers and transports anchored in Banka Strait, from which the landing had been made. Japanese fighters went off in hot pursuit of the Australian pilots, but the boys managed to give them the slip in the clouds.

It was weary work clambering over the rocky spurs and ridges, some of which were masked with heavy undergrowth. But we had worked out a plan of campaign from the old map which we had brought with us, and were determined to get over a road which ran across the island some twenty miles from the hotel, before darkness fell.

Banka Island is rather like a shrimp lying alongside the great fish which is Sumatra from which it is separated by Banka Strait, the strait varying in width from ten to twenty-five miles. Banka itself is 138 miles long and 62 wide and is covered with various series of granite hills and ridges from which many rivers run in deep valleys to the sea. The guidebooks remark that "in their upper courses they form extensive marshes". We made a personal study of this feature, involuntary but thorough.

In peace time Banka produces well over 20,000 tons of tin per annum and is, for its size, by far the richest tin-mining area in the world. The natives are chiefly Mohammedans and are closely allied to the tribes found in Sumatra. At the stage when we set out on our forlorn attempt, the monsoon, which brings heavy rain between November and February, was nearing its end; but we found that it rained either day or night at least once in each twenty-four hours. We decided to press eastwards across the island towards the opposite coast from Muntok; then, having got well clear of the coast and the main Jap forces, to turn south, struggle across the central range marked in our map, and get a boat in which we could row down one of the rivers flowing from the range, until we reached the coast again well south of Muntok.

Checking our bearings every few minutes with the compass and praying feverishly that the antiquated map still held good, we made rather slow progress for the first eight hours, for our course lay across a seemingly unending series of ridges and hill shoulders. We did not dare to keep to the tracks in the valleys and hollows because, from our knowledge of the Nip in Malaya, we felt certain he would spread patrols fanwise throughout the island. The older members of the party were emphatic that we could not afford to take chances with any of the natives, particularly as there had already been much evidence of local collaboration with the Japanese. In the interests of speed, which I felt to be vital, I was for taking the risk and using the native paths; but I was overruled. This was probably just as well in the light of subsequent events.

About two o'clock, high up on a hillside where the vegetation was not unlike that of the Dandenongs at home, we struck a kind of path and, since all were wearied by the constant battle with scrub and undergrowth and since it ran approximately in the right direction, we followed it until, without warning, it emerged on a cart road. At that moment a native on a bicycle rounded a corner and on sighting us stopped dead in his tracks, then turned round and pedalled off in the opposite direction as if his life depended on it. We took rather a poor view of this, but since the road was fringed by most inhospitable jungle we stuck to it and moved very fast for the next hour.

Then we met an old native who courteously conducted us to his kampong, a structure typical of this part of the world, with a bamboo floor some five or six feet above the ground, supported by stout bamboo posts. Here we were given water and some unhusked rice in a bag.

One of the Naval Reserve officers, a red-haired Welshman named Wade, spoke Malay fluently, and he acted as interpreter on most occasions, for the rest of us had little more than a sketchy knowledge of the language. The old man knew that Japanese were scattered over the island, but could not tell us much more. However, he guided us down the road until eventually we came to a large rubber plantation extending to some depth on both sides of the road: here we parted company. We were rather worried about two cyclists who had followed us for a while observantly and then gone off at high speed ahead of us. So we turned off the road into the rubber and went across to a native hut from which smoke was visible.

Two youths, a middle-aged woman and some small children were in the hut, and the woman made us welcome and proceeded to cook rice for us. We were trying to get eggs, salt and sugar, but the natives were very short of all these commodities and, since we had no Dutch guilders but only Malayan dollars, we could obtain nothing.

As we sat sipping tea waiting for the rice to cook, Kinnear called our attention to the fact that the second of the two youths had now disappeared, as his companion had done immediately after our arrival. However, we were very tired and not unduly alarmed until Wade, who had been talking to the woman, let out an exclamation: the woman had just told him that a patrol of twelve Japanese had lunched in this hut and had said they would be back for another meal at six o'clock; but they might now be back sooner if the boys had gone to look for them. It was twenty-five minutes past five, and we did not stay upon the order of our going. The woman, unquestionably sympathetic, gave us a heavy iron pot full of red, or unpolished, rice and we went off at right-angles to the direction from which we had approached.

We had just reached a small creek at the edge of the rubber estate when Norman discovered that he had left the precious map behind. We had a bad five minutes while he sought for the rubber-tree under which he had left it. In this part of the world, looking for a particular rubber-tree in a rubber estate is rather like needle-seeking in a haystack. But luck was with us and when Norman arrived back at the run we set off again, our tiredness forgotten.

Just as it was getting dark we came to a patch of swampy marshland from which the trees had been cut away. Across the swamp, not more than five hundred yards from where we stood under shelter of the trees, there was a lookout tower manned by what we decided, after one look, was unquestionably a Japanese sentry with a machine-gun. We therefore decided to wait until the light had almost gone before attempting to cross the swamp. In the meantime we had a spoonful of pork and beans each and a little condensed milk, the first of our food we had eaten since starting.

The last light was fading fast when we set out on hands and knees among the fern and stunted undergrowth which covered the strip of open ground. The first serious barrier was a narrow but swift stream, the bottom of which we could not reach with a stick. As far as we could see in the gloom, the sentry was facing in the opposite direction, so I took a chance and made a running leap at the stream to try to reach a projecting foothold of stone and mud in the middle. A moment later I was up to my armpits in water, my feet sinking in treacherous soft mud. It was not at all a good moment for we knew that this area abounded with quicksands and bogs which would suck a man under in a minute or two. However, after some desperate floundering, I managed to seize a bough projecting from the opposite bank and clambered ashore with no worse damage than the separation of the sole of one shoe from its upper.

After a careful reconnaissance, we found a better fording point for the others, but then found ourselves confronted with a wide billabong of uncertain depth. We lay in some rushes on the edge of this until the twilight had deepened to a point when we could not distinguish the sentry on his tower. Then in Indian file we struggled across the backwater which proved to be no more than waist-deep.

On the other side of the marsh was a native pineapple plantation and after much searching we located two small rather green pineapples. Added to the massive iron pot they made it a formidable burden, so we transferred it among us every half hour as we fought our way through dense scrub not unlike the coastal tea-tree at home.

It was now completely dark, but in the distance ahead we suddenly caught the note of a car's engine and presently a gleam of headlights showed us where the road lay, apparently not more than a mile away. We had begun to think of this road as something swallowed up by the jungle since our ancient map had been drawn, because we had been moving almost without pause for over fourteen hours without striking it.

Unfortunately, we now found ourselves descending into a hollow, although the road lay above us. The next hour was pure nightmare. There was no path of any kind and when the solid wall of vines and shrub yielded for a moment, we found ourselves up to our knees in liquid mud. We were loath to use our torch continuously, for we had only two small batteries, but the undergrowth hedged us in all round and was just too high to enable us to see anything. We made casts first to the left and then to the right, but only plunged deeper into the treacherous morass. Finally, disregarding direction, we headed for higher ground and, after a wide detour, broke away from the heavy thickets around the hollow. The moon now lent us a little light and after a long climb we found ourselves at last within thirty yards of what was obviously the motor road.

Here we held a whispered conference, because we felt fairly certain that the Japanese would be maintaining constant patrols along this, the only main road in this part of the island. Finally two of us crept silently up to the steep bank at the road's edge, dropped down it, raced across the road where a patch of shadow gave some protection from the moonlight, and scrambled up the bank on the other side. Then, one by one in quick succession, the others followed suit.

We had now reached our first objective, but were agreed that it was dangerous to camp within half a mile of the road. Unfortunately the jungle on the far side of the road was almost impenetrable and we made a fearful threshing noise as we tried to batter our way through the matted network of interlacing branches, vines and thorns. Little Tommy Marr, who was far from well, had been doing his turn with the iron pot down in the swamp, and was now utterly exhausted. So after half an hour's battling, during which we managed to get perhaps two hundred yards beyond the road, we decided to call it a night, as the ground again began to trend downwards and we could hear the sound of running water in front of us.

We decided that each man should act as picket for an hour. We should have liked to light a fire but felt that we were still too close to the road. We had just wrapped ourselves in what blankets and spare clothes we had—for the night had turned very chilly and wet—when there was a low whining sound which turned into a snuffling roar some twenty yards off to the left. The natives had told us that there were tigers and mountain leopards in the jungle, and I must admit that for the next hour I was more worried about man-eaters than about the Japanese. However, there was no further incident during the night, although the picket who woke us before dawn, at half past five, reported that a large animal had come crashing up the hillside from the stream below us after he had thrown a heavy stone down the hill.

As soon as there was any light we lurched sleepily down the slope and, after ten minutes of awkwardly picking our way across a series of tiny rivulets, climbed up another ridge and resumed a course roughly parallel to the road. In daylight the jungle was not nearly so formidable as in the darkness, for which we were duly thankful, our faces, hands and arms having been painfully scratched and lacerated during the preceding night. After about an hour we found a track which obviously led back to the road. If we were to adhere to our intention of describing a kind of horseshoe, it was obvious that the road which turned sharply here had to be recrossed, so we decided to get it over there and then. Once again, after a swift reconnaissance, we made a dash across, but were not more than a few yards into the jungle when we heard voices on the road. We crouched down where we were in a little natural arbour made of dead branches and rotting tree-trunks while one of the party peered out on to the road. A party of some twenty natives, some of them armed and on bicycles, streamed past, chattering shrilly. Had they come a minute earlier they must have seen us.

Half an hour later we came to an underground spring and decided that the clamour of the inner man could no longer be denied. So we built a fire at the bottom of the hollow by the spring, praying that the smoke would be sufficiently diffused by the tree-tops to escape observation. Then we proceeded to bathe and attend to our cut and blistered feet while the rice boiled merrily on a good fire. We there and then appointed Norman as cook, and well and nobly did he perform that office during the trials of the succeeding weeks.

Norman has had a variegated and colourful passage through life. As a boy, after serving his apprenticeship on the *Worcester*, he spent three years before the mast all over the world, ranging from Sierra Leone to Sumatra and from Barbados to Bombay. He served in Mespot. and subsequently with Dunsterforce during the war and then managed a pantomime company on tour through the British Isles. Coming out to Australia, he farmed for a while in the Albany area in W.A. and then came east and went on the stage again. During the thirties he spent most of his time in the radio game with various stations between Toowoomba and Melbourne. Just before the war, he completed a 1200-mile overland journey through Queensland and New South Wales with packhorses. In bushmanship and general knowledge of dodges for combating nature in such circumstances as we were in he ran rings round the rest of us, and I do not know how we should have got through without him.

After an enormous meal, which taught us just how much plain boiled rice one can eat when one is really hungry, we plunged on and at length emerged from the jungle and found ourselves amidst a chain of abandoned tin-mines inundated with water. In the late afternoon we came to some cleared land with a handful of scattered native kampongs. On the raised veranda of one of these we were hospitably entertained with tea and boiled rice. However, an aerial fight overhead between an Allied reconnaissance machine and Japanese planes scared the natives, who immediately made haste to speed us on our way. They were very alarmed lest the white uniforms of the naval officers should be spotted from the air and bring bombs or bullets spattering down on their huts. About five o'clock we found ourselves in a forest where lumber work had been proceeding and, finding a small spring with clear flowing water, we bivouacked for the night. The mosquitoes were ferocious, but we were so tired that we all slept like the dead until roused at first light.

Tuesday, the third day, found us again in very bad jungle. For three hours in the morning we battled our way painfully through some of the worst tropical vegetation I have seen in Java, Burma, Thailand or anywhere else. I doubt if we covered more than a mile in the three hours, and probably did not make two hundred yards in the right direction. Thousands of tenuous trailing vines, many of them spiked with countless thorns, stretched their tentacles lovingly around us at every step. Clumps of bamboo and thorn-bush hemmed us in so that at times we just stood and hacked for ten minutes on end without progressing five yards. A parang, or heavy native knife, which we had picked up in an abandoned hut on the previous afternoon, was worth its weight in gold in this country.

In the afternoon we ran slap into another hilly belt and spent all the rest of the daylight in climbing up precipitous rocks and along the slippery faces of ridge after ridge. When we finally got clear of the range, we bivouacked at the confluence of a number of small rills and mountain streamlets. There was a furious debate here about the wisdom of lighting a fire, for we were overlooked from many surrounding hills. However, the Warmth and Light Party won the day, for which I was duly thankful during my picket hour just after midnight.

I had heard some animal come down to water about forty yards from our camp-fire and could hear it splashing about in the stream. Suddenly there was a snarl followed by a series of hair-raising screams and a tremendous threshing among the bushes on the bank of the stream. For about three minutes there was what I judged to be an all-in fight or, perhaps, slaughter in which the combatants seemed to be some sort of pig and some carnivore of the cat family. Then suddenly the pig's screaming ceased, and silence descended once more like a blanket over the jungle.

There are doubtless intrepid sportsmen who feel that I should have investigated the matter personally and joined in the fray, but I am not sure that even they would have been quite so alive to the sporting interest at that particular hour of the night God-knows-where in the Banka jungle, particularly if they had been armed only with some three feet of stick.

In the morning we discovered a considerable quantity of blood and fur on the bank of the rill where the fight had occurred, but there was nothing to indicate the nature of the pig's assailant.

We tramped on for about four hours and then, as it was raining heavily, took refuge in a disused native hut in the middle of a large plantation of tea and wild maize. Since leaving the hotel we had spent forty-five hours out of seventy-seven in battling our way through the jungle, and since we had some rice, four eggs which we had obtained from a native, and a couple of nearly ripe jack-fruit, we decided to lie up for the day and try on the Thursday to reach the river which would take us down to the coast.

Now for the first time since we had set out we had time to talk and take stock of each other. Kinnear, the chief officer of the *Siang Wo,* was a thin, lithe, sun-tanned fellow with a wide experience of ships, ports and men in the waters east of Suez. Little Tommy Marr, his number two, was a Glaswegian, who delighted us on this and later occasions with a spirited rendering of "Dear Old Glasgie Toon". Wade, the Welshman, was a robust, freckled tin-miner from somewhere up in the Malayan peninsula.

The other two members of our septet were, unfortunately, to prove themselves quite unfit for such a desperate venture as that on which we were engaged. One of them, in peace time a scientific research worker, undoubtedly meant well; but he was completely out of his depth in such an emergency and as the days went by he became increasingly a sore trial and handicap. Later, in Serang jail, he informed two Australian Y.M.C.A. girls that he was a professor, although I have since learned that he was no more a professor than I am; but for purposes of the narrative we shall call him "the Professor" henceforth. The seventh member of the party did a good job in the Banka jungle with the compass, but after that the less said about him the better. The final straw which fractured the camel's spine for the rest of us came when we discovered him smoking the reserve ration of cigarettes which had been put aside for the future. As the Professor and I had voluntarily abandoned our share of the cigarettes to the others whose tobacco craving was greater, we took a poor view of it when we finally discovered that this gentleman had smoked more than two-thirds of the total cigarettes we had with us.

The fifth day in the jungle, Thursday the nineteenth, was a day that seemed to come right out of the Deadwood Dick horror stories of jungle adventure which we all read in our youth. In the morning we obtained half an egg each and some *ubi kayu,* or tapioca roots, from a native kampong, but in following this native's directions as to the whereabouts of the river which we were seeking we ended up on a broad road. Following this road we heard voices in the distance and hastily turned off and traversed an unoccupied tin-mine, with dredging gear and many signs of current usage. We learned next day, through Wade's conversation with a native, that a large bicycle patrol of Japanese had been in the native village from which we had heard the voices.

Unfortunately, beyond the mine we found ourselves in a treacherous swamp and, in the space of half an hour, in seeking a way across we had got ourselves into one of the most wretched predicaments I ever hope to face. The swamp was intersected by a maze of deep, swift-flowing streams strewn with snags. On two occasions members of the party crashed headlong from their slippery footholds into these streams and were rescued only by sheer luck. Treacherous quicksands, or rather quick-mud, into which one sank without warning up to the thighs, hundreds of rotten logs and decaying branches projecting out of the bog, deceptive grass concealing deep pools, and the unreliability of every branch and plant on which one attempted to gain a purchase, made these hours like some fantastic dream from which one struggles in vain to release oneself.

Once when Kinnear slipped from a wet rock and slithered headlong down a muddy bank, I felt sure that he had broken a leg at least; but somehow our luck held good. Just as we were beginning to abandon hope of ever getting out of the morass, and with darkness rapidly enveloping everything, we struck firm ground and presently saw the land trending upwards ahead of us.

Too utterly exhausted and miserable to care about caution, we lit an enormous fire and cowered around it almost naked trying to dry our mud-sodden clothes. Mosquitoes and gnats descended on us in swarms, but we cooked our rice and opened one of the three remaining tins. By this time, I had begun to think that our river was in the Never Never Land well known to explorers. It seemed impossible that we should have laboured along through the jungle for five consecutive days without striking any of the three waterways shown on our map as running down to Banka Strait from the ridge of mountains which we had crossed on the third day.

I knew from the information that had come into the Cathay in the last hours before we left Singapore that Japanese convoys were spreading southwards and I was wondering if our route to Australia via Java might not be already cut off. We had been told by the natives that the Japanese were shooting all Europeans on Banka, but we did not yet know that the commandos landed on Banka had been the perpetrators of the ghastly massacre of Australian nurses on the Muntok beach a few hours earlier this day.

These girls had swum ashore, or been carried to the beach on pieces of wreckage, after their ship with many of the crew and their fellow passengers had been lost through enemy bombing. Eighteen girls belonging to an Australian General Hospital were among other survivors assembled on the beach not far from the point where the *Siang Wo* had been stranded. Suddenly a party of Japanese, armed with rifles and tommy-guns, came running along the beach, seized all the men in the party and marched them round a point. Five minutes later they came running back with their bayonets and clothes spattered with blood.

They ordered the girls to enter the water and forced them to line up with their backs to the shore. Then they tommy-gunned them so that they all pitched forward on their faces in the water. The last girl in the line, Nurse Bullwinkel, was taller than the rest and the traverse of the tommy-gun caused the bullet to strike her in the shoulder. She fell forward with the rest, but when the Japanese had rushed off down the beach to deal with another batch of shipwrecked troops, she crawled out of the water and hid in the jungle.

Subsequently she met a stranded sailor and, with the aid of the natives, the pair managed to survive until some sort of law and order had been established in Muntok, when they gave themselves up. Nurse Bullwinkel was put in the hospital and was subsequently taken to Palembang where she told her story to senior Allied officers.

Although rumours of the atrocity were common throughout all prison camps in the southern regions, I did not hear the full story until I reached Kanburi in 1945, when I met a New Zealand naval officer who had been at Muntok and Palembang and had been told the whole tale by the nurse herself. This was indeed the hush-hush story of the prison camps, because it was felt that if the Japanese ever got wind of it they would unquestionably shoot Nurse Bullwinkel out of hand.

Actually, as we learned later, the officers who surrendered at Muntok Hotel were not shot by the Japanese. They had the good luck to surrender to an N.C.O. who was willing to take prisoners. But there is no doubt that short shrift would have been accorded to seven white men picked up in the jungle by one of the roving patrols.

Next morning we progressed for a while across cleared fields around a native kampong with perhaps a dozen huts. Norman and I were very keen to seize one of the fowls which were running about everywhere, because we were ravenously hungry and had had no meat since leaving Singapore. But the Englishmen apparently thought that the old school tie would be sullied by the kidnapping of a native fowl, and refused to assist us in the hunt; so finally we were forced to go on empty-handed. We met a native who was emphatic on the point that the river was only two or three kilometres ahead, but the direction which he indicated involved the crossing of another swamp. This took us nearly two hours but, apart from a bad fall sustained by Kinnear, it was nothing like the nightmare of the previous afternoon.

Early in the afternoon a torrential downpour soaked us to the skin; but we were in such a mood of bitter anger at the way in which the native's "two or three kilometres" were stretching that we kept going until we arrived at a native house. A most obliging native then conducted us to another kampong where a friend of his, despite the downpour, immediately volunteered to conduct us to a place on the river where we would find canoes. This seemed too good to be true, and after he had been going for an hour without any sign of river or canoes we began to resign ourselves to another disappointment. Then, without warning, the ground dipped suddenly and there at our feet was a deep stream with a current flowing rapidly westwards towards the coast. This was only a branch of the main stream, but we had a ticklish time in crossing it by means of a broad tree-branch which stretched entirely across the black torrent swirling viciously between rocks fifty feet below. As I had to negotiate this with not only my own gear but with the ponderous and awkward rice pot, it took me nearly twenty exceedingly unhappy minutes to edge my way, inch by inch, across to the far bank.

But it was labour repaid a thousandfold. Fifty yards farther on, among a clump of high rushes, our guide suddenly discovered for us no fewer than three small but strongly built native prahus, carefully moored on the edge of a channel leading to the main stream. Then, without waiting for our thanks, he vanished. At that moment I would have given him my widow's mite, half my kingdom, or even our one and only parang, which at that moment was worth more than either.

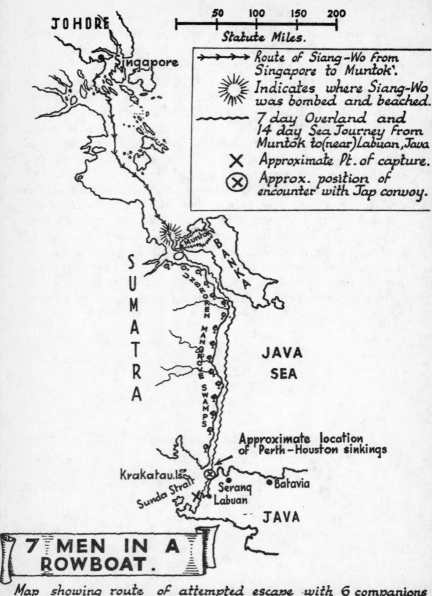

JOHORE

Singapore

50   100   150   200
Statute Miles.

→→→ Route of Siang-Wo from Singapore to Muntok.

☼ Indicates where Siang-Wo was bombed and beached.

〰〰 7 day Overland and 14 day Sea Journey from Muntok to (near) Labuan, Java

✕ Approximate Pt. of capture.

⊗ Approx. position of encounter with Jap convoy.

S
U
M
A
T
R
A

Muntok

BANKA

BROKEN MANGROVE SWAMPS

JAVA
SEA

Approximate location of Perth-Houston sinkings

Krakatau Is.

Sunda Strait

⊗

Serang   • Batavia
Labuan

JAVA

7 MEN IN A ROWBOAT.

Map showing route of attempted escape with 6 companions from Muntok to Java Feb. 15 to Mar. 7 1942.

Total distance covered, with deviations 400-450 miles.

CHAPTER V

SUMATRA HO!

His steps are not upon thy paths,—thy fields
Are not a spoil for him,—thou dost arise
And shake him from thee; the vile strength he wields
For earth's destruction thou dost all despise,
Spurning him from thy bosom to the skies,
And send'st him, shivering in thy playful spray
And howling, to his Gods . . .

—BYRON, *Childe Harold*

THERE was a house only a few hundred yards from the boats across a field of maize, and I strongly suspect that the Chinese whom we saw around it would not have been unduly pleased with our proceedings. But we were in no frame of mind to consider the rights and wrongs of annexation and, having selected the two best boats and transferred paddles and stretchers into them from the third, we embarked without more ado, four in one boat and three in the other. This was the end of the Odyssey-by-land and the beginning of the Odyssey-by-water.

At first we had a fair current behind us and our main anxiety was guiding the boat past the many snags and round the elbow bends of the narrow stream. We soon found ourselves in a setting which reminded me strongly of the scenes from the prehistoric age in Disney's *Fantasia*. Firm ground disappeared altogether and, on both sides of the channel as far as the eye could penetrate into the palms and swamp trees, there was nothing but an unending expanse of liquid, bubbling grey mud. The very trees and plants sprouting from this ooze seemed to have a dead and flaccid air, as if they had no truck with ordinary living things. It was eerie, uncanny, haunting; as if one had suddenly been swept back to the beginnings of

Time when life in the most primitive form first emerged from the slime.

The illusion was heightened by the presence on either bank of thousands of hideous spike-backed fish and repulsive reptiles which seemed to spring from the pages of scientific books on the Palaeozoic Era. They lay there gaping inanely at us as we swept by, or scurrying soundlessly across the mudbanks in a way which sent shivers coursing down the spine. I felt with the Ancient One:

> O Christ!
> That ever this should be!
> Yea, slimy things did crawl with legs
> Upon the slimy sea.

By this time we were so drugged with weariness and so miserable with hunger, that at times I asked myself whether the whole business was not some gigantic hallucination, born of exhaustion; but the comments of the others convinced me that we were all seeing the same pre-human world.

Gradually the channel broadened and as the day began to dim we were swept out on to the bosom of a wide river perhaps three hundred yards across. But by now the tide was obviously on the turn and the current was soon pulling against us. We hugged the right bank, keeping as close as we dared to the willow-like strands which hung down in profusion from the trees along the bank. Some fishermen whom we passed told us that there were Japanese in a village near the mouth of the river, but it was getting dark by this time and we hoped to slip past them unnoticed in the darkness. The natives had added that it was only ten kilometres to the mouth but, after our previous experience of their estimates of distance, we knew that it might be anything up to a hundred.

By the time night had fallen, our arms felt as if at any moment they must depart from their sockets. In the other boat they had two pairs to change at the oars, but Tommy Marr, who was in our boat, was ill, so we let him steer all the time while we rowed continuously. Six days of jungle trekking without one square meal a day is not the best preparation for paddling a heavy native boat for long hours against the current. At the end of six hours, first my rowing mate and then I suffered agonies of cramp. But as the night wore on we became anaesthetized so that the action of driving the paddles through the water became purely mechanical and we knew that we could keep going until we collapsed unconscious.

The stream was broadening now and, since the moon had risen, we became very worried about detection. When a boat was heard approaching we drew hastily into the overhanging branches of the bank and emerged only when its paddles were not even a faint rustle in the distance. Towards midnight we neared what was obviously the river's mouth, and then were alarmed to see first several lanterns moving on the opposite bank and then a stationary light some distance inland on our own side. If only the current had been with us we could have stopped rowing and drifted, but as it was we had to go on trying strenuously to imitate Deerfoot who, according to Edward S. Ellis, used to drive his canoe along with the speed of an arrow in absolute silence. I must admit that I shall be very glad to buy Deerfoot or anyone else a very large pot of beer if he can drive a Banka prahu against the current, in absolute silence, at any speed at all.

At last the banks fell away on either side of us and, risking the moonlight, we summoned up our last ounces of energy to strike out and round the sand-bar and so southwards down the coast for another half mile. Then at last we ran the canoes, which were both leaking badly, in through the surf and up on the soft white sand of the beach. I have never felt anything so good under the feet as that sand. We tried to lug the canoes up the beach into the shelter of the trees but the effort was beyond us and finally we collapsed, incapable even of setting a picket, beside our boats. It was half past one and we had been rowing continuously for nine hours.

The sun was already above the horizon before anyone awoke and then we hastily dragged the boats up the beach and concealed them in the heavy bush which fringed the shore. After that, feeling extraordinarily elated and a little light-headed with hunger, we set off down the beach in search of an opening in the bush where we could light a fire and boil the few handfuls of rice we had left.

While this was cooking on a sheltered hillside some fifty yards inland, I went back to the beach and met a Malay fisherman who was standing knee-deep in the water and catching fish like garfish on a line and rod at a great rate. In a fine mixture of pidgin, broken Malay (very broken) and the universal language of signs, I gave him to understand that I took a more than piscatorial interest in his catch, and twenty minutes later went triumphantly up to the others brandishing a huge banana leaf on which glittered some forty of these very delectable fish.

I have eaten meals in some of the most famous cafés and eating houses in London, Paris, Moscow, Vichy and other cities famed for good eating, but I never remember enjoying the pleasures of Lucullus with such gusto as I enjoyed that boiled rice and grilled garfish in the next hour. There was to be one occasion when perhaps I ate even more; but that is another story.

My friend the fisherman was apparently very impressed with my multilingual description of our distress, for he went off at high speed to his kampong and returned a couple of hours later, not with a host of Nips, but with several pounds of rice, half a dozen eggs, some small cakes and a host of urchins who in their turn brought us coco-nuts, bananas and sugar-cane.

By five o'clock that afternoon I had given up counting the number of meals and snacks I had had, but if anyone really wants to see the rosy side of life I recommend taking a jaunt similar to ours of the past week, and then at the end of it lying stark naked in the sun in a wind-sheltering copse on a bed of white sand gently sucking and masticating several feet of luscious sugar-cane. The gods in Valhalla know nothing like it.

Our fisherman friend returned again in the afternoon bringing the headman of his village, who had formerly been a policeman in Java and knew a few words of English. With him we negotiated for a boat suitable to take us across to Sumatra and if necessary down the coast to Java, which we judged to be a good three hundred miles away. He said he had a boat which had been a government motor patrol boat. This sounded very good until we discovered that it was now minus the motor and that we would have to make our own mast. However, having no choice, we finally agreed to give him my watch in exchange for the boat, which would be brought round before dark. As this watch was my wife's wedding present, I was the hero of the hour. I didn't feel very happy about it, but reasoned that if she had had to choose between the watch and me she would, all things considered, have sacrificed the watch.

The boat duly arrived about eight o'clock. It was about seventeen feet long, seemed both cumbrous and unwieldy, and was obviously leaking in two or three places. However, our expert mariners pronounced it (*a*) probably seaworthy and (*b*) better than nothing; with which expert view no layman could venture to differ.

So after rigging up a mast to which we attached my blanket—I was apparently in an exceedingly quixotic mood this day—and loading aboard all the stores which our kind friends from the fisherman's village had brought us, we set sail for Sumatra about 9.30 p.m., Saturday 21 February.

We were all in high spirits at having got clear of the hated island and its marshes, after what seemed an infinity of struggling. A light breeze stiffened towards midnight, and even with our scanty rag of "sail" we were able to abandon the oars, confident that we were speeding across Banka Strait on a diagonal south-westerly course. We felt so relieved to have set out on the sea at last that the perils of the deep seemed a mere bagatelle in comparison.

After a couple of hours the wind became very choppy and even contrary and we took up the oars again. When daylight arrived we found that land, in the shape of small atolls or promontories, was visible at all points on the horizon. There was some dispute about which land we should head for, since we did not want to be caught out in the open sea by patrolling naval craft or air reconnaissance. Finally, after much debating over compass and map, the mariners set our course. Unfortunately this seemed to be directly against the current which appeared diabolically determined to prevent our reaching the haven of the land. The sun grew hotter and hotter and we became increasingly exhausted; but the distant tree-tops did not seem to grow any bigger.

It was at this stage that we discovered that two of the septet had never pulled an oar before. Wade, the Welshman, chopped energetically at the water rather as one would attack an obstructive root with a hatchet, while the Professor had so little idea of the whole procedure that it was felt better finally to confine his activities to bailing our leaking craft.

At first sight, and again later, our worry had been about the smallness of the boat when confronted with the tropical storms of this zone. But this morning, trying to lug her through the water against the current, she seemed to me nearly as heavy as the *Queen Mary* and twice as clumsy. My rowing had been limited to two months on the Isis during which I alternated with kaleidoscopic rapidity between the Balliol Seconds (one day only) Balliol Thirds and the Balliol Fourths. Even though I was coached in a tub pair by Bob Sherriff, celebrated author of *Journey's End*, my oarsmanship was of a standard which caused one Oxonian veteran to say dismally: "He may work all right, but I think he'd be happier with a spade!"

However, old Norman—he could give any of us about a decade—was a tower of strength, and we found as the days wore on that most of the work devolved on the two of us, for Marr remained very ill and Kinnear developed a touch of dysentery, while no one was quite sure whether the Professor was propelling the boat backwards or forwards at any given moment. As to the Welshman, with his deracinating stroke, I felt it was a case of: "All rowed fast but none so fast as stroke."

Our watches crawled round to noon and the sweat ran off us in buckets; but still the land seemed over a mile away. We had three oars, all very long with thin blades such as the

Malays always use in these parts. We also had a piece of broken wood which might once have been an oar; but that was a matter of faith, hope and charity, and I had none of the three when I was called on to use it. We steered by means of a long broken sweep lashed to a rudder post, the steersman (usually Tommy Marr) sitting there with his feet on our water tins, the sweep in one hand and the compass in the other.

When at long last we ran into the shore we found it was not firm land but mangrove swamp of a particularly glutinous and unpleasant variety. However, we had been rowing without a break for nine hours, so we tied up to a tree and, sitting as best we could on the roots which projected from the mud, we ate a meal.

We had been there perhaps half an hour when suddenly a steamer appeared, nosing along Banka Strait. She carried no distinguishable flag, so we did not know if she was a Jap transport or one of the ships from Singapore. We waved tentatively at first, but Kinnear, who had been unanimously elected skipper, decreed that she was probably a Jap and that it was safer to take no risks. As this was actually a week after the fall of Singapore there is no doubt she was a Jap. We now rowed along the coast, keeping just clear of the snags and sandbanks, until we came to a strip of attractive white beach fringed with coco-nut palms behind which huts were visible. As the rain, which had been intermittent, now came down in a deluge, we hastily moored the boat and raced up to the nearest hut.

We had just started to peel off our sodden clothing and collect wood for a fire when the native occupants, apparently Chinese-Malay halfcastes, returned. They immediately began to jabber excitedly to Wade who suddenly exclaimed, "Christ Almighty! We're back on b—— Banka!" At first we were incredulous, the mariners, both of whom had their first mate's certificate, maintaining stoutly that this was a physical impossibility. But the natives were adamant and pointing across the water kept saying, "Sumatra! Sumatra!"

We had forgotten the effect of adjacent metal on a compass. Our master mariners had brought us round in a full horseshoe, and we were only a few miles from Muntok from which we had set out seven and a half days before.

It was one of those moments when neither a Mintie nor a Red Capstan would have been quite adequate. We had all utterly exhausted ourselves pulling against the current to get back to the island from which we had so joyfully believed that we had finally escaped. I am afraid that one or two bitter things were said, but no one could have been more miserable than the navigators themselves.

Now at last we paid attention to what Wade was saying. It appeared that Japanese troops were in the native village only a few hundred yards away and that some of them might appear at any moment. For an instant one or two of our party were so mortified and disappointed that they spoke of giving themselves up. But the natives were most emphatic that we should return to the boat immediately and get away lest the Japanese appear and shoot not only us but the natives also. They were very friendly but obviously panic-stricken, and very soon, loading the boat with fresh coco-nuts, they had dragged it down the beach and into the water and we were battling at the oars once more.

We had just got round the first point and were perhaps five hundred yards from the shore when, without warning, a single-engined Japanese plane came flying low down the coast and immediately swooped over us and then circled. This was one of the Bad Moments. We were quite sure that we did not look like native fishermen and expected to hear the crackle of machine-guns at any moment. He swung round in a wide arc and then came down over us at perhaps two hundred feet. Fortunately I was the only one with fair hair and I had clapped on a huge Chinese coolie hat, which someone had acquired, as soon as the plane appeared. I am still not satisfied as to whether that pilot failed to recognize us or was simply out of ammunition. At any rate, to our immense relief, he finally droned off down the coast.

The weather, which had been increasingly threatening, now gave us considerable anxiety. The wind was rising and heavy, inky-black clouds were sweeping up from the east. The squall that heralded the coming storm burst without warning and we only just had time to tear down the patched blanket before it struck our little boat. Within two minutes the waves began to present a most formidable aspect and we started to ship water so fast that very soon we had two men bailing constantly. The wind rose to a continuous roar and, with evening descending rapidly, we could see no sign of land and had no choice but to drive helplessly before the gale.

Kinnear organized us with admirable coolness. Tommy Marr stayed at the tiller through four mortal hours during which the boat was buffeted like a cockleshell by the immense walls of dark water that swept down upon us in unending succession. Although at times they came from unexpected angles, Marr kept the nose of the boat heading into the waves in a fashion which seemed miraculous to a land-lubber, and which seems even more so in retrospect when I remember the hopeless clumsiness of that long sweep in a swirling storm. Kinnear himself stayed by the mast in front, ready with a paddle to trim the boat against the seas or to fend us off from the tiny atolls and patches of rock which loomed up from time to time in the darkness as we were driven helplessly forward. The storm and the buffetting opened up the seams and we took it in turns, two at a time, to bail furiously. Even the Professor in this emergency handled the bailing tin as if it had been a beaker in his beloved laboratory.

I have since learned that the waters between Borneo and Sumatra, including Banka Strait itself with its powerful and treacherous cross-currents, are regarded by all seamen as being fraught with considerable menace. I have no idea how much alarm a normal passenger experiences on the deck of a liner in one of these hurricanes. But sitting on the ribs of a tiny native boat with fourteen inches of freeboard, the spectacle of the wind-lashed waters was perhaps the most awe-inspiring I have ever encountered.

For some reason, whether it was our mental and physical exhaustion, or the sense of our own utter helplessness, one did not feel fear so much as a certain fatalistic resignation. It needed only one of the curling monsters which raced down on us to strike us off balance and we should all have been floundering in the water, and then even for the strongest swimmer the end could not have been long delayed.

We sat there, clinging to the gunwale, sodden from head to foot, with the gale lashing through our thin shirts like a stockwhip; but somehow we were not miserable or tremulous, but rather exalted. The situation had a certain primitive appeal. Here were seven men, in the middle of the twentieth century of the Christian era, without one more aid or comfort than the first man who ever put to sea in the first wooden boat and found himself caught in a storm back in the dimmest vistas of our human story. In retrospect, I would not surrender that experience for much fine gold.

After nearly five hours the storm abated almost as swiftly as it had arisen, and at last we began to think of our acute physical discomfort and to long for rest and warmth. I don't know how far we had been carried that night, but the first moonlight showed us a long fringe of darkness to starboard which could only mean land. We pulled at the oars almost joyfully in our attempt to set the circulation going again, and in due course found ourselves in almost still waters some hundred yards from what was obviously heavy mangrove swamp.

A mist now seemed to sweep out over us, enveloping everything in its fine smoky haze and, as we rowed along vainly seeking some trace of human habitation or some break in the swamp, the events of the past twenty-four hours began to take their toll.

At first, when it happened, I tended to rub my eyes and think that there really were shapes coming towards us in the mist. We did actually strike one long-disused and rotten fisherman's hut standing on high stakes well out of the water. It was real and tangible enough and I climbed up the rotting steps and clambered across the broken floor above to see if this could afford any sort of refuge for the night. But the holes in the roof and floor were such that it was out of the question and the others, frightened by the groaning and swaying of the frail structure at my every movement, kept calling me down. So, reluctantly, we paddled on.

Then similar tall huts kept looming up in front of me in rapid succession. Usually they seemed to be forty or fifty yards in front and came steadily nearer until sometimes it seemed that the nose of the boat was about to bump into the shadowy outlines of the structure's bottom. And then again there was nothing but the swirling tendrils of mist. Presently I began to see not only these bamboo fishing frames but still more vividly a tall fence covered with creepers and honeysuckle which used to separate our backyard from the front garden of our home at the Melbourne University, where I lived as a small boy. I could see the details of this hedge with great clearness, including the rickety green gate and the slope of the slate roof of the kitchen which adjoined the fence.

I kept telling myself that it was obviously an hallucination and a will o' the wisp, but always as it loomed up again, I could not repress the sudden feeling that it really was there this time. I said nothing to the others until Norman broke out: "Well, bless me, that's extraordinary. I keep seeing eastern archways with strange designs. We always seem to be approaching them but never quite getting there." Then it turned out that not only Norman and I but three or four of us had been having a similar experience in the mists. One was seeing a little cottage amidst Kentish apple orchards where he had spent many happy holidays in his youth. All of us continually had the feeling that another fisherman's hut was hovering in the mist just ahead.

This was, of course, the fruit of the past ordeal; hallucinations coloured by our longing for rest and warmth. Since this I have had another experience of which I shall tell later, and have spoken to many others who have had similar visions after extreme privation and weariness. It was fascinating, uncanny and unforgettable.

At last, about two in the morning, another set of fishing stakes did actually present itself. The dwelling above, if there had ever been one, had long since succumbed to wind and weather, but we were by now so tired that we were content to lash the boat to the posts and call it a night. We opened our last two sample tins, chewed a piece of coco-nut and then stretched out as best we could in the bilge water which kept seeping into the boat. The boat was far too small to give us all lying space so we literally lay piled on top of each other, enormously grateful for the warmth which this gave to our frozen bodies. To be lying on the sharp ribs of a native boat, with one's side immersed in water and the weight of two or three other bodies pressing against one's own, may not sound like a recipe for coping with insomnia. But within five minutes I fell into one of the soundest sleeps of my life and knew nothing until dawn.

CHAPTER VI

WITH OAR AND "SAIL"

Poor naked wretches, wheresoe'er you are,
That bide the pelting of this pitiless storm,
How shall your houseless heads and unfed sides,
Your loop'd and window'd raggedness, defend you
From seasons such as these?

—*King Lear*, Act iii, sc. 4

At this stage we decided that our best policy would be to keep rowing down the Sumatra coast until we came to some river or break in the mangrove swamp which offered a chance of getting inland and contacting Dutchmen. After the way our little craft had ridden the tempest, we felt that with care she might carry us for several days; but the slowness of our progress, when every hour was precious, suggested that any chance of other means of transport should be seized with both hands. We had no idea as to how things might have developed in Sumatra or even farther south, but in fact the Japanese had already seized Palembang which is the main town of this region, some sixty miles inland from Banka Strait, and their patrols were now spreading over the whole area.

We had by this time exhausted most of the food provided by our friends of the fishing village and had only a few coconuts and a little rice left. Therefore we were very pleased when after some hours of rowing we came up to two fishermen's huts which bore evidence of occupation. As we drew nearer we saw a number of men and boys congregated on the farther one, on the platform which is used for drying the catch.

We rowed across and Wade began his palaver. This sort of thing was to become a main feature of each day's proceedings. The essential words in the dialogue, as I seized them,

were *macan* and *ayer*—food and water. This time we seemingly
got the right response and, at the natives' behest, rowed across to
the other hut, where some of the men immediately joined us and
helped to start a fire on which we could cook our rice. Once
they realized that we had no intention of taking anything of
theirs, they became very generous and soon we were squatting
happily round a barrelful of dried prawns, while fresh baked
fish and beautiful white rice steamed over a roaring fire.

An hour later we were all, as Jorrocks would say, "full o'
beans and benevolence". The natives told us of a big naval
fight in the strait a few days earlier, but did not know what
Japanese forces lay to the southwards. They appeared non-
plussed at the turn of events which had converted the "tuans
besar", or white bosses, into refugees seeking food and shelter.
We were not the first to have called at this hut in the past
week, so we knew that other ships from Singapore had shared
our fate and that others like ourselves were making their
way down the coast as best they could.

We learned years later, in the Japanese prison camps, that
some forty-nine vessels, ranging between a few hundred and
fifteen thousand tons, had been sunk or rendered useless in
these waters between 9 and 19 February. The bulk of the
survivors got ashore either on Banka, Sumatra or one of the
smaller islands. A very large number, with Colonel Albert
Coates of the 13th A.G.H., went down the Indregirry River
somewhat to the north of where we were hit, and eventually
reached Padang. These included many hundreds of Australian and British troops who had left Singapore on 15-16 February and also a number of civilians, including women. It has
been estimated that, leaving out those who died subsequently
in Japanese prison camps, over five thousand people lost their
lives in the attempt to escape from Japanese captivity, the
losses being much heavier than those involved in the evacua-
tions of Greece and Crete.

Banka Strait and its approaches, instead of being the escape
gate from the Singapore trap, were converted into a gigantic
Passage of Horror where few ran the gauntlet successfully. A
fleet now lies on the bottom of this sea and beside them lie the

bones of men and women who stayed until it was too late. Here was one of the greatest tragedies of the Pacific War. Once again in our history somebody had blundered, and this time it was not only men who died.

The Malay fishermen were very vague as to where we might contact Dutchmen, but they did indicate that there were several rivers with settlements of a kind at intervals along the coast ahead of us. They warned us that we could expect sumatras, or storms similar to that of the night before, on four days in each week at this time of year. They advised us to lie up whenever such a storm was brewing, and seemed rather surprised that we had survived the previous night. These Malays were good friends to us in our hour of need and, as they regarded our Singapore dollars as quite useless, there was nothing with which we could repay them.

We now entered upon a period of toil which was not measured by hours or by day and night. Our hands blistered quickly, but with the aid of salt water they also calloused rapidly and our main discomfort was caused by the hardness of the ribs and thwarts on the softest parts of our anatomies.

We usually rowed in hour-long shifts but, since Marr was never strong at the best of times and Kinnear had developed dysentery, I felt that, being the youngest and in many ways the fittest, I should do most of their work at the oars. We adopted the system of rowing as much as possible during the night and resting in the heat of the day. I found that, provided I got at least two meals a day, seven or eight hours at the oars were quite possible. Things were not so good when, as sometimes happened, we went twenty-four hours without food, during which time we had to battle against storms or currents for long hours without being relieved at the rowing seat.

For the first four days the contrary current setting northwards up the strait was our main problem. At times, even with some assistance from the breeze, with two men rowing at the thwart and two more paddling, perched on the gunwale on either side of the mast, we did not make much more than a mile an hour.

On the good days we usually found fishermen's huts some

hundreds of yards out from the shore, or huddling at the edge of the swamp by the mouth of a creek. Often after the natives had given us a meal, we stretched out on their straw mats, which seemed like beds of the most palatial luxury after the ribs at the bottom of the boat. Yet on an average we were on the water for twenty hours in every twenty-four.

We received most assistance from the occasional Chinese, who are intermixed with the Malays along this coast. They were always generous and anxious to help us although their resources were usually very limited. Indeed, the standard of living along this most inhospitable of coasts accounts for the sparsity of the native inhabitants. The only thing of which the fisherman is assured is his diet of dried fish. For rice, oil, sugar, salt, textiles, smokes, and other supplies of every kind he is dependent on the native traders who ply up and down the whole archipelago at irregular intervals. His only commodity for barter is his catch and if, through seasonal disturbances or migrations of the fish, he is empty-handed when the trader arrives, the only thing he can do is to tighten his belt and pray for better days. Inevitably, from the point of view of bargaining, he is more or less at the mercy of the traders.

We found these people much more hardy and independent than the population of Malaya. Once they recovered from their initial fear and distrust at the irruption of seven bearded white men into their isolated world, they often treated us with the greatest friendliness and generosity. I only wished that we had with us means for repaying them to whom so little would have meant so much.

It is, I think, a good thing that at least once in a man's life he should be entirely dependent on the kindness and charity of others. Some people may think this merely humiliating, but that seems a very superficial view. For twenty-five years I had never lacked anything of real importance to comfort or happiness. I now discovered that, lacking everything, one could still attain a very considerable degree of happiness and some measure of philosophic contentment, providing that at intervals one managed to obtain warmth and rest for the body and food and drink for the inner man.

Our major anxiety during these days, apart from the storms, was the morning and evening reconnaissance by Japanese aircraft based on the Muntok airfield. We soon discovered that about half an hour after dawn a plane would drone slowly down the Banka side of the strait, returning along our side perhaps twenty minutes later. The same ritual occurred towards evening. We therefore made it a practice to pull inshore and hide up at first light until the aircraft had returned to its base. During this whole period we saw no shipping of any kind, although occasionally small native sailing boats passed us at a speed which emphasized the clumsiness of our craft and our lack of a proper sail. After about five days we obtained from an old Chinese—he had a face as full of character and experience as that of the famous Doge of Venice painted by Bellini—a section of torn sail patched with an old native sarong, which at least had the merit of being twice as big as my small blanket. But even so most of the work had to be done with the oars.

The natives always told us that Java was only four or five days' "sail" away; but that was in their craft, not in ours. About 26 or 27 February, we got clear of Banka Strait, from which point the Sumatra coast trends due south for well over two hundred miles until one reaches Sunda Strait which separates Java from Sumatra. But we had failed to find any trace of Dutchmen, and always the fisherfolk told us that the nearest of the Dutch was *jalan jalan*, or farther on.

We investigated the mouths of one or two rivers which lie just south of Cape Kait, including the River Lumpur, but there was nothing to encourage us to row up them. One day at the mouth of a river we were hospitably entertained by a Sumatran and his family, which included not only his own and his wife's parents, but various cousins and in-laws and innumerable children. Here, for the first time, the woman of the house not only cooked for us but also served the meal. Usually these people, being Mohammedans, kept their women-folk out of sight. Indeed one of our main grievances with the Professor, who was becoming a sore trial in many ways, was that he would wander round the native huts and platforms, apparently bent on some form of "scientific" investigation, in a manner which irritated and alarmed our hosts.

The Sumatran at the river mouth produced a great cruse of native *gulah*, which was the first sugar of any kind we had obtained since leaving Banka. So violent was our craving that we all ate four or five platefuls of steamed rice covered with huge quantities of this thick sweet treacle. Indeed, by the time we were finished, the pot, which must have held three or four pints, was so depleted that the good fellow gave us the remainder to take with us. It was only after we had finished the meal that he told Wade that, on the previous day, a large warship had anchored off the mouth of this river and four or five pinnaces or motorboats crammed with Japanese armed with machine-guns, mortars, etc, had gone upstream. He seemed to think that as there was very little at the head of the waterway they would be coming back at any hour. So, once again, we departed with considerable alacrity.

A couple of hours later we were crawling along one of the worst pieces of coast we had seen as yet. We were making very heavy going of it, against wind and current, when suddenly Kinnear said: "I think we're in for it again." Eastwards across the Java Sea great chocolate and black clouds were racing up from the horizon. We were only fifty yards from a rocky hostile coast strewn with snags, and the moment we stopped rowing, the boat, yielding to the pull of wind and water, started to make rapidly for the rocks. We immediately turned her nose towards the incoming storm, and having fought our way out for perhaps a hundred yards, we attempted to down anchor.

We had just flung the pick over the side when the storm struck us and within three minutes the sea, which had been choppy but innocuous, was lashed into a living fury. The pick immediately began to drag and the boat started to drive head on for the rocks. We seized the oars, but so fierce was the wind that the boat was still carried shorewards. Within a few minutes we were within a chain of the foaming cauldron which marked the presence of a reef. At this moment we managed to touch bottom and succeeded in driving in two long poles which we had brought with us for just such an emergency.

Then the fight began. Even with two men at the oars and two paddling, the boat started to drift again and the poles began to drag. It was a truly desperate situation, because the violence of the storm seemed to increase at each moment, and our boat was doomed beyond all hope once it touched the swirling vortex. After that, even if we got ashore alive, the end on that barren impenetrable swamp would be certain.

Kinnear now tried to get a hold with the anchor pick once more. He was clinging to one of the poles and, as the anchor rope slipped out, his leg was caught. I dropped my paddle and flung myself on top of him, seizing the rope just as he was half overboard. At that moment a fresh squall struck the boat and the next two minutes were hectic beyond description. But this time the pick caught and, straining madly on the rope, we managed to draw the boat inch by inch away from the foaming rocks. For the next two hours the seven of us battled unceasingly, two rowing, two paddling, one pulling on the anchor rope and watching the poles, while the sixth held her nose to the gale and the other bailed for dear life.

When at last the storm abated, we were not fifty yards from the spot where we had been when it began. We opened our greatest "find" so far, a bottle of Johnny Walker Black Label which one of the fisherfolk had been persuaded to hand over in exchange for a Singapore ten-dollar note, but we were so exhausted that within ten minutes of the end of the storm, half of us had fallen asleep where we sat.

Next day, the Professor capped earlier achievements. We were tied up beside a fishtrap some distance from the shore, and the Professor was about to go off with two native boys in search of coco-nuts and fresh water. He clambered down the steps to their boat and then, instead of stepping firmly into it, put his foot on the gunwale and capsized both the boat and himself. Norman and I were trying to light a fire in the little hut on top of the fishtrap when one of the others came in, helpless with laughter, to say that the Professor was in the water. Someone asked, "Can he get out?" and someone else answered, "Let's hope not;" but presently a whining, sodden figure came crawling in to the fire. What we had christened our "white man's burden" was with us again.

That afternoon, having been without food other than two coco-nuts for twenty-four hours, we were caught by the most prolonged sumatra that I remember. It began at two in the afternoon, and, when it finally diminished in violence, it was succeeded by some of the severest rain of the trip. Sodden and bitterly cold, totally exhausted and tortured by hunger, we rowed hopelessly on until just before midnight we sighted what appeared to be a jetty about midway between ourselves and the shore, which was four or five miles off. There was a river mouth here and we had to use our last ounce of energy to force the boat towards the light, against the ebbing tide. Driving rain beat down with renewed fury as we got close, and it was not until we actually bumped against the side that we realized that this was no jetty but a big junk, or fishing lugger.

Then someone sighted us—they could not hear our shouts against the noise of the rain—and a dozen willing hands helped to pull us aboard more dead than alive. We had not been dry for ten hours and felt that we would never get warm again. However, the crew on the lugger—mixed Chinese, Malays and Indonesians—were kindness itself and within half an hour we had thawed out around the grandest fire I ever remember. Then we sat down to heaped plates of steaming rice and grilled steaks from big schnapper-like fish straight out of the nets.

This, I think, was an even more memorable meal than any of the others. It was almost thirty-six hours since I had touched food and for the last ten of them I had been rowing almost continuously. That fresh fish tasted better than anything they ever served at Maxim's. The natives, seeing the way I dealt with grilled fish, rice and the dried fish they had put on the side, kept piling new filets, straight from the fire, on to my plate. The whole performance, which lasted for over an hour, was an epic worthy of a Brobdingnagian. My crew mates were as impressed as the natives, who had never seen anything like it in their lives. I'm afraid my mind used to go back to that repast very often during the days of starvation that were to come.

Our party was divided into two sections: the one believing in hugging the coast as closely as possible, the other maintaining that we were safer when well clear of the rocks and sand-bars. Tommy Marr, who did most of the steering, tended to carry us far out to sea each night so that when dawn came we had to spend precious hours pulling back inshore where we could hope to come upon fishing huts with food and water. Norman and I regarded this as futile and wasteful of time, and believed in keeping close to the coast.

On one unforgettable evening, when I was steering, I followed this policy too literally and in due course ran us aground on a mudbank with the tide ebbing swiftly. Knee-deep in mud, we made frantic efforts to refloat the wretched tub, but we could hardly move her an inch and soon she was high and dry with the water yards away.

There followed two of the worst hours I have ever known. Myriads of gnats and mosquitoes seemed to rise from the very mud itself to assail us, while obscene-looking mud-fish flopped and plopped on the squelching mud around us. Swathed to the eyes in clothing and blanket, I was bitterly conscious that the infuriating attacks of the insects were not half as virulent as the shafts of resentment being unleashed against me by the other occupants of the boat as they sat sweating and fuming under their covering while the insect horde hummed maddeningly in their ears.

But there were other hours that were different. The best would come in the clear starry nights after midnight when one's shift at the oars was finished, and one could lie flat on one's back watching the top of the mast swaying lazily against the golden lamps suspended in the rich blue of the tropic sky. This was the hour of peace and beauty, bringing balm after the long struggle of the day, while the water lapped softly against the sides and the beauty of the night took possession, until one murmured with Keats:

Bright star, would I were steadfast as thou art—
Not in lone splendour hung aloft the night
And watching, with eternal lids apart,
Like nature's patient sleepless Eremite,
The moving waters at their priestlike task
Of pure ablution round earth's human shores.

But the days were fleeting past and the small native prahu, which came up from the south on 5 March, brought word that *orang Nippon* was everywhere, and that Batavia was *habis* or finished. We thought the three men who brought these tidings a shiftless cut-throat gang, and suspected them of being Japanese agents. I was unwilling to believe, after all the strong talk I had heard in Batavia and Sourabaya at the beginning of January, that the Dutch were not making a fight for it. Some of the others, however, were inclined to believe that the Japanese had already forestalled us, and they were right.

On the afternoon of 5 March, we drew in to a sandy spit, the first big break in the monotonous unfriendliness of mangrove and mud. We soon learned from the natives here that an Allied plane had been forced down on this spit a few days before, and that on the previous day a number of Japanese officers had arrived in a pinnace and had taken the wrecked plane away with them. We ate a meal sitting round the same fire where these natives had entertained the Japanese less than twenty-four hours before.

Then we rowed on, and kept rowing all night, which was one of the wettest of the trip. At first light, as I was relieved at the oars and crawled up forward, I caught sight of what appeared to be a white man at the edge of the shore, perhaps half a mile away. A minute or two later other figures came running down to join him. We started to pull towards them, but were not free from suspicion that they might be Japanese. At length when we were within hailing distance, I let out a prodigious coo-ee and we were enormously relieved when, at about the third repetition, a faint answering call, unmistakably English, came drifting back across the water. A few minutes later we had run the boat ashore and were eagerly grasping the hands of the first white men we had seen in nearly three weeks.

CHAPTER VII

THIRTEEN MEN IN A BOAT

> Sure, I rose the wrong way today, I have had such
> damn'd ill luck every way.
> —Mrs Afra Behn, *The Town Fop*

THESE six men were all in a bad way. They had had no food
for four days, their feet were badly cut and swollen, and they
were without boots or socks. We had managed to obtain some
dried fish from the natives at the spit where the plane had
crashed, and now, as we set about cooking this for them, we
heard their story.

They had left Singapore on Friday the thirteenth in a motor
torpedo boat. Two New Zealanders, an officer and a rating
belonging to the crew of the M.T.B., were among our six.
The others, a colonel of Engineers, who was being sent to
join Wavell's staff in Java, two survivors of *Repulse*, and a
private soldier, were among the two hundred evacuees crowded
on the M.T.B.

They were well down Banka Strait when dawn came on
Sunday the fifteenth. Then, as the light began to make things
visible through the morning mist, the alarm was suddenly
given on the bridge. A Japanese destroyer lay barely two
hundred yards ahead.

The Japs opened fire immediately and scored a direct hit
with their first salvo, smashing the bridge and silencing the
three-inch gun in the bows of the M.T.B. Within a few minutes the little vessel was sinking rapidly, while most of the
people aboard who were still alive were struggling helplessly
in the water or clinging to the one or two boats and rafts
which had not been smashed by the destroyer's shells.

The M.T.B. went down within a few minutes of being hit,

and those who could swim began a long struggle towards the shore, which they could see in the distance six or seven miles away. Our six were among fourteen who finally got together on the Banka beach. There they got in touch with a Dutchman who said he could get them a boat from Palembang. He set off immediately, but that was the last they saw of him.

In the next few days they were well cared for by some Chinese in one of the local villages. The colonel, who had had much experience in China, spoke Chinese fluently, and the shipwrecked band were fed like princes and accorded every attention until, finally despairing of the Dutchman, they decided to set off for Java in a lifeboat which had been washed ashore.

In this boat they made good progress until they reached the spit where they saw the wreck of a plane. They went ashore, learned from the natives that the crew of the plane had set off for Java in a rubber boat, and helped themselves to one or two instruments from the control panel of the wrecked machine. After a meal, they started rowing southwards again, when suddenly a junk bore down upon them under full sail. When it was within fifty yards, a burst of fire came from it and they realized that it was packed with Japanese. For the second time in a fortnight, they abandoned ship and started to swim for the shore with tommy-gun bullets kicking up the water around their heads. All but two of them apparently reached the beach and succeeded in scattering into the jungle and mangrove swamp.

The Japanese managed to capture two men who were wounded, but finally abandoned their search for the others after darkness had fallen. Next morning our sextet met, as agreed, but could find no trace of their other companions. They then set off southwards, hoping to find a river and a native boat, or to be picked up by other refugees.

For four days they had been trudging through the swamps, often waist-deep in mud, seldom making more than three or four miles a day. The treacherous mud had claimed their boots and shoes, hidden roots and sharp rocks had lacerated their feet and legs, and at times they had been without even water for over twenty-four hours. One man went down with a heavy attack of malaria, and on the day before our arrival they had decided to lie up at the tiny stream which ran inland at this point. They had been making strenuous attempts to catch fish in a hand-made trap, but had had no luck.

Years later, in a Siamese prison camp, one of them told me that he did not know what they would have done if we had not turned up at that moment, because they were absolutely at the end of their resources. He said that the meal of dried fish and rice which Norman Carter prepared for them was the best thing they had ever had in their lives.

One of the six, a stoker from *Repulse*, had what I think must be the record for sinkings over less than three months. *Repulse* had been sunk under him on 10 December. A few weeks later in Singapore harbour, a lighter, which he was operating, was set on fire by Jap bombing and once again he had to swim for his life. Then the M.T.B. was blown out of the water by the Japanese destroyer in Banka Strait; and finally he had been forced to swim for it a fourth time when the Japanese junk started machine-gunning his lifeboat. As a considerable proportion of lives were lost on each of the four occasions, he has reason to consider himself one of the world's luckiest men; but few will envy him his record.

As it was impossible to leave these men in their debilitated condition, we decided by unanimous vote to try to pack them all into our small boat. The first step was to haul it up on the shingle and to attempt with clay and river mud to repair some of the worst leaks, which had now become a major problem.

Finally, about ten o'clock on the loveliest of calm, sunny mornings, we embarked once more, our six rescued lying packed together in the middle of the boat between the rowing thwart and the mast. We could see a tall mountain, faint and purple in the distance, rising from the sea to the southward, and knew that at long last Java was in sight. It was the thirteenth day since setting out from Banka, and we were now thirteen men in the boat.

After about two hours' rowing, we met a native trading boat, well stocked with rice and fruit and with only two natives aboard. It was a big seaworthy boat with two masts and wide, square-rigged sails. While two of us were bargaining with the natives for food, the others began a fierce debate as to whether we should seize this craft for the crossing of the notoriously dangerous Sunda Strait, which lay directly ahead. Our own boat, despite our attempt at repairs, was making water badly and, with thirteen aboard, was loaded down almost to the gunwale. None of the sailors liked the prospect of facing anything approaching a storm in our present plight, and we land-lubbers liked it even less.

There is no doubt that this trading boat afforded our last chance of salvation. Already, some days before, Norman and I had been anxious to seize a trader's boat at one of the fishing stakes, but the other five were still opposed to any such lawlessness. Now once again we argued forcibly that if the strait was to be crossed, this was obviously the boat to do it in. Furthermore, if the Japanese had landed on Java, we must be prepared to make an attempt to go on to Australia, and that was out of the question in our tiny, leaking boat.

Once again, most of the others were fearful of the consequences if these natives succeeded in getting friends ashore to set out to help retrieve their property. The argument I opposed to this was that we could truss the natives up, and take them with us. In our dire extremity, it seemed to me a case of a chance of life and freedom against almost certain capture and death. But once again the majority was hesitant and, finally, Norman and I were overruled.

So the two natives went their way, having gained my Swan fountain pen in exchange for a very limited amount of fruit and dried fish. We decided that, since the weather promised fine, we might as well head directly across the strait immediately, and take our chance of being caught by a storm well away from the coast.

All that afternoon and throughout the night we laboured at the oars, some of the stronger of the rescued men taking a turn in the latter stages, by which time the food they had received had lent them some strength. By two o'clock in the morning we found ourselves within a couple of miles of the Java coast, which was clearly visible in the moonlight. But at this stage we were caught in the grip of the very strong current which races down Sunda Strait at about four or five knots. With the wind also against us, we found it absolutely impossible to pull inshore and, instead, the boat was carried steadily southwards and slightly away from the land. We only just missed the outcrop of rock on which the Dutch have perched a tiny lighthouse as a guide to mariners in the midst of these treacherous waters.

At one stage, we found ourselves in the middle of a huge pool of oil fuel, which obviously marked the grave of some ship. In later days, I often wondered whether we had rowed over the last resting-place of H.M.A.S. *Perth* or U.S.S. *Houston* or one of the Japanese vessels that they took with them down to Davy Jones's locker.

Apart from the two hours ashore where we had picked up the others, we had now been rowing continuously for thirty-six hours and were all dog-tired. It was maddening to see the goal so near at hand after the long weeks of striving, and to find ourselves helpless when so close to the shore. We now saw a number of twinkling points of light among the heavily wooded slopes that rose directly from the water. There was much speculation as to whether these were the bivouacs of Allied troops waiting to prevent a landing, or of Japanese who had already landed. By this time I had ceased to be optimistic.

At length, just before dawn, the current swept us round a point in the lee of which we again managed to make progress towards the shore. There was quite a big bay here, but I have not yet been able to discover exactly what point on the west Java coast we had struck. We were certainly in the region of Merak or a little farther south.

As the first light of dawn began to grey the east, we became tremendously excited, for there in a corner of the bay less than half a mile ahead of us lay thirteen ships of varying sizes.

We had just started to pull towards them, and were within

four hundred yards of the nearest vessel, when Kinnear, in a dead voice, said quietly: "I was afraid so. They're unmistakable. They're Japs. I've seen dozens of them with that peculiar rig at Yokohama."

Still hoping against hope, one man pointed out what looked like a Swedish flag at the stern of one vessel; but whether she was a Swede or not, this was unquestionably no Allied convoy. We were too close to the ships now to turn back, and the current which had changed was sweeping us towards them. Kinnear ordered all of us to lie flat on the bottom of the boat with palm leaves and strips of attap partially concealing us. Two men remained at the oars, both dark-skinned and heavily sunburnt, while Kinnear himself, who by this time looked like a Malay, handled the steering sweep. The other ten of us were piled on top of each other in the most acute discomfort, expecting every moment to hear challenging shouts and the patter of machine-guns.

We actually passed within sixty yards of one vessel and less than a hundred yards from another, and Kinnear could see clearly one or two men leaning over the side on the deck of each. The minutes dragged by like years as we rowed slowly past the ships heading for the southern shore of the bay. It is impossible to believe that we were not seen, for the sun was already making the sky rosy in the east. But apparently they thought that the three visible figures, the oarsmen rowing native-fashion and pushing the oar against the rollock instead of pulling it towards them, were merely native fisherfolk returning after a night's trawling.

At any rate, by some miracle, we passed right through that Japanese convoy without a shot or even a challenge. Half a mile beyond the last ship we ran inshore behind the shelter of a rocky point. A heavily camouflaged warship, either a small cruiser or a large destroyer, was patrolling this strait at high speed and, just at this stage, what was unmistakably an air-raid siren sounded from the ships or from some post ashore, where increasing numbers of Japanese troops could now be seen going to and fro from the jetty where a ship was being unloaded.

We longed for the sight of Allied bombers which would reassure us that we were hitting back against this landing force; but it proved to be a false alarm and no planes were sighted.

We now settled down to a conference. The current had carried us down the coast away from Batavia, and we knew now that a large Japanese force was in possession of this area. Our boat was leaking worse than ever and it seemed certain that the thirteen of us could not go much farther in her. Wade and another member of our party decided that they would make an attempt to go overland to Batavia, since they felt that the boat was doomed. Efforts to dissuade them having failed, the remaining eleven of us decided to row on until we could turn round the south side of the island where we hoped to pick up a larger boat in which we might reach Allied occupied territory, or even Australia. Some of those who had been so hesitant the day before bewailed the failure to seize the traders' boat. But the tide had not been taken at the flood.

We rowed on, hugging the shore and keeping a watchful eye on the patrolling cruiser which must have been able to distinguish us quite clearly with telescope or field-glasses. Eventually, we rounded a point, somewhere near Labuan, I think, and passed a lighthouse on a long white beach fringed with coco-nut palms. Farther on we went ashore, got some coco-nuts, and talked to a group of excited natives who assured us that the Japanese had sent several patrols down the road which we could see between the trees, and that the Dutch had retreated a long distance inland and eastwards.

We rowed on, aided by a favourable breeze, until we came to the mouth of a small creek where a number of Javanese in long native prahus were fishing. Here we ran the boat ashore. I jumped into the water to handle her through the shallows before we reached the bank and placed my wallet with all my money, papers and credentials on the rowing thwart. I didn't think of the wallet again until we were dragging the boat up the beach amidst a clamorous horde of natives. By that time it had gone.

None of our setbacks or misadventures had depressed me

as did this loss. In retrospect, I realize that it marked the beginning of the end and was not of great importace. But while the others relaxed on the sands and chattered to the natives, who plied them with coco-nuts, I wandered round hopelessly in the trail of one of the headmen who had taken it upon himself to investigate the loss of my wallet. I felt I would have had as much chance of recovering it among the crowd at Epsom Downs on Derby Day, and of course his inquiries proved futile.

The natives were very anxious that we should keep going, as they expected Japanese to arrive at any time and did not want to be held guilty of collusion with us. But our boat was now in such a bad way that we felt it impossible to go on without attempting some repairs. Furthermore, a storm was rapidly blowing up, so we collected gear from the boat and, having made it fast to the other side of the creek, went on to a large cave which the Javanese showed us, perhaps a hundred yards along the beach.

We had just had time to start a fire and to notice that one of our light-fingered friends had removed our only parang and a small hatchet that we'd acquired, when the storm burst with great fury. When it was over the Professor, who had insisted on going up to the native village—since Wade's departure, he was, unfortunately, our Malay spokesman—returned to report that the villagers had become very hostile, that they had refused him rice, and that other natives had come into the village waving a Japanese flag. As the natives had been perfectly friendly on the beach, we realized that the Professor had put his foot into it again.

A few minutes later the cave was surrounded by a horde of yelling Javanese, brandishing parangs and long, wicked-looking knives, and waving Japanese flags. Two of them had firearms of a kind, but the vintage was such that I thought they were at least as dangerous to their owners as to anybody at whom they were aimed.

However, it became abundantly clear with more and more natives coming up every minute that we had to leave the cave and return to our boat. The attitude of the crowd outside, which had swollen to about eighty, was now markedly hostile. When we got to our boat we found it more than half full of water, but even so we attempted to empty it and refloat it. But just as we were getting in the natives seized the boat, dragged it across to the other side of the creek, and then flung themselves on us.

We were without even a club or a knife to defend ourselves, were utterly worn out, and three of us could scarcely walk. To resist in the circumstances could lead only to murder. So the word was passed to take it quietly and do nothing to exasperate the natives who were already beside themselves with a mixture of Japanese propaganda, local oratory and a good deal of native toddy.

They were binding us pretty roughly with great lengths of boat rope when the Professor decided that this was the moment to protest. He said something rude in Malay, and tried to push away the man who was looting his pockets. He was immediately knocked down, or rather fell down after receiving a punch on the face, and there, by the grace of God, he at last lay quiet, whimpering to himself. It was perhaps just as well for him that we were helplessly trussed by this time. It was certainly lucky for us that he lost heart so quickly, because knives were being brandished within a few inches of our throats, and it only needed a foolish gesture to precipitate a massacre.

The sands of time had run out at last. The struggle which we had entered on twenty-one days before had ended in defeat. It was about eight o'clock on the evening of Saturday, 7 March.

CHAPTER VIII

NIGHT IN HELL

"I am ready; but let the reckoning stand till day:
I have loved the sunlight as dearly as any alive."
"You shall die at dawn," said they.
                    —NEWBOLT, "He Fell Among Thieves"

WITHIN ten minutes, my arms from wrist to shoulder were bound with about thirty yards of rope so tightly that my shoulders began to ache immediately with the pressure, and within half an hour my bare arms were galled as with fire. Everyone having been secured, they started to drive us forward. Many shouts of "Nippon" and gestures of shooting and throat-cutting indicated quite clearly the particular picnic that lay ahead.

Night had descended swiftly and now, as we marched through the village and on to the main road, we came under tall, heavily foliaged trees where it was very dark indeed. I was being led along in front and could see nothing of the others. Three natives walked with me holding various ends of rope from the miscellany bound round my arms, while a fourth with a bicycle and a shotgun dogged my footsteps. I was so weary that I could hardly push one foot in front of the other, but every time I lurched or stumbled the point of a parang would be pushed against my back or brandished under my nose.

Presently one of my keepers, realizing that I was just about all-in, pushed a thin native cigarette, the tobacco rolled in rice straw, between my lips. He continued to do this as fast as I could smoke them. I almost loved that man.

The colonel, who had a shocking gash across the ball of

one foot, was limping painfully and soon bleeding at every step, so the natives were content to proceed fairly slowly. Unfortunately, this was a doubtful blessing because, although we kept trudging forward, our conductors kept saying that it was still "two-three kilometre". They kept promising that a car was coming to meet us, but at the end of two hours we realized that this was just eyewash. We were being walked back along the road that ran parallel to the coast, retracing the ground we had covered in the boat during the day.

Presently Norman came up alongside me. He and I were the only ones who had a pair of shoes left, and my shoes were already in such a condition that the soles seemed to have little liaison with the uppers. Then the native who appeared to be the leading spirit in the round-up came alongside us with his bicycle. He had not been on the beach when we were seized, but was apparently the chief fifth columnist and Japanese agent along this section of the coast. We soon learned that he had served for some years with the Shanghai police and knew a good deal of English. He was crammed to the roots of his hair with Axis propaganda which he prattled at us almost incessantly for the best part of two hours. At first it was amusing, then it became irritating, and finally in our exhausted state, with nerves raw, it was rather like a dentist's drill on the nerve of your tooth. His monologue went somewhat like this:

"Bloody English! All no good. All run by Jews. Chamberlain—Jew, Churchill—Jew, all Jewish money. All Englishmen rotten with too much whisky-stingah. You like whisky-stingah? Nippon give you whisky-stingah. You like gin? You get plenty gin in one-two hours. All British same Dutch, no bloody good. Dutchman here take everything, give Javanese nothing. Now Nippon come, Dutchmen all finish. Soon Nippon take all Asia. Hitler take Britain. Soon all British become coolies. We are masters. We have many hundred Europeans working coolie for us. Very good, no? . . . Hong Kong finish, Singapore finish, Batavia finish. Many white men already dead bang-bang. Maybe tomorrow morning you get shot too. You no like to be shot? Nippon shoot all white men verree quick, verree quick. . . ." And so on *ad infinitum, ad nauseam.*

Towards midnight, this human gramophone got weary of persecuting us and dropped back to the others. I was now so done that often I was actually asleep on my feet, until the sole native who was still holding my rope would give it a twitch, producing the most excruciating pain on my galled wrists, which were bleeding. Presently, when we got to a native village, he went off somewhere leaving me in the charge of another man who did not bother to hold the rope but merely walked beside me, wheeling his bicycle. He seemed a bit inattentive, and presently, in the shadow of a big tree, I managed to drop off a large length of rope which I had been steadily loosening and unknotting for the past hour. A little later I repeated the performance, until at length there were only about six feet of loose rope around my wrists and my arms themselves were no longer bound.

Norman had now begun to walk on fast with his guard, then rest on a bank until the others came up. I decided to join him, but dropped back first to see how the colonel was bearing up. One of the New Zealanders, who had had malaria, was also in a bad way, but they were both getting along somehow. One had to admire their courage. The only groans and moans came from the Professor who had been saying for the past ten kilometres that he could not go another step.

Seeing the state that the others were in, I now suggested a sit down strike to try to obtain a rest. I set the example by squatting firmly in the middle of the road and refusing to budge. At first the natives tried kicking me and hauling on the ropes, and when I still refused to move they called up the human gramophone, who informed me that they were going to cut my throat. There followed a considerable barney during which I had the satisfaction of telling him that he'd be hanging from one of the coco-nut palms as soon as the Allies took the island back. Then one of the others made a swipe at me with his parang which I only just ducked. However, the colonel and the others kept saying that it was hopeless, that I could achieve nothing, and would certainly get cut up if I went on sitting there. So I let them pull me to my feet and lurched on after Norman. At least we all had three or four minutes' rest.

The road from now on ran across what seemed in the dim moonlight to be a series of tin-mines. Then the padi country, all under water, appeared again on both sides of the road.

As on several previous occasions during our Odyssey, I kept thinking how similar it all was to some of the adventure stories of Ballantyne, Henty, Stevenson and others that I had read as a boy. Here we were, thonged and guarded on our way to the cannibal kraal or the Indian village, and it would not be long now before we reached the stake or, more probably, the shooting party.

I think most of us were already in that state of extreme exhaustion which takes you beyond the realm of worry or anxiety. I told myself that this was probably the last night I would ever see, and that I was looking at the stars for the last time, but somehow fear seemed to remain at a distance. I had had no more than a snatched doze during the past seventy-two hours, and now the only important thing seemed to be that one should at last be able to lie down. Whether one lay down with a native knife in the back, or with a Japanese bullet through the brain did not seem of overwhelming importance.

I now joined Norman on his forced marches ahead of the main mob. After about another hour, during which we managed to lie down for a couple of minutes on two or three occasions, I noticed that our guards, who had diminished steadily in number as the night wore on, were some distance behind.

I seemed to have got a second wind by this time and began to speculate about the possibility of dropping off unobserved in the shadow of one of the big trees. The trouble was that water of an unknown depth stretched for at least a hundred yards to right and left of the road. In the course of the next half hour, I mentioned my plan to Norman and one of the others, but they both strongly opposed it, saying that I had no chance of getting away. However, as I felt fairly certain that the Japanese would shoot us, I decided that once we came to any country which offered a chance of running, I would make a break for it.

But before we got clear of the tin-mines and swamps of this section our guards had returned to us, and no further chances of making a get-away presented themselves. In any case, any such attempt would have been doomed to failure, even if I had eluded my immediate pursuers. The Japanese were by now in control of the whole area, every native village was swarming with Japanese agents, and even at this moment arrangements for the surrender of all Allied forces on the island were being completed by the Dutch Government.

By three o'clock in the morning, I was aching from head to foot, even though the guards now let me drop the last piece of rope so that my hands were free again. Now, staggering from side to side of the road, I began to see visions. The end of a wharf, or jetty, swathed in mist, kept looming up amidst the darkness ahead. There seemed to be a woman standing on the edge of the wharf stretching out her arms and trying to peer into the darkness. I could not determine whether the woman was my wife or not, although the hallucination must have occurred at least a score of times.

After a spell, I started seeing great stacks of wheat bags or wool bales such as one sees on any Australian wharf or siding. This went on until we came to some sort of roofed-in meeting-place at the end of the native village and here, at long last after nine hours on our feet, we were allowed to rest.

I fell asleep within a minute, and it seemed that within the same minute we were being hustled to our feet again; but actually, by someone's watch, we had twenty minutes' sleep which gave us a new lease of life.

So, somehow, we managed to keep going until the tropic dawn swept up with its usual extravagant splendour. I kept muttering bits of Newbolt's "He Fell Among Thieves", which seemed singularly appropriate and oddly comforting. All my worldly possessions had been stripped from me when we were dragged out of the boat, except my passport and two ten dollar bills which were in a hip pocket that the searching fingers of the looters had failed to discover.

Now the road opened up ahead where it ran into a bigger and wider motor road. A minute later two trucks swept past along the main road, and I recognized Japanese heads. Then there was a shout, the trucks braked to a standstill and, waving rifles and bayonets, half a dozen Japanese came rushing down the road towards us. There followed a tremendous palaver, during which our captors were obviously informing the Japanese what a magnificent feat they had performed in capturing us, and the Japanese, listening to them with half an ear, were devouring us with curious eyes.

The Japanese indicated that we should climb aboard the truck, which we did gratefully, collapsing on the top of sacks of rice which seemed like the downiest of beds. Then we proceeded at high speed down the road until we came to what was obviously a big supply dump on the edge of a park, or public square.

There were a number of Japanese here unloading stores from a fleet of army trucks. A mob of natives of every nondescript breed gave us a rapturous welcome, which suggested to me the howling mobs round the guillotine when the tumbrils arrived. They were all busy gesticulating (in a language that needed no interpretation) that we were about to be executed, although there seemed to be a division of opinion as to whether decapitation or shooting was to be the *modus operandi*.

We were ordered down from the truck and made to line up, at attention, in single file in the roadway. Then a detail of a dozen Japanese, hastily loading their rifles, came doubling out from a neighbouring villa and were formed up a few yards from us, while the mob howled for blood like a League crowd in the last quarter of the Grand Final in Melbourne.

At this moment two trucks were backed out from a ditch, and it seemed obvious that this was where we should be lined up before the shooting party, so that the bodies could be covered over without much trouble. Very soon we should at last be able to lie down indefinitely. I felt so certain of death, that I understood what Newbolt means when he speaks of being "untroubled of hope". This was our dawn, our last dawn.

I looked across at Norman and caught his eye. I knew that he was sure of it too.

PART TWO

GUESTS OF NIPPON

CHAPTER IX

THE BLACK HOLE OF SERANG

Fetter'd in hand, but joined in heart,
'Twas still some solace in the dearth
Of the pure elements of earth,
To hearken to each other's speech,
And each turn comforter to each
With some new hope, or legend old. . . .
—BYRON, "The Prisoner of Chillon"

THE first ray of hope flickered across my mind when an officer came out from one of the houses and addressed us courteously in English. Then he began to take down personal details. He was immensely impressed with the fact that we had rowed down to Java from Banka and it was obvious that this gave us a standing which we should otherwise have lacked.

It now became clear that whatever might happen later they had no intention of shooting us at present. The officer informed us that as soon as some medical kit arrived at the supply dump our wounds and cuts would be seen to. We were very glad of this, for the feet of the shoeless were in a bad way, and my legs were covered with festered sores and small ulcers as a result of scratches and mosquito bites infected in the swamp mud.

We then sat down by the side of the road, while all but two of our guards were dismissed. We were given the Japanese "hard tack" ration which consists of a cloth bag containing about a pound of small, hard, water biscuits, with a few parti-coloured pieces of boiled sugar scattered among the biscuits. In the meantime the native audience, which had been bitterly disappointed over the Japanese failure to execute us, began to ebb away. I must admit that at this time, and indeed until we got to Serang, I did not feel the smallest ill-will towards the Japanese, but would have given a great deal to have been able to lay my hands on some of the Indonesians.

Towards noon some medical supplies came to hand, and our cuts and sores were dressed by a medical orderly on the veranda of one of the villas which the Japanese had taken over. We were then conducted into the shade of a huge mango-tree, where we were able to stretch out at full length. Presently the long-promised meal arrived. It consisted of a Japanese ration bucket, made of wood, which was full of excellent rice, another bucket with dried fish, and then a great oil tin with about two gallons of the thickest stew I have ever seen. The villa in whose grounds we lay boasted a large poultry yard, and the Japanese had decimated the stock to produce a tremendous stew with chickens, ducks, geese and a turkey or two. We had been living on coco-nut through the past forty-eight hours, and it was not surprising how fast pint after pint of that solid poultry stew with its thick gravy was devoured. The Japanese did the same for us that night and again next day. These were the only really good meals I received from the Japanese during three and a half years.

All these Japanese officers were particularly courteous, and one of them said to one of our party, referring to our Odyssey, "You are very brave men; we would like to do all that we can for you." That evening we were told to bed ourselves down on the veranda of the house where the officers were sleeping. A group of officers, sitting at a table, called me over and asked me if I knew the news. They then told me that Singapore had fallen on 15 February, that New Guinea and New Britain were in Japanese hands, that the whole of the Dutch East Indies had been overrun, that Japanese had occupied Batavia and Sourabaya, and finally, in great triumph, they announced that the forces on Java had surrendered unconditionally that day—8 March.

Some of my companions, when I retailed this a few minutes later, refused to believe it and said it was propaganda, but as a journalist I felt sure that the Japanese were telling the truth as far as they knew it, and I felt fairly sure, during subsequent weeks when there were big rumours of Allied triumphs in Java, that all resistance had ceased as the Japanese said. This proved correct.

These Japanese, like all others we met in the coming months, were literally drunk with victory. They asked me where my wife and family lived, and expressed regret for my sake that they would be in Melbourne within a fortnight. I expressed polite scepticism, at which they laughed confidently. Throughout the whole interview they made no attempt to pump me for information and when I pleaded tiredness after a few minutes, they let me go immediately. One of them, who had already bought us bananas out of his own pocket, asked if there was anything we lacked, and I made a request for mosquito-nets. He promised to get them next day but, unfortunately for us, orders came during the night for all these officers to move on and, when we awoke in the morning, out of the whole unit there was only a handful of N.C.Os and privates left.

This was the first and also the last occasion when I was treated with consideration and decency by the Japanese. The favourable impression created among most of us was soon to be erased by ensuing events; but, to bear fair testimony, no British officers could have behaved with more courtesy or consideration than this particular set of A.S.C. officers on the west Java coast.

Next day the fittest of us were asked to assist in moving some furniture for the Japanese, and then Norman and I were requested to write an account of how we became Japanese prisoners. We confined ourselves solely to events from the time when our ship was sunk, events which could have not the smallest military significance.

Norman and I had already decided that it would be fatal to disclose any connexion with the Malaya Broadcasting Corporation. Now and henceforth we stuck rigidly to the story that I was simply a journalist and newspaper correspondent, and that Norman was a war historian and dramatic producer. Had Japanese Intelligence ever discovered any connexion between Rohan Rivett and Terry Goulburn, of

Singapore Radio, this book would never have been written. Norman and I both felt that the Japanese would do their utmost to make us broadcast in their interests, as in fact they did with other captives. We also knew a good deal about their methods of "third degree" and, while prepared to be shot as the penalty for capture, we were not anxious to die a lingering death in the torture chambers of the Japanese Gestapo.

That afternoon the Professor and another member of the party were pronounced by the Japanese to be suffering from malaria. They then announced that we were being sent to Serang, where we would find ourselves among other Australians, British and Americans. About three o'clock in the afternoon we were all placed in a truck and driven through village streets packed with jeering Indonesians, until we arrived outside what was apparently a dilapidated native cinema at Serang, the biggest town in Java, west of Batavia.

Here the native mob was in the same derisive mood, but the attitude of the Japanese we now met was very different. We gathered from other captives, also lined up with us to give their particulars, that there had been many brutal bashings of captives by the Japanese, and that conditions inside the cinema were very grim indeed. We also discovered that we were about to join some hundreds of survivors from the Australian cruiser *Perth* and the American cruiser *Houston*, sunk off Java by the Japanese a few days before.

A few minutes later we were thrust into the dark interior of the building. Neither the scraps of information, nor the changed attitude of these Japanese, had prepared us for what we saw inside. Seated on the bare stone floor in rows, packed together like penguins or seals on one of those rocky beaches which the publishers of natural history books love to photograph, were hundreds on hundreds of Europeans, most of them unshaven and incredibly dirty. With few exceptions, they were stark naked except for a small calico loincloth.

A guard cleared a space for us with the butt of his rifle and told us to sit. If we spoke to each other or to anyone else, we should be punished.

I suppose that with normal seating that cinema would accommodate perhaps five hundred people. About three times that number were now jammed into it. It soon became obvious that the handful of guards at the back of the cinema had no chance of enforcing the no-speaking order if one were careful. So we rapidly learned something of the history of the sailors around us, which is told in detail in the next chapter. Some of the men had been in this cinema since 3 March without being given a chance to wash even their hands or faces. Food was limited to a small issue of almost uncooked rice of the poorest quality in the early afternoon, and a similar issue or a small loaf of white bread in the evening. There was nothing else of any kind at any time, and everybody who had been in the place for twenty-four hours was ravenous.

Several of the boys from the ships were badly wounded, but they were lying on the filthy floor like the rest of us, having received no bandages, dressings or treatment, despite repeated protests and appeals to the Japanese. The majority of the other sailors, particularly the *Perth* boys, were covered with a thick coating of oil fuel, which had also got into their eyes, causing pain.

On the balcony, at the back of the cinema, the Japanese had a machine-gun mounted, and at times a second gun was also trained on us from this point. The only egress allowed from the cinema hall was by a door on the left which gave on to a narrow strip of yard covered with rubbish. At the end of this, perhaps twenty yards from the door, a large pit had been dug, and across this half a dozen boards and beams had been carelessly laid. This open cesspit was the sole latrine accommodation for over fifteen hundred men. A high stone wall fringed with spikes and broken glass and with barbed wire entanglements beyond, separated this yard from the neighbouring buildings. Altogether, it was as unsavoury a hole as I have ever been in, and with this massed horde of unwashed humanity packed inside, things became more unpleasant with each succeeding day.

Here are same daily jottings which I made on the backs

of pink paper cinema slips which were issued to us in lieu of toilet paper. I smuggled these notes out of the Serang jail five weeks later, and copied them in Batavia. Since then they have passed through many vicissitudes in the course of evading over a hundred Japanese searches. But the diary entries give some impression of the Black Hole of Serang.

13 March. Another Friday the thirteenth! On the last one, last month, we were bombed all day from just after dawn until the ship was put out of action and we were beached on the Banka coast. This has been nearly as grim. We've had no food all day until four o'clock this afternoon, when we got exactly eleven spoonfuls of boiled rice (almost raw rice would be more accurate). We hope we'll get another similar ration before midnight, but there's no sign of it yet (8 p.m.). . . .

We had to "sit to attention", which means sitting bolt upright in silence, for two hours before the meal this afternoon while the Japs tankoed (counted) us. On the first nine occasions their counts varied between 1620 and 1483. They've now decided after several more counts on some intermediate figure, but their system of counting is so weird and wonderful that I doubt if they really know to the nearest fifty just how many of us they've got jammed in this b—— hellhole.

When we were at last allowed to talk again after the meal, had a great yarn with half a dozen of the boys. Tom Mooney, of Burnley, a torpedo gunner, Bill Briscoe of Williamstown, Vic Duncan of Sydney, Jacko Jackson of Tasmania, Corky Corcoran of Albert Park, Writer John Rockey of Bexley, Butcher Alf Thomas of Sydney, Alan Gee of Beechworth, Slim Hedderick of Mordialloc, and Bob Bland of Fremantle, are the lads I've come to know. We had a tremendous discussion about the rival merits of Rugby League and Rugby Union which led to the inevitable dog-fight as to whether Aussie rules is better than rugger, soccer and the rest, as most of us from the southern States believe. When I left them a few minutes ago they were still going hammer and tongs about test cricket and bodyline. You'd think they were sitting in lounge chairs in the Australia instead of being huddled together in this hole where none of them has had a square meal in the ten or eleven days they've been here.

The *Perth* boys are grand with their six or seven wounded mates who have to be carried to and from the wretched latrine day and night. If we stay here much longer on this ration, which is less than one eats as a sweet for one meal at home, there won't be a man here who can carry anybody but himself. Still no bandages, antiseptics or treatment for these boys, although it is now thirteen days since *Perth* was sunk. But their spirit is unbeatable and, except for one chap who is in constant pain, not even a groan escapes them.

The Black Hole of Serang

Later. The Yanks from *Houston* are a bit better off than the rest of us, for some of them got ashore with some money and the guards are now letting them send money out to buy from the native vendors. The guards are getting a rake-off of anything from 200 to 1000 per cent, but at this stage any of us would cheerfully give a pound note for a few bananas or a small loaf of bread. Some of the boys have scrounged old tins and a bit of wood and are trying to cook among the rubbish dumps which lead to the hole in the ground which serves as a latrine. There was a fortunate break for half a dozen, earlier today. A plump cockerel appeared on the top of the wall which separates the latrine area from the adjacent buildings. After standing there tantalizingly for perhaps ten minutes, he yielded to the blandishments of a Texan who is tall, dark and handsome enough to make his fortune in Hollywood, and came fluttering down on our side of the wall. Within five minutes, sections of the unfortunate bird were already stewing, grilling or roasting on a dozen sticks and pieces of tin around the fires. I'll bet the Japs ban the fires tomorrow.

Our friend the frog-faced Jap officer came in again today and again started threatening some of the fellows with his revolver. On his last visit he asked one of the English naval officers if he would commit hara-kiri there and then if he lent him his gun. This strutting Puss-in-Boots is just itching to put some lead into one of us, but so far hasn't been able to find any excuse. He has struck several men across the face and kicked one Englishman on his bandaged leg. He keeps up a constant jabber in Japanese, Malay and broken English, but they are all equally indistinguishable to us.

Some of the boys were taken down to the river this afternoon and given the first chance that any of us has had to wash any part of his body since we've been here. One night when it rained, about thirty of us risked shooting by sneaking out among the rubbish by the latrine and getting under the water spouts falling from the eaves, but most of the boys were not so lucky.

Things are worse at night. With some of the boys up on the stage and others, including the worst fever cases, sleeping outside right on top of the latrine, there's just room for us to lie down if we each lie on our sides. The trouble is that it's a physical impossibility to leave the one hip bone pressed against the bare stone for hours on end. Inevitably you have to turn over and this involves half a dozen of your immediate neighbours turning over, for we're lying chest to spine right through the place.

The Japs have only one machine-gun mounted on the gallery above us now but they must realize that even though by a concerted rush we could take the cinema and kill the twenty or thirty guards with our bare hands, we'd have no earthly chance of getting far out of this town, let alone of getting a boat down at the coast. It isn't the Japanese guards who keep us prisoners, it's the fact that every one of these teeming millions of Sundanese and Javanese acts today as a Japanese agent. I'd give a month's pay to get my hands on the swine who seized us and took all my photos and private letters. However, I suppose we were lucky they didn't cut our heads off. Some of the *Perth* and *Houston* boys saw other shipwrecked mates decapitated as soon as they were washed up on the beach.

After some days one of the Japanese officers gave me a book, the only one in the building. It was *Come and Get It* by Edna Ferber. This seemed to me just the thing to help to distract the wounded sailors. They were pathetically grateful when I started reading it aloud to them. Then I organized a relay of readers so that they got about four hours a day. They would have enjoyed it even more if the text had not been full of descriptions of tremendous meals.

One morning a guard came inside calling out my name. I was taken out to a room adjoining the hall, which probably served as a foyer to the cinema normally, but was now the kitchen where four Americans helped to prepare the food for our guards. Here a small, spectacled Japanese introduced himself and informed me that he was a war correspondent representing the *Asahi Shimbun*. He said he had heard of our exploit in rowing down from Banka to Java, and asked me to write an account of it. I did so while, by order of the correspondent or one of the guards, I was given bread, bananas, an egg and even a water-ice—probably more vitamins than I had received in the previous week. This correspondent was hopeful that our names could soon be sent home to let our people know we were safe. This had been our main pre-occupation, for we knew what anxiety must be weighing on our families since our last cables from Singapore.

At the end of the second week since the first of *Perth's* survivors had been placed in this prison, small quantities of dressings and antiseptics were brought down from the neigh-bouring jail, where other Europeans were confined, and the worst of the wounds and sores received some treatment.

My legs were now in rather a mess, the starvation rations in the cinema having weakened the body's resistance to the

poison in my system. At the end of our attempted escape, I
had been as tough as whipcord, and probably fitter than ever
in my life. Now there was the inevitable reaction to what
we had been through, and the lack of any nourishing food
played havoc with a number of us. Just how weak I had
become I discovered on the afternoon of 17 March, when
Norman, the Professor and myself were marched across the
town to the native jail where other members of our party
had already been sent.

We believed that no change could be for the worse after
the cinema, but a few days in this jail convinced us that we
were wrong.

CHAPTER X

H.M.A.S. *PERTH* AND U.S.S. *HOUSTON*

And the sun went down, and the stars came out far over the summer sea,
But never a moment ceased the fight of the one and the fifty-three.
Ship after ship, the whole night long, their high-built galleons came,
Ship after ship, the whole night long, with her battle-thunder and flame; ...
For some were sunk and many were shatter'd, and so could fight us no more—
God of battles, was ever a battle like this in the world before?

—TENNYSON, "The Revenge"

H.M.A.S *Perth* left Australia on her last voyage on 17 February 1942, when she drew out of Fremantle harbour and sailed northwards towards Java as escort to a small convoy of supply ships. Presently a radio signal ordered the ships to return to Fremantle, but a later signal told *Perth* to resume her original course alone. In all, *Perth* was recalled on three occasions, and then each time the decision was reversed. She finally reached Tanjong Pryok, the port of Batavia, on 24 February. On this and the following day Japanese planes raided the harbour, but their formation was broken up and the effectiveness of the raid was largely nullified by the barrage from *Perth's* six-inch guns and smaller armament. The blast from *Perth's* big guns was such that hundreds of windows in the warehouses along the wharves were shattered. The one plane on *Perth* was ruined by blast from the four-inch guns of H.M.A.S *Yarra,* moored alongside. Apart from damage to a small oil tanker, all the Japanese bombs missed their objectives. On 26 February *Perth* joined other cruisers and destroyers in Sourabaya.

That evening, the Allied fleet under command of Admiral Doorman of the Dutch Navy, flying his flag on H.N.M.S. *De Ruyter*, sailed from Sourabaya to intercept a Japanese convoy reported to be approaching north-eastern Java. The Allied

ships were two eight-inch gun cruisers, H.M.S. *Exeter* and
U.S.S. *Houston*, one six-inch gun cruiser, H.M.A.S. *Perth*, two
5.9-inch Dutch cruisers, H.N.M.S. *De Ruyter* and *Java*, as well
as three British destroyers, *Electra*, *Encounter*, and *Jupiter*,
and four American and two Dutch destroyers.

H.M.A.S. *Perth* had already seen more action and sailed
farther on active service than any other cruiser in the Australian squadron. Commissioned in June 1939, she was diverted
on her way home to Australia at the outbreak of the war to
the West Indies Station, and spent the following months patrolling the central Atlantic and Caribbean Sea. *Perth* arrived
in Sydney for the first time in March 1940, but after some
months in Australian waters was sent to the Mediterranean.
She was almost constantly in action in the eastern Mediterranean during the first half of 1941, and won distinction by
her work off Greece and Crete and during the Syrian campaign. In August 1941 she was refitted and then carried out
patrol duties in Australian waters until sent to Java in the
third month of the Pacific war. *Perth*, of 6980 tons, carried
eight six-inch and eight four-inch guns, apart from torpedo
tubes and lighter armament. Her complement when she went
into action in the Java Sea was about 680. She was commanded
by Captain H. M. L. Waller, D.S.O. and Bar, who had built
up a magnificent record as commander of the Australian Destroyer Flotilla in the Mediterranean.

The fighting power of U.S.S. *Houston* had been already
diminished, one of her gun turrets being out of action, thanks
to enemy bombing in the Flores Sea. Japanese aircraft
shadowed the Allied ships during the morning of 27 February,
but no contact with enemy vessels was established until the
middle of the afternoon, when Japanese cruisers and destroyers
were sighted.

It has been estimated that the initial Japanese force in
the battle of the Java Sea, which now commenced, com-
prised five cruisers and thirteen destroyers. But there are
indications that at least one Japanese battleship and other
cruisers took part in the later stages of the action. It is known
that a number of Japanese submarines were operating in the

area, but whether any of these were responsible for the tor-
pedoing of Allied ships, or whether all torpedoes came from
the destroyers, has not been established.

Fire was opened by the heavy cruisers of both sides at
30,000 yards. The light cruisers and destroyers joined in as
soon as they were within range. *Perth's* second salvo hit a
Japanese destroyer and the enemy flotilla retired into a smoke-
screen. When the smoke cleared, the enemy destroyer was
seen to be ablaze and there is little doubt that she sank.

Perth came under very heavy fire from one of the Japanese
heavy cruisers, but neither then nor later in this action was
she damaged in any way. Her next job was to effect a smoke-
screen with destroyers around H.M.S. *Exeter* which had been
badly damaged in the engine-room by an enemy salvo. The
Dutch destroyer *Witte de With*, screening Exeter, twice hit
a Jap destroyer with her salvos, but at this stage a torpedo
struck the other Dutch destroyer amidships so that she broke
in two and folded up like a jack-knife.

Admiral Doorman now made an attempt to get behind
the enemy and attack his transports, and the Allied destroyers
went into attack. As the light failed it appeared that H.M.S.
Electra battered an enemy destroyer with her gunfire, but she
herself was then mortally hit. She stopped, and one by one
her guns were silenced, until she sank just before dark.

The Japanese destroyers made another torpedo attack on
Perth without success. One of the enemy vessels was hit and
perhaps sunk during this attack. *Perth* then began a duel
with an eight-inch cruiser and scored a series of hits. When
the cruiser was last seen she was on fire and at a standstill
with her stern well down.

Darkness now veiled the battle, in which contact between
the ships had become very spasmodic. H.M.S. *Jupiter* was torpedoed on the starboard side and put out of action. She sank
before midnight.

The damaged *Exeter* with H.M.S. *Encounter*, the four
American destroyers and the surviving Dutch destroyer, managed to reach Sourabaya that night. The other four cruisers,
having seen *Exeter* into safety, turned about again. Just before

midnight *Perth* had another brush with the foe, scoring hits with at least two salvos on an enemy cruiser. Then disaster struck the Allied squadron.

The ships were proceeding in line ahead with the Admiral's flagship, *De Ruyter* leading, *Perth* next, then *Java*, with *Houston* bringing up the rear. Suddenly there was an explosion on *De Ruyter*, and *Perth* had to swerve to avoid the stricken ship which lost way and was soon aflame from stem to stern. A few minutes later there was a second explosion and *Java* dropped out of line.

Captain Waller, now left alone with *Houston* out of the fourteen ships which had opened the action in the afternoon, took violent evasive action immediately. It seems probable that the Dutch Admiral had run straight into a submarine trap and paid the penalty for having his ships in line-ahead formation. It is believed that a few score survivors from *De Ruyter* and *Java* subsequently reached the Java coast, but the majority of their crews were lost.

Of the ships which had returned to Sourabaya, only the four American destroyers escaped. *Witte De With* was bombed and sunk in Sourabaya harbour. *Exeter* and *Encounter*, which left on the night of 28 February, reported next morning that they had sighted a force of enemy ships. This was the last word received from them.

Perth and *Houston* reached Tanjong Pryok before noon on 28 February. Neither vessel could replenish the depleted stocks of ammunition for their bigger guns, but they did take on board some four-inch ammunition, oil fuel, additional fire fighting equipment and a number of small rafts, which were to prove invaluable.

At Batavia Captain Waller conferred with Commodore J. A. Collins, formerly of H.M.A.S. *Sydney*, senior Australian naval officer in Java. It was decided that *Perth* and *Houston* should endeavour to pass through the confined waters of Sunda Strait during the night and then make for Tjilatjap, on the southern coast of Java. It was probably intended that they should evacuate Allied army and air force personnel who had been left on Java.

A report from Dutch headquarters which reached Captain Waller before the cruisers left Tanjong Pryok stated that aerial reconnaissance had failed to discover any signs of the enemy in Sunda Strait or its approaches. This report is one of the unexplained enigmas of the defence of Java. That evening *Perth* personnel plotted over two hundred vessels—presumably all enemy—in the waters north of the island.

The superstitious had some grounds for feeling queasy before the Australian and American cruisers left port for the last time. In the first place, *Perth* had been recalled three times en route from Fremantle to Java. Secondly, there were two chaplains aboard—a bad omen. Both cruisers had taken on board a supply of rafts, a wise precaution but scarcely an encouraging one. The picture of Lord Nelson hanging in *Perth's* wardroom had dropped from the bulkhead in the Battle of the Java Sea and had not been restored to its place, but was left lying face downwards. Finally, the ship's mascot, a tabby cat named Red Lead, beloved by the crew, made repeated attempts to leave the ship before she sailed from Tanjong Pryok.

As the two cruisers drew out of the harbour, the horizon was clouded with billowing cumulous clouds, red in the sunset and shot through with lightning.

The last hour of February 1942 should find a permanent niche in the naval histories of Australia and the United States. Seldom since Sir Richard Grenville went to his death off the Azores has there been a fight against such odds as those which *Perth* and *Houston* faced in the hour before midnight in Sunda Strait.

Just after eleven o'clock, three hours after leaving Batavia, one of the lookouts on *Perth*, which was leading, reported a dark object to starboard and, a few minutes later, the Australian cruiser opened fire from her forward turrets. *Perth* signalled that she had sighted a cruiser near Sunda Strait. This was the last word received about *Perth* or *Houston* until June, when a letter of mine, read over Batavia radio by the Japanese, informed the people at home of the glorious final chapter in the history of the two cruisers.

Events now occurred with kaleidoscopic rapidity. It soon became apparent that a great number of enemy vessels lay around the two cruisers at the northern entrance to Sunda Strait. Almost immediately enemy salvos were screaming over the Allied cruisers from many directions.

The gunners of *Perth* and *Houston* found targets looming up through the darkness at almost point-blank range. It appears that a huge enemy fleet, comprising aircraft-carriers, cruisers, destroyers, transports, tankers and supply ships, was about to launch the main Japanese landing on the north-west corner of Java in the region of Merak, at the entry to Sunda Strait. The transports and supply ships were drawn up in close formation in a huge crescent. *Perth* and *Houston* passed between ships and shore, belching shells from every gun that they could bring to bear. The enemy warships furiously replied.

At such range, even in the darkness, it was inevitable that both sides should wreak execution. However, thanks to Captain Waller's clever manoeuvring and the fact that he kept his ship down to half speed, nearly all the Japanese salvos fell in front of the ships, causing no damage. But *Perth* and *Houston* had the kind of target which gunners dream about. As one of *Perth's* torpedomen said to me, "You could see them now and then barely a mile away, dozens of 'em."

One of *Houston's* officers, who was on the bridge throughout the engagement, said, "There was just a solid wall of enemy ships. You didn't have to sight. You just blazed away." *Perth* used all her torpedoes, and it seems probable that most of them found their billets.

Despite the tornado of fire to which the Allied cruisers were exposed, it was twenty minutes before *Perth* was hit. The first shell to come aboard damaged the forward funnel, carried away a lifeboat, and wreaked havoc on the port pom-pom and flag-deck. Thereafter, both *Perth* and *Houston* were hit repeatedly, and about midnight two torpedoes struck *Perth*, the first on the starboard side, the second in the forward engine room. At the second hit the vessel began to lose way, and on the bridge Captain Waller exclaimed: "That's torn it!"

Perth had now fired the last of her four-inch shells and had only a half-dozen six-inch left. The gunners kept blazing away with star shells and practice ammunition. *Houston* was also virtually out of ammunition. So close did Japanese destroyers come during the action that on several occasions the cruisers opened fire with their machine-guns. After the second torpedo hit *Perth*, Captain Waller gave the order, "Abandon ship; every man for himself." He was last seen standing on his bridge watching the last of the Carley floats thrown into the water.

As the vessel began to sink, she was hit by a third torpedo on the port side towards the stern. A fourth torpedo found its billet while some of the men were still clinging to her side as she began to slip more deeply into the water. She finally sank about 12.15 a.m. on 1 March. The tornado of enemy fire was now concentrated on *Houston,* and in the space of a few minutes she too was in a sinking condition. Less than twenty minutes after *Perth* had disappeared, *Houston* followed her to the bottom of Sunda Strait.

Houston was the crack warship of Admiral Hart's Far Eastern Fleet. President Roosevelt had spent several days aboard her during his term of office, the ship being fitted with a special lift to enable the President to go below decks to his stateroom. A few weeks before she was sunk Houston had put up a splendid show in defending four transports carrying Australian reinforcements from Darwin to Timor. The names of *Houston* and *Perth* must have an honoured place in the records of naval actions in this war. They went down, but they took tremendous toll of the foe before their flags sank below the waters of the Java Sea.

Naval officers on a Japanese destroyer, which picked up some of *Perth's* survivors after the action, said that the Allied cruisers had accounted for three cruisers and nine destroyers. What is certain is that men from *Perth* and *Houston* themselves saw three enemy transports and one converted aircraft-carrier down by the stern and practically beached. The Japanese claimed that one of their vessels which overturned was a hospital supply ship, but it was not lit up and there was no means of distinguishing it in the night action. Probably the full tally of Japan's losses in the Battle of the Java Sea, and the subsequent Battle of Sunda Strait, will never be known unless records are found in the Navy Department at Tokyo. But the Japanese were tremendously impressed with the deadliness and valour of the two cruisers in their hopeless fight against overwhelming odds.

On both *Perth* and *Houston* a large number of officers and men were trapped below in the engine rooms and magazines, and went down with their vessels. A number of those who got into the water perished there as shells and torpedoes exploded against the ship's side. The men struggling in the water found themselves in the middle of a great pool of fuel oil which got into their eyes and covered them from head to foot. Clinging to Carley floats and life-belts, those who survived made desperate efforts to reach the shore, only to be thwarted by the same swift and treacherous currents we met with in these waters a few days later. Some men on life-boats or floats spent over twenty-four hours on the water before they managed to reach the shore. Others, who had been wounded, or who could not cling to the rafts, perished in the sea.

About two hundred survivors were picked up next morning by a Japanese destroyer and transferred to the transport *Som-dong Maru*, where they were quite well treated until they were put ashore and handed over to army guards at Serang.

Another large party who got ashore on the beach, after burying some of their comrades, struck inland in an attempt to contact Allied forces. Most of them had lost all their clothing or had it ruined by the oil fuel, and were clad only in sarongs, loin cloths and other odd garments obtained from the natives. This party, footsore and hungry, finally reached a village near Pandeglang, where they were seized by the natives and handed over to the Japanese, who looted them and allowed a clamouring mob of natives to beat them with sticks and bamboo rods before taking them on trucks to Serang.

At least two of the men washed up on the west coast of Java are known to have been beheaded by the Sundanese with their parangs, and this may have been the fate of others. Altogether, about 330 men from *Perth* and 350 from *Houston* survived the action, but many of these were to die subsequently in Japanese prison camps and ships.

There is little point in attempting a postmortem on the events of 27-8 February 1942. But many will regret that the handling of the Allied squadron was left to a senior officer whose gallantry was unquestioned but who had no experience of actual warfare. It is many years since the Dutch Navy has taken part in a fleet action, but on the Allied ships there was, in Captain Waller, a man with an experience in this war which few men could equal. The tragedy—for the glory of the end cannot conceal its bitterness—is that in the interests of seniority, his talents were exploited only in a subordinate position.

CHAPTER XI

NATIVE JAIL

Prison chaplain (intoning from Lovelace):
    "Stone walls do not a prison make
      Nor iron bars a cage."
Convict (dolefully): Maybe not, Guv'nor, but they 'elps,
    y'know, they 'elps.

THE Serang jail was crowded as never before in its history. The normal complement of native convicts had been herded into one wing of the prison, while in the other cells the Japanese had placed Dutchmen, their women and children, officers and men from *Perth* and *Houston*, odd soldiers and airmen, Dutch and British picked up in Western Java, and various stray captives like ourselves.

No attempt was made to make accommodation. As long as the cell doors would close, new arrivals were pushed within. In the first cell in which Norman and I found ourselves, there were thirty-seven Allied officers and civilians. An hour later we were transferred to another cell containing thirty-four Australian, American and English officers. The legend in Dutch above the door stated that this luxurious chamber was designed for eight native convicts.

A narrow gangway ran down the middle of the cell from the iron grille doorway. Stone slabs, about six feet wide, reached from the gangway to either wall and on these the prisoners lay stretched on the bare stone without blankets, mats or any other bedding, resembling nothing so much as fish in a fishmonger's window. Even fish could not have been jammed more closely together. On one side of the gangway the raised slab ended a few feet from the barred door, and in this space there was a wooden bucket in which we received water once a day, and a similar wooden bucket which acted as a latrine for all occupants of the cell.

During the first few days we were never allowed out of the cell into the stone courtyard. The cell door was opened only to admit the tin plates carrying our scanty issue of rice twice a day, and to allow the latrine bucket to be emptied. The Malay convicts used to disport themselves around the well in the courtyard, pouring gallons of water over their bodies, while we were without enough water to wash even our hands and faces. Later, this situation improved, and we were allowed to draw water from the well for bathing, but in the crowded cells conditions were always unpleasant, particularly after many men began to succumb to the ravages of dysentery due to the uncooked rice and the general filth.

In this cell I met a number of officers from *Perth* and *Houston,* including Lieutenant Roberts, of Adelaide, Warrant-officer Cecil Vowell, of Ivanhoe, Lieutenant John Martin, of Perth, and others. Later, in another cell, we met Lieutenants Gordon Black and Bill Roberts, of Melbourne, Claude Woodley and John Ross, of Sydney (Ross, a veteran of Gallipoli on loan from the Royal Navy), Frank Hawkins, Schoolmaster "Tiger" Lyons who did wonders in the last days in obtaining food for his cell from the native market, and Lloyd Burgess who had been at Scots College, and afterwards with Huddart Parker in Melbourne before joining *Perth*. American officers in my cell included Lieutenants John Stivers, George Winslow, "Red" May and Joe Dalton, all from *Houston*.

It was at this stage that I met a thin, bearded *Perth* survivor with a bandaged foot, to whom I started chatting casually about nothing in particular. To our mutual amazement and delight, we discovered that we had both been at Queen's (Melbourne University). This was Chaplain Keith Mathieson of Ivanhoe, Cavendish and Monbulk, Victoria, who was on his way to join *Hobart* when *Perth* was sunk. He had left Australia on his first seagoing commission on 16 February and had been sunk twelve days later. At one stage, at Tanjong Pryok, *Perth* and *Hobart* were in harbour together and the padre entered a boat to go across to his new ship. Then the

Japanese raided the harbour, and afterwards *Perth* put to sea before the transfer could be effected. We did not know, at this stage, whether he would have been back in Australia or at the bottom of the ocean if he had gone across to *Hobart*. Despite the Japs' stories about sinking everything, a number of our people believed that *Hobart* had got home.

This meeting with Mathieson was the beginning of a close friendship which grew and ripened in succeeding years. In the prison camps of the Burma jungle, few men were to do so much to maintain morale and aid the sick as the slender, bearded figure who became known to one and all, quite simply, as "Padre".

One or two notes from my diary offer a sidelight on how we passed the days in the cells.

We've organized a series of first-rate lectures in this cell. Bill Ditmar, a Dutch Catalina pilot, shot down over Sunda Strait, gave a fascinating talk today on international water-polo, at which he has represented the Netherlands. One of the Australian officers made an amusing attempt to instruct the Americans from *Houston* in the intricacies of cricket, in a very would-be Oxford accent which is what my beloved Damon Runyon would call "the phonus bolonus".

We're all growing a nice line in beards now. Mine has been sprouting since I last shaved in Singapore on 11 February, and is vastly better (or worse) than those of these naval laddies which have only been under way for three weeks. When we were allowed out for the so-called "medical parade"—this consists of the *Houston* doctor telling you what you need for your skin sores, fever, stomach troubles or dysentery and that he hasn't got it—someone made the crack that I came round a corner in three stages. First came the glow, then came the monstrous red beard, and finally I hove into sight myself. It certainly is not the sort of thing I would care to wear when walking with my wife down Collins Street. I wonder whether the Japs have any intention of ever giving us a razor or a pair of scissors?

. . . Of course most of us still think of food about half the time that we're awake. I keep seeing visions of the meals at the Café Richelieu opposite the corner of the Faubourg Montmartre in Paris, where Laurie Hogben (New Zealand Rhodes Scholar) and I used to gourmandize on *escargots bourgognes* and *moules marinières*. The white burgundy at about a bob a bottle was the sort of wine you can't buy in Australia for love or money, although, as I was arguing this afternoon, a lot of our wines are grossly underrated.

In the cinema, most prisoners used to spend hours each day devising the menus of the gastronomic orgies they would enjoy upon release. On the last night in the cinema I had found myself solemnly listing all the foodstuffs with which I would stock my boat on a private cruise that I hoped to do some day.

For some reason, I found that although our food in the jail was just as bad and as totally inadequate as in the cinema, my obsession of hunger began to diminish as time wore on. We were all getting visibly thinner all the time, but obviously the stomach was beginning to get resigned to the fact that it was not going to be filled. I can now well understand the religious fanatics and Gandhis of this world finding that the greatest temptation and suffering come in the first fortnight; after that the desire diminishes as the body itself becomes weaker. The whole business of virtual starvation during these five weeks at Serang, on top of our privations after leaving Singapore, afforded a fascinating study of one's mental and physical reaction to undernourishment. When I arrived in Batavia, exactly sixty-one days after leaving Singapore, I weighed seven stone thirteen pounds, which meant that I had lost forty-four pounds in that period.

At the time, I did not enjoy it at all, but later I came to regard it as an immensely valuable experience. If any one wishes to embark on a clear and detached analysis of himself and his past life, with a view to seeing things in perspective, I strongly advocate some self-denying ordinance, although I trust he will not find it necessary to go to the same limits of physical misery as those to which we were reduced.

Many of us developed a series of private dodges, more or less honest, to try to bolster up our rations. The Dutch were feeding bountifully through outside buying, but would do nothing to assist the other prisoners. Finally, Norman contacted a Cingalese gentleman who took pity on the grey beard which Norman had sprouted and obtained for him some of the Dutch surplus bread. Thereafter Norman and I used to visit this gentleman, Norman first removing his teeth. The combination of the white beard and the toothless mouth was too much for the Cingalese, and almost invariably bread was forthcoming. We would then bolt around the corner, Norman suddenly becoming surprisingly active again. He would reinsert his teeth and we would enjoy the luxury of a crust of white bread. Norman has acted on many stages throughout the world, but I am sure that he has never succeeded in looking so old or so pathetic as he did on our visits to the bread donor.

One night when we were all rather depressed and miserable there was an amazing interlude. A Japanese guard, whom we had not seen previously, appeared at the cell door and began to speak to us in English. He was the first private we had met who knew any English. Presently, to our amazement, he broke into a soft but word-perfect rendition of "God Save the King". During that night and the following one, when he was on duty, he smuggled into our cell some bowls of rice and vegetable from the Japanese kitchen. Unfortunately, he must have been detected in one of his acts of kindness, for next day he was removed from the jail and we never saw him again. It was only later, when we came to know the Japanese better, that we realized how rare a specimen was this guard who gave most of his week's cigarette ration to men in our cell.

We spent twenty-four days in this cell before we were transferred to another, where conditions were a great deal better. In the first cell, only three officers had any money, and the rest of us were deeply indebted to those three, particularly to Bill Ditmar, the sole Dutchman in the cell, for the occasional banana or native rice cake which we obtained. At Easter, we each had one duck egg which was, by far, the most appreciated Easter egg we had ever had. When Bill managed to induce the guards or the Indonesian turnkeys to bring us a few native cheroots, we used to sit around in groups of half a dozen, passing the cheroot from one to the other, each taking a few draws somewhat in the manner in which the ceremonial pipe of peace is passed around in a Red Indian wigwam. For the inveterate smokers, whose craving for tobacco outran their lust for food, these were the big moments in the drab monotony of the tedious days.

The worst feature of life in the jail was the confinement of more than a hundred Dutch women and children. These were packed in cells, just like the rest of us, with only one small bucket of drinking water each day. They had no privacy at all, and when they were allowed a little water for washing the Japanese guards kept snooping round the doors to see what they could see. Inevitably, the children were fretful and miserable in these incomprehensible conditions, but the women met the ordeal with a courage and fortitude that was beyond praise. Two Australian Y.M.C.A. representatives were among the other women in this jail. When the Dutch women and children were released in April, they were sent on to Batavia to an internment camp.

Fortunately the Dutch received much better food than we did, being able to buy extensively outside through the good offices of the native warders. Also, they were allowed out for exercise in the yard twice each day.

A feature of life in the jail was the wild rumours disseminated by some of the senior Dutch officials, who claimed that the reports had been received from San Francisco radio through a set operated by loyal Indonesians in Serang. The American Pacific fleet, which I knew to be on the bottom of Pearl Harbour, was alleged to be shelling the main cities of Java, and this was believed by practically all in the jail, including certain naval officers. Big landings of Allied troops on Timor, Bali and Java itself were widely credited. Finally, early in April, we were told on the authority of the Dutch Resident, who was one of the prisoners, that four million British, American and Canadian troops had landed in the region of Bordeau and that the total defeat of the German armies in Europe was only a matter of days. This was exactly thirty-seven months before the German capitulation!

One discovered that in conditions of extreme adversity, a large percentage of normally sane people are capable of the grossest wishful thinking. This phenomenon recurred constantly in the succeeding years, and it was not confined to the Dutch or to the troops and junior officers among the prisoners.

Medical officers in the jail had told some of us privately

that if there was no improvement in conditions serious epidemics were inevitable, and that, in any case, if the ration continued to be so utterly inadequate, more than half of us would be dead by the end of May. Dysentery soon broke out, and by the first week in April some hundreds of men were so weakened that they could scarcely crawl the few necessary paces to the latrine bucket. The Japanese contribution towards combating the outbreak was to isolate thirty-seven of the worst cases in a cell designed for six Malay convicts. There was not room for everybody to sit down properly, and at night most of them had to stand to let the others lie down. Anything worse for a man with acute dysentery than having to stand up for most of the night cannot be imagined. Our medical officers told the Japanese that unless some attempt was made to improve the food, most of the men with dysentery would be dead in three or four weeks. There is no doubt that many of the men imprisoned in Serang died subsequently in Burma and Siam largely because their resistance had been so severely taxed during this ordeal.

I noted in my diary:

The Japs allowed some of us to spend last night out in the yard so that we could crawl across to the gutter which serves as a latrine. In between innumerable visits there, Keith Mathieson, Lloyd Willey, who works in a grocery store in Hollywood with many film star clients, and I, planned a motor tour all over the States and Canada, from the Golden Gate to Halifax, and from Toronto down to Mexico. I only hope we get out to do it. . . .

Met Dave Manning, eighteen-year-old Melbourne boy from *Perth*. He has been subject to blackouts since the sinking. A torpedo exploded against the ship, just as he was about to jump into the water. He was flung into the sea, never having swum in his life, but managed to reach a float.

Later. Have been moved to a new cell in which we found three officers of the 2/3 Machine-gunners, part of the Australian force left here under Brigadier Blackburn. These three, Captain Jack Kennedy, of Hobart, Lieutenants John Hayne and John Redward, of Adelaide, were sent out on reconnaissance in an armoured car and were captured. They have all been badly beaten up and tortured by the Japanese, who were attempting to extract information from them. Hayne's eye has been badly affected by one blow, but otherwise they've come through it remarkably well. My neighbour here is Brian Fihelly, a flying-officer from Ascot, Brisbane, attached to a British Blenheim squadron. After over thirty operational flights in the Western Desert, Brian was transferred to Sumatra, but was shot down. It seems possible that his plane was the one which we heard about from the natives on the sandy spit during our trip down the coast. He and his crew-mates managed to row down to Java, only to be captured here as we were. . . .

Later. The Japs are allowing a sing-song in the cells at night, and we had quite a concert here yesterday. There was something a bit too nostalgic about songs like "There's a Long Long Trail" (I'm afraid a very long one for us), "Tipperary" and "Waltzing Matilda", but at the end we "Rolled Out the Barrel" and fell asleep more cheerfully than for weeks.

We had just been allowed to build an oven for baking bread and had enjoyed our first batch of loaves, as an earnest of better days, when a rumour arose that we were to be transferred to Batavia. It was confirmed next day, when Captain Kennedy and two other officers were taken to the house of the Japanese commander in this area. They were regally entertained on an exotic but delicious diet of bread, cream, honey and Japanese beer, and told with a string of very Japanese "So sorrys" that the commander knew that things had been shockingly bad in the jail, but that they would be much better in the new camp to which we were being taken in Batavia.

On 13 April we were removed from our cells and carefully searched to see that we were not taking with us any of the native convict sarongs with which we had been issued in the last few days. However, as these were the best part of our issue, which consisted otherwise of ill-fitting green shirts and shorts, looted from the Dutch stores, several of us managed to smuggle them through the search. I hid mine inside my trousers, covering my shrunken flanks, and got away with it. Then we were piled into trucks and bade an unregretful farewell to Serang.

I doubt whether any of the men who spent those five weeks in the jail, or cinema, will ever forget the experience. We were all suffering from acute malnutrition and claustrophobia and most of us had had dysentery or chronic diarrhoea. We felt fairly confident that whatever lay ahead it could not be worse than Serang.

CHAPTER XII

THE BICYCLE CAMP

Who never ate his bread in sorrow,
Who never spent the darksome hours
Weeping and watching for the morrow
He knows ye not, ye gloomy powers.
                    —GOETHE, translated by Carlyle

THE journey by truck to Batavia enabled us to see that, although some bridges, power installations and other valuable property had been destroyed by Dutch sabotage, a great deal had been allowed to fall into the hands of the Japanese undamaged. Remembering the thoroughness of the Russian scorched-earth policy over the past months, one could not help contrasting the attitude of the two peoples to the war. All the Dutchmen whom we had met seemed to feel that, since they had no chance of defending Java successfully, their immediate surrender was the right thing, and now all they had to do was to sit back and wait resignedly until their allies won back their country for them. We had abundant evidence during our five hour journey that the bulk of the population welcomed the island's conquerors, and were emphatically anti-European.

The main Dutch barracks, known to our troops as "the Bicycle Camp", was the site of our new quarters. Here we found the majority of the A.I.F. 7th Division and Corps troops, who had been left in Java under the command of Brigadier A. S. Blackburn, V.C. They included the greater part of the 2/2nd Pioneers, the 2/6th Engineers, and some members of the 2/3rd Machine-gunners. Also here were a number of troops from Singapore, including the 2/3rd M.T. unit, evacuated on 9 February. Two sections of this unit had done sterling work throughout the campaign on the Malayan Peninsula. Also at Batavia were a number of R.A.A.F. personnel, mostly from No. 1 Squadron—a Lockheed-Hudson Bomber and Reconnaissance Squadron—which had struck the first heavy blow against Japanese landing forces at Khota Baru, in northern Malaya in the first hours of the Pacific war.

Prisoners had been pouring into this camp since 23 March and finally there were over 2000 Australians, about 800 Americans and perhaps 500 British of all three services. The British were moved about a month later to a camp at Tanjong Pryok, the port of Batavia. Apart from 300 *Houston* survivors, the Americans were all members of the 131st Field Regiment, a Texas artillery unit. It was odd that, by the merest coincidence, practically all the Americans taken prisoner in Java should have been Texans, for that State had provided most of *Houston's* crew.

A number of senior Allied officers, including the Dutch High Command for the Indies, had been interned in another section of these barracks, but it was possible for most of the time to keep in touch with them. Brigadier Blackburn was C.O. of troops in the Bicycle Camp, and Colonel Searle, U.S. Army, was camp commander. On learning of our position, Brigadier Blackburn invited Norman Carter and myself to join the officers' mess. He extended to us honorary commissions for the term of our captivity.

Most of the prisoners had had some weeks of comparative freedom on the other side of the island near Lelas since the capitulation on 8 March. They had fed fairly well and they brought to Batavia with them a number of truckloads of rations which helped to eke out the inadequate Japanese issue of rice and vegetables. We were supposed to get about two ounces of meat per man per day, but one rarely saw any sign of it, a large part of this meagre issue coming in the form of hide, bone and entrails.

The state in which we arrived from Serang aroused the practical sympathy of everyone. The Serangites, or "Old Dysenterians", as some wag christened us, showed out like negroes among a host of albinos against the fit and well-nourished men who had come in from Lelas. The result was that we were given a royal welcome and had an exclusive monopoly of all "back-ups" or "gash", as the *Perth* boys called second helpings. The soldiers ransacked their own kit to provide clothes and bedding for the sailors from the *Perth*, and in the American compound the artillery boys looked after the *Houston* survivors in the same splendid fashion. For the first week after we arrived from Serang, we had all we could eat. To us, after the starvation issues at the cinema and the jail, the quantity of rice and vegetable provided at Batavia seemed miraculous; but these things are only relative, and after a few weeks we felt as dissatisfied with the monotonous diet as everyone else.

The Japanese turned the prisoners out daily in working parties. At first the majority of these went to the wharves at Tanjong Pryok, unloading supplies from Japan on to trucks, or loading some of the loot which the Japanese were preparing to ship home to their own islands. Captured Allied war materials, crated aeroplanes which had never been assembled, petrol drums, motor-cars and vehicles of all kinds, sugar and other foodstuffs, and furniture and treasures from the villas and mansions of Java were crowded indiscriminately on Japanese supply ships for transport to Japan. Other working parties were sent to the Shell Oil refinery and factory.

On 25 April, when the Japanese commemorated their fallen, we were paraded in front of the guard-house by the main gate of the camp and addressed by Captain Sezuki, the Japanese commandant, who promised us a tightening of discipline. All day we had a series of "tankos" to check our numbers, but the Japanese did at last promise us a canteen through which we could supplement our ration.

Four days later we were paraded on the main road of the camp with instructions "to send our humble salutations and respectful thoughts to His Imperial Majesty"—the occasion being Tenno Heika's birthday. While planes roared low overhead and did sweeps in formation to impress the populace of Batavia with Nippon's might, we stood in silence at attention for two minutes. With a curious unanimity those of us who did not think of home throughout this enforced period thought "——— the Emperor!" and then forgot about him. It was the first major illustration we had of that infantility of mind which extended not only through the ranks but to the higher command in the Japanese army. We had not yet realized that, to the Japanese, we were ignorant, dumb creatures with coolie mentality who should be obsessed daily with wonder and gratitude at the Imperial clemency in leaving us alive. However, from now on we learned rapidly.

The Emperor's birthday was remembered by the prisoners because it marked our first death at Batavia, Sergeant Caldicott, A.I.F., dying of dysentery. Standing rigidly at attention, watching the coffin carried slowly down the double line of khaki figures, one was overwhelmed with a presentiment that here was the symbol and shape of things to come. Almost a third of the men who lined the road that day were themselves to perish before our imprisonment was over.

At this stage we set going a comprehensive scheme for educational classes, to occupy the men's minds and afford vocational training and some sort of preparation for degrees and diplomas which they wished to secure after the war. I was asked to take an intermediate and a beginners' French class, and also the English class: but I finally handed the latter over to Norman, who was at a loose end at that time. Meeting for an hour, three or four times a week, we made considerable progress during the next two months. The men, many of them *Perth* sailors who had not studied for ten or fifteen years, tackled the French with gratifying enthusiasm, and I was beginning to feel very happy about our progress when the Japanese clamped down on the whole scheme and forbade further classes.

As at Serang, wild rumours constantly circulated through the camp. The Allies seized Timor, as a preparatory step towards taking Java, at least once a fortnight. On one occasion, so absolutely did the men believe in an Allied landing on the Java coast that a party made plans to break out of the camp that night to join the landing force. They were stopped by the hut commanders and officers of their own units only with

the greatest difficulty, and for some days many still believed
that the Allies were retaking Java. Actually, Allied troops did
not set foot on Java until after Japan surrendered in August
1945. But wishful thinking was rife, even among the officers,
and Padre Kellow, of the Pioneers, was much abused because
he insisted on being realistic about the situation.

Being the only war correspondent in the camp, I was
repeatedly asked how long it would be before we were free.
I had no powers of divination and said so. But I came to
realize that, owing to a series of lectures I was giving throughout the camp, considerable and unmerited weight was
attached to my opinions. I was not prepared to lie, but at
the same time I did not see that a blunt statement that I felt
things would move very slowly, would be very helpful to
morale. Usually, if pressed, I said that we could expect things
to start happening from September 1943 onwards, and was
usually told more or less politely that I was a sanguinary
pessimist.

After the first month at Batavia, we got news regularly,
thanks to a wireless set which some of the men had made.
The immense anxiety about Australia, which weighed like a
leaden burden on the better informed, was lifted only when
we got news of the Coral Sea Battle and, after some anxious
days, realized that the first big drive against our homes and
families had been smashed.

The canteen did provide a reasonable range of tinned goods,
eggs and fruit, but only a small percentage of the men had
money. Japanese pay to the working parties was long-deferred
and amounted to only ten cents per day. Prices in the canteen
were: eggs five cents, tinned milk fifty-five, jam sixty, margarine thirty-five, and cigarettes eighteen to twenty-five cents
a packet.

Tea, coffee and cocoa were obtainable at quite reasonable
rates, and sugar was only ten cents a pound. Some tinned
fish and fruit was sold at between seventy cents and a guilder.
However, since a large number of people like myself were
entirely dependent on the charity of friends, the canteen
ceased to interest us much after the first few weeks.

In the lines, particularly among the Australian troops, things went very well for a time. Nearly all the big money in the camp was in the hands of the Americans, but supplies coming in were divided on a hut quota basis. Large numbers of *Perth* boys and the A.I.F. resold their issue to the Americans, who were only too glad to pay double and treble the price for goods. But for this, our sailors, who were all destitute, would have fared far worse.

In the officers' section a mess was formed and everybody was asked to put all his money, except two guilders, into it. As in all communal schemes, the extent of one's participation in this depended largely on the philosophy and integrity of the individual, and the results caused some heart-burnings. But for four or five months the monotonous and sickening Japanese ration was somewhat improved and every officer did obtain a small amount of fresh fruit.

In the early months at this camp the working parties did rather better than anybody else, and there was keen competition among both officers and men who were anxious to be sent out on certain assignments. Dutch women made up large parcels of food which they smuggled to prisoners or handed over with the connivance of complacent guards. Some of the guards permitted considerable buying from native vendors, and for a time work parties were returning with quantities of food hidden in their clothing, rucksacks or hats.

The most profitable racket was the smuggling in of spirits looted from the godowns on the wharves. A bottle of whisky could be sold to the Dutch senior officers, who were rolling in money, for sufficient guilders to keep an Australian in eggs, tea and sugar for many weeks. However, inevitably, the Japanese soon discovered what was going on, and four Americans who were caught were brutally and humiliatingly punished. Steps were then taken to search all parties on their return to camp.

On 6 May the first officer died. This was Lieutenant Ross, U.S. Navy, who had contracted dysentery at Serang.

The lack of meat and shortage of sugar were our greatest worries at this time. One day the Americans decided to cope with their meat-craving by rounding up all the cats in the camp. Next day, Americans were vending baked "alley rabbit", stuffed and garnished, for two and a half guilders. As this was twenty-five days' pay on the Japanese scale (promised but still unpaid), few could afford to enjoy the feline delicacy. In the officers' mess, the cooks one day made a determined but misguided effort to thicken the anaemic vegetable water, which was the only accompaniment to the ever-recurrent rice. We thought the stew tasted a bit queer but most of us, being hungry, managed to push it down. It was only later that afternoon that someone discovered that the thickening in the stew had not been flour but ten pounds of plaster of Paris!

The hospital in this camp, while lacking all proper beds, bedding, toilet requisites and other essential gear, was so much better than the so-called hospitals in the jungles of Burma and Siam, that in after days we came to think of it in a relatively favourable light. The units who came to this camp brought a considerable quantity of supplies and medical instruments in their panniers, and for a time the Japanese allowed us to obtain additional drugs from Rathkamps, the main Dutch wholesale chemists. The hospital was conducted with great efficiency by a devoted band of medical officers, among whom Captain Jim Goding, of the 2/2nd Pioneers, Captain Daniels, British Army, Surgeon-Commander Epstein and Surgeon-Lieutenant Burrows, of *Houston*, Flight-Lieutenant Black-ledge, R.A.F., and Captain Lumpkin, U.S. Army, and a Melbourne ear, nose and throat specialist, Colonel N. Eadie, were prominent.

Thanks to the strict policing of sanitation and hygiene by Colonel Searle's camp administration, there was little dysentery in this camp and, considering the paucity of the food, the general health was very good up till the time when most of us were moved in October. In this period there were only six deaths among the 3000 prisoners. Apart from an epidemic of dengue and a good deal of appendical trouble, possibly aggravated by rice husks, health was not far below normal army standards, although at the end of six months on Japanese rations no man had the strength which had been his before captivity.

In the middle of May, after we had been joined by a fresh group of Australians who had hitherto been detained in a Batavia school for Chinese and in the Boeiglodok jail, the Japanese started to take away certain A.I.F. officers for interrogation by their Intelligence officers. The men taken away were confined in separate cells in the Konigsplaein jail, where the diet consisted of rice and a filthy bean curd stew. Prior to this, Air Vice Marshal Maltby and Commodore Staten had already been tortured by the Japanese in an attempt to extract information about Allied plans, strengths and dispositions. Now, over a period of several weeks, the Japanese took away twenty or thirty officers, including Colonel John Williams, commander of the 2/2nd Pioneers, and a number of other officers of his unit.

Several of these officers now learned at first hand about Japanese third degree and methods of torture. Colonel Williams was repeatedly threatened and struck during his interrogation, but continued to refuse to answer questions. The Japanese were particularly foolish in imagining that they could get information about Australia's defences from Pioneer officers who had left Australia over eighteen months before. Both Colonel Williams and Captain Ross, of the Pioneers, were tortured, cigarette lighters being held under their noses, and both being strapped to chairs and beaten. Colonel Williams, after being starved for a period, was given a bowl of rice covered with salt. He managed to eat some of the rice but it was mixed with an emetic, and he vomited violently. At another interview, water was forced down his nose. This water torture was also used on other prisoners.

Captain Stuart Handasyde, of the Pioneers, was tortured by having a pencil inserted between the finger joints, pressure being applied in a manner which caused exquisite pain, so that his fingers were useless for many weeks afterwards. Flying-officer Norman Platt, Adjutant of No. 1 Squadron R.A.A.F., was repeatedly beaten and tortured by these inquisitors seeking information about planes, aerodromes and R.A.A.F. dispositions. But the Japanese were universally unsuccessful in extracting information of the smallest value by these methods.

They only succeeded in arousing the hatred of all their prisoners, who were united in their pride in the officers who defied the Japanese Gestapo.

On 22 June all the interrogated officers were brought back to the Bicycle Camp. At the jail, among many male prisoners, there had been a Dutch woman with her baby. She had been jailed by the Japanese for throwing a brick at a Jap soldier who was interfering with her child. Although treated no better than the men, she was cheerful and indomitable, and the Australians admired her immensely.

There was one comic incident during the interrogation. The Japanese had expected to find, on Java, the bulk of the Australians from the Middle East and at least one division of Americans. The presence of one lone artillery regiment from the U.S. Army puzzled them greatly. One Jap officer said to Major Rogers, of the 131st Field Regiment, "But it is absurd! How could your Government think to stop the great Nippon Imperial Army with one regiment?" Major Rogers shook his head. "It is madness," the Japanese went on. "Did they think they could stop our army with six hundred men?" Major Rogers: "Maybe next time they'll send seven hundred."

At the end of June Norman Carter, who had started to organize a camp concert party, put on the first Batavia concert. These shows went from strength to strength, not only through the excellence of the talent available in the camp, but because of the sterling work done in the theatre by carpenters, electricians, engineers, scenic artists, costume designers, tailors and others. Among the many whose performances in these concerts will always be remembered gratefully by all of us in Batavia were the late "Doc" Clark, a born comedian from Sorrento, Victoria, who achieved a *succès fou* as "Nellie Nellie with the Rice-belly"; "Willie the Winner", a clever Dutchman who sang marvellously, and could use his black eyes more effectively than any Parisian coquette; Fred Quick, a professional crooner from the States; Bob Martin, a bearded Texan who made a name for himself as "Nostradamus"; Jim Anderson, of Hampton, Victoria, whose splendid baritone voice was to be an inspiration to many during the dark days in the jungles; the late Jock Milligan, of the Pioneers, who wrote a song about Australia which swept the camp like a flame; Arnold Westgarth of the same unit, who revealed real brilliance as a musician; Jack Altman, leader of the hard-working band; "Poodles" Norley, of H.M.A.S. *Perth*, female impersonator; "Fuglehorn Freddie", a Dutchman, who was a master with the trumpet; and many others.

Norman Carter excelled himself with the production of *The Monkey's Paw*, by W. W. Jacobs, in which every ounce of horror and tragedy in the piece was drawn out by a particularly well-trained cast. Norman himself played the mother, Colonel Chris Black was the father, and they were excellently supported by Captain Ted Campbell and Lieutenant Peter Rossiter of the Pioneers. As one American officer said afterwards, "I've spent many good dollars on entertainment that wasn't half as good."

"Tex" McFarlane and a group of Americans put on one or two good shows, including *Mexican Fandango*, in which the properties, scenery and costumes were a triumph for all the unselfish, unseen workers behind the stage who conjured excellent effects out of old bits of rag, carved wood and a box of coloured chalks.

Star feature of one concert was an illuminated sign which was suddenly flashed on before the lights went up at the end of the first half of the programme. The only tobacco available in the camp was crude native weed which we called "wog", a word used by the boys from the Middle East to denote anything belonging to a native race. Suddenly, out of the darkness of the shed in which the concerts were held, thanks to a clever arrangement of lights behind a carefully cut out screen, a neon sign reading "When in a Fog, Light up Your Wog" flashed out at the audience in a fashion worthy of the most sophisticated film palace. For a moment everybody gasped, and then there was long and sustained applause. It was a triumph.

Australians like the Neighbour brothers from South Australia, Frank Purtell, brother of the jockey and formerly attached to J. C. Williamson's wardrobe department, the late

Hut sing-songs were very popular, but in the late stages of our captivity were seldom allowed.

Ron Hovenden who painted the scenery and did brilliant sketches as an accompaniment to Fred Quick's crooning, and Captain Harry Bishop, who commanded the band of electricians and engineers responsible for the lighting, laboured tirelessly to make these concerts a real means of escape from the sordidness and boredom of the prison camp, and earned the lasting gratitude of the men they entertained. By the time we left Batavia, Norman was probably the most popular man in the prison camp.

Towards the middle of June Brigadier Blackburn was informed by the Japanese that officers could write letters that would be broadcast home to their families. At first it was decided to refuse this offer, but later, in the interests of the sick, and because it was felt that there was no other way of allaying anxiety at home about men captured in Java, it was decided that letters should be written. The first was sent off by Captain Jim Goding, and a few days later Captain Ted Campbell, also of the Pioneers, was sent for, and wrote a letter in which he said "conditions in this camp are comparable to those at Dudley Flats" (referring to a notorious Melbourne slum area). The Japanese thought this was a compliment and sent it off. This gave me the idea of using the letter to get word home to Australia that three hundred of *Perth's* crew had survived. I also wished to convey to the authorities and public at home something of the toll taken of the Japanese flotilla by shells and torpedoes from *Perth* and *Houston.*

Therefore, when I was sent for on 20 June and taken down to the Batavia studios where these letters were written, I had a plan for sending as much information as possible to the Department of Information at home, who, I knew, would be monitoring the Batavia broadcasts. Therefore, after writing a description of the way in which the seven of us had reached Java, I wrote:

Here at Serang were nearly all the survivors from the gallant Australian cruiser *Perth* and the American cruiser *Houston*, sunk in a terrific battle against superior Nippon forces at the entrance to Sunda Straits on the early morning of 1 March. I have heard the Nippon sailors on a destroyer which picked up some of the 300-odd *Perth* survivors pay a generous tribute to the wonderful fight put up by the two vessels, surrounded by great numbers of Nippon cruisers, destroyers, submarines and transports. Nippon officers themselves paid generous tribute to the deadly efficiency of *Perth's* gunners, both in that last action and in the action on 26 February in the Battle of the Java Sea.

I felt that, with luck, the Japanese might fail to see that although our people were already well aware of our own losses, this was the first word they had had of the enemy's losses. In fact, the Japanese sent it home word for word and the report was published by the Press of all States. In the actual broadcasting of these letters, the Japanese often cut out some of the derogatory things we said about the food and conditions, and put in one or two flowery sentences about "the courtesy of the Nippon authorities", but on the whole the bulk of the letters were broadcast as written. They cut out from my letter the description I gave of our treatment by the Javanese who captured us, and by the Japanese at Serang, but this was not surprising, because I had not pulled my punches.

From first to last perhaps a hundred men of all ranks and all nationalities had letters broadcast, while at the same time the Japanese were also transmitting the names of all those in the camp at the rate of twenty-five names every two days. It was a painfully slow business, but it was better than nothing, and those of us whose names were sent home were much luckier than tens of thousands of others in Japanese hands, whose people did not hear that they were prisoners until late in 1943.

On 27 June the Japanese, little knowing that we were getting B.B.C. bulletins from the secret radio, started to post typewritten Japanese news, in English, on the camp notice boards. This was the time when Rommel was threatening Alexandria, and the Japanese bulletins claimed a tremendous naval victory involving the sinking or crippling of twenty-eight Allied warships off the Solomons. So great is the power of the printed word that a certain number in the camp, particularly some men who were depressed by sickness, seemed to believe this bulletin; so a number of us set out to debunk the Japanese version of the battle, and soon it became known through the camp that actually it had been an Allied naval victory.

On 27 June also, the Japanese informed Brigadier Blackburn that all prisoners would be required to sign an oath of allegiance to the Imperial Japanese Army. The brigadier protested that this could only be done "in so far as it did not conflict with our oath of loyalty to our King". This the Japanese refused to accept, and the question reached a crisis on American Independence Day, 4 July.

In the morning hut commanders were paraded and ordered to sign the oath and to force their men to sign it. Already bashings and kickings of prisoners by guards had broken out all over the camp, and it was obvious that the Japanese were prepared to go to any lengths to enforce obedience. The entire camp, without exception, stood firmly behind the brigadier and Colonel Searle in refusing to sign. At lunch-time the camp was placarded with notices telling everybody that they must come to the Japanese office to sign the oath. The lives of those who failed to do so would not be guaranteed. Not a man signed.

So in the afternoon the whole camp was paraded and first hut commanders and then the rest of the officers were separated from the other prisoners, while outright threats of mass execution were levelled at the commanding officers. Finally, the brigadier, seeing the Japanese were prepared to go to any length, and realizing that duress had been amply proved, gave the order to sign under protest. After the men had signed, the officers who had been segregated in a long shed, were brought to the office.

Four officers representing army units and *Perth* refused to sign until they knew that all their men had signed. They were forced to kneel on the ground in front of the Japanese guardhouse until nine o'clock that night, and were beaten up by Sezuki, the camp commandant, and other Japanese. They were then flung into cells but remained adamant in their refusal until they received a direct order from the brigadier that they were to sign as all other prisoners in the camp had now done. These four officers were Captains John Kennedy, Bronte

Edwards and Harry Bishop, A.I.F., and Lieutenant Frank Gillan of *Perth*. The whole affair left a nasty taste in the mouth of many of us, but further resistance could only have led to Japanese reprisals in which our sick in hospital would have been the first sufferers.

A list of punitive measures had already been issued by Sezuki, including the banning of the buying of medical supplies and canteen goods, the discontinuation of educational classes and religious services and the abrogation of the few liberties left to us.

The camp became conscious of the fact that a harsh new epoch had dawned. Armed guards maintained a constant patrol through the huts, and everybody had to stand rigidly to attention from the moment they came in sight until they had passed on. Men who failed to notice sentries approaching were savagely bashed and kicked.

On 6 July a particularly brutal bashing with a split bamboo rod was dealt out to one of the cooks on night shift. The Japanese sentry, finding him on his bed, did not stop to discover the reason. There was an order that prisoners should not be on their beds in the daytime and that was enough. When a protest was made by the prisoners' administration, the Japanese said it was a mistake, and next day the sentry, a confirmed sadist who rejoiced in the apt appellation of Dogface, brought round a slice of iced cake as a conciliatory gesture to his victim. It was poor compensation for the merciless beating of the previous day.

It was quite obvious that the sentries were being sent through the huts in pursuance of a definite blitz against the prisoners' morale. When the guards could not find a genuine excuse for bashing prisoners, they invented one. In our hut, Brian Fihelly was standing rigidly to attention, but his feet were not at the exact angle of forty-five degrees prescribed by the Japanese. A little runt of a sentry tried twice to strike him, but found the tall Queenslander towering feet above him. He therefore led him outside and made him stand in the gutter, while he stood on the step and struck the Australian across the face.

The consequence of all this was that our nerves were always on the *qui vive*, and a day in the huts, having to spring to attention several times each hour and stand motionless for considerable periods, was often as exhausting nervously and physically as a hard day's work. It is difficult to exaggerate the atmosphere of the camp during these weeks. Some of the guards, given an opportunity of venting their brutality on men who could not strike back, had a royal time, but the real culprits were the Japanese officers who licensed this organized sadism.

In mid-August there was evidence of much increased aerial activity. A brownout was enforced throughout Batavia, while immensely complicated Japanese instructions about A.R.P. were promulgated through the camp. On one day at least a hundred planes manoeuvred over the city, while sirens put us through constant air-raid rehearsals day and night for four days. We had no evidence that Allied planes had come over Batavia but it was obvious that the Japanese were expecting something. The optimists immediately declared that a landing was imminent, but received a set-back when our radio operators picked up a statement by Prime Minister Fraser of New Zealand that we would not start hitting back effectively in the Pacific for another twelve months.

Sezuki left us in mid-August, and a month later his successor was replaced by Lieutenant Sonai. At the same time the entire personnel of our guards was changed, and Koreans, the bullies of Japanese-occupied China, took us over. Immediately there was a fresh outbreak of violence in all parts of the camp, officers and men being mercilessly beaten merely because they had moved after the sentry had caught sight of them. Protests fell on deaf ears, and some of the severest bashings occurred in the officers' compound. The new commandant strutted round the camp in polished jackboots, delighting in the infliction of every possible humiliation, interference and restriction on the Allied officers and men under his command. Every time the sentries passed along the central road of the camp, all activities in the compounds had to cease, while everybody stood frozen at attention. The camp resounded with shouts of *"Kiwotski"*,

"Yasmae", *"Kiri"*, *"Nauri"*, *"Kasira Migi"*—Japanese commands given by the nearest prisoner as sentries came in sight. As one veteran soldier said, "Shellfire in Flanders was much less nervous strain."

The long-promised Japanese pay for workers finally arrived in September, but officers' pay, which was supposed to be at a rate equivalent to Japanese pay, was still not forthcoming.

At the end of September an arts and crafts exhibition was held in the officers' mess. This produced an astounding collection of skilfully worked articles, made by prisoners in their leisure hours. There were model sailing ships, yachts, speedboats and warships, twenty varieties of model aircraft, various new patents of mouse-trap and rat-trap for coping with the increasing hordes of rodents in the camp, a microscope, a washing machine, cigarette machines, holdalls, jewellery made from bones, plastic and glass, inlaid chess and cribbage boards, wood cuts, inlaid coins, ash-trays, clocks, woven belts, leatherwork, wood carvings and a wooden Ford engine. There was also an art exhibition with some excellent sketches of camp personalities and scenes from Javanese life.

During September rumours of a general break-up of the camp gained strength daily. We had been joined at the beginning of August by twenty officers and twenty-five men, under Colonel Bill Leggatt, from the Australian force captured at Timor. Most of these were sent off to Singapore in mid-September, and by the end of the month it was known officially that most of us would be following them very soon. Speculation as to our destination ranged over the whole Japanese-occupied area. Borneo and Malaya shared favouritism for a time, but a large number thought we should be taken straight to Japan. We did not know what Allied submarines were operating in these waters, but American claims already indicated a heavy toll on Japanese shipping.

The only people who really regretted departure from this camp were the gardeners whose crops of tomatoes were just beginning to ripen nicely. Some of them, determined to reap a part of the fruits of their labour, took buckets of green tomatoes with them when we left.

Injections and inoculations were now the order of the day. Our arms were treated like pin cushions, but we did not know how effective the Japanese antidotes to cholera, smallpox, typhoid and tetanus might be.

On 3 October two hundred men, with Lieutenant Cal Mitchell of the Pioneers and three American officers, left the camp. The officers' mess decided to eat, drink and be merry on the carefully hoarded tins and other rations which were being kept for Christmas. Finally on 6 October it was announced that all prisoners except 160 would leave the camp in two batches. On the next day we had to pack all our gear and spread it out on the main road of the camp for inspection. I had a lot of diary, notes and the manuscript of a novel, but I managed to get these through the search. Lieutenant Bill Tilney, 2/2nd Pioneers, did even better, concealing a revolver between his thighs. The Japanese concentrated mainly on taking hatchets, tools, and mosquito-nets, but when a protest was made most of the nets were returned.

There was a reveille at one-thirty next morning, and after endless counting on the camp road we finally marched off carrying our gear to the main Batavia station where we entrained to Tanjong Pryok, the port of Batavia. The optimists now said we were being put on a boat for exchange at a neutral port, but there were not many of us who could believe that anything so pleasant lay in store.

CHAPTER XIII

WHAT HAPPENED IN JAVA

The thing that's wrong
About the Dutch,
Is giving too little
And asking too much.
—Nineteenth Century jingle in South Africa

THE attempt to defend Java, proudest jewel in the Dutch crown of empire, was carried on from the hour when the Japanese launched the war on 8 December until the first Japanese landed on Java on 1 March, after the destruction of the Allied fleet. What happened on the island itself was merely a miserable and unpleasant postscript to the failure of that attempt.

The activities of Dutch submarines against Japanese communications and supply lines, the Dutch planes which had fought from Singapore bases, the joint American and Dutch destruction of the Japanese convoy in Macassar Strait, the final brave but hopeless fight of the Allied cruisers and destroyers in the Java Sea, these had been taken by the world as the prelude to a tough and bitter resistance on Java itself. They were no prelude; in the event, it was proven that the handful of planes, now whittled down to the point of non-existence, and the warships now on the bottom of the Java Sea, were all the defence that Java had.

The much publicized army of the Dutch on Java, supposed to amount to between sixty and a hundred thousand trained troops, existed only on paper and in the minds of the propagandists. To all intents and purposes, the Dutch did not fight on Java, and their surrender, a few days after the landing, involved the capture of several thousands of Australian, British and American soldiers and airmen.

This has led to much bitterness in the minds of many of those thus left "in the bag" and even more in the minds of their relatives and friends at home. It is senseless, at this stage, to seek to cover up the mistakes that were made in the last days of February 1942. But some explanation of the factors involved and the reasons for decisions taken may serve to diminish the misconceptions which abound regarding the defence of Java.

When I passed through Java at the beginning of January 1942, I found the Dutch very resentful against their American allies, on the grounds that they had been let down, thanks to American unpreparedness at Pearl Harbour, and that since then the long promised help in ships and planes had not been forthcoming. After the fall of Singapore, the British became the main offenders. In the subsequent years of captivity in the prison camps, it became fashionable for Dutchmen to maintain that, by their sacrifices, they had saved Australia. Left virtually unsupported by their allies, it was, they said, the deeds of their sailors and airmen which procured the delay needful to protect Australia. This view of the Dutchman, returning good for evil and perishing gallantly on the altar of his allies' interests, is absurd and unrealistic.

The plain truth is that the Dutch, with only eight million European Dutchmen in the world, and only a quarter of a million free outside their conquered homeland, never had any chance of holding their huge island empire against Japanese invasion, unless other people pulled the Dutch chestnuts out of the fire. Some anti-British Dutchmen have talked glibly about the favourable terms they could have made with the Japanese if they had not been lured to fight by Allied promises which were never fulfilled. Fortunately, no such view prevails among the better balanced members of the Dutch community, who realize that the Japanese would have overrun and then bled the Indies in the interest of their own war effort, whether the Dutch were nominal enemies or not.

Neither the British Empire nor the U.S.A., in the first months of the Pacific war, had the troops or the materials to defend the Indies for the Dutch, although they were quite prepared to do all they could. With our gross inferiority in air power, the naval disasters at the beginning of the Pacific war, the overrunning of the Philippines, and the fall of Singapore, the loss of Java became as inevitable as the succession of night to day.

The Dutch have never been in any position to start throwing mud at their friends, because, without the protection of Britain and America, the Dutch Colonial Empire would have been swallowed up many years ago. The Dutchmen who died before the surrender of Java did not die to save Australia, but to protect their own homes and interests, as hundreds of thousands of other men were dying in all parts of the world for just that reason.

When General Wavell assumed command of the Allied forces in Southern Asia, he made Java his headquarters, and this, inevitably, aroused the belief that the island would be held at all costs. The rapidity with which the Japanese tentacles reached southwards, and the fall of Singapore ten weeks after the outbreak of war, rendered all this so much moonshine. To defend Java a force of at least five hundred fighters and bombers, constantly reinforced, was necessary. There existed only the remnant of the Dutch Air Force, a few Blenheims, Hudsons and Hurricanes, salvaged by the R.A.F. and R.A.A.F. from the aerodromes on Singapore and Sumatra, and a handful of Flying Fortresses and Curtiss pursuits which were all that the Americans had been able to get into operation from Java's air fields. When the Japanese convoys appeared off the Java coast, total serviceable aircraft available on the island did not exceed fifty. Scores of others stood about the airfields in need of repair or wrecked by Japanese bombing, while a number of Flying Fortresses still lay in the crates where they had been landed.

The shattering of the naval force on 27-28 February effectively ended any idea in the minds of the Dutch Command of any real resistance to the invader. It is very doubtful whether senior Dutch officers ever intended to fight out the issue after General Wavell and his staff had left the island on *Orontes*, at the beginning of the last week of February.

Unhappily, it had apparently been felt necessary by the Allies to make a political gesture, even if an unmilitary one, by leaving a token force on Java. This force consisted of three Australian battalions from the Middle East, composed of seasoned troops who had seen action in the Western Desert and in Syria, part of an American artillery regiment, and a British tank company. In addition there was an Australian M.T. unit, evacuated from Singapore. Whether somebody really believed that this heterogeneous force would induce the Dutch to put up a fight, or whether it was felt that, in the interests of prestige, the Dutch could not be left to surrender alone, is not clear. In any case, the failure to evacuate these troops cost the Allies seasoned fighting men who would have been invaluable to Australia in her hour of need. Worse still, there were left on Java about 5000 R.A.F. and R.A.A.F. technicians and ground staff and a small group of pilots.

It is easy now to emphasize the absurdity of throwing away these men, too few in numbers to be of any value in halting the Japanese; but perhaps, the sacrifice was not made in vain.

The Japanese Intelligence apparently believed that all three Australian divisions from the Middle East plus at least one American division were being sent to Java. In this belief, they landed on the island between 1 March and 8 March approximately ten divisions, including a strong armoured unit. Had the immense convoy, totalling between two hundred and three hundred vessels, which brought these forces to Java, gone on to Australia and landed in the region of Fremantle, few would have felt hopeful of defending Perth successfully.

It has been claimed that Wavell's going to Java was nothing but a gigantic bluff from the first, to distract Japanese attention from Australia. If this were the case, the hoax was tremendously successful, and even the sacrifice of such valuable personnel was well worth while. But it is more probable that the Allies did their best to bring aid to Java, and that it was only when Wavell realized that Java, like Hong Kong and Singapore, was doomed to provide more case history under the "too little, too late" heading, that the idea was abandoned.

The political gesture, if such it was, achieved no purpose

whatever, for the Dutch regarded the few thousand Allied troops as a distinct embarrassment in the business of coming to terms with the enemy. There is abundant evidence that there was a sorry lack of frank speaking between the Dutch Command and senior Allied officers when the decision was taken to leave this paltry force on the island.

It has been said that, had all Allied troops been evacuated from Java in the last days of February, Japanese agents, who were scattered through all parts of Java, would have informed the approaching enemy forces, which might then have been diverted elsewhere. This view takes no account of the small time available for any such major switching of objectives. At no stage in the first year of the campaign was there any hint of flexibility in the grand plan of Japanese strategy.

The truth is that the Japanese High Command swung a terrific haymaker at Java, in the belief that there they could knock out the chief forces remaining to the Allies in the southern regions. Precious days and weeks were wasted before they realized that they had been misled and that the foe was recuperating his forces in another corner of the ring. It is possible that this blunder cost the Japanese as dearly as Hitler's decision to go on to Paris, instead of attacking Britain, cost the Germans in May 1940.

But these considerations can scarcely compensate the men who felt they were sacrificed so purposelessly on Java. The circumstances attending the last days before the Dutch capitulation did nothing to allay their bitterness.

The senior officers of the Australian and American units were not, at any stage, given any indication that the Dutch had no intention of fighting. They made their dispositions in accordance with the wishes of the Dutch High Command, in the belief that the Dutch troops ahead, on their flanks and in the rear, were ready to enter upon a serious conflict with the invader. In fact, at the first hint of an enemy landing, many of the Dutch units melted away like mists before the sun. Liaison between the Allied C.Os and the Dutch Command deteriorated from bad to worse, and it was impossible for senior A.I.F. and American officers to obtain any satisfactory picture of what was going on in any zone outside their own immediate area.

The only effective resistance to the main Japanese landing on the western extremity of Java was put up by the Australian 2/2nd Pioneer Battalion, west of Buitenzorg, at a place called Leeuwilliang. They inflicted at least five hundred casualties on the enemy, while their own losses were negligible, until one company was cut off and almost entirely killed or captured. The Pioneers, being left without support, were eventually forced to fall back on Bandoeng.

Under threat of Japanese bombing of the undefended capital, the Dutch Command now decided to surrender immediately. The Allied troops retreated according to plan into the hills beyond Bandoeng, where it was hoped to continue guerrilla resistance. But, at the request of the Dutch Command, it was finally decided to abandon this plan. The Dutch Command's surrender covered all forces on Java.

For several days it had been hoped that at least a section of the Allied forces would be got away from the ports along the southern coast; but the main port, Tjilatjap, was blockaded by Japanese submarines and surface craft from 4 March onwards and most of the last vessels to leave this port were sunk within a few miles of the shore. It was believed that R.A.A.F. Catalinas would endeavour to evacuate certain key air force personnel and senior officers, but a Japanese raid put out of action the only flying boats available. Eventually the bulk of the Allied soldiers and airmen on Java assembled at Lelas, where they remained for a month before the Japanese took them over. The majority were then brought to prison camps in Batavia, while others were incarcerated at Bandoeng.

The worst incident of the whole gloomy story occurred at Kalidjati, main British aerodrome in northern Java. A Japanese landing was expected at Cheribon, and British and Australian air force officers had been told that considerable Dutch forces, ensconced in pill-boxes and prepared positions, would defend the aerodrome. Yet the first word of the Japanese landing that the pilots and ground staff at the aerodrome received came when Japanese armoured cars and motor-cyclists started to stream across the edge of the field.

A handful of men, dashing to their planes, managed to get some of them off the ground as the approaching vehicles opened fire. The majority of the men on the aerodrome were rounded up or ambushed on trucks and a large number of them were killed. Whatever the difficulties of Dutch resistance to the landing forces, it should have been possible to get word to the aerodrome to avert this catastrophe. As a result of the entire absence of any warning, a large number of planes, either ready to take off or only temporarily unserviceable, fell into the hands of the Japanese undamaged.

In defence of the Dutch forces on Java, it can be said that they were up against hopeless odds, and that their own units contained only a leavening of trained troops. The unfortunate thing was not that they failed to fight, but that they failed to maintain any liaison or adequate communication with the Allied units stranded in their midst.

The bravery displayed by the small Dutch Navy and Air Force at the beginning of the Pacific war, did not serve to maintain Dutch prestige with the Indonesian population in view of the débacle of the Army which took place under their eyes. Herein lies a major cause for the anti-European demonstrations which prisoners met with in western Java. The same loss of prestige has been a factor in the strength and violence of the Indonesian nationalist uprisings since the end of the war.

CHAPTER XIV

IDLE THOUGHTS OF A PRISONER

I am a part of all that I have met;
Yet all experience is an arch wherethro'
Gleams that untravell'd world, whose margin fades
For ever and for ever when I move.
— TENNYSON, *Ulysses*

I HAD been a prisoner of war for exactly seven months in Java when we were marched down to Tanjong Pryok. The following entries from my diary are drawn more or less at random, to indicate something of our reactions to captivity.

In Serang Jail. It's now a month since we were captured, and lying on your back, watching the big bluebottles crawling over the filthy bandages on your legs, there has been plenty of time to begin to see the whole stunt in perspective. There's no doubt that the six weeks after leaving Australia were a purple patch. I wonder if anyone else has had the experience of spending eighteen months in the A.I.F. without hearing a shot fired, and then, a fortnight after discharge getting to a hot spot like Singapore on the eve of its destruction? I don't regret anything except the suffering that those at home must be undergoing, not knowing if we're alive or dead. If only we knew a little more about the invasion of Australia of which these beggars are so confident! Having seen something of their mentality and methods, you have moments when you want to bang your head against the stone wall of the cell at having to lie here helpless when they may be bombing or shelling home at any moment. . . .

It is ironical to remember that in the intervals when I got a rest from the oars in rowing across Sunda Strait on the second last day, I was scribbling out a cabled dispatch which I hoped to send from Batavia within twenty-four hours. The others were busy planning the menu for a celebration feast at the Hotel des Indes. We certainly did not think that we should be lying here watching the hours crawl by like some sluggard tortoise, each man wondering if the rice issue for tonight's meal will be a little better than the half dozen spoonfuls we had for our first meal today.

Idle Thoughts of a Prisoner

... This is one of those peaceful sunny mornings when the sordidness and misery of this place seem absurd and out of place. I have been standing by the cell door, looking across at the papaya palms, the tops of which over the prison wall are the only growing things I have seen for weeks. Then the courtyard was invaded by the mob of native convicts, one of whom insisted on washing the private parts of his anatomy in the gutter immediately in front of our cell. They are a wretched gang, very amused at the fact that they are fed about five times as well as we are. ...

I started reflecting about that last tranquil Sunday morning in Paris just before Hitler attacked Poland. Sitting in the Tuileries, watching the birds and bees darting about the flower-strewn beds, and the lovers parading arm in arm across the carefully kept lawns I found it incredible that we should all be expecting bombs from the sky within the next few days. The one good thing about the misery and destruction of this war so far is that Paris remains relatively untouched. I suppose my chances of ever seeing Paris again would seem rather remote, but if she is to be mutilated and desecrated like London, I think I would rather keep the memories which I have today. The fishermen sitting so patiently like carven images along the banks of the Seine, never really expecting to catch anything. ... The bookstalls along the footpath by the parapet where I used to browse for hours. ... The Luxemburg gardens at twilight, and the girl in black who sat crying on a park seat because her evening paper told her that war was inevitable. ... The tombs of the immortals in the Parthenon, especially the tomb of Lannes, the former apprentice dyer from Gascony who died as a Marshal of France, having stood on over thirty victorious battlefields and never on a losing one. ... The Opera at night with the lights glittering at a million points from the crystal chandeliers along the great mirrored promenade. ... The little newspaper kiosks with the boys shouting *"Ce Soir—Paris Soir—L'Intran"*. ... The old legless woman selling violets in the Place des Ternes. ... Champagne in big silver buckets at Dupont's with Laurie. ... That song of Coward's, simple and almost trite as it was, said all there is to say. Once you love Paris, she will always remain mistress of your heart however many other charmers attempt to beguile you.

Bicycle Camp, Batavia. 20 April. Since arriving here I have been looked after like a new-born babe by Don Hanna who was at Wesley with me, and another flying-officer, Don Hackett of Adelaide. I arrived weighing seven stone thirteen pounds, but must have put back nearly a stone already. Unfortunately, I've had no chance to do much about my appearance and move about the camp looking like one of the characters in that canvas depicting Burke and Wills just before the end, ragged, dirty, bearded and starving. My trousers despite my patching attempts really flaunt defiance to decency. The large holes burnt in them one night on Banka when we were trying to dry our clothes are patched in an amateurish fashion which would give mother the horrors. However, although I've been unable to get a razor and toilet gear, I've had the beard rigorously trimmed so that it does look a shade less villainous. I can easily borrow a razor to take it off, but with blades scarce and razors precious, and no money of my own it is unfair to ask anyone to give me his razor daily, so it looks as if the beard stays for a while. . . .

Met Doug Harris, from Hay, who is an overseer on a station at Isis in Queensland, also two friends of his, Snowy Davis and Don Stuart, a veteran of the Black Watch in the last war. All three are members of the 2/3rd M.T. Doug Harris has kept a diary record of his section's job in the show all the way down Malaya from the Thailand border to Singapore. An excellent story. All these men cannot say enough for the Argyles and the Ghurkas who bore the brunt of the fighting in their sectors. When Norman and I were out at the Argyles' camp in Singapore in the first week in February, I remember officers and N.C.Os praising the work of this Australian M.T. unit. I believe General Heath had accorded them special recognition. The C.O. of the unit, Lieutenant-Colonel C. M. Black, who was Supply Chief for Blackforce in Java, is among the prisoners here. . . .

Have been spending a lot of time yarning with some of the officers from No. 1 Squadron R.A.A.F.—Doug Howie, George Evans, Gerry Alderton, Don Capron, Alec Dobbie, Bert Sinfield and Bill Moore. Some of these chaps did splendid work in the show at Khota Baru where four Japanese transports were sunk and many landing craft destroyed with great loss of life before we were forced to evacuate the aerodrome.

Subsequently they did what was known as the "clay pigeon" run—in daylight without fighter escort—against Japanese objectives in northern Malaya from Sembawang aerodrome on Singapore Island. They operated later from a secret airfield at Palembang, Sumatra, until that was seized, and were finally captured on Java after almost all their planes had been destroyed.

17 May. We have had to fill in a long and detailed form dealing with birth, parentage, education, work, hobbies, interests and so on. The Japanese passion for forms and details is more acute than among our own bureaucracy. Norman and I are still a bit worried as to what they think of our status. They know I am a war correspondent and they know that we have the status of lieutenants. As long as they do not connect us with Singapore Radio I think we'll be left in peace. . . .

The boys back from working party today saw another Dutch woman beaten up by Japanese soldiers because she made the V sign towards the prisoners' truck. Two Japanese rushed at her and struck her several times across the face. These incidents make us black with fury at our own helplessness. They also bring home exactly what has been hanging over Australia. (In code) The Coral Sea battle seems to mark the first turning of the tide. Since we heard the news, I've not been worrying each night after lights out as I did at Serang and when we first got here. One can't help wondering whether everybody in Britain realizes what it would mean to Australia if the country was overrun by the Japanese even temporarily.

21 June. Started a novel about university life this afternoon. I've had the idea for about five years and, if it serves no other purpose, it'll be good to set down on paper one's thoughts and conclusions after the years at Queen's and Balliol. I'm calling it "Undergraduates in Love". As things are at present, I can write either in the mess or on my bed throughout the afternoon.

. . . We've now got eighty books for the officers' library, but as there are about a hundred drawing from it some people inevitably miss out. The books are an absolute godsend and, as librarian, I'm doing my best to exchange them when possible with those from libraries in other huts.

13 July. Our new bakehouse under Captain Wiley has turned out its first batch of loaves. They were excellent and represent a tremendous amount of hard work by all concerned in building the ovens and mixing the bread. . . .

30 July. Several officers and N.C.Os were paraded today to give their impressions of conditions to General Kito, commander of all P.O.W. camps in Java. They were asked: "Why are you fighting Japan?", "What is the attitude of the Australian people?", "Are you learning Nippon Go (Japanese)?" and so on.

4 August. Have spent the last few days in Hospital with dengue which has ravaged our hut in the past fortnight. For the first two days you ache everywhere, particularly in the legs and behind the eyes, then for two days you seem much better, until on the fifth day the fever hits you with a terrific wallop and all you want to do is to lie still without moving, eating, talking or hearing anything.

The Timor boys, mainly 2/40th Battalion, who have just come in have reason to feel that they did everything they could against impossible odds. The Japanese landed on 19 February, and our fellows held on, despite a parachute landing in their rear, for four days; but with no air support and no prospect of relief continued resistance could achieve nothing. Once again it was a case of "too little, too late". We'll start winning this war only when we start getting our blow in first.

9 August. Norm had a grand vaudeville show last night. The jazz band and the ballet were outstanding and Hal Hamlyn of *Houston* put on a puppet show about "Dangerous Dan McGrew" which was a riot. The Japs are now issuing a few cheap native cigarettes which we've christened "stinkadoros" because they are full of some stuff that smells like cheap incense. Having smoked some pretty grim things in various parts of the world, I give the palm to these saffron night-mares. One would give them away, if one had a cent to buy any other smoke, but when you're as broke as I've been in this camp you've got to make the best of anything. The only decent cigarettes we've had, I've swopped to get some sugar. This helps the rice down and helps to offset the constant craving for sweets.

Many of us have started making jam from the rind of papayas and pomelos with the aid of ginger-root and whatever sugar we can lay our hands on. The result is surprisingly good, but oh, what I'd give for a decent bag of sugar.

. . . Am now lecturing not only at night but quite often during the eleven to twelve recreation hour, which the Japanese have enforced. The brigadier has asked me to assist the officers running this, and I've been organizing quizes and spelling Bs which occasion an amazing amount of amusement and rivalry. Must have given over fifty lectures in this camp by now on the trip to Russia, Paris, test cricket, and a talk on possible developments in Australia in the coming years. This last serves to stir up great controversy over such questions as immigration, abolition of State Parliaments, continuance of White Australia, nationalization and the effect of war-time inflation on the buying power of the pound. I've been given a great reception in all huts, and the whole business has at least given me the satisfaction of feeling that I'm doing something to help the lads to kill a few hours of this grim period of waiting. Audiences have been so large that I've been warned there may be trouble with the Japs. At one lecture I started with 300, but was told there were 1000 at the end. The other night down in the Americans' hut, I was just starting to talk about Paris, when a voice from the darkness at the back of the crowd drawled, "Excuse me, Mr Rivett, are you gointa talk about Paris, France, or Paris, Texas?" (Uproarious laughter.) It appears that Paris, Texas, has a population of about 800.

In the officers' mess when it was my turn to talk I lectured on the political reasons underlying the military collapse of France, using the material I collected for articles to the *Argus* from France.

3 September. Major-General Saito issued a manifesto telling us that he was in command of all prisoners of war and that we must not lose our national pride. There is no danger of this. The more we see of the Nip and all his ways, the more contemptible he appears and the prouder one feels of Australia and all things Australian.

6 September. The camp commandant has forced everybody to have his hair cropped short, "not longer than his own", which means that we've all been shorn in the past twenty-four hours. Some hideous sights now meet the gaze on all sides. I look like nothing so much as a bearded egg and the only consolation is that there are dozens of other monstrosities. Colin Mathieson of Nilpeena station says it's the biggest insult the Nips have inflicted on us yet, and I'm inclined to agree. . . . There's no doubt that for some months we've been treated like inveterate criminals, and now a good many of us look the part.

. . . "Slug" Wright, a Texan with a superb sense of humour, tells a good story against himself about the search the other day. Slug, who is in charge of the Americans' Q. store knew that a case with many thousands of guilders in bills was hidden amongst the ration pile. His presence, loitering round the pile might only draw suspicion, so he went off to the wood heap which seemed the quietest and safest place in the compound. When the search was over in the Australian lines, an Australian came down and started searching among the wood where "Slug" was sitting. After a minute, he produced four Mills bombs, stowed them in his pocket and walked calmly away.

20 September. The wet season now seems to be under way and we've had some really heavy rain. Today was a red letter day because I finished the novel. I determined I'd write at least two hundred words a day and haven't fallen down on that except when I had dengue, averaging well over a thousand. Have also written three short stories, one of which has been liked very much by all who've read it. They say nice things about the others, but I'm afraid they're tripe. Now the question is, how will I manage to keep the bulky MS. of the novel through the rest of the captivity? I'd hate to see it torn up by the Japs, although even if I get it home nobody may read it except Gwyth [my wife] and the family. It's given me a tremendous kick writing it every day and has been a marvellous escape from the continuous strain of these prowling guards and continual "Kiwotskis" (Japanese for Attention!). Some of the dialogue is quite good, I think, but in parts the whole thing is so thin as to be almost diaphanous.

. . . It seems certain now that we're going to move. (In code) I wish I could feel that there was some prospect of our release before 1944, but in all honesty I can't believe in it. If we're put on a ship there is a good chance of our being torpedoed by one of our own submarines, but the chances of being picked up afterwards or given a chance to get hold of a boat to set out for Australia again are just about nil. All we hope is that we don't get taken to Japan. Anywhere else there is always some prospect of release before the end of the war. A number believe that the Japanese will shoot their prisoners before surrendering them, but it seems to me quite futile to worry, although there is no doubt that they are not only capable of it, but that most of them would love to do so if they could get any sort of authority for it.

. . . Custom may bring resignation to some, but I'm afraid that I am not one of the lucky ones. Each week of captivity seems just as galling as the last. I wonder where I'll be writing this in a month from now?

CHAPTER XV

THE UNKNOWN JAPANESE

To begin to understand the Japanese mentality and to penetrate
his mind it is absolutely essential to grasp to its uttermost significance this fact: the Japanese are convinced, they are even more
than convinced, they *know* that they are descended from the gods.
—TAID O'CONROY, *The Menace of Japan.*

IT is impossible to form any accurate picture of the conditions
with which the prisoners of Japan were confronted without
turning our attention to the study of the captors themselves.
Seldom in the world's history, during recent times, has there
been so much ignorance and muddled thinking about a large
nation as prevailed about Japan and the Japanese prior to this
war. The average Anglo-Saxon or European was inclined to
regard the Japanese as something in the nature of a joke,
even if the joke appeared at times to be in rather bad taste.
His stature and general appearance in Western eyes tended
to emphasize the comic side, and to lead to gross miscalcula-
tion of his ability, tenacity, ruthlessness and fanaticism. Even
the events of a decade in China did not serve to arouse a large
section of the public to much more than a feeling of rather
bored resentment.

Several of the books published with a view to presenting the
Japanese—his thoughts, his beliefs, his ambitions—to the
English-speaking world were treated as somewhat biased
propaganda; to a great extent, the sentimental eulogies of flat-
tered visitors and of novelists enraptured by cherry blossom,
the glamour of Bushido and the tales of the Samurai, still held
sway.

The attack on Pearl Harbour shocked the world, not only
because of the efficiency and deadliness of its execution, but

because of the tremendous self-confidence and ambition revealed by the attack on the world's most powerful nation, at a time when Japan should have been sore and exhausted after four and a half years of inconclusive struggling in China. The sinking of *Prince of Wales* and *Repulse* completed the revolution in the thinking of many. What Hitler had failed to do had been done by the little despised men from the islands of Nippon. At last people began to ask themselves whether the Japanese militarists were not as grave a menace as the Nazis. In those first months of successive disasters there arose a tendency to overrate the Japanese nearly as much as we had formerly undervalued him.

The men captured in the first months of Japan's southward drive did not begin by hating their captors. Many of them admired the courage and efficiency displayed in the Japanese attack, and were severely critical of the blunders and failures made by ourselves. Most prisoners were inclined to be sceptical of anti-Japanese propaganda and were prepared to take the Japanese as they found them.

The process of our education as prisoners was gradual. About some things we were slow to believe the evidence of our ears and eyes. But as the lessons were hammered home by scores of Japanese in varying circumstances, we came to understand something of the strange and, to us, fantastic being we were up against.

Over the years, in Java, Malaya, Burma, Siam and other occupied areas, it was brought home to the prisoner that the Japanese has a greater capacity for self-delusion than any mortal on this earth. His whole training throughout childhood and in the army has brought the Japanese to a state where he can easily and consistently believe that right is wrong and wrong is right, just as it suits his book. Again and again, Japanese of all ranks made statements to prisoners indicating a complete certainty that they were a divine race, as superior to other peoples as man is to the other members of the animal kingdom.

In the truest and ablest analysis of the Japanese that I have seen, *The Menace of Japan*, Professor Taid O'Conroy, who lived in Japan for a large part of his life and who married a Japanese, presents the Japanese as he really is with a fidelity which no one with less experience could hope to emulate. The pity was that we, of the democracies, did not, until it was too late, listen to him and to others with similar knowledge.

Tens of thousands of us—Australians, British, Americans and Dutch—saw, day by day, year by year, with our own eyes, the arrogant ruthlessness of the Japanese in power. Step by step, we came to realize that we were dealing with a people with whose thoughts and ideas we had nothing in common.

All of us are familiar with dishonesty. It is as old as the world and common to all peoples in all ages. Even so, to find habitual and flagrant intellectual dishonesty the keynote of the thinking of all members of a race was at first staggering and later, after endless repetition, nauseating. We discovered that so perverted have general education and publicity become in Japan, that beliefs held by every other educated race are ignored or rejected. Most achievements of modern science and engineering are attributed to Japanese. The belief is deeply ingrained in the Japanese population that their buildings, their ships and their trains, like their army, navy and air force, are all vastly superior to anything outside Japan.

Time and again we saw Japanese officers, N.C.Os and privates deny knowledge of incidents which had happened before their eyes a few minutes earlier. Slowly, but at last with unshakable conviction, we came to realize that the Japanese can hypnotize himself into believing anything, however absurd. We discovered that here was a race which almost universally lacked a sense of humour.

We were more taken aback by the absurdities to which this lack could carry the Japanese than by their brutality. At length, most of us were forced into a state of mind in which we avoided all contact with the Japanese that was not absolutely unavoidable. Certain officers and men, throughout the captivity, chatted freely to Japanese guards and officers, whenever opportunities presented themselves. The majority of us found any such association as repugnant as unnecessary contact with a disgusting disease.

The evolution of this feeling was due to the multitude of experiences set forth in this book, but to establish any picture of the Japanese as he saw himself, it is necessary to turn to his own announcements and speeches.

In the early months of our captivity in Batavia, the camp commandant caused the following notice to be placed on the notice board in the officers' mess. Beyond need of comment, it reveals under its comic wording, the abysmal ignorance of the Japanese about the pride, loyalty and patriotism of his prisoners.

TO THE PRISONERS OF WAR

1. Reply honestly about what the Japanese forces asks you. If the answer is incorrect, you will be punished seriously. Example: (*a*) If you know that a certain part of Australia cannot be passed by motor-car or foot on account of forests or marsh and you answer that it can be passed. We go to the place and suffer hardships believing your answers. (*b*) In spite of knowing there is a traffic organization believing your answer "there is none" we find the traffic organization in the district.

2. But for the lying propaganda of the senior men of your countries, you wouldn't have met with the hardships as prisoners of war.

> Because you believed them,
> You came here to fight against us
> You surrendered
> You are prisoners of war
> I am sorry for that.

3. DAI NIPPON is a just country and does not use lying propaganda. Do everything honestly, and be well repaid.

—BY COMMANDANT SUZUKI.

One of the most illuminating notices, promulgated in Batavia, announced an essay competition for which a prize in cigarettes would be donated by Lieutenant Kitemura, one of the camp administration. Eight subjects were listed for the choice of competitors. Subjects 1 to 7 were quite conventional —My Home, My Job, A Love Story, etc. Subject number 8 made us catch our breath. It was—Mr Kitemura! I don't know if any of the men who wrote essays ever thought of writing this one, but I doubt whether anybody in the camp knew, or cared, enough about the gentleman to string together three sentences.

But we did not really come to appreciate the elephantiasis

of the ego, which seems to be universal among Japanese officers, until we came to work on the Burma-Siam railway. Those of us who worked in Burma were harangued on our arrival by Lieutenant-Colonel Y. Nagatomo, commander of 10,000 prisoners, in a speech which reflects the Japanese mind as fully and as representatively as any other single statement.

It is a great pleasure to me to see you at this place, as I am appointed Chief of War Prisoners' Camp in obedience to the Imperial Command issued by His Majesty the Emperor. The great Asiatic War has broken out due to the rising of the East Asiatic Nations whose hearts were burnt with the desire to live and preserve their nations, on account of the intrusion of the British and Americans for the past many years.

There is therefore no other reason for Japan to drive out the anti-Axis powers of the arrogant and insolent British and American from East Asia in co-operation with our neighbours in China* and East Asiatic nations and to establish the Greater East Asia Co-prosperity Sphere for the benefit of all human beings and to establish everlasting peace in the world.

During the past few centuries, Nippon has made extreme endeavour and made sacrifices to become the leader of the East Asiatic nations who were mercilessly and pitifully treated by the outside forces of the American and British; and Nippon without disgracing anyone has been doing her best for fostering Nippon's real power.

You are only a few remaining skeletons after the invasion of East Asia for the past few centuries and are pitiful victims. It is not your fault, but till your Government do not wake up from the dreams and discontinue their resistance all of you will not be released. However I shall not treat you badly for the sake of humanity as you have no fighting power at all. His Majesty the Emperor has been deeply anxious about all the War Prisoners and has ordered us to enable opening of War Prisoners' camps at almost all the places in the southward countries. The Imperial thoughts are unestimable and the Imperial favours are infinite and as such you should weep with gratitude at the greatness of them and should correct or mend the misleading and improper anti-Japanese ideas . . .

Living manners, deportment, salutation and attitude shall be strict and according to the rules of the Nippon Army, because it is only possible to manage you all who are merely rabbles, by the order of military regulations. . . . My biggest requirement from you is escape. If there is a man here who has at least one per cent of a chance of escape we shall make him to face the extreme penalty. If there is one foolish man who is trying to escape, he shall see big jungles toward the East which are absolutely impossible for communication, towards the West he shall see the boundless ocean and above all, in the main points of South and North our Nippon Army is staying and guarding. . . .

At the time of such shortness of materials, your lives are preserved by the Military, and all of you must reward them with your labour. By the hand of the Nippon Army railway works to connect Thailand and Burma

* Shades of Chiang-Kai-Shek!

have started to the great interest of the world. There are deep jungles where no man comes to clear them by cutting the trees. There are also countless difficulties and sufferings but you shall have the honour to join in this great work which was never done before and you should do your best efforts. . . . In conclusion I say to you "Work cheerfully" and from henceforth you shall be guided by my motto.

This farrago of nonsense, lies and absurdity was not only pronounced by the colonel himself to every batch of prisoners which arrived to work on the railway, but was printed and issued throughout all camps.

More revealing of Japanese inhumanity and disregard for their prisoners was this speech made by Lieutenant-Colonel Yanagida on assuming command of the largest P.O.W. group in Thailand in 1943. Many hundreds in this group had already perished, and thousands more lay wasted with disease and malnutrition when Yanagida took over. Instead of concerning himself about the appalling state of the prisoners entrusted to his care, he issued the following "Instructions":

I have the pleasure to lead you on the last stretch of Railways construction Wardom with the appointment of the present post. In examination of various reports as well as to the result of my partial inspection of camps, as to present conditions, am pleased to find that you are in general keeping discipline and working diligently. At the same time regret to find seriousness.

It is evident that there are various causes inevitable for this end but to my opinion due mainly to the fact for absence of firm belief as Japanese "Health follows will" and "Cease only when enemy is completely annihilated".

Those who fail to reach objective in charge by lack of health or spirit is considered in Japanese Army as most shameful deed. "Devotion till death" is good yet still we have the spirit "Devotion to Imperial cause even to the turn of life in incarnation". The spirit which cannot become void by death.

You are in the act of charge in colleague with JAPANESE ARMY.

You are expected to charge to the last of the work with good spirit and taking care on your own health. Besides you are to remember that your welfare is guaranteed only by obedience to the order of the Imperial Japanese Army.

Imperial Japanese Army will not be unfair to those who are honest and obey them, but protect such. You are to understand this fundamental spirit and to carry out the task given you with perfect peace of mind under protection of the Japanese Imperial Army.

Nearly as striking as their inhumanity and indifference to suffering was the façade of lies and false promises put up by

Japanese officers and N.C.Os in dealing with P.O.W. requests and grievances. The prisoners' own administrations ran into an impenetrable barrier of falsehoods and equivocations, which immensely complicated all attempts to secure some measure of justice and improvement of conditions.

In Batavia Brigadier Blackburn was held responsible for maintaining discipline within the camp. But on the caprice of two privates he was publicly slapped and forced to carry slops from the cells where prisoners were undergoing special punishments.

Inconsistency was a thing that worried the Japanese not at all. In Batavia hut commanders were paraded and told it was quite wrong that prisoners should stand with their hands behind their backs. "Only prisoners stand like that in Japan," our officers were informed. When they pointed out that they were prisoners, they were told: "You are not prisoners, but the Emperor's guests. Besides, you might have a pistol concealed behind your back."

As the years went by, we grew accustomed to the Japanese of all ranks promising things without the smallest intention of fulfilling those promises. If you reminded a Japanese on Friday of a promise made on Tuesday, he would say he had not *promised* anything but had *hoped*, etc. Curiously enough, Japanese or Korean privates were usually more honest in their dealings with individual prisoners than officers and N.C.Os were in dealing with the P.O.W. administration.

The curious blindness to the beliefs and reactions of others extended from the most ignorant coolie to the best informed Japanese. One could attribute it only to the obsessions which dominate the Japanese mind. I had an excellent instance of this about six weeks after writing the letter to my people at home.

One day I was sent for by camp headquarters and told that a Japanese staff car had called to take me away. Our officers believed that it was the Gestapo and that I was being taken to the Konigsplaen jail for questioning. They told me to get my sarong and personal odds and ends in preparation for a term in the cells, such as other officers had been subjected to.

However, the car took me to the broadcasting studios, where prisoners were writing their letters, and I was told again to write a letter home. I could not understand this, but imagined that it might be connected with the change in the control of the Batavia station of which we had been told. Presently I discovered why they wanted me.

Mr Mitsui, who was allegedly a Yale graduate, entered the room where I was writing and told me that he had taken charge of broadcasting and was running a special programme to Australia to try to give Australians some true knowledge of the Japanese. He knew I was a journalist and wished me to write the introductions to this daily programme.

I told him that this was propaganda for the enemies of my country and that I would have nothing to do with it. He said it was not propaganda but an attempt to establish a real basis of friendship between the Japanese and the Australian people, who were fighting Japan without reason. He added that if I would co-operate he would at the end of a month secure my release on parole from the prison camp; that I would live with the rest of his staff in a flat in Batavia; and that life would be much better than in the camp where things were likely to get even worse than at present.

I said to Mitsui that, as a man with some knowledge of the West, he must know that his proposition was out of the question. I said he could put me in front of a microphone with a pistol in my back and perhaps succeed in making me talk, but he could never make me write anything that was worth while. He tried to persuade me, saying significantly that "there was no thought of coercion at this stage". He pointed out that concessions for prisoners might be made on his representations if I helped. I replied that it was a matter of honour and that in no circumstances would I be connected with any work of that nature.

All this time I was wondering whether Mitsui had discovered my connexion with Singapore Radio, but it turned out from his questions that he knew nothing except that I was a journalist. Finally, he gave up and sent me back to the camp with orders to tell another journalist among the officers to come to the studio.

I went back and reported the whole interview in detail to Brigadier Blackburn. That was the last I heard about broadcasting, and Norman and I were not subsequently pestered.

As time went by every one of us became an eye-witness to Japanese delight in torturing and tormenting animals. It soon became evident that this form of sadism was not confined to a few perverts, but was general through all ranks of their army. Not even the bashings dealt out to ourselves infuriated us so much as the deliberate cruelties to helpless beasts. No single action of the Japanese emphasized so strongly the abyss which separated our mentalities. A large group of Japanese will always gather round whenever pain is being inflicted on some helpless creature. Their expressions and enthusiasm show their delight in its agonies. The catalogue of the things which prisoners witnessed would make painful reading to anyone, even if he had no love for animals. We saw trussed pigs tortured for an hour before execution, by having boiling water poured down their ears so that they screamed like demented souls; fowls packed helplessly in a crate had their eyes gouged out by gloating guards using pointed slivers of bamboo; a dog, more dead than alive after a senseless beating, was buried up to the nose in a bed of quicklime. Any prisoner can add endlessly to the list. To listen to the cries or barks of the victims used to make many of us experience a wave of hatred and nausea, such as persecution of ourselves never induced. As one P.O.W. said: "I'd rather they kicked me in the stomach than have to listen to them amusing themselves with a dog."

It was not until we reached Burma and began to read *Greater Asia*—a Japanese newspaper published at Rangoon, in English—that we realized to the full the credulity, blindness and utter lack of humour in our captors.

All Japanese newspapers were an unending source of amusement and delight to prisoners, at a time when we had very little of either. Their stories went from the wildly improbable to the utterly impossible without the journalists concerned batting an eyelid. We discovered that the best way to deal with Japanese communiqués was to divide the Allied losses they claimed by anything from five to ten, and to take the Japanese losses as the figure quoted for the Allies. By the time of what the Japanese called the "Third Battle of the Gilbert Islands", they had destroyed three times as many battleships, and twice as many aircraft-carriers as the United States had ever built.

But it was the stories that provided the real joy. I only hope that some of the copies of *Greater Asia* and other Japanese papers of 1943-4 can be found and preserved for exhibition in the museums.

One reporter gave us a glowing account of the enthusiasm with which the elephants of Burma had hailed their delivery from the cruel British who abandoned them, and their appreciation of the Imperial Japanese Army. He said that the elephants were now experiencing better treatment than they had ever known before, and that he had just seen a parade of elephants "raise their trunks and let forth a resounding trumpet of salutation in honour of their deliverers, the heroic Imperial Army, whom they loved". The prisoners in Burma were naturally tremendously impressed with this story, for they saw nearly all of the working elephants along the railway line ill-treated or starved to death by the Japs within a few months.

Then there was the Japanese submarine which proceeded on the surface into an Allied port, full of cruisers and destroyers, sank a merchant ship and sailed out again in broad daylight under a hail of fire, without a scratch.

But the feats of the Japanese airmen, or "Wild Eagles", were the stories which the papers loved. No Japanese plane was ever shot down by the enemy. Such trivial losses as were admitted were always due to the fact that the pilots "crash-dived into their objectives". A lovely touch provided in many reports dealing with raids a fortnight old was—"Six of our planes crash-dived into their objectives, or have not yet returned to base." As one R.A.A.F. pilot remarked, "Some of these Nip pilots must go for a pleasure cruise for a week or two on their way home."

In the air battles over Burma, one Japanese pilot, being

out of ammunition, shook his fist at the British plane. The British pilot was so terrified that he immediately landed his plane in a padi field, in accordance with the Jap pilot's wishes. Another Jap pilot secured victory over his opponent by covering him with a pistol, so that the cowardly enemy hastened to land his plane in Japanese territory.

In New Guinea, a Japanese forced his enemy down in the jungle. He then landed his own plane (apparently in the jungle tree-tops), ran back to the British plane, overpowered the enemy pilot, tied him up with jungle vine and marched his captive back through the jungle to a Japanese aerodrome.

Facts of time, space, speed and elementary aeronautics did not disturb the Jap scribes. One of the most famous stories told under bold headlines is how a Japanese pilot, out of ammunition, found himself pursued by a huge Liberator. The pilot, with great gallantry, hurled his rice-cake at the pursuing plane, causing it to crash ignominiously into the sea.

The finest performance was that of another "Wild Eagle" who, though out of ammunition, wished to attack a British destroyer. He dived at the warship upside down, making straight for the bridge. Then he drew his Samurai sword and, leaning out of his cockpit, valorously decapitated the commander of the destroyer as he swept past.

Finally, we had the hero who, after shooting down innumerable foes, returned to his base with less than half his plane, one complete wing being missing. He staggered to the operations room and reported in detail to his commanding officer. "It was only after he had finished," the report ran, "having fulfilled his entire commission, that it was discovered that Lieutenant—was dead."

CHAPTER XVI

THE HORROR OF THE HELLSHIPS

And below the ships are prisons, where with multitudinous griefs,
Christian captives sick and sunless, all a labouring race repines.
And many a one grows witless in his quiet room in hell
Where a yellow face looks inward through the lattice of his cell.
—G. K. CHESTERTON, *Lepanto*

WE arrived at Tanjong Pryok station at dawn on 8 October 1942, and were marched to the dock across an area covered with scrap from wrecked aircraft and motor vehicles. Our first view of the vessel which was our destination was not reassuring. She was a squat, grey freighter of about 5000 tons and it was difficult to see just where the 1500 of us were to be stowed, particularly as large quantities of freight were being loaded aboard. This was Japanese supply ship No. 674, *King Kong Maru*.

I finished the journey to the ship's side barefoot, because the improvised sandals, made of leather straps and string, which were my only foot cover, had proved unequal to the strain. I had no pack for the miscellaneous canvas and other odd gear which constituted my entire possessions and, with odds and ends bound up with cord, I resembled nothing so much as a walking junk shop.

At the foot of the gangway leading up from the wharf to the deck we were paraded and counted and then started to scramble up the narrow swinging steps. At the top, sentries herded us towards the top of the hatch where a perpendicular steel ladder gave access to one of the holds. Negotiating this with all one's personal gear was not easy, and as usual the sentries were yelling and screaming in a high state of excitement. Peering down into the hold we were amazed to see that it was already packed with Bren-carriers. We were now driven down among these. Although the entire deck space at the bottom of the hold around the carriers was soon full, the Japanese continued to push men down until 189 of us were packed in. Prisoners had to get under and between the carriers but were not allowed to bestride them. We could not help thinking that, in the event of a sumatra, appalling carnage might ensue, for the machines were not secured in any way. We had seen enough of the storms in these waters to know that this boat would be flung about like a cork; and no one relished the idea of having a score of steel juggernauts sliding about like live things among men so packed that there was no chance of dodging.

In No. 2 hold, which was a good deal bigger, 744 men were crowded so that not all had sitting room and sleep was only possible lying literally one on top of the other. The remaining 567 prisoners were jammed into No. 3 hold at the other end of the vessel.

It was nine o'clock in the morning when we clambered down into the hold. We remained there for the next ninety-six hours. Well before midday the heat at the bottom of the hold became almost intolerable, there being no ventilation. We soon discovered that the total issue of liquid was one and a half pints of tea per man per day. No water for drinking or washing was allowed, although we were bathed in sweat and soon indescribably dirty. Yet the Japanese on deck used to frolic and play under the hoses for hours on end through the worst hours of the day.

Three times a day buckets containing rice and soya soup with a little radish floating in it were lowered to us. We were not particularly hungry by Batavia standards, because we still had the tinned rations from camp stores that were issued before we left the Bicycle Camp. But our thirst was intolerable and grew worse as the long hours of the day wore slowly by. We moved away from the wharf to the mouth of the harbour, but did not leave until just before dark.

The harbour itself was strewn with shipping destroyed by bombing or sabotage. One or two boats had been turned over and now lay with their sides and keels protruding foolishly above the water. All that could be seen of several other vessels was the tops of their masts as they rested on the bottom of the harbour. When I thought of Tanjong Pryok as I had seen it at the beginning of January en route for Singapore, bristling with ships of all nations, with naval launches, submarines and flying boats arriving or departing amidst the shoals of freighters and liners, it seemed as if the port itself had died. The wharves were virtually deserted, and everywhere the eye encountered only wreckage, desolation and the reminder of what had once been. It was amazing that after seven months of occupation the Japanese should have done so little to put this great port in working order again.

My view of the harbour was obtained only by loitering on deck for a few minutes on the pretext of going to the latrine. This was the only excuse under which one could get out of the hold for a moment. The latrines consisted of three small boxes on the starboard side of the ship into which a tall man had to crawl like an animal. These had to serve the needs of the thousand prisoners in the first two holds, many of whom, in the succeeding days, developed dysentery and diarrhoea. It was not surprising that men sickened quickly in the fetid, stinking atmosphere at the bottom of the unventilated holds.

Representations to the Japanese on behalf of the sick produced vague words but no results. During the night of 9-10 October, less than forty-eight hours after coming on board, an A.I.F. man died. He was the first of scores whose deaths were directly attributable to the sapping of their resistance through dysentery in the hellships, although some did not die until months later in the Burma jungle.

Those with compasses told us that we were heading northward, and Singapore was now the goal favoured by popular rumour, which this time proved correct. After anchoring for some hours off the Rhea Archipelago on the tenth, we steamed slowly through many mine-fields to the examination anchorage at Keppel harbour, where we dropped anchor towards noon on 11 October. We were all kept below until late afternoon when we were allowed on deck to gaze at the neighbouring island of Blakangmati and at the beaches where scores of Chinese volunteers had been massacred with machine-guns after the capitulation.

There was more evidence of life in Keppel harbour than at Tanjong Pryok, with boats, ferries and lighters chugging to and fro; but to those of us who had known it in other days this harbour, too, seemed to have lost its vitality and something of its soul.

Next day we tied up at a wharf and at noon, after many "tankos", were piled on to trucks. We passed many 8th Division A.I.F. prisoners rolling oil drums along the wharves, but were not allowed to talk with them.

As we drove around the eastern coast of the island towards Changi we saw little evidence of the wreckage which parts of the town had undergone through Japanese bombing and shellfire. Many of the ruined buildings had been cleaned up, and men from the Middle East who had not known the city before were surprised at the fewness of visible scars. We drove along New Bridge Road and then through the heart of the city, along Victoria Road, past Kalang air port and so northwards up the east coast of the island towards Changi.

A number of the shops were still shuttered and closed, but most were open, although business seemed very poor, which suggested that most of them had little to sell. Groups of Japanese soldiers wandering round the streets were the only new feature, but the crowds seemed smaller, quieter and more idle. Once again, as in Batavia, one felt as if a blight were hanging over the city. One could understand how London must have seemed to Pepys and his contemporaries during the Great Plague.

I suppose that superficially there was still something left of the colour and bustle that had made cosmopolitan Singapore, with all its ugliness and vice, so pulsatingly alive. But an indefinable shadow seemed to lurk over the city even in the more crowded thoroughfares. There was brought home to those of us who had lived there before a feeling as if a dead hand had been laid on the very throat of the city. We were to see more of this in other cities before long.

The Horror of the Hellships

Whatever the fine words spoken about the "co-prosperity sphere" and the brotherhood of all Asiatics, the Japanese Army had no hope of inducing this feeling in the occupied areas until from the highest general to the lowliest private it had undergone a transformation and change of heart. You cannot preach love to a people when you constantly assert your dominance with ostentatious arrogance backed by ruthless brutality.

There is no doubt that in both Batavia and Singapore Japanese discipline was far better than it had ever been in the occupied cities of China. No orgies such as had marked the capture of Nanking had followed the occupation of these cities.

Yet the very system of military training and the beliefs instilled into the Japanese rank and file by the military caste, while excellent for securing obedience and fanatical devotion in the field, made it impossible for them to fraternize with the peoples to whom they claimed to have brought deliverance. No other Asiatic is prepared to swallow the conceit of the Japanese that he is a member of the Chosen People and under divine protection. Whatever blunders and mistakes the white man has made in the Orient by his failure to study the viewpoint and customs of the Asiatic population, no European race ever flaunted its sense of superiority more stridently than did the soldiers of Japan's armies. In a few weeks they undid most of the work so carefully done by Japanese agents and propagandists during the preceding years.

It may not have been surprising that the Chinese of Singapore did not take kindly to their Japanese overlords. The Chinese were knitted by close bonds to their fellow countrymen in the motherland ravaged and persecuted by the Japanese through the past years, and they had stood loyally and courageously behind the British in their struggle to defend the city. But the Japanese were no happier in their relationship with the other Asiatic races with whom they came in contact.

It was on this day in Singapore that I first came to the comforting and cheering belief that the Japanese were in fact the best propagandists for British rule that one could find. I felt

that two or three years of Japanese occupation of Southern
Asia might well prove sufficient to destroy, for generations
to come, all illusions about Japan as the liberator and bene-
factor of the peoples of Asia. They might not like British
domination, but they would know that things might be far
worse.

We stopped on the bare wind-swept plateau which sur-
rounds the grim stone walls of Singapore jail at Changi. All
men were ordered out of the trucks and lined up for a tanko.
Pessimists were already offering ten to one that the jail was
our destination, when the order came to climb aboard again,
and the trucks proceeded through the Changi barracks to the
extreme north-eastern tip of the island where we stopped
below the peace-time barracks of the Gordon Highlanders.

Here we spent the next day and the following morning,
renewing acquaintanceships with thousands of members of
the 8th Division and of British units who were quartered
around us. All the officers in the Java party were the guests
of British messes.

At Changi we found a far greater degree of freedom and
comfort than we had ever known in Batavia. Japanese sentries
seldom appeared inside the large area in which prisoners were
confined. Sikh guards were seen occasionally, and movement
from section to section of the area was restricted, but after the
incessant persecution of Batavia, Changi appeared to us like
a P.O.W. heaven.

The feeling was strengthened when we discovered that a
Red Cross ship had arrived a few days before with 1700 tons
of supplies for the prisoners. We sampled some of this at mess
and an issue of foodstuffs was made to us before we left on
the morning of 14 October. The most ragged of us also
received khaki shirts and shorts from the British Q store which
had been left entirely under British control by the Japanese.

After the hold of *King Kong Maru,* these hours in
Changi were like a holiday, and we were bitterly disappointed
when we learned that our stay was to be so brief.

The Australian officers were visited by Colonel "Black
Jack" Callaghan, A.I.F. C.O. in Changi, who told us that

8th Division morale had never been higher, and that the boys were ready to play their part as soon as the British were ready to retake Malaya. It was cheering, although some of us felt that the end was still a long way off.

In Changi, in accordance with British Army tradition, a very determined attempt had been made to maintain discipline and morale with a strict observance of military custom. Saluting was still the order of the day, both between officers and men and among officers themselves. Some of the Americans from Java did not take kindly to this state of affairs, and this led to a famous episode. A very senior British colonel was walking down the road when he passed a man who, like most of us from Java, was dressed in very ragged and nondescript fashion and carried no insignia of rank, these having been removed in Batavia by order of the Japanese. The pukka colonel barked gruffly: "Well, my man! Don't you know that you should salute?" The American ensign thus addressed stared at the glowering officer in bewilderment. "Don't you know who I am?" thundered the Britisher. "I'm Deputy Acting ———— ———— of Malaya Command." "Pleased to meet you," said the Yank imperturbably, "I'm Ensign H——, Acting Admiral for the American Pacific Fleet, Changi area." Legend does not disclose the sequel, but I can vouch for the truth of the story.

On another occasion, some Americans in a mess became increasingly irritated to hear two British officers lauding General Rommel. "After the show he's put up, I hope to goodness he comes through alive," said one. "We can't afford to lose a military genius like that. After the war—" "After the war," interrupted one American drily, "I suppose you'll take him to England for stud purposes."

On the morning before we left, we were all issued with a card on which we could write a 25-word message home. This lifted a great weight from the minds of many, for we were told that the cards would go home immediately. So we went down to the harbour again more cheerfully than might have been expected. Alas, for our hopes; the letters did not reach Australia until September 1943—eleven months later.

As our trucks sped through the Changi area, scores of slouch-hatted Australians came out of their tents to wave to us. We cheered them and waved back; but a minute later, on our left, we passed a grim reminder of the stern realities we were facing. This was the cemetery where all those who had died in Changi since the capitulation lay buried. Many of these graves belonged to men who had been mortally wounded in action, but one couldn't help wondering how many of these dead might have been saved if we had not been under the Japanese.

As we passed the Kalang air port, Singapore's civil aerodrome, from which a handful of Buffalos had sought to defend the city until one by one they were eliminated by the enemy's overwhelming numerical superiority, we noticed that the Japanese had laid down two broad asphalt landing strips across the field. I remark on it because it was the only piece of Japanese military work which we saw in three and a half years of captivity which really looked a good job.

At the docks the Japanese sentries were in a particularly vicious and truculent frame of mind and a number of men were bashed as we were herded on board *Mayebassi Maru*, Japanese supply ship No. 722. Our party of 1500 had now been augmented by the 200 men who had left Batavia five days ahead of us and also by some Dutch. We left a handful of the sickest men in the P.O.W. hospital at Changi. In all, 1799 prisoners were crammed into two holds forward and one aft on *Mayebassi Maru*.

We had imagined that nothing could be worse than conditions on the trip up to Singapore; but two minutes on the *Mayebassi* convinced us that we had been wrong. A I peered over the shoulders of those in front of me at the edge of the first hatch, I saw that two upper tiers in this hold were already occupied by Japanese troops. From the lower of these a forty-foot ladder descended to the very bowels of the vessel, where the floor space was already half covered by piles of Japanese gear, boxes, bed-rolls and other miscellaneous articles, including a tractor. The actual area of the hold was 75 feet by 48, and into this 650 prisoners were now driven.

From the bottom of this pit the patch of daylight at the top of the hatch seemed as remote as the clouds from the depths of the Grand Canyon, and it was obvious that nobody would be able to lie down in comfort. A group of us climbed on top of the highest pile of gear, perhaps twenty feet above the bottom of the hold, and there we perched precariously in the pious hope that we were at least a little nearer to fresh air.

No written words could convey the depression which seemed to settle on us in the depths of that pit. We did not know how many days lay ahead of us, and previous experience had taught us that we should be confined here until the end of the trip, however long that lasted. Suddenly, a lad from Wagga, Micky Cavanagh, called out in a ringing voice, "Don't let them get you down chaps. We can take it! Are we down-hearted?" The Japanese, crowded along the rail of the tiers above, like visitors at a zoo peering down into the animals' pit, must have been amazed at the vigour of our response. The spell had been broken. The boys were not going to be licked, however grim things might become.

For the next fifty-four hours we lay sweltering in this unforgettable hole without a breath of fresh air. The ship lay stationary in Keppel harbour so that the canvas vent in the prevailing dead calm brought no air to us in the depths. What little air filtered in at the top of the hold was drawn on first by the two hundred Japanese quartered in relative comfort above us. We had thought the *King Kong Maru* an inferno. We realized now that it had been only one of the outer compartments of the Jap P.O.W. hell. Now we were in the central torture chamber—the grill *de luxe*.

Within an hour most of us stripped to the skin, but even so the perspiration rolled down us in streams, and on the precious occasions when we got half a pint of tea or hot water to drink, it seemed to escape through our pores within three minutes. For acute and sustained physical discomfort, the holds of *Mayebassi Maru* beat even Serang to a frazzle.

At night some of the men simply lay on top of each other. Those of us who were on top of the gear tried to sleep with our heads perhaps three feet above our feet dangling below. My head and back were on a sloping roll of coir matting while my calves and feet tried to retain a precarious purchase on the bonnet of a small tractor feet below. Any man who got two hours of sleep in the twenty-four was doing very well.

By the Friday evening, 54 hours after coming on board, we had begun to think that we were doomed to rot slowly on the bottom of this wretched boat in the middle of Keppel harbour, for such days as remained to us in this world. So it was at first with incredulity, and then with hoarse cheers, that we heard the anchor being taken up. As the vessel at last moved forward a first trickle of fresh air came down the vent into our purgatory. With it came hope and an incredible rush of cheerfulness.

As we steamed slowly westwards and out into Malacca Strait, I could not help thinking of third-class and tourist cabins I had occupied at times on various ships, and of the complaints I sometimes made about the conditions. I realized now that even in the ill-ventilated inner cabin which I had shared with four others on a Russian boat in crossing from London to Leningrad, I had been cruising in the lap of luxury. Wanderlust may carry me into some strange places on some very odd ships, but I don't think I or anyone else enjoying Nippon's hospitality on that particular pleasure cruiser will forget its fragrant memories.

When we turned northwards up Malacca Strait on the evening of 16 October 1942, Destiny had obviously dealt out the hands for all to see, and there could no longer be any doubt that Burma was our destination. In Changi we had heard of a railway project in the Bangkok area, and we knew that a number of prisoners from Changi had been sent up there earlier in the year. Burma had been mentioned by the guards in Batavia, but it was only now that we came to realize that we were probably going to be employed on the construction of a railway to link Bangkok with the Burma coast and the Bay of Bengal.

The Japanese allowed us on deck for periods of twenty minutes or half an hour at dawn, and again in the evening.

Jap torture in Siam. This man was later beaten to death with a sledge hammer

Our worst trouble was the entire absence of water for washing. A number of men, who sought to wash in the trickle from a deck hose or at the leak in one of the pipes, were mercilessly beaten up by Dogface, the worst of the Batavian guards, who accompanied our party. On two occasions, for brief periods, we did get permission to turn on the deck hose and by this means hundreds of men had their only wash in ten days after leaving Changi.

The latrines were similar to those on *King Kong Maru* and, with the number of dysentery cases increasing daily, they were soon in an appalling state and almost unusable.

The ration of water, at first two pints a day, was later improved; but the meat throughout consisted of Australian mutton carcasses from the Singapore Cold Stores, bearing the dates 1931 and 1935. This meat might have been all right while frozen but *Mayebassi Maru* had no refrigeration, and the meat stank to high heaven, so that only those with the strongest stomachs could tackle it.

The scanty medical supplies brought by the party were liberally used by the crew and guards for the pettiest ailments. The senior M.O., Colonel Eadie, of Melbourne, was beaten up for refusing to allow a Japanese to fool with his microscope while he was using it. We eventually secured permission to place the worst of the dysentery cases on top of the hatch, so that they could be near the latrine, but scores of men who were becoming weaker daily had to face the grim climb up to the deck.

Every now and then the Japanese indulged in orgies of bashing, usually on the flimsiest of pretexts. Prisoners were hustled down into their stinking inferno at the end of the short periods on deck with blows of rifle butts, and sometimes, for hours on end, even the sick were not allowed access to the latrine.

Yet somehow we got through the days as the vessel crawled slowly along the green Malayan coast with its low, swelling hills. We were naturally anxious about torpedoes, for we knew that British submarines were operating in these waters. The Dutch P.O.W. ship which followed us a week later was attacked by a British submarine, and we were amazed at our own luck in getting through. At the bottom of those deep wells, with only one rickety ladder leading to safety, and two hundred Japanese who would unquestionably panic and jam the only companion-way leading to the deck, the chance of escape in an emergency was slim in the extreme.

We devised various methods for killing time. Those who had books were lucky. I read *Café du Dome*, Anna Reiner's picture of the refugee community in Paris in the years before the war, and thought it a great book because it lifted me completely out of my physical miseries and brought back the atmosphere of Paris so vividly. Its realism in presenting the sufferings and sacrifices of those Germans who risked their lives in underground activities against the Nazi regime seemed just the type of fare one needed in one's own travail. Re-reading the book in easier circumstances later, I still felt that this was one of the great European novels of the decades between the two wars.

A bridge school helped four of us to preserve our sanity. The other three were Bill Clements, Fred Mathieson and the late Alf Flessor, all Brisbane members of the 2/3rd M.T. We had the oldest and dingiest of packs and, since we always played through the hottest part of the day to try to distract our minds from the roasting, the cards soon became so many pieces of sodden pulp. But somehow I think those games were worth more to us and were more enjoyed than any games we may play in the comfort of our own homes with a jug of iced beer at our elbows. Ely Culbertson never envisaged that his beloved Contract would be played in such circumstances, but I doubt whether he has ever had four more fanatical devotees. Unshaven, bathed in perspiration, incredibly dirty, we bid our slams, finessed and put each other down with a zealous enthusiasm that was never equalled in any international bridge tournament. If a game is good enough to hold you like an opiate in such conditions, it is not a bad game—and let all those who decry Contract howl derision as they may!

You can't stop the Australian from finding something to

laugh at even when you're stewing him alive. One day a roar of laughter swept the ship from stem to stern. A very small Japanese, who, because of his stature, friendliness and smattering of English, was regarded by the boys as something of a mascot, sought to descend into the upper section of the hold just as a mob of Australians were coming up for their evening breather. He found himself completely surrounded and hemmed in by tall men towering over him. Suddenly, in a shrill falsetto voice he screamed, "Please, please, make way for the little boy!"

Then there was the evening when Jim Anderson, of Hampton, Melbourne, came and sang to us. It had been a particularly gruelling day and the air at the bottom of the hold was so thick and so laden with tobacco smoke that it was difficult to breathe. Jim, who had been ill himself, came across from one of the other holds, perched on the ladder which led down into our hell, and began to sing. Within two minutes he commanded a rapt audience, including score upon score of Japanese who crowded into the upper section of the hold, gazing down at these amazing captives. Jim sang "Legion of the Lost", "On the Road to Mandalay"—very appropriate— and a number of other songs beloved by baritones, and the boys roared back the choruses. At the end, he received an ovation in which the Japanese joined tumultuously. He will probably remember that night long after he has forgotten other triumphs.

Even the slowest hours and days draw to an end at last. On 22 October we steamed into the mouth of the Irrawaddy, and slowly up its broad, muddy stream between brilliantly green padi fields, past innumerable warehouses, to anchor at the Rangoon docks. We were not allowed on deck from the time we anchored until sunset, but it was one of those sunsets that makes anything worth while. As the great orange ball of the sun sank into a bed of golds and purples, night descended rapidly on the river. Against the background of light and colour which changed each minute, we stared fascinated at the thronging river-craft. Heavy barges and ferries chugged slowly upstream against the swiftly flowing current. Slim lateen-rigged fishing smacks glided gracefully past. Heavy prahus and sampans of all sizes laboured painfully upstream, driven by the tireless arms of sturdy native oarsmen, or slid rapidly seawards in the grip of the coursing stream. Red, green and blue lights appeared on the ever-changing stream of craft as the last lights of day faded. We stood there entranced, drinking it in as eagerly as the cool evening breeze which brushed our faces. Then the guards decided that we seemed too happy, so we were thrust down below again.

This was the worst night of the lot. It was not merely that we were stationary and that the air vent was not working; millions of mosquitoes filled the holds so that one could not move one's hand without brushing against scores of tiny, hovering bodies. The droning buzz from these countless invaders beat against one's eardrums relentlessly. We wrapped ourselves from head to toe until we nearly stifled, but sleep was an impossibility. For nine hours we sat or lay or stood in misery; but, except for the handful who had mosquito nets, I don't think one man had an hour's sleep.

Next day we were told to collect our gear and, after assisting the Japanese to extract all their goods from the hold, we left the ship and were marched along the wharves. It was obvious that first the Japanese and more lately British bombers had been having a busy time over Rangoon's extensive dockland. The river was littered with the masts of sunken shipping and with fragments of wreckage. Many of the godowns had been gutted or blown to fragments, and the docks themselves had suffered considerably.

While we were waiting to climb the gangway of another ship—*Yinagata Maru*—we watched gangs of handcuffed coolies moving rails on the wharves under the direction of Japanese taskmasters. The nature of the treatment meted out to these Burmese and Tamils as they toiled suggested that the Jap was not likely to make himself any more popular in Rangoon than in Singapore or Batavia.

From the docks we could see a number of the main buildings and thoroughfares of the city. The same curious atmosphere of inertia and deadness, emphasized by the absence of motor vehicles, seemed to exist here. Directly opposite us, the Hollywood Hotel, its architrave bedecked with red and yellow figures of Mickey Mouse, Donald Duck and various other film personalities, brought back startlingly another world in which hellships, coolie labour and bullying Japanese had no part.

Aboard *Yinagata Maru* we found ourselves placed in a hold on top of a cargo of gravel, which had the great merit of being flat, and provided by far the most comfortable billet I had yet found in a Japanese ship. Here we were issued with six and a half biscuits per man. That afternoon we raised anchor and, to our surprise, were all allowed on deck until after nightfall, while the boat moved slowly down the Irrawaddy and out across the Bay of Mataban towards Moulmein. Our last view of Rangoon, like the first, was of gold-topped pagodas glinting miraculously in the late afternoon sunlight to remind us that in the unchanging East the overthrow of Empires and the coming of new conquerors impose their influence only on the surface of things.

It was on the following afternoon that we drew slowly in to the mouth of the Salween River, a much narrower stream than the Irrawaddy, and knew that, at last, journey's end was in sight. We passed a number of native kampongs amidst fields of lush corn and rice, and then towards evening found ourselves, again amidst pagodas, dropping anchor off Moulmein.

After dark we went ashore on a huge floating platform towed by motor tugs. It was a beautiful moonlit night, marred only by the screaming and ranting of the Jap sentries who found occasion to indulge in some brutal kickings and beatings before the first batch was landed ashore. After the misery of our passage, it was good to stretch out full length on the metal pavement of the road where the Japs held us for an hour before we were marched off to the Moulmein jail. It was seventeen days since we had lined up on the road in the Bicycle Camp—days in which many men were murdered as surely as if a knife had been thrust into their vitals.

All things considered, we were tremendously lucky that

the epidemic, which the M.Os dreaded, did not sweep the crowded holds. The fate of the 1500 Dutch P.O.W.s who left Batavia a week behind us proved how uncheckable was infection under such conditions.

These prisoners never left the ship through twenty-two days and nights of hell from Batavia to Rangoon. After taking ten days to reach Penang, they lay stifling there for nine days, following a submarine attack. Dysentery, already bad, now spread like a bushfire, and by the time they reached Rangoon, fourteen were dead and scores more on the verge of death. A Japanese doctor made a cursory examination of the sick at Rangoon but made no attempt to succour the dying men. All prisoners were herded into the Rangoon jail where on the first night the worst dysentery cases, in batches of sixty, were locked in bare stone cells with nothing but a little straw on the floor. They were left all night without food, water, pans, buckets or anything else. This was a death sentence for many. Within a few days more than half the total force was virtually incapacitated by dysentery.

Constant appeals by senior Dutch officers were met by the Japanese with abuse, refusals and sometimes blows. The Japanese provided nothing whatever for the dying men except tools for their comrades to bury them, for the captors were mortally afraid of an epidemic involving themselves if the corpses were not hastily shovelled underground.

Even at the cemetery, crosses bearing the names of the dead were deliberately changed around by the Japanese in a final childish attempt to spite those who had passed beyond the reach of their inhumanity. Throughout the whole period at the jail, no milk or sustaining light food of any kind was given to even the worst cases, although the Japanese had plentiful supplies captured after the British evacuation. The diet for all prisoners consisted of plain rice pap without even soup to help it down. Despite all representations, only about sixty of the worst cases were taken from the jail to a hospital, and then only when it was often too late to do anything for them. In any case, little more attention was given in the hospital than at the jail.

On 20 December, when the strongest of this force left for
Moulmein to work on the railway, they left behind 200 dead
and 450 more incapable of movement. Even then they carried
with them many who could not walk. In the grinding work
along the railway line, numbers of these men succumbed,
while in Rangoon itself the total of Dutch dead reached 260,
or more than a sixth of the party.

One has only to see a man dying slowly of dysentery, becoming more and more emaciated as each day passes, to feel
that his plight would draw blood from a stone. But our hosts
of Dai Nippon Gun, with their vaunted code of Bushido,
cared nothing and did nothing as these men rotted to death
before their eyes.

PART THREE

BURMA RAILWAY

CHAPTER XVII

FROM MOULMEIN INTO THE JUNGLE

For the temple-bells are callin', an' it's there that I would be—
By the old Moulmein Pagoda, looking lazy at the sea.
—RUDYARD KIPLING

THERE was an eerie silence over Moulmein as we trudged
through the moonlit streets between white shuttered houses.
Now and then a shadowy figure could be glimpsed on a
balcony above us, or a shutter would open softly and dark
eyes would peer out into the street. But there must have been
a curfew in the town for, apart from some Japanese soldiers
at the far end of the street, we met no living soul.

We came at length to the high stone walls of the Moulmein
jail. This is divided by a network of intercepting walls into
compounds, in each of which stand several barrack-like
wooden buildings, divided into dormitories. Each man sleeps
on the floor with his head in the slot of a raised block of wood,
which resembles nothing so much as the guillotine block.

As we stretched out wearily, I could not help wondering
about our predecessors who had rested their heads in this same
spot. For what crimes had they been incarcerated, and how
long had they spent behind these stout wooden bars that
formed a lattice-work against the brilliant moonlight
drenching the prison yard outside? I began to think that after
a few more native jails I should be qualified to write a book
"Jails of Asia I Have Known". Compared to Serang, this was
a jail *de luxe*. You could even roll over without touching the
man next to you.

At first light, I climbed to the top of the building and, true
to Kipling's promise, the dawn came up like thunder; and
there behind and above us, its bells tinkling faintly in the gentle

morning breeze, was a golden-topped pagoda, its quaint spires catching the first sun. Red overlapping roofs ascended the hill-side in endless series, interspersed with the green fronds of palm-trees and lattices covered with red, white and purple blossom.

Much argument and research have never disclosed whether this actually is Kipling's pagoda from "Mandalay". It is certainly the biggest and highest pagoda in Moulmein and it does look out towards the sea, although Kipling's geography is a little astray about China being "acrost the Bay".

We remained in this jail four days until dawn on 29 October. During this period we were fed only on rice and innumerable melons, with a scrap of meat in the last day or two. Some of the men made contact with five political prisoners—one old white man who had lived in Moulmein for so long that he refused to be evacuated, and four civil servants, all Indians. They said that their conditions were not too bad. They were not fed at all by the Japanese or by the Burmese turnkeys, but friends in the town brought them plenty of food. We saw nothing of the native convicts and apparently nearly all of them had been released by the Japanese.

On the third day at the jail we lost Vaudan Heggaton, of the 2/3rd M.T., who had contracted dysentery on the hell-ships. His passing cast a shadow over everybody, for he was not only a splendid Australian who would unquestionably have made his mark in the political life of the country, but he was tremendously popular. Many men felt that his passing, so soon after our arrival in Burma, was a foretaste of the days to come. In the months that followed, hundreds of those who saluted as Heggaton's remains were borne past were themselves to be buried in Burma soil.

It was still dark when we set out from the jail on the next lap of our journey. Eight hundred of us, under Lieutenant-Colonel Chris Black, were to go to the farthest P.O.W. camp yet established in the jungle along the projected railway track. The remainder, under Lieutenant-Colonel J. M. Williams, were to follow next day and occupy another camp five kilometres nearer base.

The events of the next hour are indelibly imprinted on our memories. In Java, from first to last, we had met with little but derision and jeers, or at best, indifference, from the native population. Now, having to pass right across the town to the railway station on the other side, we were prepared for a similar reception.

But, to our surprise, we were literally swamped under the most spontaneous and generous demonstration of sympathy and friendliness that I have ever witnessed. The people of Moulmein had no word of our coming, but as soon as we appeared in the streets in the first hour of daylight, they started to tear tobacco, cheroots, fruit and foodstuffs of all kinds from the stalls. Disregarding the guards, they ran up to us and thrust them into our hands. As we passed what appeared to be mission schools, I saw many women and girls standing crying, while others came running out of their houses with trayfuls of fresh, hot rice-cakes and native biscuits, which they were baking for the day. In the whole four-mile march there was no discordant note and, after the mockery and hostility in western Java, it was almost unmanning. Whatever the strength of the irredentist movement in other parts of Burma, there could be no shadow of doubt that in the hour of acid test, with nothing to gain and much to lose at the hands of the Japanese occupying forces, the people of Moulmein gave a demonstration of loyalty and adherence to the British·cause that could not have been bettered in the streets of any British city.

At the station we were loaded into cattle trucks and one passenger car with wooden seats, and in due course set off along the track which runs southwards from Moulmein to Ye. Our destination was Thanbyuzayat, forty miles south of Moulmein, the point from which the new railway was to run across the Siam border to link the Moulmein-Ye line with the main Singapore-Bangkok line running up the eastern coast of the peninsula.

We passed through banana groves and occasional rubber estates until we emerged into more open country, covered with monstrous bark-grey water buffalo which moved cumbrously over the lush fields or wallowed in the numerous waterholes and mud patches which dotted the fields. Early in the afternoon, we ran into Thanbyuzayat, the small station being surrounded with store sheds, piles of sleepers, rails and material of all kinds. We marched up a road running west-wards towards the coast for perhaps a hundred yards and then turned into a camp of rough native huts, made entirely of bamboo with attap roofs. This, we soon learned, was the base camp for the Burma P.O.W. labour force. Here was Brigadier A. L. Varley, who had come up from Singapore in May 1942 with 3000 Australians. After working at Victoria Point, Mer-gui and Tavoy, most of this force, known in Singapore as "A Force", had now come up to Thanbyuzayat and, since Sep-tember, had been working along the projected track running south-eastwards towards the Thai border.

By the time the last prisoners had come up from southern Burma, the total P.O.W. group under Brigadier Varley's com-mand, including some 4600 Dutchmen from Java and Sumatra, numbered nearly 10,000. This group was known for the next two years as No. 3 Thai Prisoners of War Branch. The only other group of Allied prisoners to work in Burma during this period was No. 5 Branch, consisting of 2000 Aus-tralians, Americans and Dutch who had been with us in Java but who did not come up to Burma until January 1943.

At Thanbyuzayat, we found Brigadier Varley's headquar-ters' staff, about a hundred camp workers, and several hun-dreds of sick men, occupying a group of half a dozen dilapi-dated, dark, weather-beaten huts called by the Japanese "The Hospital". These huts had no flooring but merely bamboo platforms raised a couple of feet above the earth, with a gangway about eight feet wide running down the centre of the hut. On these platforms the sick were crowded, a man to a metre and, as more and more men fell sick in the jungle camps, the overcrowding grew worse week by week.

We left behind here some of our sick, including two officers, Padre Keith Mathieson and Flying-Officer Don Hackett, and the rest of us were told to be prepared to set off at dawn for a camp forty kilometres into the jungle called Beke Taung.

But before we departed we were treated to the address already quoted from Colonel Y. Nagatomo, commander of all prisoners in No. 3 Branch. Here, our force, designated Blackforce, was divided into "kumis", or platoons, which were to serve as working units along the railway. There was a kumi for the thirty-four officers and sixteen other kumis made up of N.C.Os or privates, with forty to fifty men in each. Officers in charge of a kumi were called "kumichos", while another officer commanding two kumis was christened a "hancho". Special armbands were issued to all officers carrying appointments on the camp staff or in charge of working platoons.

The whole parade, and especially Nagatomo's farrago of pompous nonsense, was so comic that we had great difficulty in keeping straight faces. But many felt a sense of foreboding as they heard the stories of grim conditions in the jungle and saw the pitiful accommodation accorded to our sick in this base camp. It was clear that we were entering on a struggle for very existence and that the Japanese had already loaded the dice against us.

That evening Brigadier Varley sent for me at his headquarters. He told me that he wanted to place me, as a war correspondent and representative of the Ministry of Information, in possession of the full facts concerning the execution of eight Australians by the Japanese at Tavoy on 30 May 1942.

These eight men, seeing the conditions which faced the one thousand prisoners of A Force landing at Tavoy, decided to attempt an escape, but were soon recaptured by Japanese and their Burmese agents. In defiance of all international law, the Japanese then announced that they were to be shot. Brigadier Varley went to the headquarters of the Japanese Command in the Tavoy area with the *Manual of Military Law* and cited the Geneva Convention and the Hague Agreement, to the latter of which Japan was a signatory. The Japanese officers remained adamant that the Australians were to be shot. The brigadier then warned them that he would hold them all responsible, and that after the war they would be tried by an international commission and punished for an act of murder. All his representations produced nothing except a threat against his own life and, a few hours later, a group of prisoners was forced to dig a pit, on the edge of a clearing, to act as a grave for the condemned.

The brigadier and padre were ordered to attend the execution, but neither was allowed to speak to the men. However, as they were placed on a truck to be carried to the execution ground, the brigadier put his head out of a car in which he sat with Japanese officers and yelled out, "You're for it, boys!" in the hope that they might be able to make a break for it. But either they did not hear or did not understand, and a few minutes later they were rushed to the field and ordered to kneel down along the edge of the pit.

Face to face with the inevitable end, they called out "Good-bye, sir" and other messages to the brigadier, and then awaited the volley from the shooting party with a defiant courage beyond all praise. The brigadier said, "In the moment when they died I have never been prouder of being an Australian."

A few days later at Mergui, where another party of a thousand Australians belonging to A Force had been landed, two more Australians were executed after being found outside the wire; and on 30 July a man who had been outside the Mergui camp attempting to trade with the Burmese was also shot. All these executions were in flagrant violation of all international law and justice.

When the first party of prisoners arrived at Thanbyuzayat to commence work on the railway, the Japanese informed Major Charles Green, of the 2/4th Machine-gunners, who was in charge of the party, that all men must sign an oath that they would not attempt to escape. Major Green refused to pass on such an order, and was immediately confined in a small cell with nothing except rice covered in salt and a little water. He was told he would be kept there until he died, unless he agreed to sign the oath. Major Green remained adamant until Brigadier Varley arrived to take command. The brigadier joined Major Green in confinement to prove duress, before agreeing to sign. He then ordered all officers and men to sign the oath. Major Green was released after enduring seven days of appalling conditions, although he was a sick man at the time.

After the brigadier had given his oath not to escape, he told Nagatomo that it was understood throughout the world that an oath extracted by duress was not binding. Nagatomo, beside himself with rage, threatened to put the brigadier in solitary confinement until he died or changed his mind.

I left the brigadier's hut feeling that in Nagatomo we had struck the extreme type of Japanese military fanatic, and that prospects for the thousands of white men now going forth to labour in the jungle, under the worst coolie conditions, were forbidding in the extreme.

CHAPTER XVIII

JUNGLE DAYS

This slavery is surely of the devil,
And only grief and harm can come of it.
—E. E. Stopford, *The Slaves of Rose Hall*

On the morning of 30 October, some of us in trucks and others on foot, we set off into the jungle. Camps along the new line were known by their distance from Thanbyuzayat. At this stage prisoners occupied the 4-kilo, 14-kilo and 18-kilo camps, but we were now going out much farther, to the 40-kilo mark. We all had to walk the last five kilometres to our new camp, but many walked a considerable part of the first thirty-five kilometres before the trucks came back to pick them up. Distances between camps were measured along the straight railway line, but by the road along which we walked it was considerably further.

Our first sight of our new camp suggested that here at least we were not going to suffer from claustrophobia, for the fence hardly existed. The huts had been erected by the Burmese, Malay and Tamil coolies who had cleared the jungle back along the projected line. They were filthy but, by the standards of native huts, reasonably weatherproof and sound. There was no well in the camp and water had to be drawn either from a native well, five hundred yards away, or from a tiny stream which crossed the road a similar distance below the camp. This meant an enormous amount of extra labour for the cook-house staff which was augmented by a force of water carriers.

The Japanese wasted no time, and on 31 October we were aroused by the bugle before dawn and all fit men were hustled out to the track. Breakfast consisted of plain boiled

A working party

rice without even salt, and anyone who has not been forced to rise by moonlight, on a cold jungle morning, to face a breakfast of dubiously cooked boiled rice, has no cause for early morning ill-temper.

It was discovered that the job was on a task work basis, 1.2 cubic metres of earth having to be dug up and carried about a hundred yards to the railway embankment by each man on the party. In practice, some dug all day with spades, picks and chunkels (heavy native hoes or mattocks) while other men in pairs carried the earth in baskets suspended on a bamboo pole between them. Where the soil was soft, and the "carry" to the embankment was not too far, 1.2 cubic metres per day was reasonable; but it was not to remain at this figure.

A handful of the men who went out to work that first day in the jungle managed to work through, month in and month out, until the job was completed eleven months later. The great majority were to be worn out by the monotonous strain of the job, coupled with the niggardly ration of coolie food.

Up and down the line, through untracked jungles, across dizzy ravines, astride rivers which became destructive torrents in the rains, through jungle-choked mountain passes, over rocky cliffs and through treacherous swamps, the toiling thousands of prisoners and conscripted Asiatics built this railway in conditions and under treatment which, if inflicted on animals at home, would produce an outcry from every decent man and woman in the community.

It did not matter to the guards or to the engineers who laid down the daily task how hard or difficult the ground, or what natural barriers obstructed the work. The fixed task had to be completed whether it meant seven hours of toil or ten or twelve. Day by day as, stretched over four hundred kilometres of jungle, the men from two score camps picked and dug, chunkeled and carried, the long hours and the fierce sun slowly drained away their resistance, never bolstered by a single square meal.

Worse even than the embankment work was the bridge building. The wooden piles to support the rickety bridges had to be driven in by the most primitive of methods. Gangs of men, straining on ropes, raised the heavy "monkey", or iron weight, then let it thud down on the top of the pile, repeating the process endlessly until at last the great beam stood securely in the river-bed. Some men, detailed to this work, spent many hours each day for months on end standing waist-deep and sometimes shoulder-deep in the rivers.

All work was carried out under an incessant barrage of shouting and screaming, usually quite incomprehensible, from guards and engineers. Men were struck with pick-handles, with bamboo rods, with anything the guards found to hand. Officers seeking to protect their men from the bashings and kickings of sadistic guards were themselves beaten yet more brutally. The method of the Japanese in charge of our bridge building kumi was to follow all orders by hurling iron spikes and tools from his vantage point on top of the bridge, at the heads of the officer and his men labouring below. The strain of each day's toil would not have been nearly so great if engineers or guards had attempted to be reasonable or to treat the prisoners as fellow workers and not as ignorant slaves or beasts of burden.

Our main worries in this camp were the shortage of all medical supplies, the absence of water in the camp and the totally inadequate quantity of vegetable and meat received in the daily ration with the rice. The meat, consisting of Burmese cows, came up on the hoof from Thanbyuzayat, while other supplies came by truck.

Our M.O., Captain John Higgin, of Cronulla, Sydney, soon had his hands full as men went down with fever and dysentery. The swarming flies which surrounded the heaped tins of boiled rice in the cook-house were our most dangerous enemies, for it was they who carried the dysentery bacillus. We were pitifully short of all cooking gear and boiling containers, and no covers were available to keep the flies from the food.

A few days after our arrival, I went down with an attack of dengue and for five or six days lost all interest in the camp, the jungle and our problems. This was perhaps the most depressing illness that I remember. Under the influence of the fever, the jungle seemed savagely hostile and forbidding, and one could see no prospect of liberty for many long months ahead.

On 8 November we lost our first man at this camp, when Corporal Burrows died. Twelve days later there was another dysentery death. The hut which we had decided to use as a hospital filled rapidly with men who had been in poor health since the gruelling on the hellships, and who now went down like ninepins with dysentery and malaria. Within three weeks nearly half the force was too sick to work. Fortunately, the Japanese in charge of us was a decent little lance-corporal named Hunda, who was himself appalled at the poorness of our rations and the failure, despite our urgent appeals to base, to give us any medical supplies.

It should not be thought that these conditions were peculiar to our camp at this time. They were paralleled in the camps closer to base, although the prisoners in these fed slightly better through contacts with native traders operating in their area. In an attempt to better conditions, we sent off endless notes to headquarters, but Brigadier Varley and his adjutant, Captain Ray Griffin, could secure little co-operation from Nagatomo or from his medical officer, Heguchi. We started sending our sickest men down to the base hospital, and were joined by a second doctor, a Dutchman named Dr Hakking, who had been dealing with tropical disease in the outer islands of the N.E.I. for many years. The doctor soon established himself as a great favourite in the prison camps through his habit of collecting all Australian vulgarities, swear-words and slang, writing them down in a little black notebook and using them on all possible occasions with the utmost relish, with an accent and intonation that used to send even the sick men into fits of laughter. Unfortunately, like many of the funniest things in the prison camps, the doctor's sallies are quite unprintable.

Japanese efforts to improve our food ration were farcical. One day a large party of men was sent out looking for a jungle root known as lily-root, which was supposedly edible.

This "vegetable" was also sent up in our ration from the Thanbyuzayat Q Store; but after the M.Os had watched its effect for some days, they ordered Captain Charles Howitt, of Murrumbeena, who was in charge of our cook-house, to jettison all further supplies. On another occasion, the Japanese took a party of eighty men to a neighbouring swamp, or pond, to obtain fish for the camp. As a result of an all-day effort dredging the mud, they got a basketful of very small fish adequate to feed about eight men out of our eight hundred—and no miracle of the loaves and fishes happened to help us out.

One evening we pleaded energetically with the Japanese to shoot one or two wild cattle which were wandering in the jungle around the camp. However, they rigidly refused. But after dark a party of us were roused from our beds and told to come and help in catching a cow. The beast was carefully surrounded and with ropes and sticks the net closed in to secure it. Suddenly out of the darkness, without any warning, a fusillade of shots rang out. Most of us had seen enough of the guards' handling of their rifles, and as one man we flung ourselves to the ground. The Japanese had fired at the cow at about ten yards' range and, while only two bullets had actually struck the beast, the others, by a great mercy, missed us also. After that we did not urge any more hunting parties after dark.

I took up the job of economic officer for Blackforce, which consisted of handling the daily Japanese pay returns for the 610 Australians and 190 Americans who composed our force. It involved going to base each month to complete the returns and collect the pay for the camp. The rate at this time was only ten cents per day for privates and fifteen cents for N.C.Os. At the price of eggs at base, this represented one small duck egg for a day's back breaking coolie labour—and up in the jungle eggs were unprocurable anyway. I had a considerable amount of time to myself and spent most of it in digging garbage pits in the camp area, and in making long expeditions into the surrounding jungle, as the order about keeping close to the camp could not be very strictly patrolled in the early days. However, on 22 November, twenty additional guards arrived and egress from the camp soon became far more strictly controlled. At no stage in Burma did the risk deter men from slipping out beyond the fence, although the Japanese said they would shoot anybody found outside the prescribed area.

The most interesting feature of life at Beke Taung was the work of the elephants, or "hathis". Three of them came into our camp one night and proceeded to clean up the stumps which studded the camp area with an intelligence and efficiency that surpassed the work of any machine. First the elephant would kneel down and press with his trunk until the stump was pushed over and its roots loosened. Then, if he could not prise it up and carry it off with tusks and trunk, he would wait for a chain to be passed round the stump and then tug it out of the ground.

These elephants were the only "mechanical" aid to human muscle which the Japanese provided for the construction of embankments and cuttings. They worked splendidly, with an understanding that was almost human; but maltreatment and starvation in the Japanese tradition gradually took toll of them.

Lieutenant Yamada, the only Japanese officer in the Burma prison camps who had any claims to respect from P.O.W.s, came up one day from Colonel Williams's camp to visit us. He bemoaned the fact that it was nearly seven years since he had seen his wife and children in Japan, and that mail often did not reach him for six months at a time. He listened gravely to our complaints about food, medical supplies and conditions, but we knew that he could do nothing for us while Nagatomo was opposed to any alleviation of our lot.

On 26 October Colonel Black and I went down to Thanbyuzayat to a conference between Nagatomo and the C.Os and economic officers of all camps. This was farcical. Nagatomo had a monstrous vanity, as he had illustrated at our "welcome" parade. In Indo-China he had picked up some French, and he insisted on airing this at the conference, although the Dutch interpreter, "Cor" Punt, spoke Japanese.

The result was that everything said by one of us in English was translated in Japanese to Nagatomo, who replied in French, which "Cor" Punt had then to translate back into English for the assembled Allied officers. It was all the more ludicrous because Nagatomo certainly understood 90 per cent of what was said in English. We secured nothing tangible in the way of increased food and medical supplies, Nagatomo being mainly concerned with threats about shooting anybody who tried to escape or who was found outside the camp area, since three Dutchmen had got away a couple of weeks before. However, it was confirmed that our force should be brought back from the 40-kilo camp where the sick rate had been so high, to a group of coolie huts at the 26-kilo mark, called Kun Knit Kway.

The main reason for evacuating Beke Taung was the drying up of the small stream below the camp which had provided our water for cooking and bathing. A few days before we left thirty or forty of us were washing as best we could in the rocky creek-bed where there was now less than a foot of water. Suddenly one of the working elephants appeared on the bank. After contemplating our ablutions for a while, he shouldered his way slowly into the middle of the only good waterhole in the creek-bed, churning up the mud and making himself thoroughly at home. As some of us still persisted in trying to share the creek with him, he filled his trunk with muddy water and squirted it generously over everybody within ten yards. Snorting delightedly at the consternation and confusion which followed this stratagem, he proceeded to answer the calls of nature there and then. This completed our rout and, dirty and unwashed, we hastened to leave him in sole possession of the pool.

Most of the force had to walk to the new camp at Kun Knit Kway, carrying all their gear on their backs. On arrival we found that the Tamil and Burmese coolies, who had just evacuated the camp had left it in a state of filth that defied description. Excreta and other dirt of every kind covered the bamboo slats in each hut. We had been warned that there had been cases of cholera in this camp, but we were not prepared to find two unburied corpses lying in the bushes on the edge of the camp only a few yards from the nearest hut. While we were burying them, we found another one a little farther up the hill.

The attitude of the local natives and of the Japanese to cholera victims had been shown at Beke Taung. An Indian there was left dying on the side of the road without food or water. Passing natives never turned aside to lend him succour of any kind, and when we asked the Japanese if something could not be done for him, they forbade us to go near him and said he would soon be dead. Nevertheless, some of the boys kept him supplied with water and rice from their own scanty rations until, after four days of exposure, he died. Even then the Japanese would do nothing about the festering corpse, which was immediately attacked by swarms of maggots and other insects. Finally, a party of prisoners was allowed to bury the body.

Kun Knit Kway had a group of huts rather worse than those at Beke Taung, but at least there was a well in the camp. In view of the menace of dysentery, a sterilization point was established where all men could immerse their dixies and pannikins in boiling water after each meal. Thanks to this policy, which was rigidly enforced by our own camp administration and medical officers, the dysentery scourge was kept in check and the general sick rate both then and later in our other camps was much lower than in many British camps in Siam, where no such precautions were taken.

At Kun Knit Kway we were joined in the middle of December by nearly a thousand Australians from Tavoy under Lieutenant-Colonel George Ramsay, of the 2/30th Battalion. Colonel Ramsay, as senior officer, now became C.O., but Blackforce and Ramsayforce retained their own administrations. With the exception of the senior officers who joined our own officers in a hut which we built ourselves, and which by reason of its slightly improved comfort was known as "Buckingham Palace" or more irreverently, as "B——t Castle", the whole of Ramsayforce was billeted in the group of huts on the other side of the road from our own camp. The road was the lowest point in the area, hills sloping sharply upwards to thickly timbered crests on either side. To the west the ridge was quite high and extended for some miles roughly parallel to the road. In the trees along it troops of gibbons used to scream and play at all hours of the day, the hills echoing and re-echoing their discordant clamour.

As at Beke Taung the working parties saw and often killed snakes of many kinds, chiefly green rice-snakes about three feet long. For some mysterious reason, although many men worked bare-legged and without boots, no man in any of these camps was bitten by a snake. Our chief casualties from insects and reptiles were inflicted by the numerous scorpions, hairy repulsive Arachnida with claws like a lobster and a poisonous sting in the tail. They often reached a length of six or seven inches, and their bites, although never fatal, were sometimes extraordinarily painful. The young scorpions climb on to the mother's back, and are carried about under the guard of her tail until able to look after themselves.

There was abundant bird life in the jungle. Brilliantly coloured parakeets, hawks of many varieties, a type of black raven, and innumerable miners and sparrows were always to be seen. The top of the rocky ridge to the west of the camp was a favourite haunt for eagles, but an even bigger bird was the giant hornbill. Flying over the camp, even at a height of several hundred feet his tremendous pinions made a heavy beating sound which immediately caught the ear.

At this camp we had the Kun Knit Kway Comedy Trio. This consisted of a small nannygoat, her kid and a brindle puppy. The three were practically inseparable and used to play together throughout the day. The pup used to dash towards the kid with a great show of ferocity, only to sheer off at high speed as the nannygoat swept towards him with her curving horns. The speed at which the trio used to bound and leap over the hill-side was a constant source of amusement and delight to the men.

But neither the screaming of the gibbons, the howling of the pariah dogs around the camp, nor the shrill screeching of some of the birds disturbed us as much as the shattering shrieks

with which the guards at the guard-house on the road saluted
the passing of an officer's car. The frightful falsetto yell which
indicated that a car with the blue flag of a lieutenant, the red
flag of a captain, or the yellow flag of a field officer, was
passing, reminded me of the ecstatic screams of George Duck-
worth, the Lancashire wicket-keeper, appealing for a catch.

Apparently, in the Japanese Army, the degree of respect is
indicated largely by the promptitude and volume of the yell.
Our guards were intensely respectful, for day and night alike
were made hideous with the most raucous and soul-searing
yells which, coming without warning, were not amusing to
work-weary men trying to sleep a few yards away.

On the whole, by the Japanese standards in the jungle, Kun
Knit Kway might have been considerably worse, although it
was not until afterwards that we realized this. The chief problem, as the old year died and we entered 1943, was the increasing exactingness of the labour on the railway and the
continued vitamin deficiency of our rations. The rice ration,
which varied between 700 and 1000 grammes per day, would
have been sufficient if backed up with adequate quantities
of greens, and some meat. As it was, the vegetable ration consisted almost exclusively of melons, pie-melons, sweet potatoes,
white radishes and other root vegetables lacking in the vitamins and iron which we needed. One saw an occasional scrap
of meat in the stew more frequently than at Batavia, but we
would have given much to sit down just once a week to the
sort of meat meal that we ate twice a day at home.

In December the Japanese increased the daily work to 1.4
cubic metres, and a little later it rose to 1.8. As the ground was
now often very hard, and the "carries" often long, there were
many nights when the men, who had paraded for work at the
first light of dawn, did not get back to their huts until well after
dark.

As the weeks wore on, the strain of the monotonous toil
began to tell on all. The Australians, perhaps unwisely but
very naturally, flung themselves at each day's task with a fierce
energy, being determined to finish it at the earliest possible
moment. No navvy in a working gang at home could have

worked harder than many of the men. But they forgot that they were white men working in the tropics, and that the ration was not only one to which they were completely unaccustomed but utterly deficient in the animal fats, proteins and vitamins which they needed most.

Attacks of malaria put a man off the job only for so long as he was taking quinine; but men failed to take into account the extent to which their strength and vitality had been sapped under the ravages of high fever. The doctors were under continual pressure from the Japanese to send out as many men as possible to maintain the strength of the working parties. Colonel Ramsay, Colonel Black, their adjutants, Captain Arthur Hence and Captain Ron Winning, and the doctors attached to the two groups, fought the Japanese tooth and nail to prevent sick and convalescent men from being hounded out to toil for ten and twelve hours under the broiling, enervating rays of the tropical sun.

At the end of November and throughout the next three months the monsoon swept the area, bringing violent changes of temperature. The nights, which had hitherto been comparatively mild, became suddenly bitterly chill to men most of whom were suffering already from malnutrition, whose blood was thin, and who were, with few exceptions, pitifully short of warm clothing and of bedding. Whereas one sweated profusely through the heat of the day, one found that soon after dark the temperature dropped very rapidly, and from the small hours of the morning until well after dawn it was freezingly cold. An icy breeze made its way through the many apertures in the flimsy bamboo huts and attacked us through the bamboo slats of the platforms on which we lay. Many men were without blankets of any kind, while all found their thin, worn tropical shirts no protection whatever against the bitter cold. It became an established thing for scores of men to sit up over such fires as were permitted at the ends of huts, sacrificing the hours of much needed rest for the sake of warmth.

All of us went to bed wearing every scrap of clothing or wrapping on which we could lay our hands. Even when wrapped in my entire wardrobe, consisting of two aged shirts, a pair of shorts, a pair of slacks, a sarong, plus woollen socks and a thin blanket, I found that I often awoke long before dawn and lay shivering, too miserable to be able to get to sleep again. There were hundreds who did not have even this much protection against the severity of the nights. Inevitably, bronchial attacks descended on many and colds paved the way for other kinds of tropical disease. Beri-beri and tropical ulcers, the malignity of which was enormously increased by our miserable and ill-balanced diet, now began to spread widely through our ranks.

The senior officers and M.Os were already gravely alarmed at the prospect facing us when the heavy seasonal rains would break over the jungle in May. It was clear, from the experience of those who had worked farther south in Burma, that the rains would render all transport difficult, and the appalling state of the road which carried such rations as we were receiving suggested that under heavy rain the supply situation would deteriorate rapidly. One needed no knowledge of medicine to realize that the general health of the whole camp was falling off month by month, and that over-work, tropical disease and malnutrition were sapping the resistance of all.

A bright spot in a gloomy picture was the existence in our camp of a secret radio smuggled over from Java by Leading Aircraftsman Arch Caswell, of Murgen, Queensland. This had been transported in a waterbottle, from which, when uncorked, water flowed in the normal fashion. A supply of valves for the set was brought across from Java by Don Stuart, who strapped them around his waist inside his belt. Arch Caswell had operated this set from the first days of our arrival in Burma, and bulletins were distributed through the camp at regular intervals. We learned of Montgomery's brilliant advance across the Western Desert culminating in the capture of Tripoli towards the end of February. We followed with eagerness and anxiety the gigantic clash in Russia, which now reached its turning-point with the cutting-off and eventual annihilation of the German Sixth Army at Stalingrad.

The effect of this news on all of us was incalculable. The good news from the world, which seemed incredibly remote to those toiling day long in the dust and heat on cuttings and embankments, came like a great light to pierce our darkness. It brought hope and comfort to weary men, exposed daily to the brutalities and incomprehensible whims of brutal guards; it helped to stiffen morale when we were overwhelmed with the hopelessness of our conditions and the calculated inhumanity of our captors.

Right through our days in Burma, Arch Caswell continued to operate this set, and the men of his camps and of other camps supplied with news from the same source owe to him, and to all those who assisted him, a debt that cannot be repaid. It was a tribute to the care and discretion used in dissemination of this news that, during fourteen months in which the set was operating, the Japanese never managed to get hold of it. On one occasion, at the 75-kilo camp, a foolish note sent by one soldier was intercepted by the Japanese, and the gear of Flight-Lieutenant Ken Smith, senior R.A.A.F. officer, who controlled the handling of the news, was searched; but the Japs found nothing. Many subsequent searches proved equally fruitless, and throughout even the darkest days the words of the B.B.C. announcers in London brought strength and comfort to thousands of men struggling for existence in the Burma jungle camps.

We were fortunate at Kun Knit Kway and later to have with us Chaplain Keith Mathieson of H.M.A.S. *Perth*. "The Padre", despite his own illness, was untiring in his attention to the sick men lying miserably on the bare bamboo slats of the "hospital" huts. His ready smile, his kindness and unflagging energy, were an inspiration. He organized discussion groups and Bible study circles in addition to the normal church services, whenever the Nips would allow us to hold them. Gathered round the camp-fires at Kun Knit Kway, our sessions lighted by the stars and the brilliant yellow Burma moon, we discussed social problems, questions of ends and means, ethics, love, marriage, and a dozen other subjects with a frankness and thoroughness not often possible among such groups in the workaday world at home.

At this Kun Knit Kway camp, we had a Korean guard

christened "George" by the boys. George was disliked exceedingly by his fellow guards for he had an individual and particularly un-Japanese outlook, and a sense of humour which made him unique among our guards. Often, after being ostracised in his own lines, he would come across to the P.O.W. huts and spend the evening with our officers and men. He was the only guard with whom anybody fraternized and, as far as we know, he never let us down. Some of George's sayings have entered into the folk-lore of the prison camps.

On one occasion he caught Fred Quick, the big American crooner, flagrantly violating one of the strictest of camp rules by buying sugar from a Burmese in an ox cart along the road. Both the American and the Burmese stood rigidly at attention expecting to be bashed as George came ambling up. George shook his head dolefully saying: "Someone must get slappie-slappie." Silently the other two waited, expecting immediate blows and possibly a long and unpleasant session at the guardhouse afterwards. Then George walked slowly round the ox cart, and stepping back, kicked the ox in the belly. "O.K.," said George smiling. "All men go home."

George was somewhat sceptical about Japanese propaganda. When Thanbyuzayat was bombed by Allied planes, the Japanese papers had been full of tales of the utter destruction of the American and British Air Forces operating from India. George came up to one group of prisoners saying: "George no understand. Paper say all British planes shot down. All American planes shot down. O.K.! Then George want to know—what ——— planes bomb Thanbyuzayat?"

George was always in trouble with his immediate superiors in the camp. He confided miserably one day to a group of officers that the Nippon mind—here he made a clock-wise movement round and round his ear—worked one way, and George's mind—here a vigorous anti-clock-wise movement—worked another.

On one occasion, when told to prepare tea for the Japanese W.O. in charge of the camp, he found, when the tea was ready, that his superior was missing. George saw two prisoners passing by, called them in and, with their aid, made short work of the W.O's tea and rice-cakes. When the W.O. returned, hungry and thirsty, a few minutes later the boys had gone, but George received a merciless beating. On another occasion when told that his rifle was in a state which was a disgrace to the Imperial Army, George solved this problem by taking his weapon to the creek and immersing the whole thing lock, stock and barrel. We could hear the resounding blows that he received after this performance, a hundred yards away on the opposite hill.

Most of the guards were only too anxious to pass on to the prisoners all news of Japanese victories and Allied defeats as represented in the fantastic propaganda published in their papers. After the penetration of Japanese submarines into Sydney Harbour, one guard told some prisoners in the orderly office of tremendous destruction wrought by the subs, and added, "You know big Sydney bridge? Japanese torpedo big centre support. Bridge all finish." An exasperated Australian, after seeking to explain the absurdity of this, rummaged in his kit and produced a post-card photo of the suspension bridge. The Japanese seemed doomed to loss of face, but with typical Nippon "logic" he said, "They build support after you prisoner."

We had our laughs at Kun Knit Kway. Many of them came on the occasional "yasmae" or rest days, when Norman Carter and a strong concert party, including Jim Anderson, Val Ballantyne and Norm Whittaker and his brass band, with instruments brought up from Changi, defied the utter lack of all properties and, on their bare bamboo stage out in the jungle, managed to produce roars of laughter and applause from hundreds of weary men to whom the shows provided the only relaxation and moments of escape in the long waste of dreary days. The best shows were a mock trial written and acted by half a dozen officers, and an exotic piece which would never get past any civilian censor called "The Sultan of Serang", purporting to be enacted in the Sultan's "luxurious, lecherous lounge of lust". With colourful native sarongs and bits of material carried by men who had hoped to present them to their wives and sweethearts at home, amazing female costumes and drapes for the stage were produced and the men were not slow to show their appreciation of those who worked tirelessly against heart-breaking difficulties to provide amusement for them.

The best day of all was a race day held in February. A "Melbourne Cup" meeting had been held at Tavoy some months earlier by the men of Colonel Ramsay's force, and this was the basis of an attempt to produce in the Burma jungle the atmosphere of a race day at home. The enthusiasm with which all concerned worked during their scanty leisure hours in preparation for this event attested the love of racing so strong in most Australians.

We had wooden horses with four projecting legs which prevented the rider from running at more than a fast amble. Bits of native sarongs, and odd scraps of material from women's dresses and scarves went to make up jockeys' blouses and caps. A bamboo framework and the linking together of webbing belts produced a totalizator board manipulated by hand, which recorded accurately to the nearest point the current odds on each starter, while hard-working clerks at bamboo tables behind the "windows" dealt with the queues of men anxious to wager their cents on their pals who were running in the race. Bookies' stands with amazing improvised umbrellas, and records sometimes kept on pieces of bamboo, gave us the atmosphere of the ring.

There were "girls" gorgeously dressed from our scanty stock of stage properties—and some of the minxes walked with a roll of the hips that was positively breath-taking. A prize was awarded to Micky Cavanagh as the loveliest "lady". Colonel George Ramsay attended in splendid regalia as the Governor, with the "Governor's Lady" on his arm, while impressive looking officials bustled about in superb frock coats made from hessian bags dyed black, with bamboo top-hats and huge rosettes in their buttonholes.

There was a boxing booth sideshow where boys put the gloves on for a couple of rounds, while vendors with stalls or trays sold peanuts, bits of ginger-root in native sugar, synthetic "coffee" made from burnt rice and other delicacies carefully hoarded for the day from our meagre canteen supplies. In addition, there were taxi men, touts, spruikers, "ladies of joy", professional "urgers" and hangers-on in the best traditions of the racetracks.

As these meetings were few and far between—there were only four in three and a half years—betting was terrific and sums equivalent to a month's Japanese pay changed hands over a single race. But these occasional highlights of our existence were merely the odd pebble on the dreary expanse of sand that was our habitual lot.

There may not have been so many bashings at this stage as there had been at Batavia and as we had to face at other times, but the atmosphere of brutality and persecution was never far removed, and there were some very ugly incidents. The Australian officers in Burma managed throughout to resist Japanese attempts to force them to work. Such work could have assisted the men in no way, since the task was allotted on a *per capita* basis, and it was felt that what little protective authority the officers retained would be swallowed up once the guards and engineers saw them working like coolies with the others. Instead, the kumichos and hanchos sought to act as buffers in all the incidents which arose between bullying guards and prisoners. Most of these were exacerbated by the language barrier and the lack of interpreters. One could not exaggerate the uncontrollable frenzies into which many guards lashed themselves on the smallest provocation.

Norman Carter was brutally beaten up so that his dentures were smashed and eating rendered difficult for him for the remaining years of captivity. Two flying-officers, Harry Pannifex and Gerry Alderton, were threatened with shooting by an infuriated guard one day when they steadfastly refused to work, in accordance with the agreement which the Japanese themselves had accepted. The guard pointed his rifle first at one and then at the other, and in his excitement—as happened with these guards on other occasions—the rifle went off. By the sheerest luck, the bullet passed between the two Australians, but this was no fault of the gibbering lunatic who fired it.

On another night, after a prisoner from a neighbouring camp had been found missing, the Japanese, in a state of dangerous excitement, ordered a special tanko at nightfall during which many men were struck and kicked without the smallest excuse. Finally, an ugly situation developed when a guard struck Driver Mackenzie, whose arm was broken and in a sling. The men, unmindful of the consequences, showed their resentment in no uncertain manner, and it seemed for a few moments as if an all-in brawl was inevitable. Flying-Officer Alex Dobbie, who intervened between Mackenzie and the raving guard, was himself struck and kicked, and only the interference of a Japanese N.C.O., who retained some sense of justice, averted a scene which might have culminated eventually in the massacre of many prisoners.

It was not the few dozen guards in each camp who prevented the prisoners from taking control of things and making a break for it. It was, as Nagatomo had said in his speech, the impenetrable jungles and the hundreds of miles of ocean which rendered all attempts at escape virtual suicide.

CHAPTER XIX

THANBYUZAYAT BASE CAMP

AUSSIE P.O.W.: When is a hospital not a hospital?
HIS MATE: When it's a bloody coolie hut with bandages, dressings, drugs, pans, instruments, and sterilising gear existing only in our imagination!

IMMEDIATELY after our transfer to Kun Knit Kway, I went down to Thanbyuzayat base camp to try to draw our first pay. After the returns were made up—a long and absurdly complicated rigmarole—I was ordered into hospital, for the festering sores on my legs, which had never really healed since our days in the Banka marshes, were spreading rapidly. So, when the pay arrived, my American colleague, Captain Fitzsimmons, took it back to Kun Knit Kway. I remained at Thanbyuzayat until the December pay came through in the second week in January. The legs were still in a messy condition, but I was sick of the so-called hospital and wanted to get back to my friends in the jungle.

During December the repeated representations by the camp administration and medical officers at Thanbyuzayat had at last persuaded the Japanese to build some new huts for the accommodation of the sickest men who were coming down from the working camps up-jungle in increasing numbers each week. But this work was not completed until the end of January, so that for over four months after the establishment of this "base hospital", the patients were jammed together in squalid hovels which were invaded all day by swirling clouds of dust from the camp parade ground.

Here we lay, without bedding of any kind, on the bamboo slats which can become cruelly hard when the flesh has wasted away from one's bones and one is lying day after day on the same few square feet of space, unable to shift six inches either way because of one's neighbour.

Quinine we had most of the time in reasonable quantity, which was not surprising since the Japs now controlled the world's supply area. But every other hospital requirement was either non-existent or available only in hopelessly inadequate quantities. Hard work by orderlies—chiefly from the 2/4th C.C.S., a Tasmanian unit—and the camp "Buppin", or works staff, resulted in the improvization of a scanty but invaluable stock of tables, containers, pans and tins for boiling water. The Japanese supplied a few antiseptics and a small quantity of such things as acriflavine, boracic and one or two healing agents, but there was no ointment or grease to form a base for the hundreds of dressings required daily by men suffering from tropical ulcers, ringworm, tinea and all the other forms of dermatitis produced by malnutrition in the tropics.

The problem was solved only by the gallant scrounging of axle grease from the Japanese workshops by P.O.Ws working there. Staff-Sergeant Bev Browne, of Launceston, the chemist attached to the C.C.S. unit, mixed up compounds of axle grease with a thin ration of antiseptic and this helped to draw the pus which seemed to appear with such rapidity from all sores.

But bandages and dressings to cover the sores presented a far bigger problem. The Japanese simply would not give us even one per cent of the material we needed. A man who was lucky enough to get a few yards of bandage for his legs had to use it and re-use it sometimes for months on end. Often no bandage of any kind was available, the last bandages having been cut into patches, a square inch in size, to serve as a pad to cover sores. These pads had to be held in position by means of liquid rubber tapped from some trees in the vicinity. I had three lengths of bandage at the beginning of December, but my legs needed continuous dressing daily for months afterwards, and it was not until April that I got another few yards of waste to replace the worn-out rags. They had been washed and rewashed times innumerable, but

Dysentery death house.

remained a dirty brown through stains and dust. Even so, I was luckier than most.

But the miseries of the men whose legs and bodies were covered with sores paled by comparison with the lot of those with dysentery. The Dutch medicos, professing an expert knowledge of tropical disease, and particularly of dysentery, had charge of all dysentery cases, in a filthy, dark, airless hut, which soon rejoiced in the name of "the Death House". The Dutch took the view that no man with dysentery should wash. So dozens of wretched men lay week after week in the stench of this hovel, without even receiving the opportunity to wash their hands and faces. Unshaven and incredibly filthy, racked with the pains of bacillary or amoebic dysentery, many men died wretchedly in the last weeks of the year, before Australian protests swelled to such a chorus that our own overworked medical officers took over our dysentery cases as soon as the new huts were constructed.

Unfortunately, a number of Australians had already died in the Death House. Among them was Leading-Aircraftsman Brown, of Kew, who had set an inspiring example to all other orderlies in our jungle hospital at Beke Taung by his indefatigable care for his sick mates long after he himself had being stricken by disease.

I remember on Christmas Eve organizing some extra water for some of the Australians in the dysentery hut, one of whom told me that the water had enabled him to have his first wash in four weeks. Certainly boiled water was at a premium, owing to the appalling lack of containers for boiling, but the Dutch were adamant in their refusal to allow their patients more than one waterbottle per day. In any case, the effect on the morale of the Australians of being denied the right to wash was far worse than any supposed ills which might have arisen from the application of ¬ pint of water to their skins.

In spite of the fact that Thanbyuzayat was always talked about by the Japanese as a hospital, the conduct of guards towards sick men suggested that the word was meaningless in Japanese. A few days after I was sent to hospital, Wardmaster

Paul was attending to a patient too sick to help himself. He had his back to the gangway and failed to notice the entry of a Japanese sentry. The Japanese suddenly screamed abuse at him, and then kicked him savagely with his boots on the knee and shins. Paul protested courageously and vehemently. Next day when Major Ted Fisher, C.O. of the hospital, made a heated protest to the Japanese, there were apologies and statements that it was all the result of a misunderstanding, but nothing was done to remedy the situation. Guards continued to parade between and through the hospital huts, insisting on salutes and bows, or "kiris" from all. By this time, malnutrition and avitaminosis had affected the eyesight of many, and a number of patients were almost totally blind. These men were unable to see the guards approaching, and some of them were mercilessly bashed and kicked for non-recognition. Finally, to protect them, the medical officers made all the blind or partially blind carry a Japanese sign indicating their condition.

Tankos, which had at first been left to the hospital authorities, were instituted by the Japanese, who paraded through the huts twice a day, and nearly always made so many mistakes that the count lasted four or five times as long as an Australian would have taken.

The effect of the ceaseless patrol of guards and the frequent bashing of prisoners on the morale of the sick, many of whom underwent the acute depression that often accompanies malaria, needs no underlining.

Perhaps the biggest battle in the early months at Thanbyuzayat, was to secure the right to buy, with such limited funds as we had, eggs and bananas for sick men to whom the obtaining of extra vitamins was literally a matter of life and death. Nagatomo, with a spitefulness and illogicality incomprehensible to any Westerner, refused to allow prisoners to spend their pay, or such Burma rupees as they had obtained in other ways, in supplementing their rations. The bazaar in the village of Thanbyuzayat was packed with meat, eggs, fruit and vegetables, but for a long time canteen buying was absolutely forbidden and supplies could only be smuggled in at dead of night through the good offices of certain guards who were making a handsome "squeeze" from the prices we paid the Burmese trader.

Lieutenant Hosoda, a fairly reasonable but timid officer who was in charge of the camp at this time, permitted supplies to come in in December after Nagatomo had gone off to Singapore for a conference about P.O.W.s; but he told us that this would stop as soon as Nagatomo returned.

On 8 December, anniversary of the outbreak of the Pacific War, the Japanese bedecked Thanbyuzayat and the other camps with flags and had a big day with ceremonial parades, feasting and exultation over their victories. The Imperial Rescript declaring war was read out, on the eighth of each month. It was noticeable, each year, that the enthusiasm and extent of the celebrations diminished as the war swung against Japan. But at the end of 1942 they still believed themselves to be invincible, and by nightfall they were all very patriotically drunk.

When Nagatomo left Thanbyuzayat, three Dutchmen who had attempted to escape from the Dutch camp in the jungle were confined in the cells behind the guard-house. Brigadier Varley had put up a vigorous fight to avert the death penalty with which Nagatomo threatened these men. Nagatomo's reply was that we all had signed an agreement not to try to escape, and that international law had no claims to respect from the Imperial Japanese Army. Nagatomo did not have the courage to order the shooting party himself, but sent a wire from Rangoon to Lieutenant Naito that the men be executed.

Naito, who was the senior officer in Burma after Nagatomo, was a man of some education who had occupied an important bank position before the war, and had subsequently held good staff posts in China. But drink had been his undoing, so he found himself reduced to the obscurity of the P.O.W. organization. Characteristically, now faced with an execution which he knew to be utterly indefensible, he drank himself into a state in which he could sign the order without too many qualms of conscience. As we awoke at dawn on the morning of 13 December, a detail of Japanese guards, heavily armed, swept across the parade ground in army trucks with their condemned prisoners. A few minutes later a volley of shots echoed through the camp.

It is difficult to depict the bitterness and anger of the hundreds of sick men, lying helpless in the squalor of the hospital huts, while their fellow prisoners were cold-bloodedly murdered a hundred yards away. But this was not the end. An hour after the execution, an Australian who had escaped from Wegale, the 8-kilo camp, came in and gave himself up at Thanbyuzayat after a futile attempt to reach Rangoon. This man had rather a poor record with the A.I.F., and there was little doubt that he was far from normal. In view of the fact that he had given himself up, the camp administration had strong hopes of saving his life, and our medical officers certified that he was mentally unbalanced and pleaded for mercy on grounds of insanity. The Japanese promised to consider the case, and he was placed in the hospital near his kumicho, Captain Gordon Fraser, of the 2/4th M.T., who had been held responsible, according to Japanese regulations, for the escaped man. It was believed that Naito might commute the normal sentence and hopes rose when the man was left in the hospital for the next twenty-four hours.

At ten o'clock next morning, Gordon Fraser and I were sitting on our beds a few feet away from the escaped man. Suddenly, four Japanese whom we had not seen before entered the hut and seized him without offering any explanations. He was hustled outside to a truck loaded with armed men, while we suddenly realized that all huts had been surrounded by guards who drove prisoners inside at the bayonet point. The truck drove across to the cemetery, and we waited in that grim suspense which is not really coloured with any kind of hope. Mercifully, the volley came within five minutes. The tally of Australians executed in Burma during the year had now reached twelve.

On 18 December officers, for the first time after ten months of captivity, received pay from the Japanese. Nominally they were to receive the same pay as Japanese officers of equivalent rank. However, this was paid in Burmese rupees which had a much lower value, owing to rapid inflation of the local currency, than the Japanese yen on which the scale was based. Even so, lieutenant-colonels were supposed to receive 220 rupees per month, majors 160, captains 110, lieutenants 85 and sub-lieutenants 70.83. Actually, the Japanese began by deducting sixty rupees for "board and lodging"—we computed that at the current price of rice it cost them less than five rupees a head—and then limited the money any officer could have in his possession to seventy rupees.

Brigadier Varley asked all officers to accept a flat rate of twenty rupees a month to allow whatever remained over to be put at the disposal of the Red Cross organization within the camps. The officers accepted this, and so a fund amounting to several thousands of rupees was established to buy eggs, bananas, sugar and other commodities when available, to give the sick in the base hospital and the jungle hospitals a chance to supplement their hopelessly inadequate diet, and withstand their disease. There is no doubt that this scheme was responsible for saving hundreds of lives.

Twenty rupees a month at current prices represented a buying power of a little over a pound a month at Australian standards, but as Japanese inflation continued, prices soared rapidly and up in the jungle, in the last months of the year, the twenty rupees was practically valueless. In any case, most officers set aside a considerable portion of this exiguous amount to assist friends and members of their units who were seriously ill.

Even when rates of pay on the railroad were increased to twenty-five cents a day for privates and thirty cents for N.C.Os, the buying power of the workers remained abysmally low. Even if a man remained fit enough to work throughout the month, he could not earn more than about seven rupees. At current prices, at the beginning of 1943, this enabled him to supplement his diet for perhaps a week. By this time, a year of miserable food had made most of us so grateful for small mercies that a piece of sugar or a banana, mixed up with the rice, represented relative luxury. Average prices at base in January 1943 were—eggs ten to eleven cents each, a *viss* of *shintagar* (three and a quarter pounds of native sugar in brown cakes, wrapped up in palm leaves) cost seventy cents to a rupee, bananas (very small) twenty-five cents a hand, tomatoes, when available, three to five cents each; peanuts, ten to twenty cents a mug. Occasionally at base, other things were available in small quantities, but we were seldom able to buy tinned milk, which was our greatest need for the men dying of dysentery. For a tin which costs 7½d. in Australia, one had to pay at least five rupees, equivalent to twenty days' pay at the new rates, or fifty days' pay prior to February.

Canteen supplies to the jungle camps were always totally inadequate, and dwindled to nothing on the approach of the rains. Prices in the jungle were usually anything from 25 to 200 per cent higher than at Thanbyuzayat.

The sick were unpaid and, of course, absolutely destitute. They depended solely on what extras they received through the Red Cross funds provided by the officers' pay and the generosity of their working mates. Indeed, had we had to rely on Japanese pay alone, the death rate would have been much higher than it was. Actually, most of the money circulating in the camps came from other sources.

From the first days of our arrival in Burma, we had discovered that the local population was very short of clothing and textiles of all kinds, and that, thanks to the Japanese Army's printing presses, most Burmese now had more in rupees than they had ever had previously in annas. Yet, despite the abundance of paper money, all natives with whom we could communicate said emphatically that their living standard was far lower than under the British. Many commodities, such as textiles, tools and manufactured goods, had simply disappeared from the bazaars, and food prices were mounting at a dizzy rate each month. The viss of shintagar which had cost ten or fifteen cents prior to the Japanese occupation cost five times as much by the end of 1942, and by the end of 1943 in the jungle camps we were paying eight, ten, twelve and even fourteen rupees for a viss.

The temptation to sell such shirts, shorts, blankets and other gear as they had was too much for many men asked to work long hours on a starvation diet. Practically every night one or more men would go out from each camp carrying piles of prisoners' belongings to exchange for the rupees which would buy food. The traders, who were risking their lives, naturally did very well out of it, taking a commission proportionate to the risk they ran. The result was that in all camps there soon sprang up a minority consisting of traders or men who had valuables such as watches or surplus clothing, who established a considerable store of rupees. Most of these men were generous in helping their friends and sick mates, and nearly all gambled freely so that quite soon this "illegal" money began to spread through the camps, and there is no doubt that it did, to some extent, offset the meanness of Japanese pay and the straitened state of many.

Enterprising souls, determined to supplement their rations, began to invest their capital in the establishment of "business". At Thanbyuzayat, by the beginning of 1943, we had vendors selling cakes, rice coffee, gingerbeer brewed from ginger-roots obtained through the canteen, rissoles (made of rice and vegetable), and sambals (hot sauces or pickles composed chiefly of chilis with which the Dutchmen love to season their rice). Many of these "racketeers", as they were christened by those outside the rackets, soon had far more money than any officer.

The unfortunate thing was that great inequalities of wealth and diet were thus opened up among men living cheek by jowl with each other in the huts, because not everybody had traders or friends in the "rackets" to look after him. Nor was there any way of taxing those with the money for the benefit of the sick. The canteen could not be run at a big margin of profit without penalizing the workers whose limited pay already bought very little.

Even more unfortunate was the sale of rupees, by the moneyed minority, for promissory notes to be met in Australian currency on our repatriation. Current rates on this "black market" at Thanbyuzayat varied between two rupees and one rupee for an Australian pound. Just how many of these engagements will be honoured by the parties concerned has remained a keenly debated point in the prison camps. It is difficult for an outsider, who has not been faced with starvation and who has never battled month after month for very existence, to weigh the ethical pros and cons of this matter.

At Thanbyuzayat a weekly concert in which Sergeant Bob Skilton, well known Port Melbourne footballer and radio vocalist, was the moving spirit, soon became one of the highlights. In addition to his singing, Bob developed a series of "patter" acts with an English sergeant, Les Bullock, who at intervals operated a wireless set or "dicky-bird" in this camp, as Caswell was doing up in the jungle. Some of the patter that these two put over was exceedingly witty, if seldom fit for the drawing-room.

The chief medical personality at Thanbyuzayat was a brilliant but temperamentally difficult Macquarie Street specialist with a biting tongue and a dictatorial manner which earned him the title of "the Fuehrer". It was his habit, before evening tankos, to go rapidly through the hospital area peremptorily telling all who were not on their beds: "Go back to your bed and stay there until I come to you!"

Skilton and Bullock got hold of this at one concert and took advantage of the fact that "the Fuehrer" was allegedly not only a bachelor but a misogynist. "What," demanded Bob, "will be the first thing that Major ———— says to his wife when he gets home?" "Go to your bed and stay there until I come to you!" (Uproar.)

Bob had a version of Cinderella that was never found in any child's story book, and that would have lifted the hairs on Rabelais's scalp. He was assisted at these concerts by a couple of Dutchmen who had a touch of genius in playing piano accordions, and an enthusiastic reception was given to others whose earnestness and desire to entertain the sick went far to compensate for the limitation of their talents.

On Christmas Day Norm Whittaker's band made a tour of the camps. Unfortunately when, jaded and weary, they completed their fourth concert for the day at Thanbyuzayat, Naito, who had arrived during the concert in an advanced state of drunkenness, insisted on a repeat performance. This spoiled everybody's fun and served to make our shackles bite bitterly into our consciousness even on this day when the Japanese did for once allow us a reasonable quantity of meat and vegetables, with which the camp cooks, headed by Sergeant Wittingslow, achieved a triumph. At Kun Knit Kway the Yanks caught an immense water buffalo which promised a feast on Christmas Day. But despair and gloom settled over the camp when the buffalo broke away as it was about to be slaughtered. However, three other cows were shot, and the Japanese gave the camp further animals from the reserve ration, so for one day at least our meat craving was satisfied.

The escape of potential meat, thanks to the rottenness of the only ropes supplied by the Japanese, used to make many of us want to rend our hair. The Burmese cow, a long-suffering and much abused animal, becomes unsettled and highly excited at the strange smell of the white man. The daily slaughter at the camps was often attended by an extempore rodeo exhibition, in which stockmen from New South Wales and Queensland and cowboys from Texas vied with each other in seeking to control and bring to the slaughter pit the frantic cattle. At Thanbyuzayat we lost more than a third of our cattle for over a month, and meat-hungry men used to curse bitterly when plunging beasts snapped the slender ropes and broke away irrecoverably to take refuge in the jungle.

On the other hand, many of the beasts were so emaciated that they had to be carried into the camps on trucks, being too weak to walk. The Japanese dumped them out of the trucks, their legs bound, as if they were so many sacks of salt.

The slight relaxation of discipline and oppression which had attended Christmas did not last for long. Three more Dutchmen who had attempted to escape were shot at dawn on 27 December at Thanbyuzayat, while at the 18-kilo camp Sergeant O'Donnell, of Lieutenant-Colonel Charles Anderson's force, was the victim of a shocking and cold-blooded murder, which still remains clouded in mystery.

O'Donnell had been out in the working party and had got permission to go aside into the bushes. A few minutes later work ended for the day and the rest of the party, with their guards, returned to camp. Tiemoto, a Korean, christened by the boys "Peanut", but henceforth known as "Dillinger", apparently stayed behind with O'Donnell. Back at the camp shots were heard by those in the camp orderly room, but the Koreans were so careless with their firearms that nobody took much notice. Only at tanko that evening was it discovered that O'Donnell was missing. A search party presently found the body with a bullet hole through the head and two others through the chest and shoulder. He had been shot at point-blank range from in front, which disproved the Jap suggestion that he was running away.

The men in the camp were so enraged that the smallest spark would have served to start a mass attack on the guards. Colonel Anderson made such vigorous protests to the Japanese that "Dillinger" was removed from the camp and sent down to base, where an inquiry was held. He was said to have been badly beaten up by a group of the engineers supervising construction of the railway, and when I saw him at Thanbyuzayat in mid-February his face was still swathed with bandages. I don't believe that any Japanese or Korean had a shadow of doubt as to "Dillinger's" guilt, but no proper disciplinary action was taken by Nagatomo, and after a period of some months the murderer resumed duty as a guard in the prison camps. When the Koreans saw the writing on the wall, towards the end of the war, "Dillinger"* used to walk round the camps assuring prisoners that he had not shot O'Donnell, but that it was his twin brother.

It was at this stage that the Dutch survivors of the dysentery epidemic, following their hellship journey to Rangoon, arrived at Thanbyuzayat. Their story and the mounting figures of our own sick-rate on top of the December murders did not make for much rejoicing at the passing of the old year.

However, 1943 began well, for we were issued with cards on which we could send a two-line message home. Those of us who had come through Changi in October were the only ones who had had a chance to send off a card, so this excited some hopes of allaying anxiety among loved ones at home. A

---

* I believe "Dillinger" has been shot by the Allied authorities in Bangkok since Japanese capitulation.

P

week later Nagatomo returned, apparently a changed man. He promised us improved pay, a Red Cross ship and an official canteen. Furthermore, he said that the new hospital, then being built, would fulfil all our requirements. We took this with a certain number of grains of salt, and it soon proved that we were wise.

Later in the month the second party of Australians, Americans and Dutch from Batavia, recruited by additions in Singapore, arrived on the railway and were established as No. 5 Group, outside Nagatomo's command. Arriving at Changi a few days after us, they had remained there for nearly three months before being placed on two Jap cargo boats, similar to those on which we had travelled. On 18 January, off Moulmein, two Liberators from India had swept down on the two ships. Bombing with deadly accuracy, they scored three direct hits on the first vessel, one bomb falling down the hatch of a hold which fortunately contained no prisoners but 500 Japanese. The ship began to sink rapidly and the surviving prisoners and Japanese took to the water. The planes scored near misses around the second vessel which was carrying most of the P.O.W.s.

As one of the *Perth* boys on board said to me afterwards, in describing their plight: "We couldn't hope that they'd be shot down, but we did pray that the blighters would get hungry and go home to tea."

The Japanese on the second vessel panicked badly, firing their anti-aircraft gun indiscriminately without any attempt to aim at the attacking planes. Amidst the screaming and confusion on the deck, Commissioned Gunner Ross of *Perth* and other P.O.W. officers did their best to maintain order amongst the yelling Japanese. Finally the planes sheered off and they were able to pick up the survivors from the first ship. Fifty-two prisoners lost their lives as the result of this sinking—two from H.M.A.S. *Perth*, three from the 2/2nd Pioneers and forty-seven Dutch. It was believed that more than five hundred Japanese were lost.

Some of the Japanese thanked the prisoners for their help in pulling men out of the water irrespective of nationality.

But one bedraggled little Nip told another tale. "Australians no ——— good," he said vigorously. "Every time I come up for air Australian in water push my head under again."

This news proved at least that we were beginning to hit back, but it provided a grim augury for further sea trips with Nippon. Already there were rumours that we should be moved from the railway, either on or before its completion, to Japan.

At Kun Knit Kway, Colonel Black discussed the possibilities of our being sent to Japan with Captain Fitzsimmons, senior American officer. "You know, Fitz," said the colonel, "I can tell you a way to make your boys quite safe even if we do get sunk going over." "What's that?" asked Fitzsimmons. "Just get each of your Yanks and paint on his backside 'We Won The War'. Even the sharks won't swallow that!" As this was just at the time of the American reverses south of Tunis, this was one up on the Yanks.

On 9 February Captain Mull, an A.I.F. officer with wide experience in India and Burma in the British Regular Army, made a break for liberty from the 14-kilo camp where Greenforce was now situated. With him went two others, Dickenson and Bell, both of whom had some knowledge of the jungle. The trio had laid their plans and made all preparations with great thoroughness, Captain Mull having spoken with many Indians in the neighbourhood. Unfortunately, Dickenson was suffering from fever when they left, and his condition worsened rapidly, so that, in accordance with their agreement, he finally made the others leave him behind in a native kampong. Here he was handed over to the Japanese and brought back to Thanbyuzayat where, after some days in the guardhouse, he was shot at dawn on 2 March.

At the 14-kilo camp, the Japanese seized the orderly officer, Captain Dave West, of Colac, who was known to be a friend of Mull, dragged him into the jungle and attempted to extract information about Mull's escape by beating him mercilessly with a bull's pizzle. Members of the Japanese *Kempei*, or secret police organization, arrived at the camp and grilled senior officers. The Japanese seemed astounded at the audacity of the attempt, made by an officer with a full knowledge of the Burmese jungle and its difficulties. The general verdict in the prison camps, where it was known that Mull hoped to strike across to Allied territory, was that it was almost hopeless, but that if anybody could do it, Mull would.

However, about 24 February, Mull and Bell were caught in a padi field a hundred miles north-west of Moulmein by a posse of Burmese police collaborating with the Japanese. Mull, who always said he would not be taken alive, was shot dead and Bell was captured and brought back to Thanbyuzayat, where he was shot.

He asked to be allowed to walk to his execution and to face the firing squad with his eyes unbandaged. Lieutenant Hosoda, who was present, said, "How sad it is that so brave a man should die for such a foolish attempt to escape!" Bell shook hands with Hosoda, who had done him some kindnesses, saying, "I have done my duty. Now you do yours." So passed a very brave Australian soldier and so ended a very gallant attempt to escape from a captivity which each month grew more galling and ominous. Its failure confirmed the Japanese in their view that they could afford to guard their prisoners with only a minimum of warders, because the distances, the jungles, the sea and the native population were more effective custodians than stone walls and iron bars.

On 28 February there was enacted at Thanbyuzayat a farce on a Gargantuan scale. Two A.I.F. boys had been caught during the month outside the wire of their respective camps. These were Sergeant Scanlon, of Williamsforce, who was accused of stealing from the Japanese, and Private Billy Williams, son of a well-known Melbourne boxer, who had been missing from Kun Knit Kway one night. Williams, who had gone out to trade with the Burmese of the nearest village, said he had been detained there by force. But he was unable to identify his assailants among the Burmese whom the Japs rounded up. The Japanese accused him of having attempted to escape, which carried the death penalty.

Before the trial, Naito, Nagatomo's second in command, told senior officers that Nagatomo was probably going to execute the men, but that he, Naito, would do his best to save

Preparing for the execution of an Australian prisoner of war in Burma.

them. Those present at the trial witnessed a carnival of
Japanese duplicity and absurdity. Naito, well knowing that
Nagatomo hated him and would be glad to flout him, began
with an impassioned plea for the execution of the two accused.
When evidence was called none of the Japanese paid much
attention, and at the end Nagatomo solemnly condemned to
death two of the witnesses, who were not involved in any way.
When this was pointed out by P.O.W. officers, Naito applied
again for sentence of death on the accused. But Nagatomo,
annoyed by his blunder, sought to spite Naito by announcing
that the case called for clemency and sentencing the men to
periods of confinement in the guard-house with hard labour.

That night, the anniversary of the sinking of *Perth* and
Houston in Sunda Strait, two Allied planes came over Thanbyuzayat after midnight and dropped two flares which lit up
the camp area and caused a prodigious panic in the guard-
room where face, both literally and in the Oriental sense, was
lost by guards fighting to scramble through the window into
the slit-trench outside. After circling for half an hour, the aircraft dropped two bombs near a supply dump a few hundred
yards down the road from the camp. This suggested that they
were getting information from native agents, and comforted
those who feared the camp might be bombed.

But we were to wait fourteen weeks longer for that pleasure.

CHAPTER XX

REFLECTIONS IN THE RED DUST

O western wind, when wilt thou blow
That small rain down can rain
Christ, that my love were in my arms
And I in my bed again.

November 1942 (at Beke Taung). . . . Various forays into the jungle behind the camp are beginning to teach me something about this country. The place would be an entomologist's paradise, but unfortunately we have none of the brethren with us. The butterflies are fantastic. Yesterday I saw one with wings, as large as a woman's palm, which were of the deepest purple shot with slivers of black and white. On the way home there were two, one saffron with orange whorls, the other a brilliant ocean green with a black blotch on either wing. . . . With our dearth of drugs, it is unfortunate that the only medicinal plant we have found is the cascara-tree, with its green beans often fourteen inches in length. What we need with the present wave of dysentery and diarrhoea is not an' aperient but a binder . . .

The cavalcade of native ox carts, rumbling slowly over the dry ruts of the jungle road, affords us our only glimpse of the free, and the degree of their freedom is, I'm afraid, very limited. In the silence of the jungle night you can hear the creaking of the axles and the groaning of the shafts up to a mile away. As they draw nearer, you catch the staccato cries of the native drivers, often children no higher than the belly of the patient oxen which they control. Apart from a bit of fodder and occasional loads of timber the carts seem very bare, and it is difficult for us to buy anything even when there are no guards about. . . . I said last night to Doug Harris that our part of the jungle here had a rugged, primitive beauty of its own. I pointed to the steep ridge to the north-west of the camp, with its masses of dark trees silhouetted against the moon which was just peering over the shoulder of the height. The tall trees, teak, cascara, tamarind and evergreen hardwoods, carry with them in the moonlight a close resemblance to the eucalypts of home. But Doug was up in arms. He is homesick for the good grassy plains with their straying sheep, the mulga and scrub around the little dry creek-beds, the wise sheep dog watching his every gesture, and the feel of a good horse between his knees. After nine months of captivity, we are all homesick in varying degrees. The Texans yarn constantly of Houston and Dallas, Wichita Falls and Fort Worth. . . . Yet, particularly by moonlight, the jungle has its charm. In the silence after rain you can sometimes hear the faint trickle of water over the rocks in the creek bed in the distance, but at other times the cicadas, crickets and other insects set up a droning which makes the air pulse with sound. . . .

December 1942 (at Thanbyuzayat). . . . The whole camp attended a "Challenge Quiz" at the wood pile last night when a team of hospital patients including Sergeant Scott, a teacher from N.S.W., Jim Sutherland from Prahran, Melbourne, and myself, were pitted against a team from headquarters comprising Colonel Hamilton, from Newcastle, senior M.O. in Burma, Padre Bashford, Major Peter Campbell, a Sydney accountant, and W.O. Pat Levy, a member of the Sydney Stock Exchange. Sutherland has one of those photographic memories and is a perambulating combination of the Stud Book and the Turf Man's Guide. He can tell you not only which horse won any important race in Australia in the last twenty years, but can go on to give you the placed horses, the jockeys, the time, and very often the weight the horse carried and the colours of his owner. We have several jockeys and people associated with the turf in these camps, but they seem unable to floor him. I believe he is equally good at recognizing music, particularly classical music.

The hit of the evening was made by the padre. At a critical stage in the quiz, he was asked, "What is the meaning of the word 'osculation'?" The padre sat silent while his thirty seconds ticked away with sibilant whispers of "kissing" passing among the audience around him. Then just as the timekeeper was about to rule him out Padre Bashford said quietly, "Am I right in thinking it might be described as—an act between the sexes?" (Uproar.) . . . Have now got accustomed to slopping about all day in the wooden clogs, made for me at the beginning of the month by Wally Roberts, hygiene specialist of the 2/4th C.C.S., and a last war veteran. There are a number of methods of walking in clogs. Some people prefer to insert the toes only and to clip-clop with the heel of the clog smacking against the heel of the foot at every step. I favour the school which believes in placing the strap well back. The trouble is that if your toes start protruding over the front of the clog you soon know it, because in the dark it's hard to go far in these camps without striking some root or other object in a way which produces the most acute agony. . . . (These clogs were my daily wear for the next twenty-five months. I wore them down from a thickness of three-quarters of an inch until they were almost like wafers. Constant friction with one's foot tended to produce on the surface of old clogs a high polish comparable to that of well cared for furniture at home. Most prisoners clung to clogs as long as possible, because you seldom found two pairs exactly alike, and often a short walk in someone else's clogs would produce chafing and skin sores which festered like every other abrasion in these camps.)

January 1943. Began the new year well by having my beard shaved off, for the first time since leaving Singapore. Lloyd Willey laid me flat along the edge of the bamboo platform and removed the red fungus with a safety razor. One now has the feeling of being incognito. Half an hour after the operation I ran into B——, to whom I was talking last night. I started to talk about some cricket score we had been discussing, and found him looking at me oddly. The whole conversation seemed to move very jerkily and I wondered if I had offended him. Then I made some direct reference to something he'd said, and suddenly he gasped: "By Christ! you've had your bloody beard off! I've been wondering who in the hell I was talking to!"

. . . The Japanese have now opened a brothel down in the town with their own geisha girls, imported from Japan. The guards are all on a regular roster and go down there twice a month. They come round and tell some of the boys what a good time they're going to have, apparently in the hope of inducing expressions of envy; but from what we've seen of the girls with their piled-up hair and kimonos, titupping along the road past the camp, they look jaded and miserable. Some of them were at the pictures with Japanese officers the other night. This is patriotic service with a vengeance. I can't imagine anything worse for any woman than being dumped out here in a two-ox-cart village in the middle of Burma.

Parties of prisoners are being taken to a screening of Japanese and Burmese films each month. The only programme I have seen consisted of a high-powered propaganda news-reel of Japanese triumphs in the Aleutians, a frightful would-be-musical, full of moaning native instruments, and a Burmese film in which the highlight came right at the end, just as I woke up for the second time, when the hero, a particularly nauseous type of Asiatic Valentino, got a smashing left hook to the jaw from his girl friend's father or brother. Unfortunately, he recovered rapidly, but the film ended before I could get off to sleep again. If this is the sort of thing that Western culture has done for the Burmese, I can understand the strength of the local irredentist movement. . . .

Nagatomo has now installed a pet monkey at his headquarters. One of the drivers strolled in the other day and caught sight of it. "Ah!" he said, "I see Naga has had a baby." The drivers are constantly amazed at the ignorance of the Nips about their trucks. A good deal of sabotage has been done by the men working as mechanics. One puzzled Jap officer asked an Australian to find out what was wrong with his car. After a brief inspection, the Australian told him his battery was flat. "Ah!" said the officer sagely. "What shape is it usually?"

Two new words have been added to the glossary of prison camp terminology* The melon which floats grimly on the surface of our so-called "stews" with unfailing regularity is known here as "White Death". The stew made from the small pods of the *ketju ichang* develops a nauseous blue shade and has been christened "Blue Danube". Contact with the 8th Division boys here convinces me that my observation in Batavia that "bloody" was no longer the main Australian adjective is true. Its successor is uglier and far less satisfactory, but it's amazing how many variants of the term some of the men pack into a single sentence. I overheard one cook give voice to the following gem: "I'm ——ed if a ——er can ——ing well find out where the ——ing hell he's ——ing well expected to eat his ——ing dinner."

January 1943 (at Kun Knit Kway). Five of us have formed a syndicate here, and on my birthday two nights ago we had a terrific feast with omelettes, pancakes, an amazingly edible pudding made of pounded rice (patiently thumped for an hour with an improvised pestle and mortar), lime peel, shintagar and a sarsaparilla sauce conjured out of some native beans. It was the first good meal any of us had had in Burma, so this, my first—but not, I fear, my last—birthday in captivity has rather a less unpleasant memory than I expected. Our activity around our cooking fire after dark is supposed to resemble Snow White's Dwarfs, so now we sing as we go off to cook "Heigho! Heigho! and off to work we go . . ." The group is Keith Mathieson, Norman Carter, Ron Winning, the adjutant, John Higgin, the M.O., and myself. . . . A major tragedy nearly wrecked our domestic harmony this evening. Norman borrowed John's one and only good singlet as a cloth in which to boil the pudding. Norman-like, he forgot all about it and, by the time he remembered, the water had all boiled away and the singlet was just a charred remnant and a memory. John said never a word when Norm came in tremblingly exhibiting the relic, but his expression would have brought tears to the eyes of a Gestapo torturer. . . .

. . . The Yanks here are a pretty cheerful mob and I have spent the last couple of nights in their lines yarning about the States and getting advice about the motor trip I hope to make there with Gwyth one of these days. There is a quartet of Bronx boys among the Texans, who are as unpopular with the others as a ham bone in a synagogue. They're whip-smart, and tend to run rings about some of the slow-thinking, slow-spoken Texans. But their speech grates on the ears like a rusty saw after the smooth, musical drawl of the boys from the South. Each evening at meal-time the camp resounds with a yell so distinctively American and raucous that it sets the gibbons screaming

* See Glossary.

on the opposite hill-side and scares the nesting birdfolk. The cry calling Kumi 105 cannot be produced accurately in phonetics for it has a high whine and a touch of the yodel running through it: "One-oh-faive-cummangetyah-cheow!"

These Yanks, like all others, still hand the boys a bit of salesmanship about the superlativeness of all things American. Some of the Aussies have become a little intolerant of the American attitude. The other day a truckload of Yanks was passing up the road when they came upon a group of Australians digging laboriously. One Yank called out, "Cheer up, boys, it won't be long now. Uncle Sam'll be here soon." Quick as a flash one of the Aussies exclaimed: "What! is he a prisoner too?"

Conversation piece: Guard (telling prisoners about the heroic exploits of Nippon's "Wild Eagles"), "Darwin, bomb-bomb-bomb, Townsville, bomb-bomb-bomb." The boys, "Sydney?" Guard, "Yes, Sydney, bomb-bomb-bomb." The boys, "What about Phar Lap?" Guard, "Phar Lap, bomb-bomb-bomb!"

A number of Ramsayforce officers have joined us in "B——t Castle". Among them are Colonel Ramsay, his 2 I.C. Major Merrett, Major Arch Ewart, a Sydney engineer, Major John Lloyd, of the Victorian State Savings Bank, Major Charles O'Brien, a Sydney teacher, Captain Don Cumming, a crackajack Macquarie Street doctor, Captain Arthur Hence, the adjutant, from the Commonwealth Bank at Inverell, and Red Cross Representative Keith Bostock, a Melbourne carpet importer. They are a band of good fellows and we all get along excellently.

Everybody in the camp seeks to supplement the ration by a bit of private cooking and lines of fireplaces run between each hut. The popular game at the moment is collecting the blood from the slaughtered beasts and frying it in black cakes—pancake size. It's rather tasteless, but we all believe it's good for us and compensates for some of the vitamins we're lacking. However, few Australians are prepared to go as far as the Dutch. They take all parts of the entrails from the cattle, boil or fry them, and devour them mixed up with many chilis in their rice. Hence, the names "Squareheads" and "Cheese-eaters" for Dutchmen have given way to "Offal-eaters". . .

February 1943 (at Thanbyuzayat). The most amazing thing at base, where we are now working on the pay sheets again, is the recovery of Driver Tollett who, in December, was the hospital's prize exhibit of what dysentery can do to a man. After two months of pain and suffering since contracting the disease on the hellships, he had so wasted from his normal weight of ten stone odd that he weighed just three stone thirteen pounds, and nobody expected him to live for more than two or three days. A friend of his, Driver MacAuley, also of the 2/3rd M.T., was sent down to base to be with him. His care seemed to inspire Tollett, and he began to fight back. Getting some eggs at the canteen, they put fourteen into him in a day, and since then, painfully slowly but nevertheless surely, he has pulled uphill and must now be regarded as out of danger, although I doubt if he weighs more than five stone.

The new hospital is a tremendous improvement on the old, for the huts are of wood with wooden floors about five feet above ground level. The matting windows lend an almost civilized air to the place. But the number of patients continues to mount, and in the cemetery, to the west of the new hospital, there are already over seventy graves, most of the dead being victims of amoebic or bacillary dysentery. If only we had had a supply of Emetin, all these amoebic cases could have been saved.

At conferences with the brigadier, all of us who come down monthly as pay officers keep urging the importance of making preparations for the wet season, by establishing food dumps up-jungle, improving the transport and the road, and seeking to offset the break-up of communications which we dread. Nagatomo, although more reasonable since his Singapore conference, doesn't really care two pins whether his prisoners live or die . . .

February 1943 (at Kun Knit Kway). Nagatomo has told us that our motto is "Work Cheerfully". Hence, the Japanese in most camps have banned all whistling, singing and music in our huts, even at the end of the day's work. The miracle is that most of the lads keep up their spirits in great style. (In code) Monty is the hero of the hour, with the Russians, who annihilated Hitler's Sixth Army, a close second. The Nips are tough, but I think most of these Aussies are a lot tougher.

When the pay sheets are finished each day, I get up to a little bamboo clump just behind "B——t Castle", where I can write undisturbed in a way that has not been possible since we left Batavia. Am thrashing along with the story of shipboard life on an Australia-England steamer. The story has changed its central character twice already, but I'm enjoying myself, attempting something quite different in style to the undergraduate stuff. A better effort, I hope, is a story "Farewell to Paris", which, if it stays on the right side of the fine border between pathos and sentimentality, seems rather better than anything done yet. The bamboo thicket is more of a private haven than I've had since we left Singapore. I think one of our first needs, if and when we escape, will be to get right away into the country somewhere where we'll hardly see another man from one day's end to another. However, there'll be no ban on the other sex!

Occasionally Keith Mathieson comes up here, and we have a hammer-and-tongs discussion on some religious, ethical or social problem. Keith says these talks are the best stimulant his sermons have ever had, but he'll have to be careful or he'll find Beelzebub grinning at his elbow in the pulpit.

Reflections in the Red Dust

March 1943 (at Thanbyuzayat). There is one thing about this pay-officer job which suits me very well, in spite of all the bumping up and down to and from Thanbyuzayat through the dust: we do see something of the native life here. Today the trucks brought us only to the Q store, and we had to hike through the village. Despite a general movement from Moulmein, which is now being bombed, across the border into Thailand, there has been no mass exodus from Thanbyuzayat as yet. Judging by the ox-cart convoys which we passed on the road today, most of the migrants are very short of food. But there are no signs of any scarcity in the village, and I only wish we had money to buy all that is available. I daresay the epicures at home would not be very enthusiastic about the great hunks of raw buffalo steak, covered with dust and flies, and exposed on papaya and banana leaves on the stalls. But at this stage of our history few of us are very choosy. In fact, many of us don't bother to pick out the white weevils which are served up in our rice every day. As someone said, "They all help to build up the meat ration."

It's probably very stimulating for a white man to be put on a sub-coolie diet. It should certainly be one of the prerequisites for the graduation of our philosopher kings. I'm sure that Kant, Hegel and company would have been able to put things much more simply and clearly to the layman if they'd had to live on boiled rice, and precious little else, for a year or two.

The most colourful figures in the villages and along the roads are the Burmese priests with their black umbrellas and saffron robes. However, one can't help feeling that in the life of the community they come into the category which the boys label as "bludgers". By far the most active and also, I believe, the most intelligent members of the population are the women, who seem not only to undertake all the household work, field labour, and business enterprise in the village, but also to produce children with clock-like consistency. It is quite common to see a woman passing along a street laden with her purchases from the bazaar, with three or four children of school age preceding her, a couple more toddlers dragging at her skirts, and another baby in her arms. The amazing thing about the kiddies is the way they take to cheroots. Although I've seen it a dozen times, it still gives me rather a shock to see a pot-bellied little urchin, who can't be a day more than four years old, sitting cross-legged in the dust drawing at "a whacking great cheroot" about half as big as himself. Sergeant Murray Knight, Ammunition Sub-Park, maintains that he has seen a suckling babe in its mother's arms with a cheroot in one fist, alternating a puff of smoke with a mouthful of milk—and I'm not even sure that this is only one of Murray's stories.

All the men and women wear the coloured *lungyi*, or sarong, the women wearing a white bodice, usually of lace. Their hair, which appears to be soaked in coco-nut oil, is piled up in plaits on the top of their heads. Some of them, when young, are very attractive, but I believe that they are regarded as old women by the time they are thirty.

The surprising thing is the amount of time everybody seems to find, at all hours of the day, to sit out on the verandas of their huts and shops doing precisely nothing. I suppose the men do work at times, but you have to be smart to catch them at it.

There is an epidemic of lice or "chats" here at present. Towards evening you see scores of earnest souls diligently going over their blankets and clothes, and expertly murdering the little grey monsters by crushing them between their thumbnails. The practice has given rise to a new word which I've just added to the glossary. I know bombhappy, slaphappy, and Japhappy. Now we have "chathappy". Example tonight: "Gee, Bill, I've been trying to see these beggars against my blanket for so long, that my eyes have gone on me. Guess they're chathappy."

Colonel Hamilton tells me that Hosoda has visions of running a shop in Sydney after the war. He asked the colonel his opinion of the prospect. The colonel suggested that the treatment we were receiving was not likely to improve the popularity of any Japanese enterprise in Australia. I understand that Hosoda shook his head in regretful agreement. Personally, I will hasten to invest my humble all in a life insurance policy on the first Jap from these camps who opens a shop anywhere between Cape York and the Leeuwin.

The Japanese attribute the absence of all the Red Cross goods, blankets, clothing, boots, and medical supplies they promised us to the sinking of their ship off Moulmein on 18 January. Whenever we ask for anything we are told it was on that ship and was destroyed by the "indiscriminate bombing" of our own planes. I suppose this satisfies everyone; they save face and we realize that they had no intention of producing these things for us, anyhow.

March 1943 (at Milo—75-kilo camp). This camp is rather better than we feared. There is a stream about fifteen yards wide in which most of us swim daily, while most of the huts are located on the banks of the stream between it and a steep bluff on top of which are built the Japanese and P.O.W. officer huts. They have been having a thin time here thanks to the presence of several bash artists among the guards. The most sadistic and noxious of these are the pair known as the "B.B." and the "B.B.C.", i.e. the Boy Bastard and the Boy Bastard's Cobber.

. . . Last night Ron Winning, our adjutant, had to promise Takamoto, another Korean bully, that he would commit hari-kiri if the tanko figures which he handed in for our parade were incorrect.

. . . Naito has arrived here, as usual very drunk. When two Koreans started fighting last night, he suddenly leapt through the window and gave the two combatants a terrific bashing, to the great satisfaction of the boys. . . . The Japanese have ordered all sick men, irrespective of the nature or state of their illness, to work inside the camp, and there has been a showdown. . . .

Owing to the state of my legs, John Higgin has ordered me into hospital, where I seem to have contracted a touch of malaria. The orderlies here have added a new item to their menu. A tiny streamlet runs through reed-beds between the hospital hut and the foot of the cliff behind. It is infested with water snakes which swim at incredible speed. The orderlies—such as Len Coon, of N.S.W., Andy Anderson, of Adelaide, two air force boys, "Nigs" Hansen and "Tex" Wells, of Perth, and Norm Fosdyke, of Sydney—have been organizing snake hunts, and boiling or frying their "bag". I believe that snake provides a juicy fillet which is a cross between chicken and whiting, but with this fever I don't feel much like tackling it myself. By the time we have finished with the Burma jungle (or it has finished with us) I doubt if there will be anything which runs, flies, creeps or wriggles which some prisoner or other has not tried to eat. Some of the men in the lines are already digging up bamboo roots and boiling them in hope of deriving a little extra nourishment from their fibrous wood. I doubt if a hundredweight of bamboo root would be worth one decent meal at home.

I notice that when one is sick in these prison camp hospitals, one tends to discuss plans for the future at home more keenly than at other times. Have been yarning this way with three 3rd M.T. men, Jimmy Sheehan, Dan Pritchard and Bill Toogood. Have also got to know, in the last few weeks, two fine Sydney N.C.Os, W.O. "Tiny" Cullen and Corporal Charlie Power. I suppose a hundred times a month we ask one another, "How long, O Lord, how long?" but no response seems likely to be vouchsafed in the near future.

April 1943 (at Thanbyuzayat). Was sent down here with the other pay officers on April Fools' Day, with instructions that I was to stay, since my legs are definitely worse than they have been before, pus coming from about two dozen sores on each. On the way down, the driver made a great attempt to run over a big python which slid across the road in front of us. I have no idea how long he was, because we saw only the last eight or nine feet of him. However, the wheel just missed his tail as he glided into the undergrowth down the bank at the road's edge. It took us seven and a half hours to do the trip down, the road being abominable beyond description for the first half of the distance, which by road is more like 90 kilos than 75.

Sports meetings have been inaugurated down here on a green strip at the back of the canteen, and some of the workers, who are feeling a bit better than the patients, can still show a nice turn of speed. . . . Poker schools, dice and other gambling games are now becoming general in the hospital huts, a symptom of the increased amount of money now circulating in this camp where many men have sold valuables of all kinds, including a certain amount of loot picked up during the retreat down the Malaya Peninsula. Those in possession of such goods argue that it was a case of taking them or leaving them for the Japs, and if the stuff helps to save the lives of men fighting for existence, it seems a case where the end justifies the somewhat dubious means. . . .

The new hospital is a torture chamber at present thanks to the hordes of bugs that swarm out of every crack in its boards to devour the unknown delicacy of white flesh which, to jungle bugs, must be like caviare in the Antarctic. We lie sweltering under the mosquito-netting in the hot still nights which preface the coming of the rains, but sooner or later one is forced to get up and take refuge outside, walking round and round the hospital huts in the moonlight. Last night we must have done about ten miles in the hours after midnight while Don Capron, of Coogee, and Murray Knight instructed me in the intricacies of pig-farming. At any rate we finally were so tired that we went in and fell asleep in complete defiance of the red swarms . . . Today every board in this hut was taken up and tens of thousands of the little carnivora were crushed or scalded to death with boiling water. But tonight they will be back again in undiminished numbers. The one consolation is that the long sessions in the moonlight trying to drug oneself with weariness have been productive of some of the best yarning about Australia and the future which I've heard in these camps. . . .

CHAPTER XXI

CAME THE RAINS

It was not part of their blood,
It came to them very late
With long arrears to make good,
When the English began to hate.

—RUDYARD KIPLING

As April passed, occasional sharp showers heralded the coming of the rains. The jungle camps were doing their utmost to evacuate all their least fit men to Thanbyuzayat, realizing that it might be impossible to obtain any kind of medical aid for them in the jungle later. By May even the enlarged area of the new hospital was filled to overflowing and, under Japanese pressure, the M.Os were forced to send up-jungle many men who were barely convalescent. To some of these the decision proved a death sentence.

The Japanese now decided to make a propaganda film to illustrate their humanitarianism and generosity to their captives. The making of this film was a masterpiece of Japanese hypocrisy, and I only hope that a copy of it can be found and preserved as a monument to their duplicity.

At Thanbyuzayat elaborate preparations were made. The canteen was stocked with quantities of fruits and stores which we had never seen before, and never saw again. A lorry was brought in, apparently laden high with vegetables; but when the top layer was removed empty crates were revealed underneath. A P.O.W. was made to hold a beer bottle to his lips and another was given a sheet of paper to suggest writing a letter home. Then prisoners were forced to queue up at the counters while camera men filmed the scene. At the end of the performance, most of the goods were loaded back on to carts and taken out of the camp again.

An even more shameless performance was put up for the R.A.P. Special shelves and numerous bottles, many of which were filled with coloured water, were brought into the camp. In place of our miserable dispensing tables, a modern dispensary was set up with "props" worthy of a Hollywood set. After the film was made, drugs and bandages provided for the performance were hastily rushed out of the camp again, although they would have been invaluable in the hospital's struggle to cure its patients.

A clothing issue of khaki jackets and shorts, together with new boots—an issue unprecedented during the whole term of our captivity—was made to a large number of prisoners who were then conducted to the Thanbyuzayat siding, where films were made of prisoners coming in by train and being marched up to the camp. While this was going on, a train passed containing a number of European women internees, who waved and blew kisses to the prisoners. A little later, a Japanese officer on another train saw a guard rush at one of the prisoners and start bashing him and kicking him because he had moved aside a few yards from the rest of his party. The officer jumped out of the train, gave the guard a terrific smite in the face, and apologized to the Australian concerned for the ignorance and brutality of "this coolie".

The next item in the film was a camp concert. Special building materials were brought into the camp, and we were allowed at last to build the stage which we had been asking for for months. Next, marquees and tents were erected around the stage. A piano—always denied us previously—was brought into the camp and the concert party was given unlimited scope for rehearsal. The entire band, brought down from up-jungle, was fitted out with new hats, uniforms and boots. Then all hospital patients who could walk were made to put on the best of such clothing as they had, or could borrow, and go and sit in the sun for three hours while the film was rehearsed. Nagatomo, attended by all his satellites, arrived in state and took a prolonged salute, before seating himself, with all the pomp of a monarch, in the special marquee. One could not help feeling that the whole effect could have been obtained with a troupe of well-trained orang-utans in fancy dress. The audience was carefully drilled in the timing, nature and volume of its applause, while anybody who looked too emaciated was carefully removed from the camera's zone.

Finally, after two days of rehearsals in the gruelling sun, the film was made, with nearly as many re-takes as would be demanded by the most temperamental Hollywood director. Then the tents and marquees, the piano and other properties, were loaded on to trucks and we saw them no more.

Cinema equipment was taken to one of the jungle camps so that prisoners could be shown enjoying a film. This was the first and last film ever shown in the jungle. At Colonel Williams's camp, the colonel was accused of deliberately sending his bugler out of the camp to work when the man was needed for the film. Colonel Williams was struck repeatedly, and then forced to stand at attention outside the guard-house for thirty hours consecutively, heavy rain falling for much of this time.

At the 105-kilo camp, the Japanese forced prisoners to put on a "mock" funeral. Scores of sick men, scarcely strong enough to walk, were turned out of their beds to make the film, because the Japanese were too mean to call the working gangs in from the railway. A large group of men, dolled up in the best clothing that many of them had worn for months, were ordered to parade past the cameras "singing happily" with tools over their shoulders, to create the impression that work on the railroad was a labour of joy.

The boys, who were furious by this time, sang with great gusto the A.I.F. version of "Bless 'em All" which could not be considered polite in any circles, but did exactly express how they felt about this hypocrisy. The Japanese proceeded to make a full sound track of this, before someone with a rudimentary knowledge of English realized what was actually being sung.

I do not know in how many Japanese-controlled cinemas this film was ultimately shown, but one gorgeous but quite unconfirmed story stated that the Tokyo authorities had not felt that conditions revealed in the film were sufficiently good to make the best propaganda, so the film had been withdrawn. Actually, the prison camps in the film had as much in common with reality as a *de luxe* flat has in common with a slum hovel.

It was in May that we heard for the first time of the fate of F and H forces brought up from Singapore in April to work on the railway on the other side of the border. There were over 10,000 men in the two groups, 3500 being Australians and the rest British. They were brought by train to Ban Pong, on the main Singapore-Bangkok line, the jumping-off point for the Burma-Thailand railway. Some of them were taken by rail to Kanburi, fifty kilometres farther up the line, but most of them walked from Ban Pong, carrying all their gear on their backs, little or no food being supplied on the way.

This was to become known as the "Death March", for day after day the exhausted men, getting ever hungrier and hungrier, were driven remorselessly onwards into the jungle until they had passed all the camps previously occupied in Siam. It was useless to warn staggering men, scorched by a merciless sun, of the dangers of drinking unboiled water. Without adequate food, their resistance already lowered by fourteen months of Japanese captivity, they went down like flies with fever and dysentery.

Bit by bit, the weaker men began to jettison their last precious possessions—their one change of clothing, their blanket, their one towel. Before long, scores of men, with nothing but the shirt and shorts they stood up in, their mess dixie and waterbottle, were struggling along, their raw feet hurting with each step, going steadily deeper and deeper into the enveloping jungle. Japanese guards beat and threatened to shoot any man who collapsed on the road. They drove the stragglers before them, firing occasional shots just over their heads. Inevitably, in that cholera-stricken region, they struck contaminated water. At the end of the trek, after covering well over two hundred kilometres on a ration totally insufficient for their requirements, they had to start carving camps for themselves out of the jungle. While those who could still move about laboured to erect bamboo shelters from the impending rains, their comrades began to die.

When we heard of this march, we knew nothing of the full extent of the tragedy as it developed in the following months when over 4000 of the 10,000 men perished. But we did know enough of the jungle and of the Japanese to understand that this was equivalent to a massacre. We realized that the railway was to be completed on schedule, regardless of the cost in human life. To even the blindest of optimists it was now apparent that no considerations of humanity would weigh in the scales for a moment. We did not even have the value of a slave gang, which must be fed sufficiently to keep it alive so that its owner will not have to spend his gold buying replacements in the slave market. The Japanese had many tens of thousands of captives. They had the unlimited coolie labour of Southern Asia on which to draw. They were not only unconcerned as to the ravages of disease; they were quite prepared to starve us to death as the work was done.

The dread word "cholera" swept in whispers along the packed wards of the base and jungle hospitals, conjuring up pictures of a raging epidemic which struck men down in hundreds, while the doctors were left helpless. To men scourged with recurrent bouts of fever, to men whose bowels had turned to water, to men who watched daily the slow rotting of their bodies with suppurating . ulcers, the word struck ominously like the heavy note of a gong of doom. It was in this shadow that we awaited the breaking of the rains.

In the jungle camps the Japanese had discovered that there were ways of crowding more men into a hut than merely laying them side by side on the bamboo platforms. At Milo and other up-jungle camps it was now customary to build bunks in tiers one above the other towards the roof, with only a narrow alleyway between each group of bunks. In this fashion far more men were crammed into a single hut than had ever been possible before, and the risk of epidemics and infection, already high, became proportionately greater.

There was no doubt that all along the line, right across Burma into Siam the working force was beginning to crack.

The long months of digging, shovelling, carrying and climbing along the embankments were now producing their inevitable consequences for all to see.

As the sick parades increased daily, so that the numbers available for work dwindled, the last shreds of veneer were torn aside from the face of the Japanese Beast. Up and down the line, not from ignorant coolies, not from the uneducated toughs such as you find in all armies, but from the officers in responsible positions, the class representing Japan's development, came the words, "Your sick shall starve until they die or go back to work."

The commander of No. 5 Group in Burma, Captain Mizdani, in telling his 2000 prisoners that he would not feed the sick in the camp "hospital" said: "Any sick man who staggers to the line to lay one sleeper will not have died in vain." At Milo, the 75-kilo camp, a series of blitzes of the sick began and the new camp commandant, Lieutenant Hochi, paraded the "no duty" men and pronounced the edict: "No work, no food."

A senior Japanese officer of field rank, after listening to a passionate and eloquent appeal on behalf of our sick, said quite coldly: "You do not understand us. We will build this railway if necessary over the bones of the P.O.W.s." Across the border, in the Tarsao area in Siam, an engineer officer controlling the work of several thousand prisoners announced blandly: "You will never see your homes again. You will work for the Japanese until you die."

These were not the isolated statements of unbalanced fanatics or perverts. They expressed with complete fidelity the attitude of all Japanese to their prisoners throughout the first years of the war when they believed that nothing could stop Japan. The voice was that of prison camp commanders and officers often without high rank, but the verdict was that of the highest in the land. This policy expressed the mind of the ruling class in Tokyo.

This was the situation of 60,000 Allied prisoners of war scattered over 400 kilometres of jungle across the top of the Malay isthmus, when, on 22 May, with a long preliminary sighing which grew swiftly deeper and more intense, a remorseless invader swept down over the hills and valleys, across jungle and padi field to submerge the whole land.

The rains had come.

For seventy-two hours without a break, with a relentlessness that slackened only to become again more intense, a wall of water seemed to shut out the surrounding world. In its fury, it battered on the attap roofs of native houses and coolie huts and roared torrent-like down the deep gutters of village streets; it lashed the thickly covered mountain slopes, inundating the evergreens and the bamboo clumps until each leaf streamed with moisture; in the space of hours it converted tiny dry watercourses into foaming spates; it stirred to savage life the sluggish, moribund creeks which had been wandering aimlessly along; within the first day and then with ever-mounting zeal, it widened the muddy rivers until they began to spread prodigiously and climb their jungle-fringed banks; dominating and assertive, it intruded on every conversation and even on the privacy of your thoughts; it brought change of habit to every living thing that plodded, scurried, flew, crawled or wriggled in the trees, in the rivers, on the earth or under it—not least along the narrow red scar running through the jungles where tens of thousands toiled, seeking to wrest a new highway for man from territory which had belonged to nature since time began.

Its coming meant discomforts, hardships and even death for the tens of thousands of coolies, their elephants and their oxen which had known this phenomenon all their lives. To the white men, who had never lived on rice alone, who had never toiled coolie-wise in the steaming hothouse of the tropics in the rains, who had never lacked dry clothing, warm beds and shelter from all weathers, its coming was like some gigantic turning back of the hands of time, reducing man to the same primitive level as the beasts of the field. Now for us there was to be a testing of moral and mental strengths such as battle danger and hot-blooded action had never brought.

In all the working camps, life entered on a new and yet grimmer phase. Before dawn the strident bugle roused weary men from their comfortless lying space. As soon as their un-changing breakfast of boiled rice was eaten, they went out on to the parade ground to be counted, marshalled in gangs and then marched forth with their tools to the line. More often than not it was raining when they first went out, and invari-ably it rained sooner or later during the long hours of labour. It was not now a matter of excavating, shovelling up and carrying to the embankment 2, 2.4, 2.8 or even, as on some days, 3.2 cubic metres of earth per man. It was now a matter of dealing with the same quantity of soil made immensely heavier by the saturation of the rains.

The clothes of most, if they had any clothes left, were now rags and patches. Thousands of men left camp barefoot each day to trudge often for miles to the place of work, labour all day up to the calves in sticky, glutinous mud and then trudge home again, often in another lashing downpour, when dark-ness had enfolded the jungle.

Even if a man were so fortunate as to have hat, shirt, shorts and boots, he was not much better off. They became water-logged and miserably uncomfortable while it poured, and when the rain ceased and the sun scorched down, making the moist earth and sodden jungle steam like a Turkish bath, it was impossible to wear any more than decency rendered essential. Sometimes, when it rained consistently, the men were left without a dry garment for days on end, for during the nights it was impossible to dry the sodden clothes. Very soon 90 per cent of the men wore only a loin cloth from dawn to dark, their bodies exposed equally to the slashing fury of the rainstorms or the broiling beams of the sun.

Inevitably, bronchial troubles, colds and a form of influenza came to prey on the debilitated men, all helping to pave the way for increasing fever. Instead of red dust, black mud now adhered to every scratch, sore or festered bite.

Within the first few weeks, it became obvious that our fears about the ration situation had not been groundless. The supply of vegetables, other than a little valueless radish or melon, dwindled sadly. Apart from our carefully hoarded bags of dried peas, dahl and ketjuichang, there was nothing to provide the means for even the simplest of stews. The thin stream of cattle driven up the roads to the up-jungle camps lapsed to a feeble trickle as emaciated beasts collapsed on the way, so that only a small percentage of those dispatched reached their destination.

The seasonal scarcity, the state of the roads and the shoddy mechanical work put into the Japanese transport vehicles, all served to diminish supplies. Guards and engineers along the track pilfered from trucks and from such trains as now drew supplies along the first few kilometres of laid track with a complete disregard for the prisoners to whom the goods were consigned. Many Japanese and Koreans, under the pretext of building up their own rations, already vastly better than ours, commandeered our rations and sold them to the thousands of natives, uprooted from their homes and normal food supplies to work along the railway. The cumulative effect of the rains on supplies, transport and Japanese rapacity was passed on to the toiling prisoner, already engaged in a life and death struggle.

The death rate soared by leaps and bounds. Where in each camp one or two had died each month at the beginning of the year, June saw a dozen deaths, and by August the death rate had climbed still further.

Nowhere in Burma was it comparable to the toll just across the border, where the men of F and H forces were, at the same time, seeking to meet Japanese requirements along the railway and render their own quarters at least weatherproof. Like a destroying flame through dry scrub, cholera seized on the bodies of men left without reserves after the ordeal of the march. In one camp at the end of the rains, owing to cholera, the death rate rose so high and the living were so weak that it was impossible to bury the dead and the corpses were flung, day and night, into a fire pit which blazed hungrily like some insatiable Moloch in the dim, dark ages of human history.

In the midst of our own travail, the inhumanity of the Japanese was exemplified in the treatment handed out to their own troops, forced to march along the appalling road which ran alongside the projected railway track. These Japanese soldiers, each loaded with full equipment, had to pull the carts carrying their food and ammunition and manhandle their mountain guns across a hundred miles of country where, during the rains, no truck could penetrate. Our own men toiling on the railway watched with grim satisfaction that was tinged with pity the ordeal of this Nippon cannon fodder struggling to the front in such primitive conditions. They saw privates, who sank to the ground exhausted, kicked in the face and stomach by officers and N.C.Os. These front-line troops were plucky and tough, but they were doomed. We felt a certain admiration for their gameness.

On the eve of the rains, Blackforce, Ramsayforce and Green-force were moved from the 75-kilo camp still farther into the jungle, to a camp at the 105-kilo mark called Aungganaung. Except for a handful of the very sickest men, who were packed on to trucks, the entire force, carrying all their personal possessions, bedding and cooking gear, had to march.

The move began after nightfall on 13 May. By railway the distance was thirty kilometres. By the twisting, winding road it was forty-two. When the moon disappeared the jungle trees obscured everything in pitch blackness, so that the men, for the most part bootless, stumbled and slipped on the rocky, rutted surface of the road, never sure of the next step ahead. Drunk with weariness, many men crashed with their packs down the banks on either side of the road, twisting ankles and cutting their hands and faces. The B.B. drove the stragglers on by firing shots over their heads.

At the 90-kilo camp there was a rest, but when it was discovered that cholera had broken out here, the men had to press on. From three o'clock on the following afternoon until well into the night, exhausted men hobbled into the new camp to collapse in the huts regardless of mud, filth and discomfort. In the first few days after the march, several men who had drunk from the streams en route went down with cholera. Many others were attacked with dysentery, malaria or spreading tropical ulcers which were to cost them their lives in the succeeding months.

In these weeks the Japanese completed a work which had

not been achieved by all the petty persecutions, humiliations and spitefulness of the earlier captivity. Now, in the jungle camps, as we watched our comrades die through Japanese inhumanity, 60,000 Australians, Englishmen, Americans and Dutch were knit together by the bonds of a common hatred which, strong as it was, was never stronger than the searing contempt that possessed us when we contemplated the bestiality of our captors.

CHAPTER XXII

THE TRAGEDY OF THANBYUZAYAT

Rise, take up thy bed, and walk.
—SAINT JOHN, v, 8

AT half past two on 12 June, a sunny afternoon, the planes
came over Thanbyuzayat. There were six of them, just as
there had been a few weeks earlier when they came in similarly from the north. On that occasion all patients who could
leave their beds had gone out and waved, cheered by the sight
of the big four-engined planes that we had longed for but
never seen in Malaya and Java. They had droned over and
on to some target farther down the coast.

When they came over this time I was having the sores,
which now extended from my legs to the middle of my back,
opened and cleaned by an American orderly, a car salesman
from Detroit. As soon as we had seen them we came inside
to resume the unpleasant operation and the conversation which
the planes had interrupted. I heard someone outside the hut
announce that the formation had broken into threes and that
they were wheeling round, but thought no more about it until
a sound swept through the hospital like the first impact of a
gale. I was lying flat on my stomach, spread-eagled on the
platform, my face buried in my arms, trying to concentrate on
what the orderly was saying and not on the pain I was experiencing, so I did not look up immediately. When I did lift my
head, it was to see the American diving down the steps just
beyond us, and to realize that the hut had emptied miraculously. There came a noise, once daily familiar, which I had
not heard for many months. I decided it was too late to get up,
and in the same split second realized that six or seven feet up

in the air, on the platform of a wooden hut was by no means an ideal spot when bombers had chosen you for their target.

There came a series of explosions that shook the hut, and bits of shrapnel whistled overhead or smacked through the hut walls. Then, after a pause of a few seconds, there came another packet from the second trio of planes. None of the bombs seemed very close, although far too near for comfort. They sounded as if they had fallen between the P.O.W. hospital and the level crossing where the road crossed the railway track beside the station.

As suddenly as they had come, the planes disappeared southwards, and, fairly confident that the hospital huts had escaped, we set out to inspect the damage. Then a white-faced prisoner came racing towards the M.O's quarters from the far hospital hut. "The well party—" he panted. "They got the well party."

It was the worst of bad luck. The planes had made no attempt to bomb the hospital area, and the nearest crater was just outside the fence from the old hospital huts. But apparently one of the planes had seen the well, perhaps fifty yards from the fence, and mistaken it, very excusably, for a gun post. The water carriers, whose business it was to ferry water from the well to the kitchen, had just arrived at the wellhead to begin their afternoon's labours. The bomb scored a direct hit on top of the well gear and blew all but two of the party to smithereens. Several men in the old hospital huts had been wounded by flying shrapnel from bombs which seemed to have been all 250- and 500-pounders. Altogether we counted twelve dead and fifteen injured. There were wild rumours of a bomb falling among the Japanese troops billeted all round the P.O.W. hospital, but I was never able to find evidence of more than one Japanese death.

Many of us had been expecting this for so long that we had begun to tell ourselves that our fears were groundless and that British agents had already conveyed our position to the Allied authorities in India. If these hopes were unfounded, our position was truly appalling.

Crowded into fourteen long huts, identical with the surrounding Japanese barracks and store-houses, were about 3000 sick prisoners. On one side of us lay the railway with its sidings and stores of sleepers. On two of the other three sides there were Japanese barracks and supply sheds, and right on the corner of our camp, beyond the cemetery, the Japanese had built an ammunition hut.

Nowhere in the area were huts so tightly packed in such formal military and geometric pattern as in our camp. If the air force did not know that this was a prison camp, it was certain that we should be bombed and strafed as the major military target outside the station itself.

In vain the camp administration pleaded with Nagatomo to be allowed to make P.O.W. signs or place big red crosses through the camp. There was a red cross on the ground on the far side of the camp from the railway line, but it had no white border, and from the air probably looked like two intersecting red paths. A small and dingy red cross had been draped over the roof of the little dispensing hut in the middle of the new hospital, but the old hospital huts, filled with overflow patients and the mechanics' and camp workers' huts, bore no distinguishing mark whatsoever. The only concession Nagatomo would make was to allow us to improve and extend a system of crenellated trenches along the sides of each hut.

That night every man who could crawl from his bed made his way to the cemetery to pay tribute to our dead comrades. The dead included Australians, Americans, Dutchmen and one Englishman and the service conducted by Padres Bashford, Corry and Vergeest was deeply moving. It seemed the quintessence of tragedy that these men, whose captivity was due in great measure to our total lack of aeroplanes, should now perish in the first manifestation of our new aerial might of which the B.B.C. bulletins were so full. Was bombing by our own planes to be added to the menace of a wet season's toil in the disease-ridden jungles?

The answer came within three days. On 15 June we had just conducted a dress rehearsal evacuation of the hospital to the slit-trenches, each man being told the trench he was to occupy, when alert ears caught the drone of incoming planes. An orderly evacuation of huts followed and every man was in his trench when six Liberators again appeared over the camp. The Japanese who, during the first raid, had fired·away blindly with rifles, and even in one case with a pistol, now had a number of machine-guns and light automatics at various positions throughout the area, and these opened up immediately.

We had protested to Nagatomo about camp guards firing at the planes and thus identifying the camp as a military target, in defiance of all international law. The response had been unsatisfactory, and now once again there was firing from the camp area, while bullets from the gun posts in the surrounding jungle whined over the top of the huts.

The next hour was not a happy one. This time the camp itself was the central objective. Three planes bombed and strafed it by turns, each making many runs. Coming down to a height of less than 2000 feet, one plane dropped its bombs so accurately as to score three hits down the centre of the workers' huts in the old section of the camp. The hut on the opposite side of the parade ground was similarly demolished. Sticks of bombs fell across the area between the Japanese ammunition dump and our canteen and cook-house. Other bombs sliced across the area between the new hospital huts and the old, showering both with bomb splinters. One bomb crater was only fifteen yards from the slit-trenches in which over a hundred of us from the first new hospital hut were sheltering.

At least, you could generally see the bombs coming. When the planes opened up with their cannon and sent a stream of .5s spattering over the whole area it was much less healthy. The planes treated the small-arms fire from the ground with the greatest contempt, coming down as they wished.

There was more than a touch of comedy about it all, although one was not very alive to it at the time. An English captain, brave but foolish, would insist on sitting up on top of our trench, as if he were improving the morale of a platoon about to go over the top. C. D. Smith, a tall Yank who was with us, grumbled at him and finally, as some bullets tore through the bushes around us cried, "For God's sake man, quit being crazy! Don't you know what those things are? They're lead poisoning!" But it was some minutes before the captain would condescend to stop acting as a target.

My friend, Don Capron, and I shared our end of the slit-trench with a small bullfrog. It was a moot point which of us was the most unhappy. Don would say: "Hell! the blighter's coming straight in again. Here come the eggs. They'll be close this time!" Then there would be a deafening detonation and the frog between our feet would start blowing himself up and panting at a terrific rate, while Don and I shook our heads and wished we knew as little about the effects of high explosives as our frog.

There are few things so testing of morale as being bombed in a P.O.W. camp. Men said to me that under bombing and shellfire at the front you did not worry half so much because there was a job to be done, and it was all part of the contract. But to be plastered with high explosive and machine-gun bullets by your own bombers while you were cooped up in the narrow confines of a prison camp, looking for all the world like an enemy troop concentration, seemed a little over the fence.

When the last plane had finally expended its bombs and ammunition, we crawled out to count our losses. Considering the nature and accuracy of the attack, these were amazingly light. The bombs, which had destroyed the two huts, had fallen straight down the centre of the buildings, leaving most of the men crowded in the slit-trenches outside dazed but unscathed. Altogether about sixty men were killed or wounded. Captain Ray Griffin, the camp adjutant, was caught by a delayed-action bomb as he was seeking to organize help for some of the wounded. He died almost immediately after being carried across to the hospital. Fourteen others were killed instantly or died during the day, and a number of wounded, as well as several who had been shocked by blast, died during the following weeks. One man lost a leg and Colonel Chris Black had his arm smashed by a .5 bullet. The brigadier had the narrowest of escapes from the bomb that killed Griffin, and his face was contused and discoloured for many days afterwards.

When it was learned, during the evening, that the Japanese had refused the brigadier's request to allow Colonel Hamilton, as senior M.O., to broadcast an announcement of the hospital's location from Rangoon, and that nothing had been done about evacuating the hospital, a profound gloom settled over the camp.

Staff-Sergeant Charlie Sellers, 2/6th Engineers, had an amazing escape when he was lying on the ground a few yards from the bomb that nearly demolished the canteen. The blast picked him up bodily and hurled him many yards, but he escaped without a scratch. It was his birthday, but he was not anxious for many returns of this part of it.

For some time we feared that the peculiar shape of a crater near the canteen concealed a time bomb, but the fears proved groundless. Most of the craters were between twenty and forty feet in diameter, the bombs being chiefly 500-pounders. As I was inspecting the craters, I met "Slug" Wright. He shook his head dolefully over his experiences during the raid. He said, "I ran to one trench an' it was filled, so I ran on to the next but a guy just beat me to the last place. So I said, 'Won't one of you guys make room for a feller that's reelly scairt?'" On such occasions a man with the sense of humour of Slug is worth all the sermons in the world.

That night, as the shadows deepened and darkness came stealing across the camp, we again stood in a great square, four deep, around the cemetery while our dead were conveyed to their last resting-place. Looking at the long lines of emaciated, disease-ravaged men, standing at attention in their pitiful rags against the sombre background of a lowering sky, you felt that here was being enacted one of war's grimmest tragedies.

It was not surprising that, next day, most of us tended to start at any sounds which suggested the drone of planes. Padre Vergeest was conducting a service for his flock when, groping for a word, he turned his eyes skywards seeking inspiration. Immediately the whole congregation turned their heads in the same direction to scan the horizon for approaching planes.

At last darkness descended, but not before doctors, orderlies, patients and camp workers alike had realized that our nerves were not by any means normal. One M.O. said: "The raids are doing more damage to some of the patients than months without drugs."

Finally, on the morning of the seventeenth, it was announced that the camp was to be evacuated, and the patients moved away from the Thanbyuzayat military objectives. However, the Japanese refused absolutely to provide trucks or railway accommodation to move the patients. With the exception of about fifty men who could not stir from their beds, and who were not moved until a couple of days later, every man, regardless of his condition, was told to gather up his gear and prepare to march out into the jungle. The Japanese would not even give us transport for our heavy baggage. They expected the 3000 patients to carry all their worldly possessions with them.

During the morning each officer among the patients was given command of fifty men. After a scratch meal, one batch after another, we set off. With typical callousness, the Japanese called a halt for a grand tanko which held the men in the main street of the village for a full hour. My men were halted and forced to remain at the level crossing, which was the target *de luxe* of the area, from half past two onwards, the very hour when the Allied bombers usually left their visiting cards. Finally, we were allowed to proceed, and it was with immense thankfulness that we reached the outskirts of the town.

The next hours probably helped to kill more men than the bombs. The majority of the men had not walked more than a few hundred yards for months. Many had scarcely left their beds. Now they were asked to carry not only themselves but all their bedding, kit and mess gear out into the jungle. It was a gigantic Via Dolorosa of the halt, the lame and the blind, more tragic in many ways than the swift deaths of the men killed by the bombs.

Here was an R.A.A.F. boy—one of the squadron bombed out of Khota Baru, out of Sembawang, out of Palembang, and finally captured on Java when the squadron had no planes left to fight—his legs bandaged from ankle to thigh to conceal the suppurating ulcers; here, a scarecrow in rags, one of the 2/29th who wrote Australia into the history of Malaya at Muar; a tall Yank from Texas, almost stone-blind with beri-beri; a Glasgow boy from the Royal Navy, hobbling along, his feet covered with hideous sores caused by avitaminosis; a well known Sydney athlete lurching helplessly from side to side of the road, dizzy with a raging fever; here were others of all nations, mere derelicts of the men they had been only a year before, burnt out by months of ceaseless toil under a sun which knew no mercy. These men were enduring the tortures of the damned for no failing of their own; they were paying the price for the blindness, complacency and unpreparedness with which the democracies had entered the war.

We all found that we were astoundingly weak, and that we had overrated our ability to carry heavy packs for any distance. As we swayed wearily from one side of the road to the other, a group of *Perth* boys, who had been with me at Serang, came level with me: "You'll have to put this in your book, Mr Rivett," they said. "The folks at home'll never believe it." "No, I don't believe they will," I said. "Anyhow," persisted one, "you've got to write it. Everybody's counting on you to tell our story." "If we get out alive it'll be done," I promised.

About six kilometres up the road, at the 4-kilo camp, long since abandoned by prisoners, many of the men were able to find shelter. Here the Thanbyuzayat administration remained. The rest of us were told we had to go on to the 8-kilo camp, another six kilometres by road. The men started staggering and dropping out at intervals all along the route. Those who died as a result of this grim trek from Thanbyuzayat, including my batman and friend, Driver Jack Wilson, 2/3rd M.T., were killed by Nagatomo and his officers as surely as the men they executed in the cemetery.

It was nearly dark when we finally staggered into the 8-kilo, only to discover that it was the mere shell and skeleton of a camp. The rains, the winds, and acquisitive natives had torn the attap from all but one of the huts, so that only a framework of bamboo supports remained. The huts were overgrown with weeds, and the whole camp area had already been invaded by the jungle at that breath-taking rate familiar to all who know the tropical jungle.

It was in this "camp" that nearly a thousand men, all suffering from disease or tropical ulcers, were called on to spend two weeks at the height of the rainy season. Most of us were too tired to worry much about the rain on that first night. We erected what shelter we could with odd branches and pieces of attap and then lay down on top of our gear. It rained, now heavily, now lightly, throughout the night, and in the morning I awoke to find myself lying in a pool of water. Most of my neighbours were in a similar plight, but when the sun came up we dried off quickly enough.

The first thing I saw, on staggering into the camp on the first evening, was Charlie Sellers, still resilient after the bombing and the march, organizing the serving of a few spoonfuls of rice to his exhausted fellows. This was the sort of thing that inspired you to carry on when you felt most like throwing in the towel. I prised out of my kit a rusty tin of milk which I had been carrying as iron ration since leaving Batavia, and three of us sat down there and then and demolished it with a spoon. It was ages since we had tasted anything so good.

In the morning the officers were called together by Major Colin Cameron, 2/4th M.G., and we took stock of our exceedingly unpleasant position. There were a thousand things to be done immediately and not a fit man in the camp to do any of them. For the first twenty-four hours we lacked even an M.O., and had only one small box of medical kit. All officers in the camp were patients themselves. The organization of that camp in succeeding days was a personal triumph for Major Cameron and everybody who lent a hand. Wigwams and humpies sprang up all over the camp area. Within forty-eight hours a band of hard-working cooks started to produce meals better than those at Thanbyuzayat. I got a group of volunteers to help in coping with the problem of trenches for latrines. At the end of a week, without any help from outside, we were all sleeping dry and eating as well as we had ever done in Burma.

The Japanese guards, as bombhappy as the sickest patient,

made us evacuate the camp area every day well before noon and remain in the jungle until late in the afternoon. As Thanbyuzayat was bombed five times in that fortnight and, since the planes always came directly over our camp, this was a welcome relief to strained nerves. But standing for hours in the jungle during the rains is scarcely to be recommended for hospital patients.

Amazingly enough, whether it was being able to wash in a swift, clear stream instead of in dirty water drawn from the Thanbyuzayat well, or whether it was working virtually naked in the rain each day digging latrines during that fortnight, I got rid of the ringworm, tinea and other skin sores that had been the bugbear of my life at Thanbyuzayat. When I left Thanbyuzayat I had over a hundred sores. After fourteen days in the jungle there were less than a dozen still producing pus. I hand this over to the research workers in tropical diseases. But if the rains were partly responsible for washing away the infection, I would suggest a more pleasant cure for victims of skin diseases than standing in the jungle, naked but for a towel and a pair of clogs, while a tropical deluge soaks them for hours on end.

The situation at this camp had its amusing points. It was rather comic to see the guards abandoning camp at ten o'clock in the morning and spending the next half-hour beckoning to prisoners to depart into the jungle. I doubt if ever before in the history of prison camps, guards have had to order their prisoners out of confinement.

Some of the fitter men took full advantage of their liberty to roam for some distance on either side of the camp, seeking to obtain food from native kampongs. From the top of one ridge you could see the ocean. One day I was lying scribbling in the shade of a clump of bushes, watching a Burmese tilling his field with the habitual ox-drawn wooden plough. Presently a flight of seven Liberators roared overhead and a minute later we heard the crashing explosion of their bombs in Thanbyuzayat. The Burmese did not even pause in his labour, but went on stolidly turning up the padi field as his ancestors had done for thousands of years.

That evening some of us witnessed another remarkable exhibition of the marksmanship of our guards. A big and particularly troublesome beast had been corralled in a pen we had built, and was to provide our meat for the morrow. As we had no implements of slaughter, a guard decided that he would shoot the beast for us. He took aim carefully from just outside the fence, about three yards from the bull. The first bullet smashed the animal's horn, a second missed altogether, a third lodged in the fleshy part of his shoulder. By this time the boys were almost helpless with laughter, and the guard was beside himself with rage. Finally, at the fourth or fifth attempt, he lodged a bullet in the beast's brain and, smiling complacently, waddled off. I felt, not for the first time, that it is almost impossible to hate anything which is alternately ludicrous and pathetic.

The worst feature of the days at the 8-kilo was the drafting of parties of 100 and 200 men, all hospital patients, to go into Thanbyuzayat to repair bomb damage in the railway yards, which were hit by our planes on 21, 22, 27, 28, and 29 June. Much of the work was done at night in heavy rain and many of the men were unequal to the strain of filling bomb craters and shifting heaps of rubble, particularly in such conditions.

At this camp, Bob Skilton and Les Bullock were operating their set when a Japanese walked into the canteen where they were. Bullock was lying on his bed under the mosquito-net with the headphones on, listening to the B.B.C. He leapt up, but after speaking to the guard for a moment he saw that Bob had the situation well in hand, so calmly got back under the shelter of the net and continued to transcribe the news bulletin, not three yards from the unsuspecting guard.

After a few days, we managed to send the worst of our sick off to the 18-kilo camp. By the end of the month most men had moved on there or to Retpu at the 30-kilo mark, which was in future to be the main hospital camp, extra huts having now been got ready to accommodate us there.

Many men had to walk to the 18-kilo camp, and some had to cover the whole distance to the 30-kilo on foot, although they did not have to carry their heavy gear. Others went by truck or, less happily, along the newly laid railway which now reached the 62-kilometre mark.

I took a party of men on the rail journey, our first opportunity to taste the delights of travel on our own railroad. By the end of the trip most of us were convinced that next time we should much prefer to walk. The ballast had been laid only at intervals, and the sleepers were all over the place. The train seemed to bounce from rail to rail, and at corners there was a lurching and groaning which was ominous in the extreme. But the real fun came at the bridges, forty to sixty feet above the swollen rivers swirling through the shaky wooden piles below. At one of these, the connexion of the rails leading on to the bridge was so bad that we had to make three runs before the engine could get up and pull us across. There was much evidence of the haste and carelessness with which the buttresses and the embankments leading from the bridges had been constructed. I remember watching Peter Holden of Cairns shaking his head gloomily as we crept, with painful slowness, up a treacherous gradient with a sheer drop of a hundred feet on either side. "We'll never get there," he said with conviction. "You see, I was working on this bit of track and I know the rubbish we put into this embankment. The whole thing might crumble away at any moment."

It took us three hours of jolting, shunting and flag-waving by scores of Burmese and Malay linesmen to cover the twenty-two kilometres to Retpu. Frequently, the train had to stop while coolies with crowbars jacked up sleepers. It was rather like the nightmares a child has after his first experience on the switchback railway. We all breathed an immense sigh of relief when we clambered off the piles of road metal and iron spikes on which we had sat during the journey. As someone had remarked cheeringly, they would have made pleasant associates if our truck had been derailed and we had rolled down the banks.

As one with a wide experience of Japanese P.O.W. transport by boat, rail and road, I must record the opinion that Mr Thomas Cook would scarcely be enthusiastic about any of them.

CHAPTER XXIII

PRISON CAMP PERSONALITIES

Good company and good discourse are the very sinews of virtue.

—Izaak Walton

"Tell that Dutchman," said Galloway, "that I won't warn him again. Cooking between huts is forbidden, and he's not going to get away with it alongside this hut." Sergeant Charlie Roots, of Albert Park, went out and told the Dutchman that he would have to move. But the Hollander had his tins of sambal boiling and his rice frying, so he just pretended he didn't understand English and went on stoking his fire while the smoke blew into the Australian hospital hut. Finally, Galloway sat up on his bed, drew on his boots, put the old slouch hat firmly on his head and marched heavily out of the hut and across to the fire. Once more he repeated his request. The Dutchman was contemptuously indifferent. Galloway drew back his foot and with one mighty kick dispersed fire, frying-pan, pots and sambal in all directions. Then, ignoring the Dutchman who was gibbering with rage, he stalked ponderously back into the hut.

Galloway Stewart, Light Horseman in the last war, decided that he could not stay at home in this one, although his heart should have debarred him from any kind of service. He finished up as a lieutenant in the Ammunition Sub-park. In training, he mounted a motor-bicycle, for the first time, to do a test ride down a cliff. Galloway would not admit that he could not stop the machine and his first ride ended only when both machine and rider were immersed in the sea.

Galloway strained his heart badly soon after reaching Burma and consequently spent most of his time in hospital. One of those fiercely patriotic Scots, always ready to brandish

the claymore, Galloway unconsciously preached many an eloquent lay sermon by the way in which he stood up to the
ordeals and illness of his P.O.W. days. His resounding voice
and the deep hoot of his laughter became familiar to all. His
sincerity and constant big-heartedness to others gave him far-
reaching influence over many of his fellow patients.

Other veterans of two wars among the officers in Burma
included Major Colin Cameron of Western Australia, who
went overseas as a boy of sixteen with the Light Horse and
who still retains a boyish smile and the cavalryman's rolling
swagger; Captain Bob (Poppa) Grabham, Quartermaster of
the 2/3rd M.G., who has packed a multitude of adventures in
many lands into his fifty years; Lieutenant Peter Rossiter who
did some admirable sketches of P.O.W. life and was one of
the concert party stalwarts; and, of course, the senior Allied
officer along the railway, Brigadier A. L. Varley, whose son
Jack added lustre to the family's military reputation by winning the M.C. in Malaya. The Brigadier was one of those lost
in 1944 en route to Japan.

The 2/3rd M.T. had a large quota of last war veterans who
had set their ages back five or ten years in order to serve again.
Sergeant Jim Emslie had the unenviable distinction of
spending two and a half years in German prison camps in
the last war, and so was the doyen of us all in P.O.W. experience. With Lieutenant Wally Summons, of the 2/2nd
Pioneers, who was captured by the French in the Syrian campaign, Jim held the right to call himself "P.O.W. and Bar".

Driver H. S. (Alec) Alexander, from Maryborough, Queensland, went out to work on the line day after day during our
first months of captivity. Although well into his fifties, he
stood up to the gruelling heat better than many men thirty
years his junior. An enthusiastic organizer of talks, Alec was
always on the go, even when the doctors told him he was
not to attempt further work on the railway.

Driver Peter Holden, who is as well known along the Barrier Reef as Magnetic Island, used to hold audiences spell-
bound with his anecdotes. The way Peter survived a fearsome
attack of dysentery at Thanbyuzayat, when he shrank to a

mere ghost, surprised everyone including Peter himself. It was one more case where the strength of the spirit pulled the body through.

Some of the characters best known along the line owed their celebrity rather to their idiosyncrasies than to anything else. We all became familiar with the "thousand-a-year" man who had had good jobs galore. Quite apart from the more gifted devotees of Ananias, there was no doubt that many men tried to compensate for the wretchedness of the present by exaggerating the comforts and luxuries which they had enjoyed in the past.

Then there was the large school of "Get-rich-quick-Wallingfords" who each month embraced with enthusiasm a fresh project for gaining riches. No castles in Spain were more splendid than the duck farms, pig yards and chicken runs, planned to bring their owners four-figure incomes within the first two years. One officer, who listened patiently all day to a series of these gold-spinning schemes, returned to his hut one night and announced wearily that he had a plan which was unique in the camp. He proposed to go back to the job he had left!

The Japanese had no hope of breaking the spirit of the Australians. The grimmer things became in the present, the more eagerly they reminisced about the past or conned the possibilities of the future. They delighted in mocking the wretchedness of their quarters, the tatters in which they stood and the miserable food they ate. One morning, up in the jungle, when we had been living for weeks on boiled rice and pepper water, I heard a man rouse his mate for breakfast as follows: "Come on, Bill. The eggs are done to a turn, and the steak will be overdone if you don't show a leg. Cream in your coffee?" I regret to say the reply was unprintable.

A number of those who played a notable role in camps I was in, particularly C.Os and adjutants, have appeared at various stages in this story. Many of those who were most popular with their immediate circle were unobtrusive men, little known to the majority. Others, known to many, had few real friends and intimates.

Prison Camp Personalities

All the professions had representatives in the Burma camps. I have spoken of the M.Os in another chapter. It would be difficult to magnify the importance of each doctor or the trust vested in him by hundreds of men suffering from diseases and complaints, which had been little more to them than names in books. Each doctor came under a more testing scrutiny by his fellow captives than he would ever have met in the exercise of his profession at home. It spoke volumes for the Australian M.Os in Burma that they measured up to the occasion.

Our main political figure was Lieutenant Hamilton Lamb, Victorian M.L.A., who died in a camp on the Burma-Siam border at the end of 1943.

The Bar had several notable representatives including Lieutenant Jim Lalor, from Perth. No respecter of rank or person, Jim was a fiery champion of difficult causes in the true Irish tradition. Possessed of tremendous ability and drive, Jim was probably "agin-the-government" in the cradle, and he will be very unhappy if he is not still fighting the cause of some victim of injustice when he reaches the other end of the journey. Lieutenant Des Macawley, of the Brisbane Bar, was our classical pundit, always ready with quotations ranging from Homer to Chesterton. His stories of the Bar and Irish anecdotes helped to pass many a weary hour.

Representative of the other (and better) bar was Lieutenant Bill MacFarlane of the Fawkner Club Hotel, Melbourne. Always doing a fine job despite ill-health, Bill was immensely popular, but possibly even he did not realize how many friends he had until he got back to a Melbourne experiencing a beer shortage.

In addition to Chaplain Keith Mathieson, the Church was ably represented by Padre Bashford, of the 2/4th C.C.S., who did a particularly fine job in the notorious Death House, where dysentery patients at Thanbyuzayat were confined in the early days; Padre Smith who, when cholera came to his camp, persisted in visiting the stricken despite Japanese threats against his person and his life; Padre Corry who, despite much sickness himself, served unwearyingly; Padre Kellow, of the

2/2nd Pioneers, always active in organizing sports, libraries
and other facilities; and Padre Cunningham who spoke the
broadest Scots ever heard in the Australian lines.

Particularly well known in the hospital camps were Lloyd
Willey, U.S. Marines, and Jimmy Whittaker, a Manchester
boy from one of the British 18th Division units. They made
themselves responsible for the issue of all canteen supplies to
the sick. From early in the morning until after dark, they were
always on the job looking after men too sick to be able to get
food for themselves.

Another American, J. B. Cole III, acquired fame or perhaps, more accurately, notoriety by his efforts as camp bugler.
A "swing" maniac, J.B. "hotted up" many of the military calls
until they were almost unrecognizable.

A number of characters in the jungle hospitals always carried with them a tremendous enthusiasm for their own
particular hobby or vocation. But no man ever talked, dreamed
and lived cattle so fervently as "Sack" Watts who, with his
six brothers, owns a large slab of Queensland somewhere north
of Quilpie. Sack's father was with Kidman the Cattle King,
and Sack always managed to bring the atmosphere of the
broad plains of Queensland into even the darkest hut in the
Burma jungle.

The *Perth* boys were a happy bunch, who stuck together.
They never talked, they "nattered"; there was no such thing as
the floor or the earth, there was only "the deck"; the latrine
became "the heads"; a second helping or "back-up" became
"gash"; a soldier was a "swatty", while a sailor could only
be referred to as a "matelot". One of their number, A.B. Keith
Mills, was savagely attacked by an engineer on the railway,
because he had driven in a spike crookedly. The Jap rushed
at Mills with a crowbar, which missed, Jap and crowbar
crashing headling down the embankment. Furious at this loss
of face, the Jap went off and got hold of two bullies among
the guards who immediately came up to Mills and dragged
him away into the jungle, where they beat him up with rifle
butts, breaking his jaw in three places. Mills was brought
down to base in a serious condition, but his jaw was wired

up and, although he could eat nothing solid for many weeks, he eventually recovered completely, thanks to the M.Os and to the care lavished on him by his ship-mates.

Possibly it was the memory of this affair which caused another P.O.W. to put up one hand and remove his dentures just as a guard was about to bash him. The guard stared, then suddenly burst into a laugh and turned on his heel. Unfortunately there were few guards like this.

Adelaide had two representatives who were universally popular in the hospital camps. Private Jim Roberts, of the 2/3rd Machine-gunners, had a long and tough row to hoe with dysentery and malaria right through the piece. A true Australian, with six brothers and sisters in the services, Jim's charm and quiet, unassuming manner made him friends by the score. The sympathy of all his comrades goes out to him in his tragic loss of his young wife on the very day after he had at last reached home again.

Sergeant Murray Knight of the Ammunition Sub-park had more wisecracks than Groucho Marx. His picturesque similes were all comic, pungent and—alas!—unprintable. When you sat down with Murray at a bridge game, with Jim Emslie and his dry Scottish humour, and Charlie Sellers, who was made for laughter, horrible things were done to Culbertson, but you usually laughed until your eyes ran.

Five of the finest N.C.Os lie buried today along the railway. But they will live in the memories of hundreds of their comrades.

Sergeant Frank Knight, young Melbourne engineer, had a keen, probing intelligence and a personality which assured him a brilliant future. Chronic malaria and a shocking ulcer attacked him and, despite his courage, he died in November 1943 at the 55-kilo.

Star N.S.W. Rugby League footballer, Sergeant Jack Lennox, was a popular lecturer in the camps, thanks to his wide knowledge of leading personalities in all branches of sport. He was one of our select circle who used to sit out in the moonlight, between the huts at Thanbyuzayat, preferring sleeplessness to the millions of ravening bugs which made our nights a misery.

Grand Executioner of cattle at Thanbyuzayat was "Pop" Dearden, another last war veteran from Goondiwindi, Queensland. Pop did a grand job for his sick mates and, when stricken with dysentery himself in Siam, fought on with a courage beyond praise, long after it was clear that we had no hope of saving him. Widely beloved, "Pop" was of the best that the Australian bush produces.

Sergeant Bob Jamieson won the M.M. with the 2/6th Engineers in Syria; but he was a sick man when brought up to work on the Burma railway. Through a long and bitter twelve months he fought to hold his own against the rapid encroachment of the disease which our doctors lacked all facilities for fighting. Bob was so fine a boy that a number of us did our utmost to ensure that he should always have everything in the way of food and canteen goods available, no matter who did without. Yet the end was inevitable and, as we watched him grow weaker and thinner month by month, we all knew that it was wrong to hope the end would be long delayed. Bob died at the 55-kilo camp in November 1943.

Bob was nursed with the greatest devotion by his mate, Staff-Sergeant Charlie Sellers, a last war veteran who was quartermaster to the 2/6th Engineers. A *Sydney Morning Herald* man, Charlie, never strong himself, was the friend, nurse and general factotum for scores of his sick mates in the hospitals along the line. Never sparing himself, he was a bad patient in that he could never rest on his bed when he felt that other men, sicker than he, were in need of something. Charlie came through the ordeal in the jungle and, at Tamarkan, seemed better than he had been for years. But in January 1945 cerebral malaria attacked him suddenly and he died within forty-eight hours. His passing was a heavy blow to all the men of the prison camps who knew and loved him. One of those loveable personalities who leave warmth and comfort wherever they go, he made one proud to be a newspaper man and prouder still to be his friend.

My boon companions in many adventures were Flying-

Officer Don Capron, who spent his time before the war photographing large numbers of the population of Victoria and New South Wales in all stages from nappies to nonagenarianism, and his 1 Squadron fellow-pilot Alex Dobbie, agent for a Victorian woollen mill. "Dobb" put his foot through the bed platform in every camp we were in from Moulmein to Bangkok. Like "Cappy," he showed the same distressing lack of appreciation of my singing as I have always found among my relatives and friends. Cappy, indeed, was occasionally roused to violence, but Dobb usually played the trump card by threatening to retaliate in kind. The three of us shared many things from slit-trenches, during some most unpleasant air raids, to fillets of fried python and Thai "wine"—about 90 per cent alcohol!

Few officers did a better job all along the line than Lieutenant Harry Farmer, of the Bank of New South Wales. On the long, dusty rides up and down between Thanbyuzayat and the jungle camps, we discovered a common devotion to cricket and, in recalling the glories of past afternoons at the Sydney Cricket Ground and the M.C.G., we forgot the sweltering heat, the choking dust and even the sentry squatting grimly behind us. Both before and during captivity, Harry Farmer proved himself the best type of officer that the A.I.F. produces.

A junior officer who did a particularly fine job in charge of a large force near Aperon in the Burma jungle in 1944, was Captain Osma "I-want-to-go-to-Addis-Ababa" Blau, who cherished the unique ambition of carrying on his engineering vocation in Abyssinia, after release. I doubt whether even Coleridge's maid with her dulcimer will be sufficient to draw "Ossie" to Abyssinia after three years in the jungles.

Lieutenant-Colonel John Williams, of the 2/2nd Pioneers, had the honour of being regarded by the Japanese as No. 1 bad man in the prison camps. He defied them with sterling courage time after time and, despite many brutal attacks, never faltered in his opposition to the persecution of his men. No one could have fought more determinedly or revealed a greater contempt for the physical consequences.

Three stories of Colonel Williams suggest something of the man. On one occasion the Japanese told him he must forbid the buying of fruit from natives, of which the camp rubbish-heap afforded evidence. The colonel said to his troops: "You are not allowed to buy fruit, so for God's sake see that after you've eaten it you bury the skins." On another occasion a Japanese lost his cap. The colonel said to his parade that some-one was apparently hunting souvenirs a little prematurely. A day would come. . . . When a Williamsforce officer was beaten up, on the railway, a nasty incident seemed likely to develop. Colonel Williams told the Japanese commander that if there were any more similar brutalities there would be bloodshed on the line, and the blood would not be all P.O.W.

CHAPTER XXIV

NAITO AND THE REIGN OF TERROR

Tyrants seldom want pretexts.
—EDMUND BURKE

IT was at Retpu during July and the first half of August 1943
that Lieutenant Naito converted the main P.O.W. hospital
in Burma into the ramping-ground of a dipsomaniac with a
sadistic lust to kill.

The prisoners in Burma had already seen more than enough
of Naito when drunk. At the end of April he had crowned
a series of outrages at Colonel Anderson's camp by jailing the
colonel and alleging that Captain Drower, the British interpreter, had smallpox. By Naito's order, Drower was placed in
a hut occupied by a smallpox case, and all his clothes were
burnt. He was then sent down to base and isolated with infected
personnel.

Later Naito held a ceremonial parade of Williamsforce and
Andersonforce while he swaggered round uttering mortal
threats against anybody who disobeyed his orders. A train
arrived and a chair was placed, in state, on one of the trucks.
Naito made elaborate arrangements for everybody to stand
stiffly at attention, saluting him as he departed. But as the
train started he forgot his majestic pose and proceeded to wave
frantically from the moving car and to force Colonel Anderson, who was with him, to wave too, rather like Sunday school
children waving from a charabanc en route to a picnic.

With a tremendous capacity for putting away liquor, he
could still walk about when most men would have been out to
it. It was his custom to wander round the prisoners' lines,
trying to catch some unwary prisoner who failed to recognize

and salute him. Fearful bashings, which apparently satisfied his drunken ego, followed. The new hospital camp at Retpu was now placed under this individual.

Naito was an interesting study in the more educated type of Japanese. When completely sober, he was an extremely efficient officer, and senior P.O.W. officers found him more reasonable to deal with than most Japanese. He had a veneer of the Western gentleman, but this disappeared under the influence of drink, and the primitive barbarian emerged. He was a fascinating psychological study because, when sober, he was like any Japanese whom you meet in one of our own cities.

For the first three weeks we had no serious trouble with Naito, who vented most of his brutality, when drunk, on his own terrified guards. One night an Australian P.O.W. found him standing near the bamboo urinal at the top of the camp, moodily staring at the moon. This was on the eve of Italy's collapse and Mussolini's overthrow. Naito volunteered the information that Italy was finished, Germany was losing the war and that Japan would soon have to fight the world alone. None of us had ever heard anything like this from the lips of a Japanese before. It did illustrate the difference in outlook between the former staff-officer, with a knowledge of the falsity of his High Command's communiqués, and the credulity of the average soldier.

Whether it was the bad news from Europe, or merely a new "high" in his craving for alcohol, Naito now entered upon a terrific drinking bout which lasted with scarcely an intermission for several weeks. He used to bring large, square quart bottles of Burmese brandy back with him every time he returned to the camp, and other liquor was brought to him from the neighbouring kampongs. Colonel Black who, as camp commander at Retpu, had to see him every day, never knew whether he was about to face the Jekyll that was Naito sober, or the Hyde that was Naito drunk. Fortunately for the camp, the colonel's relations with Naito were quite good, and he handled him very cleverly. At this stage, the colonel's arm, which had been smashed by a bullet in the bombing at Thanbyuzayat, was in a bad state. One day, Naito, in a maudlin state of alarm, cautioned Major Alan Hobbs, who was looking after the arm, that he would be shot if the colonel died.

Now Naito began to conduct tours of inspection through the camp, during which many men were brutally kicked and beaten up. Under Naito's instructions, the guards were more than ordinarily cruel, fearing the consequences to themselves if the drunkard was not satisfied with the punishment meted out.

A series of searches of huts was instituted, and several tanko parades. Whereas, when sober, Naito had some appreciation of the way in which hospital patients should be treated, when drunk he was the Japanese bully *par excellence*.

He now started to roam around the camp with his pistol drawn, after lights out, apparently under the illusion that prisoners might attempt to escape. One night, as he was walking between huts, yelling out in a drunken fashion, one incautious Australian, sick of the persecution, cried out, "Aw, shut up! You silly b———." Quick as a flash, Naito came running round into the hut and flashed his torch along the bunks, demanding who had called out. No one stirred. Then, furious with rage, he ordered everybody in the lower bunks outside. No one in the upper bunks moved. When the sleepy men were lined up stiffly at attention while he brandished his revolver under their noses, he ordered them all back inside and told the occupants of the upper bunks to parade. Then, without further investigation, he marched the whole lot down to the guard-house, and handed them over to his guards for "discipline".

The only redeeming feature in the situation, which became aggravated from day to day, arose from the fact that the guards feared and hated Naito even more than did the prisoners.

Naito had a love for midnight parades and drills. At Thanbyuzayat he had roused the brigadier from his bed, made him watch an exhibition of bayonet drill by guards, and had then conducted a formal inspection of the whole camp at two o'clock in the morning, although he was far too intoxicated to know what he was looking at. Now, at Retpu, he turned his guards out in the middle of the night so that our sleep was shattered with the blood-curdling yells which Japanese find it necessary to utter whenever they are drilling with bayonets.

The climax came one night when Sergeant-Major Jack Coombes, a Tasmanian member of the 2/4th C.C.S., and R.S.M. of the hospital, was suddenly pounced on by Naito when on his way to the urinal. Naito told Coombes that he was attempting to escape, and marched him off to the guard-house, where he kept him covered with his revolver while the guards kicked and beat him as he knelt on the floor. Naito enjoyed this spectacle for a long time until Coombes was nearly mad with pain. Then he ordered him to his feet. Accompanied by a guard, with rifle loaded and bayonet fixed, Naito marched his victim across the camp until he reached the path which led to the cemetery. As they started to move away from the camp, along this path, Coombes realized that he was going to be murdered. At that moment Naito spoke to the guard and a second later the latter tripped Coombes. As Coombes fell, Naito fired at him. Coombes rolled over and Naito fired again from a distance of less than five yards. The first shot missed, and the second only cut across Coombes's back. He leaped to his feet and raced back to the main hospital hut, yelling, "Major Fisher, Major Hobbs, the bastards have shot me!" The whole camp was aroused by the shots and the yell.

In the hospital they seized Coombes quickly, put a bandage against his back and hustled him into bed. A minute later a guard arrived and asked if Coombes had run into the hospital. The orderlies denied all knowledge of his whereabouts. There is little doubt that the guards knew exactly where he was, but they were not prepared to assist Naito in a drunken murder. We have never discovered whether the guard tripped Coombes in obedience to Naito's order, or in the hope of giving him a chance to escape before Naito shot him in the back.

At any rate, after an anxious night, dawn finally arrived and Colonel Black went up to see Naito and to protest. Naito, a little sobered, claimed that Coombes had been attempting to escape, although it was obvious that he did not believe this for a moment. For a long time he persisted in maintaining that Coombes must be shot. Then, brandishing his revolver, he walked down to the hospital and standing over Coombes's bed with the revolver covering him, asked Coombes if he had any idea who had shot him. Coombes wisely said "No" and Naito muttered darkly that he had better not think of any other answer. Then he told Colonel Black that he would shoot him if any report of the incident was sent down to Colonel Nagatomo at base.

It would be difficult to exaggerate the state of nervous tension produced in the hospital huts among the helpless men who now feared that they might be murdered at any moment by a drunken lunatic.

Major Edward Fisher, as C.O. of the hospital, issued a strict order that in the prevailing situation no man was to go to the latrines after lights out. With dozens of men suffering from dysentery and chronic diarrhoea, this meant that the huts themselves were fouled, but, in spite of protests, the Major held to his order, maintaining, as was certainly true, that Naito was quite capable of shooting out of hand anyone found outside his hut.

This state of affairs continued for several days, a number of guards and prisoners receiving brutal bashings from the camp commander, who wandered through the lines day and night brandishing his revolver and obviously itching for a pretext to put lead into somebody.

Then Naito went down to base. Horowishi, a Christian guard noted for his decent attitude to the prisoners, told Colonel Black that if Naito bashed him again he would leave the camp. By this time the nerves of the guards were worn as thin as those of any prisoner. An old Digger from the last war stated publicly that he was prepared to throw Naito down the camp well, and that he felt reasonably sure that the guards would back up the story that Naito had fallen down.

This was the state of affairs when Naito returned, having emptied two quart bottles of whisky on the journey up from Thanbyuzayat. Next day he held a special tanko. All men who could move were lined up outside the hut, while the very ill remained on their beds. Captain Gordon Fraser, our hut commander, said that the few officers in the hut might as well remain inside. I went on reading as I lay full length on my bed, and Naito apparently considered this an insult, for before I knew what had happened, he strode up to me and struck me across the face. Then he ordered me outside apart from the rest of the parade. I was quite convinced that the next step would be to take me down to the guard-house for one of the Naito beatings-up, but by the time the hut count was over he had forgotten all about it, and was obsessed with the fact that there was an error of one in the hut count. He sent for Captain Fraser, who explained the simple reason why a mistake had been made in the returns.

But Naito would not listen to reason and, covering Fraser with his revolver, accused him of deliberately lying and seeking to deceive him. For about a quarter of an hour, while Naito threatened and brandished his gun, Fraser sat expecting to be shot at any moment. At last the storm of abuse died down and he was allowed to depart.

The end came a few days later. One of the drivers had already taken word of the situation down to the brigadier at base, and a strong protest had been lodged with Nagatomo. Then Horowishi was beaten up again by Naito and, in accordance with his promise, left camp. Naito proceeded on one of his bashing tours accompanied by two of the worst guards, and several men were brutally struck and kicked. Next he descended on two Dutchmen who were sitting innocently on the end of their beds, and when last seen was marching them out of the camp towards the cemetery.

Immediately the rumour raced through the camp that he was about to make another attempt at murder. However, whatever his original intention, he now developed a new whim, marching the Dutchmen out of the camp and across to a native hut beyond the railway, where he bought them biscuits and sweet cakes. Then his wrath broke suddenly on two engineers who were sitting by the edge of the railway. He was proceeding to bash them, when a truck raced up and Nagatomo leapt out. Horowishi had intercepted the group commander's truck and now the colonel caught red-handed the second-in-command he had long hated. In the space of a few seconds Naito was seized, trussed and thrown ignominiously on to the floor of the truck, which then drove off to Thanbyuzayat, and Retpu saw him no more.

That night, all the guards got drunk and ordered a special concert to celebrate the ending of the "terror".

We heard that Naito spent several weeks in a hospital, where he was denied all alcohol. We did not see him again until early in 1944, when he passed through our camp in Siam on his way back to Japan. He was then full of the charges he was going to lay against Nagatomo, and of the fate that awaited that officer. Once again, he was the cosmopolitan gentleman and offered to do anything in his power for the brigadier and Colonel Black. But if he has not drunk himself to death by this time, he would do well to keep clear of any place where he may meet any of the prisoners who were at Retpu in August 1943.

CHAPTER XXV

DARK CLOUDS BUT SILVER LININGS

For while the tired waves, vainly breaking
Seem here no painful inch to gain,
Far back, through creeks and inlets making,
Comes silent, flooding in, the main.

—A. H. CLOUGH

WITH the coming of the rains and the bombing-out of Than-byuzayat, we entered upon a grim and dark period all along the line, for it was at this stage, with rations failing and the health of all prisoners visibly deteriorating each week, that the Japanese instituted the "hurry-hurry" policy, or "speedo". They had decided that the railway was to be finished by 15 August, regardless of the cost in human lives.

Thousands of Asiatics, mainly Tamils from Malaya, were lured up to the line with promises of high wages. Thousands of others were seized and used as conscripted labour, being guarded in concentration camps. The Japanese paper *Greater Asia*, published in English in Rangoon, carried glowing accounts of the privilege of working for Nippon's victory in "the Burma sweat army" whose workers were christened "Heighos" after the song from Disney's film. In fact, the Heighos, instead of being a gallant volunteer force working enthusiastically for the liberation of Asia from the hated white man, were a miserable horde of enslaved workers, systematically starved, who longed only for escape.

It was at this period that cholera swept through their camps, carrying off thousands of starving men each month. British medical officers attached to Tamil camps in Siam are convinced that at least 100,000 and probably as many as 250,000 of these unfortunate people perished along the railway. They tasted to the full the benefits of Japan's "Asia for the Asiatics" policy, getting five feet of Asia apiece. Many of them did not even receive this allowance, because the Japanese had them buried seven to a grave to conceal the full number of deaths.

The Asiatic, under sickness and oppression, tends to abandon the struggle for life far more quickly than his white brother. As thousands of men became too weak to work, the Japanese adopted increasingly barbarous methods to squeeze the last ounce from their dwindling gangs. Tamils too sick to work were driven up into the branches of trees where they had to remain, foodless and waterless, until they crashed to the ground through weakness. Others were tied up and systematically beaten, tortured with wire and fire, and exposed to every devilry that the ingenuity of the Japanese mind can invent.

The Japanese may have believed that the tale of this mass annihilation might remain hidden in the depths of the jungle. It is more probable that in their arrogance and certainty of continuous victory they cared nothing for the opinion of the peoples whose lands they had overrun.

In the P.O.W. camps the "speedo" period saw men working from dawn right through the day and on until the small hours of the following morning, sometimes doing this day after day, for weeks on end. In many camps it became the regular thing for the shifts to last sixteen, twenty, twenty-four and even, on one occasion, thirty-six hours.

While people at home complained of the hardships of rationing, and of the way in which some things had become unprocurable, their fellow countrymen were toiling day and night in the mud and incessant soaking rain in the Burma-Siamese jungles. Even strong men began to crack up under the strain. Undernourished, with every scratch and bite festering into spreading ulcers, the men began to sicken and die at double and treble the rate of the earlier months.

Of the Burma forces, those who suffered worst during this period were the men of No. 5 Group, under the tyranny of Captain Mizdani, and the mobile camps of our own group, drawn from Williamsforce and Andersonforce. Captain Mizdani refused to allow the sick men of his group to send a letter-card home when the rest of us did so. Our mobile camp workers were moved every week or fortnight, and never had a chance to build any comforts or conveniences, or to make their huts even moderately weatherproof before being moved on as ballast; sleepers and rail were extended and the track reached towards the border.

On 20 July there came into the hospital camp at Retpu 120 sick men from the mobile force. Accustomed as we were to seeing worn-out men brought into the hospital, none of us had ever seen anything like this before. Many of the men were from the 2/2nd Pioneers, and *Perth*, and I had not seen them since Moulmein jail. A number, whom I had known well, were totally unrecognizable. "Slim" Hedderick and Alf Thomas, of *Perth*, were cadaverous wrecks of their former selves. Other men had their faces so swollen by beri-beri that the features were like some cartoonist's nightmare. Many of the men had not only dysentery or chronic malaria, but tremendous ulcers on their legs as well. Naito was sober this day and his eyes filled with tears as he gazed at this human flotsam.

Fortunately, on this day we had received some eggs in our canteen and within a couple of hours after their arrival dozens of men had spent their own meagre supply of rupees to get eggs for their mates. Major Fisher who, as senior M.O., inspected these men as they were laid out on the parade ground, returned to his quarters looking years older. No one in the camp was surprised when more than twenty of them died within the first few weeks. They had been beyond saving when they arrived. The amazing thing was that some, who seemed too weak and emaciated to have any chance of life, fought back with tremendous courage and determination and, despite the poverty of food, gradually began to win back something of their former strength and appearance.

Conditions at Retpu were dishearteningly bad for a hospital camp. Many of the huts were old, and the roofs broke out constantly in new leaks under the battering of the rains. Rations were inadequate, and canteen supplies much fewer than at Thanbyuzayat.

The camp had two redeeming features. It was surrounded

on two sides by a stream of fast-flowing water and excellent bathing pools, and the prisoners were allowed to spend the afternoons in the jungle around the huts. For sick men, whose nerves were in an abnormal condition after the bombing ordeals at Thanbyuzayat, this freedom brought great relief.

Humpies sprang up under the spreading trees and amidst the bamboo clumps which fringed the stream, and some of the pleasantest hours for the sick in these years of captivity were passed in playing cards, reading, talking, or just lying quietly on a bed of grass or pine-needles through the afternoons at Retpu.

The jungle itself always had something new to offer to those who were prepared to use their eyes. The butterflies, the winged beetles, the parti-coloured spiders, the millipedes and the fascinating activity of the teeming millions of the ant world taught many a city boy lessons about nature. After the sorry business of bathing in a couple of pints of dirty water carried from the well in a hollow bamboo, it was a sheer delight to have a pool of fast-flowing water in which one could swim for thirty or forty yards. A number of small, brown fish, rather like baby trout, played in the shallows of this stream, and meat-hungry men used to sit for hours on the banks with a bamboo rod, a piece of string and a bent pin, trying to lure the fish to bite.

One day a Dutchman brought in from the jungle a branch on which two Emperor moths were mating. The female moth had wings eight inches in length and five inches wide, while the male was about half this size. The wings of both were shot with the richest and most beautiful colours in a pattern similar to the eyes on a peacock's tail. With the Emperor moth, the male dies after mating, and is then devoured by its mate.

Some of the men, disregarding threats of shooting, went far beyond the 500-metre limit permitted to prisoners, and bought meat and sometimes fowls from natives. We met a former Burmese civil servant from Moulmein who spoke English fluently. He told us that the price of all commodities was rising steeply each week, and that the Japanese were levying "squeeze" on every load of rice carried along the road. He said that, in spite of Japanese promises, the people of Moulmein and other towns were unable to obtain lungyis or cloth in any form. He added, "under the British, the padi farmer could buy a parang for 25 cents. Today the price is 20 rupees, and you just can't buy them. Most of the natives have stopped accepting or using the Japanese currency, and among themselves rely entirely on barter."

It was rumoured that many Burmese villages were in open revolt against the Japs. One of our guards was brought into Retpu on a stretcher, with his head cut open by a parang. Next day seventeen Burmese were brought to the guard-house, their wrists cruelly bound with wire, which was tightened periodically with tweezers. We believe they were all shot next day. A guard said that one of them had attacked the Jap because he was drunkenly interfering with the Burman's wife.

It was at this time that a gallant attempt to escape was made by a party of fourteen, including a colonel, from one of the worst Thailand camps just across the border. The party was led through the jungle and eventually down to the coast by a native elephant boy who had been misused by the Japanese. Several of the party fell out during the march, but the survivors managed to obtain a boat and set out towards India. They were a long distance out into the ocean when they were spotted by a Japanese reconnaissance plane and picked up a few hours later by a patrol boat.

They were seen by some of our men on their way back to their camp, where it was said they were to be shot. The elephant boy was tied up in front of the Japanese guard-house and struck by each guard every time one of them came or went. I believe the prisoners were all beaten and tortured, but we do not know their ultimate fate.

It was now that the working camps learned of the death, at Aungganaung, of Captain Ray Watts, M.C. In charge of the "buppin", or works department in Blackforce camps, he toiled unsparingly with his men, and eventually died from dysentery. A Sydney architect, awarded the M.C. in Syria for his work with the 2/6th Engineers, Ray was universally admired, and his death cast a gloom throughout the camps.

By this time we were convinced that the Japanese would

never learn that mere numbers of men was not the solution to getting a job done. One day at Retpu they needed long bamboos from the jungle for new building. All fit camp workers were already occupied, so about seventy of the "light" sick were paraded, and handed over to me with orders that I should bring bamboo from the jungle. The only tools with which we could be equipped were two parangs, one hatchet and a length of rope. Fortunately, two or three members of the party had heavy knives, or hatchets, hidden among their gear. Even so, sixty men were left sitting around in the wet jungle, while those with tools did their utmost to separate as many sticks as possible from the thick, awkward bamboo clumps. Finally, after four hours of this futility, we returned to camp with about sixty sticks. Twenty men with tools could have got twice as much in a quarter of the time, but the Japanese preferred to force a crowd of useless, sick men out into the jungle.

In the middle of August, Heguchi, who acted as Japanese doctor, inspected the Retpu patients. Most men, he said, were to be sent back to the working camps, while a handful of the very sickest would be transferred to the hospital camp established in June at the 55-kilo mark. It was a typical Heguchi inspection. The whole camp was turned out on the parade ground, and men walked up to his table. He never removed their bandages, took a temperature or felt a pulse. Sometimes he did not even bother to look at them before marking them as fit to go back to the working camps. So, at the beginning of September, many hundreds of convalescent men, including some who were still very ill, were once again sent up-jungle.

Before we left, heartening news came via the "dicky-bird". British and American troops had at last landed on the toe of Italy and, seizing on the optimistic predictions of some commentators, we believed that another army was about to cross the Channel. It would be difficult to exaggerate the optimism, partly produced by the grimness of our fight for survival, which flooded the prison camps during these months. Rumour overthrew Mussolini many weeks before the event. Sicily was ours two months before fighting ceased. Most of us expected a drive to reopen the Burma Road, and a landing on the coast in the Moulmein-Tavoy area as soon as the rains eased. When at last Montgomery, having swept right across North Africa and overrun Sicily, landed on the Continent itself, it was difficult for men whose impatience was proportionate to the hopelessness of their plight, to believe that this was not the beginning of the end. Few imagined that two more long years would drag by before release came at last.

The news that filtered into the camps, thanks to the secret radios, was the only asset which our doctors had in the long, uphill fight to bring worn-out men back from the shadow of the grave. Rumours and distortions born of wishful optimism were often potent medicine when there was none other.

In the second half of August, the discovery of secret radio sets at Kanburi camp in Thailand led to a series of rigorous, if not very skilful, searches of all camps along the line. From this period forward our huts were searched as often as twice in a week. Fortunately for people like myself who were carrying a great deal of "contraband", there was usually at least a few minutes' warning before the Japanese were upon us.

At Retpu, I twice had narrow escapes. On one occasion, three Japanese entered the hut only a few bays from my bed, and ordered us to open up all our gear for inspection. I had a mass of papers, manuscripts and private diary, wrapped in a waterproof under my pillow. It was obviously fatal to leave it there, for their initial operations were very thorough. So I picked up the dressings tray carried by one of the orderlies, placed my papers in the middle of it and paraded solemnly down the hut, past the guards and out into the jungle which began only a few yards from the hut.

After this, I kept as many papers as possible in hollow bamboos around my bed or in tins or cloth wrappings under the ground. The trouble was that one never knew when the hut might be flooded by a cloudburst.

Ugly rumours of what had happened in Thailand, after the finding of the radios, began to trickle through, but we did not get the full story until some months later when we moved to Thailand. However, we knew enough to realize the tremendous risk being run by the men operating "dicky-birds" in the jungle camps. Hitherto the Japanese had not seemed particularly interested in papers, but after the Kanburi incident, scores of diaries were seized in all camps, and as time went on very few men still possessed written matter of any kind.

The following account of the Kanburi incident is taken from the eye witness statement of a British artillery captain acting as Japanese interpreter in the Kanburi camp:

At 8.30 a.m. we were just starting our breakfast after roll call had finished when the Japanese guards entered the huts and ordered all men out of them just as they were. They then proceeded to carry out a very thorough search of all huts. They had just finished searching the last kit when a Japanese officer who was present noticed a small piece of wire dangling from the roof. This was a lead in from the local electric light plant. The suspicions of the Japanese were aroused and they proceeded to inspect the bamboos of the hut and the ground inside the hut. Batteries were dug up and a wireless set was found in a small tin of peanuts. The whole hut was then taken apart and two more sets, one in a water-bottle and one in a coffee tin, were found. The two people at whose beds the discoveries were made—Sub-Conductor C. L. A. Thew and Artificer Sergeant Smith—were then sent for. I noticed that the reaction of the Japanese Kempis taking part in the search appeared to be quite negative at the time. It was the engineers who were running the camp who vented their wrath on these two men.

Thew and Smith were stood in the sun in front of the guard-house for the next two days. Then they were each given a very heavy sledge-hammer and made to hit a piece of metal on the ground, without stopping. When they fell down they were forced to their feet and made to continue. On the fifth day Thew was very badly beaten up, and Smith was made to stand for a further period outside the guard-room. On 22 September five more officers, now implicated in the reception and distribution of wireless news, were sent for. They were so savagely beaten up that in the morning only one of them was still standing up outside the guard-house. Another had both his arms broken.

That day, four more British officers, including the interpreter, were sent for. Here is the interpreter's account of what followed:

We arrived at 2.30 p.m. At the guard-room Major Smith was lying unconscious where he had been all night without food or medical attention. We were met by Lieutenant Komi, camp commander, accompanied by the Japanese interpreter, S. Kanematsu. Our kits were searched and then we were taken to "view" Major Smith. He was completely unrecognizable except for his Volunteer topee which was lying on the ground near by him. His face, neck and jaw bone were a mass of contusions and swellings. We were then in turn subjected to a rudimentary cross-examination by Kanematsu, who confined himself to questions of identity and the existence of the sets. After this ordeal we were stood in front of the guard-room at attention until 10 p.m., when between six and ten Japanese N.C.Os and guards (Koreans) came out from a hut and led A—— (Lieutenant, 7th Coast Regiment, R.A.) about twenty yards away in front of the guard-room. He was ordered to strip down to his shorts and to hold his arms above his head. The whole area was dark except for a dim light thrown by two hurricane lamps and a flash lamp. He was then assaulted by the whole mob of Japanese simultaneously, armed with heavy split and round bamboos. After about forty blows on the back, buttocks and thighs he was violently tripped up from the front and thrown on his back. He was then turned over and the beating continued on the ground, usually about three Japanese striking him simultaneously. He was dragged along the ground by the legs across the area which was covered with gravel. After an hour of such treatment H—— (2nd Lieutenant, R.A.S.C.) was led out, stripped and treated similarly, the punishment being accompanied by all manner of insults in English shouted by Kanematsu and Komi, who were both present during the whole proceedings and who had obviously been drinking heavily.

A—— was the first to lose consciousness, but was soon revived by kicks in the back and stomach and buckets of water, which were thrown over him. He was forced to his feet and the punishment continued. He fell down repeatedly and had to be held up by the Japanese. Finally he was beaten senseless while lying on the ground, after having been dragged about all over the place on the gravel. Simultaneously H—— was receiving the same treatment and was dragged across the area and flung into a deep anti-malarial drain with about a foot of mud in the bottom, where he was ordered with kicks and blows to get out; but by this time his legs had become paralysed from the repeated blows and he was unable to move. Finally he was dragged out and the beating continued once more. Apart from a few involuntary grunts when blows fell on his kidneys, A—— made practically no sound at all. H——'s last remarks were a wholehearted cursing of the Japanese for their bestiality.

Fellow prisoners counted more than 400 blows which resounded through the camp. Both men died during the night, and their bodies were thrown into the guard-room latrine. A Korean guard told prisoners of the bodies, and two years later, after the Japanese capitulation, his story was confirmed when the remains of the two victims were discovered. Thenceforth,

Australians on the march.

the prisoners along the railway knew just what risks they ran.

Prisoners were moved from the hospital at Retpu to the up-jungle camps in a manner typical of Nippon. Here is the account of our move, no better or worse than the way in which hundreds of other batches of prisoners were moved up and down the line at this period.

8-11 September 1943. Don Capron and I, with Murray Knight as senior N.C.O., left Retpu on the morning of the eighth, after a false start the day before. There were eighty men in the party, many of whom had been in hospital continuously for six months or more. We had to carry all our gear on our backs, but were told that we would get a train at the 40-kilo mark which would take us to the 83, and from there we would go on by truck. Unfortunately, it did not work out like that.

Don had a heavy fever on him and was in no condition to walk at all. I had all my papers and diaries and some stuff I was carrying for chaps at the 105, and was in difficulties with my kit-bag before we had gone half a mile. Unless strapped on to your shoulders, a forty-pound kit-bag is one of the awkwardest things with which you can tackle a long hike. Before we had covered half the distance, Sergeant Frank Gault (2/3rd M.T.) was betting two to one that I would never make it with the assorted clobber I was trying to carry. In addition to everything else, I had got hold of some shintagar, and was trying to carry about two pounds of liquid boiled shintagar in a long, hollow bamboo, the only container I possessed. Fortunately, the three guards with the party were reasonable enough, and somehow we all managed to stagger past the old Beke Taung camp and on to the quarry beyond, where we expected to be picked up by the train. It was here that the guards announced that we had to go on to the 45-kilo camp—a total distance by road of 18 kilometres. I don't know how Don kept going. He trudged on somehow but I don't think he knew where he was half the time. A soaking rainstorm came to add to our miseries. Murray was a tower of strength, and carried the gear of Bluey Noonan as well as his own, while cheering on the stragglers.

It was only when we reached a dry hut at the 45-kilo that Murray discovered just what a good fellow he had been. He then heard Bluey Noonan arguing with Frank Purtell, about how much Purtell owed him. It turned out that Purtell had promised Noonan a rupee if he would carry his gear for him. Murray rounded on Noonan: "Do you mean to say," he demanded, outraged, "that I've been carrying Purtell's gear so that you could earn a dollar?" "Oh no," said Bluey, "I've been carrying Purtell's gear, but you've been carrying mine!" Murray says it will take him weeks to live this down.

My heels had got two great welts which festered immediately, and for the rest of the trip every step in boots was painful. However, it was blissful that first night to get the boots off and to hobble round in clogs. Cappy, Murray, Ray Kendall and I went down to the river here which has now become a swirling torrent about eighty yards wide. You couldn't go far from the edge of the bank or the current swept you away, but after the sweat and agony of the road, diving into that stream was the most exhilarating thing that you could ask for. Next morning we limped painfully and stiffly across to the siding, and after sitting in cattle trucks for three hours, an engine arrived and we went on to the siding at the 62-kilo mark. We lay there in a filthy shed bearing many evidences of recent native occupation until dark when, in pouring rain, as no train had yet come, we tramped back two kilometres to the 60-kilo camp. We had had no meal since breakfast at dawn, but all they could give us was a little pap. We all went to bed stiff, wet and empty.

One of the party had run a long bamboo splinter into his foot on the previous night, and was crippled and in great pain. Doc. Hakking was willing to keep him in his hospital, but the Dutch interpreter interfered and finally we had to make a stretcher and carry the wounded man with us. It was just as well for the interpreter that the Japanese guards were beside him. He has been a thorn in our flesh all along the line, and after this needless brutality some of the boys were itching to settle accounts with him.

We spent another long, tedious day without food at the siding. Towards nightfall we at last set off in cattle trucks, and were soon climbing into the mountainous country around the 70-kilo mark. The jungle is so thick here that a man escaping, who did not want to use the railway track, would be lucky if he made 500 yards in an hour. The train had to stop three times owing to the steepness of the gradients, which were apparently beyond the scope of our two engines operating on wood fuel. For the last hour it poured monotonously, but at long last we drew into the 82-kilo siding. Here, after being denied admission to an engineers' camp, where our guards tried to secure accommodation for us, most of us were forced to spend the night on the wet ground in an empty shack close to the line. Murray, with twenty others, went to a P.O.W. drivers' camp up the hill and brought us down some rice and hot stew. We were ravenous, but there were only about eight spoonfuls each. All night we lay jammed together in this malodorous hut, fighting off the incessant attacks of millions of mosquitoes and sandflies. I don't think many of us got any sleep. We were then told that part of our heavy gear, and the eleven sickest men would go on by truck to the 105, while the rest of us would march—about 28 kilometres by road. Owing to the state of my heels, I was going by truck, but Christiansen, one of the orderlies, was so groggy with fever that I put him on and hiked.

I don't know whether the Japanese set out to undo any good that a spell in hospital may have done their prisoners, but to be compelled to enter on these long hikes on leaving hospital is about the worst thing for many of these chaps. About noon we passed the 95-kilo mark, where No. 5 Group are at present. At the 100-kilo we were marched off to a Japanese kitchen by the river-bank, where a quantity of rice and stewed vegetable was cooked for us. For the first time since leaving Retpu the ration was sufficient. It rained through most of the afternoon, and for the last hour or two we seemed to be climbing all the way, but we finally staggered into the 105, just before five o'clock, and a few minutes later Keith Mathieson and some of the others came out to greet us. It has taken us three and a half days to cover less than fifty miles, and three-quarters of us are going to be laid up for several days. But at least I won't have to put my boots on again for a while, and just at the moment that is more important than anything else.

CHAPTER XXVI

HIPPOCRATIC STRUGGLE

. . . the Crisis is fleeting, Experiment risky, Decision difficult. Not only must the physician be ready to do his duty, but the patient, the attendants and external circumstances must conduce to the cure.
—HIPPOCRATES, *Aphorisms*

THE breaking of the rains in May, 1943 ushered in the beginning of a struggle, that was to determine the fate of the prisoners in Burma and Thailand. There ensued an epic battle in which no quarter was given or demanded. The antagonists were, on the one side, tropical disease supported by overwork, appalling conditions and malnutrition; on the other the fifty-odd doctors scattered through the jungle camps, backed up by the orderlies who served under them. The latter were cruelly handicapped by the lack of all those drugs, foods and equipment necessary to them in these circumstances.

All that had gone before had been only the preliminary sparring. Now the combatants met, toe to toe, in the centre of the ring, hitting with an intensity that waxed with every passing month. The ending of the rains, in October, brought no abatement. The prize was the living bodies of the 60,000 white men toiling between Thanbyuzayat and Ban Pong.

What happened in Burma is typical of what was occurring in all other sectors along the railway. More men perished in the area around Konkwita and Nikke than in the Burma camps. But Burma's hospitals were representative of all.

The problem of the P.O.W. M.Os in Burma was made immensely harder by the attitude of the Japanese "doctor" responsible for the 10,000 prisoners. This officer, Heguchi, was a dentist who had been given three months' medical training. He never acted in the interests of the sick, but solely as an agent recruiting labour for the railway. Our doctors were frequently overridden, and sick men whom he classified as fit were sent out to the working camps to their deaths. Heguchi's medical ignorance was abysmal and, on many occasions, he made no pretence of examining the men he pronounced as fit.

He lied constantly to Nagatomo about the quantity of medical supplies which he was furnishing to the camps. There is little doubt that he made a handsome rake-off on the medical supplies which he never delivered to the prisoners. When Colonel A. E. Coates, brilliant Melbourne surgeon, after repeated failures by Heguchi to provide emetine for the amoebic dysentery cases, sent in a stinging protest to Brigadier Varley for transmission to Nagatomo, Heguchi denied that there was any evidence of amoebic dysentery in the camps. He said the complaint was only "hill diarrhoea". Colonel Coates challenged him to examine the slides which proved the presence of amoebic dysentery, but Heguchi would not admit to Nagatomo that he had lied.

There is no doubt that if the Japanese had appointed a capable, honest doctor, the sick rate in the Burma railway camps would have been greatly reduced and more men would have been available for work. It was one instance more of the Japanese tendency to cut off the nose to spite the face.

At the camps of No. 5 Group, the death rate had reached alarming proportions, thanks to the group commandant, Captain Mizdani, who insisted that the sick should not be fed. Hospital cases, who should have been moved only on stretchers, were driven along the road from one camp to another, Mizdani himself personally striking and kicking many men who collapsed through pain and weariness. The letter sent by Surgeon-Commander Epstein, U.S. Navy, to Brigadier Varley, imploring his assistance, and explaining that he was literally destitute of all needed food and medical supplies with which he might save his sick men, was a damning indictment of the administration of this group. However, since the Japanese were intensely jealous of their separate commands and since bad feeling prevailed between all Japanese units, little could be done by the officers of our group to assist Commander Epstein and the other doctors of No. 5 Group. One of these doctors, Captain Lumpkin, U.S. Army, lost his life through his devoted work for the sick.

When the No. 5 Group hospital was evacuated towards the end of the year, the patients were brought to our camp at Aungganaung. Many of the men were so wasted and debilitated, or so hideously swollen with beri-beri, that they were not recognized by mates who had shared the same quarters with them only a year before. For some, such as that brilliant comedian "Doc" Clark, the move to the 105 served only to hasten their deaths. We had little to offer them, and, although everything that was available was given to them by men who needed it sorely themselves, a number of these men died within a few days. Of the 2000 members of the group, 535, or 27 per cent, were dead by March 1944.

Commander Epstein had a dry, bitter sense of humour. At Thanbyuzayat, just before his transfer to the No. 5 Group hospital, when visiting the wards one day, he stopped before one of his patients. "Do you like tomaytoes?" asked Commander Epstein. "Yes, sir," replied the Australian, "but I haven't any money to buy them." "I see. Do you like banann-ers?" Again the affirmative. "Well, you jest eat all the tomaytoes, banann-ers, peanuts, eggs an' papayas that you can git." The commander strode on leaving the Australian wondering whether this was an injunction to break the Eighth Commandment, or whether the commander expected the "tomaytoes" and "banann-ers" to materialize out of thin air.

On another occasion, the commander, after inspecting a sick man, turned to the orderly accompanying him and reeled off a prodigious list of drugs and potions to be administered at intervals to the patient; then he moved off towards his quarters. A bewildered orderly came panting after him: "But, sir," he stammered, "we haven't any one of those drugs you prescribed for ———." "I know," replied the commander grimly, "but if he's going to live, that's what he needs."

The main battle for the sick of our No. 3 Group from July 1943 onwards was waged at the sick dump established at the 55-kilo mark. It opened inauspiciously when Colonel Coates, the chief M.O., was carried into the camp on a stretcher. Thanks to the devotion of Captain John Higgin, the colonel was nursed round so that, within a few days, he was hobbling through the wards on a stick, and had started the series of operations to which many prisoners owed their lives.

Before even the most elementary provision for drainage and hygiene had been instituted at this camp, the men who had been broken up by the "speedo" which coincided with the coming of the rains began to pour into the camp. As everywhere along the line, the Japanese would not allow more than a small fraction of the orderlies, cooks and camp workers necessary to look after these sick. Proper attention was an impossibility. Soon there were 2400 seriously ill and dying men in the camp, of whom 800 had deep and growing tropical ulcers. The food, which went from poor to bad, gave the men no strength to resist. Many men developed diarrhoea, dysentery or malaria concurrently with their ulcers, thus further weakening the body's resistance.

The handful of doctors and orderlies was literally submerged by the influx of suffering humanity. There were no beds, no sheets, no bandages, no antiseptics, no instruments, no sterilizing gear. Men, too weak to crawl out to the latrine, lay for hours in their own mess, because there were no pans and no one was available to clean things up.

In this emergency, Major Joe Harris, 2/4th M.T., organized all officer patients who could move from their beds into a working team to look after the sick. Then began a night and day struggle to make something out of nothing.

Bamboo provided crutches, washing mugs, buckets, trays, tubes, boxes and a dozen other vital necessities. Beds for the worst cases were constructed with rice bags on bamboo frames. Bandages and dressings were improvised from all rags, scraps of clothing and the bottoms of mosquito-nets. Tin cans and other discarded junk were beaten into bowls and containers.

When the scant supply of antiseptics gave out, the ulcers were dressed by placing salt on the raw wounds. Many of the ulcers laid bare the leg bone for several inches, and on some men the ulcers extended from knee to ankle.

It is generally considered that, apart from dysentery, the tropical ulcer assisted in the deaths of more men in Burma than any other single factor. According to a textbook of tropical disease, the tropical ulcer is "found chiefly among slave gangs working on a starvation diet in disease-ridden jungles and marshes." No more telling indictment of our conditions could be found.

No anaesthetic was available for the curettage or "gouging" of ulcers. Many of the ulcers penetrated destructively, attacking flesh, joints and tendons until they ate their way to the bone itself. Daily curettage was a grisly business which caused untold agony, but it did help to save the legs and the lives of many. Owing to the lack of instruments, spoons and even pieces of bent tin had to be used for scraping the pus from the raw flesh. In the later months, the Japanese supplied a spray and pump for hosing the ulcers with potassium permanganate.

Many of the ulcers soon reached a stage where it became obvious that they were draining away the patient's life. Colonel Coates decided that to give these men a chance he must amputate. No ether or general anaesthetic of any kind was available, and repeated urgent pleas to the Japanese proved unavailing. A Dutch chemist, named Boxal, succeeded in extracting a Novocain solution from some cocaine which Colonel Coates was carrying. Inserted at the base of the spine, it acted as a local anaesthetic for the lower part of the body for about an hour.

No operating theatre was available, so a rough table was constructed under a bamboo lean-to. All the equipment of a modern operating theatre was lacking, and conditions were comparable with those in which surgeons operated in the Crimean War. No surgical instruments could be coaxed from the Japanese, and Colonel Coates had to operate with the butcher's saw, which was duly returned after each operation, to cut up the camp meat ration.

In these circumstances, between July and November, Colonel Coates carried out 115 major amputations of limbs. Inevitably, a large proportion of the men were too weak to withstand the shock imposed on their worn-out systems; but dozens of others fought back and recovered. All these men must have died if amputation had been long delayed.

A further sixty men had tendons excised. Hundreds lost fingers or toes. No anaesthetic of any kind was available for these minor amputations. Colonel Coates would walk through the ward with an ordinary pair of steel scissors. Sometimes he would stop and say, "That toe's doing you no good, lad. I think it had better come off." There would be a quick snap of the scissors, a yell from the patient, and the toe lay on the floor. On some occasions, nervous men did not even know what was intended until the operation was completed.

The courage of these men was astounding; their confidence in Colonel Coates absolute. He would say, as he bent over a hopelessly eaten-away leg, "It's no good, laddie. I think we'll take it off for you and give you a chance. When would you like it done?" "Right away, sir, and let's get it over." Within the hour, the injection would have been given, the patient, smoking one of the colonel's own cheroots, would have witnessed the removal of his leg, and would be carried back to his bed. As one man said, as he surveyed the stump, "Gosh, that feels good. It's the first time in months that I haven't felt my ulcer."

On one occasion, after the operation, the colonel was displaying the joints and muscles of the severed limb to the orderlies and intending surgeons, who watched his operations. The patient sat up and said calmly: "That's the first time in months, you've b——d about with my leg without hurting me."

One day, on the train journey down to Thailand, the joke was on the colonel. Turning over sleepily, he touched a leg. "Who's that?" he murmured. The owner's voice came clear and emphatic: "That's one leg *you* are not going to get!"

Boxal, the Dutch chemist, proved himself a tower of strength with a series of improvizations. By careful separation and extraction of components of the scanty store of drugs available, he obtained others which were unprocurable. From some extract of ipecacuhana he produced a solution of emetine.

Unfortunately, the extract was not available in sufficient quantities to enable much to be done, but all cases treated with the extracted emetine showed immediate, marked improvement. The same chemist also succeeded in preparing surgical gut, suitable for sutures, from the entrails of cattle. The recipe for this was devised by Colonel Coates. The stripped bowel was cut in ribbons, twisted and then sterilized by heat under the kwali ovens when the fires were raked out.

Right through the rainy season and on to the end of the year, the struggle at the 55 continued. The hopelessly inadequate ration was increased for many through the activities of "traders" who bought meat on the black market outside the camp, and thus secured steaks and red meat for men whose resistance could not be maintained on rice alone. By sheer unremitting hard work, services of a kind in respect to cleaning, washing, and the making of beds were obtained for all who were too weak to look after themselves.

In the space of five months 330 men, of whom more than four-fifths were Australians, were buried at this camp. It was a magnificent personal triumph for the doctors, orderlies, camp workers and convalescent officers who assisted them that the number was not three times as great.

Desperate as were the conditions faced by the doctors who spent most of their time in the "hospital" camps, still more heartbreaking were the circumstances confronting the lone M.Os attached to each working force. It would be invidious to discriminate between the men upon whom the entire personnel in Burma depended so absolutely. The Australian medical officers won unbounded praise from men of all nationalities. All told, there were thirteen. Colonel Tom Hamilton of Newcastle was senior M.O. in Burma. Major W. E. Fisher, a consulting physician from Sydney, and Major Alan Hobbs, Adelaide surgeon, carried the burden at Thanbyuzayat until that hospital was broken up by the bombing. After that, M.Os were nearly all interchanged between the hospital and working camps. Major Krantz of Adelaide, shared most of the surgical work along the line with Colonel Coates and Major Hobbs. Colonel Norman Eadie, Melbourne specialist, served with Williamsforce until he became ill himself, when he was moved to Retpu and later to the 55.

Except for short periods at the 55-kilo camp, Captain John Higgin, of Sydney, Captain Don Cumming, of Sydney, and Captain Claude Anderson, of Perth, remained with Blackforce, Ramsayforce and Greenforce respectively, throughout our servitude in Burma. How much is owed to these three men and to the orderlies behind them, by these forces, the men who have come home well know. Captain Rowley Richards, of Sydney, Major Chalmers, of Hobart, Captain White, of Sydney, and Captain Tom Brereton, of Sydney, who had the misfortune to become virtually blind, completed the splendid team.

These men served their fellow prisoners with a devotion in keeping with the highest traditions of their profession. Often racked with illness themselves, they insisted on resuming duty at the earliest possible moment, often long before they should have left their beds. There must have been times when one and all felt that, in face of their lack of everything essential to the adequate performance of their task, the whole struggle was hopeless. But they concealed their feelings and carried on with a grim earnestness and sincerity that often inspired a fierce will to live in the men to whom they could offer no proper treatment.

In many cases the only weapon in the hands of the doctor was his knowledge of human psychology and his ability to build up the patient's faith in eventual recovery. It was a stern school of medicine, both for the young who had just left their universities and for those who were already well on into middle age. It exacted each day far heavier demands than the biggest practice at home would ever make. Of the way in which its representatives stood up to the most onerous ordeal of their lives, the medical fraternity of Australia has every reason to feel immensely proud.

Across the border in Siam, three medical officers attached to the 2/2nd C.C.S., captured in Java, worked together as a team throughout the construction of the railway, and made an immense impression among all prisoners in Siam. Many

British Army officers, normally disinclined to emphasize the
virtues of "colonials", could not find words adequate to express
their admiration for these men whose names will be remembered by thousands, not only in their own country, but in
every corner of the United Kingdom. These three were
Colonel E. E. Dunlop of Victoria, Major Moon and Major
Corlette, of New South Wales.

Yet, despite the sterling work of the doctors, many of the
men who have survived their sentence of hard labour on the
railway would not be alive today but for the work of hundreds of men who knew little or nothing of the arts of healing.
Some of the orderlies, particularly those of the C.C.S. units,
had a considerable knowledge of the care and tending of the
sick. Many others who served with tireless enthusiasm had
never assisted at a sick bed before. Most of the M.Os will agree
that some of the best orderlies in the jungle camps were men
who had had no medical training in the army or in civil life,
where they may have been artisans, professional men, truck
drivers or salesmen.

The sick of the ill-fated F and H Groups at this period
were packed across the border to a hospital at the 50-kilo mark
where Major Bruce Hunt, of Perth, with his assistants fought
desperately not only against the prevailing diseases but also
against the shattering effect of days without food, water and
ill treatment in packed rail trucks. We saw the trucks passing
our camps en route to the 50-kilo. Strong men sickened at
the sights within. When the trains at last reached the camp—
sometimes five to eight days after setting out—many men were
lifted out dead while others were beyond human aid.

In the opinion of many of the British, the great strength of
the Australians in the jungle lay in their ability to adapt themselves to the most adverse circumstances, and in the strength
of the "cobber" bond between individuals, especially between
men of the same unit. Part of this could undoubtedly be
attributed to the Australian system of recruiting men for each
unit from particular districts and areas. There is no doubt that
many men owed their lives to food and money given to them,
or sent down from up-jungle, by their mates.

The rice cooks. The kwali or rice hat with its wooden lid rests on
the mud brick fireplace made by P.O.Ws.

Every Australian unit in Burma and Thailand had funds contributed by officers and men for the benefit of the sick of their unit. But despite all this organization, the bulk of the provision for the sick in many instances came from individuals, who sacrificed their own meagre comforts because a cobber was in greater need. Generosity in such circumstances brings its own reward. There were certain officers, and some of the men with money, who never went near the hospital huts or sought to aid the sick in any way. But they were a minority. The thoughtfulness displayed and sacrifices made during the captivity helped to forge bonds between men which will endure for the remainder of their lives.

One of the main problems facing the doctors was to induce the sick to eat their rice. However deficient rice might be in proteins and certain important vitamins, it was obvious that men had no hope of maintaining their strength unless they ate a sufficient quantity of the one food available. To men racked with malaria, and groggy with quinine, the tackling of plain boiled rice demanded the utmost will-power and perseverance. The rice, which was often ill cooked, showed a maddening disposition to go round and round in one's mouth without being swallowed. Major Fisher each day used to demand of his patients, "Are you eating your rice?" Colonel Coates framed the dictum, "Your ticket home is at the bottom of your dixie." But even under constant urging, some men seemed incapable of forcing their rice into their stomachs, and in a number of cases the failure cost them their lives.

The attitude of men who, sick or well, knew that morning, noon and night would bring only the inescapable rice was well expressed in a poem by Captain W. Store, of the B.E.F. Written for the prisoners at Mergui in 1942, it expresses the experience of all of us in our years in Burma and Siam:

> At the prison camp at Mergui,
> Conditions were not nice
> And we fed on a diet
> That was wholly, solely rice.
> Not rice as mother knew it,
> Nor done as she used to do it—*No!*

Behind Bamboo

Not baked rice nor flaked rice
With-sugar and with-milk rice,
Not cooked rice that looked rice
And all as smooth as silk.—*No!*
We got glued rice, half stewed rice
Stone cold rice, grown old rice
Unfit for even dogs
The sort you throw to hogs.
We got broken rice, outspoken rice
That argued with your plate,
Unpolished rice, abolished rice
Some few years out of date.
We got burned rice, that wasn't rice
That tasted just like cinders
And brittle rice, sharp little rice
Like bits of festered tinders.
We got boiled rice, quite spoiled rice
And kerosene-drum-oiled rice
That no one could call rice.
We got baked rice and caked rice
That weevils made their bed in.
We got bad rice, sad rice
That filled you with its sorrow.
We got podgy rice, stodgy rice
That meant no latrines tomorrow.
We got limed rice, grimed rice
And ought-to-have-been-crimed rice,
Disrupted rice, corrupted rice
Undischarged, bankrupted rice.
We got sloshed rice and squashed rice
But never any washed rice,
Half caste rice, half mast rice,
And lots of jungle-grassed rice.
We brewed rice, we chewed rice,
The lucky ones they spewed rice . . .
We starved on, but we lived on
In spite of everlasting rice.

It is to be regretted that the four lines before the final couplet have to be omitted, owing to censorship, but hundreds of those who heard and cherished this poem so descriptive of our feelings will fill in the missing quatrain for themselves.

The worst of the medical struggle ended early in 1944. A base hospital was established at Nakom Paton, some miles west of Bangkok, for all seriously ill men along the railway. Here, for the first time, the Japanese did make some effort to provide better quarters for the sick. It became one of the largest hospitals ever established, having at one time 8000 patients, with an average of 5000, including all the chronically ill and the maimed of the Burma-Siam railway.

Lieutenant-Colonel Coates was chief M.O. All thirty-five doctors—Australian, American, British and Dutch—met twice a week for discussion of their manifold problems.

Particularly fine work was done by Major Marsden (British) in pathological and biochemical investigation. Anaemia due to chronic malnutrition was a scourge and many lives were saved through the 1500 blood transfusions given with defibrinated blood.

The surgeons did nearly 1000 major operations of all kinds. The results of such routine work as hernia and appendiceal operations were as good as in any civil or military hospital. Excellent artificial limbs were made and fitted to nearly all the 178 men who had lost legs. Physiotherapy—massage, exercises and P.T.—had a good effect on morale. The apparatus for exercising patients was improvised from ropes, bits of board, bamboo and leather straps.

The main factor in the success attending the efforts of doctors and orderlies in this camp was the eking out of the drugs and medical materials received from the American Red Cross in May 1944.

All who took part in the medical work, administration and care of patients shared in the achievement of reducing total stretcher cases to 400 by the time Japan capitulated. Of the 10,000 patients brought to this hospital the total mortality was only 2.8 per cent.

Nakom Paton might have shocked people at home but compared to the jungle hospitals it was a Rockefeller Foundation.

CHAPTER XXVII

DEARTH IN THE JUNGLE

> I saw their starved lips in the gloam
> With horrid warning gapéd wide,
> And I awoke and found me here
> On the cold hill side.
>   —JOHN KEATS

AUNGGANAUNG camp, known to all Burma P.O.Ws as the "hundred-and-five" or the "one-o-five", will not be forgotten by the prisoners who spent their worst months of captivity in its huts. The 105 was like one of the Borgia women, beautiful but murderous. It was situated amidst tall trees on a hill slope, in a position which suggested that it was the finest camp we had seen. Yet scores of men rotted to death in this camp, while many more were carried from it in a shocking condition to be buried at the 55-kilo hospital camp.

For the "Old Dysenterians" of Serang, even the 105 failed to equal their first weeks of captivity. But those who had not been at Serang had never experienced anything like it, and none of us would ever wish to face similar conditions again. For in that camp on the lovely hill-side, not during the rains, but afterwards when communications by road and rail were open, every prisoner was slowly but surely starved, until each hut was riddled with malaria and ulcer cases, and the "Last Post" sounded dismally from the cemetery each day, sometimes four or five times in the twenty-four hours.

Yet this was not a hospital camp, but a working camp from which over a thousand of the sickest men had already been evacuated, so that, nominally, only the fit and strong were left.

The 105 had been first occupied in the middle of May 1943 by all members of Greenforce, Ramsayforce and Blackforce not in hospital. From the earliest days it acquired an unpleasant reputation, owing to the immediate crop of cholera victims after the grim march from the 75. The water position was acute and, at first, all water had to be drawn from a creek three-quarters of a mile away, the men carrying buckets on the chain system.

Food was short from the beginning, and large parties of "light sick", that is, men unable to work on the railway but still capable of moving about, had to march down the line to the 95- and 100-kilo camps to carry up rations on their backs. These grinding journeys in the mud and continuous rain took heavy toll, and dozens of men had to be sent to hospital.

In the middle of June a cholera scare caused the hundreds of Burmese who were living in their ox carts close to the camp to disperse without taking their cattle. For a few days parties of prisoners found "important business" in the *ooloo* or jungle where the deserted beasts wandered. In the lines there was a meat orgy, and for a few days many had more meat than they had seen in all the preceding months in Burma.

But the Japanese would not allow any beasts to be caught and coralled and, as the supply of beasts from Thanbyuzayat had dwindled almost to nothing, a long succession of months without meat set in. Periodically, boxes of meat came up from Moulmein, but the journey often occupied several days, and nearly all of this meat had to be buried hastily upon arrival.

When we arrived in September at the 105, we found that, although all the worst cases had been evacuated, the hospital was full and there were already over twenty graves in the cemetery. One of the main troubles was the hopeless inadequacy of all medical supplies—even more acute than elsewhere. This was aggravated by the policy of the fat, spiderlike monster who sat in the camp commandant's hut all day, eating Red Cross foods which should have come to us, and bartering precious medical supplies for men's watches and personal valuables. He had a large glass jar of iodoform on his table. Men used to come to him with their most precious trinkets to try to obtain a little extra food and a few spoonfuls of iodoform to help their mates, who were facing amputation and possibly death through the unchecked spread of their ulcers.

This Japanese officer rejoiced in the name of Hochi. When he left the camp in December, the entire camp was paraded to bid him farewell. Before he strutted out himself, he was preceded by no fewer than twenty-six boxes, trunks and bundles, most of them laden with the valuables he had extorted from starving men in exchange for a few eggs, worthless rupees or a little iodoform.

A tremendous fuss was made by the Japanese over their first distribution of Red Cross goods since we had been captured. The issue was really magnanimous; three small packets of cigarettes per man, a little margarine which all went to the hospital, and a small tin of condensed milk divided between eleven men. That was all the Red Cross issue that most of us saw in fifteen months in Burma, although a little more tinned stuff went into the hospitals in December.

Under this pearl among camp commanders, we had one of the choicest collections of barbarians and robbers ever assembled as guards in any camp.

There was "Buffhead", a hideous Korean, who dealt out some ferocious beatings, but who was normally too dumb to know what was going on around him. There was "Pinhead", or "The Snipe", a shrewd, scheming little N.C.O. who acted as commandant when Hochi went down to Moulmein. He was a master of petty persecution, and delighted to keep the weary and emaciated prisoners standing for long hours on the parade ground while tankos were conducted. Every humiliation that a clever mind could conceive for prisoners was practised by this specimen.

Then we had "Mickey Mouse", a vicious little dwarf with a colossal vanity and a delight in airing his abominable English. He used to parade through the officers' hut at all hours of the night, screaming for the orderly sergeant in a shrill falsetto that would have roused the dead. Then there was "The Bull", a giant bully who seemed to spend his entire waking hours in seeking opportunities to bash prisoners. He relieved the monotony now and then by beating up his fellow guards. No pretext was too flimsy for the Bull. If he came through the hut on the prowl, you were bashed if your clogs at the foot of your bed were out of alignment.

To complete the collection, we had those two unamiable thugs, the B.B. and the B.B.C. The B.B. probably considered a day ill spent when he did not beat up several prisoners. With the sadist's delight in torment, he loved to hold his victim standing rigidly to attention for many minutes while he lashed himself into a rage, with a string of Japanese and broken English blasphemies and obscenities.

These guards and some of their fellows organized a thorough and ruthless robbery of the limited ration of oil and sugar which reached the camp for prisoners. On several occasions, everything except our rice was removed from our rations and placed in the Japanese cook-house. Of a month's ration of palm oil for cooking, we received a half tin out of twenty-four.

On the two or three occasions when goods of any kind became available for our canteen, the squeeze was absolutely shameless. Once, when a native trader had brought a cartload of sugar and cheroots to the camp, the guards asked our canteen officer how much he could afford to buy. They then took all his money and, squatting down on the floor, four of them divided most of it among themselves and pocketed it; only then was the balance handed over to the trader. This was done under the eyes of at least twenty Australian officers, who knew, by bitter experience, that any protest would lead only to the removal of the goods.

The one decent guard in the camp was a Christian who was christened Holy Joe. This appellation gave rise to the following discussion. Holy Joe: "Australian soldier call me Joe?" Aussies: "That's right." Holy Joe: "Joe a good name?" Aussies: "Yes, all number one—Joe Stalin, Joe Chamberlain, Tojo." Exit Holy Joe, ecstatically happy.

Between attacks of malaria, I went out with the working parties until my legs again lapsed into a bad state, owing to the atrocious diet we were getting. The main work at this stage was quarrying for stone and breaking it up for use as ballast along the line. It was monotonous, irritating work and, watching the men tapping patiently at the stones, I thought that we were much worse off than criminals sentenced to hard labour at home. At least they were better fed, and they did know the term of their imprisonment.

When my legs got too bad, I organized a series of lectures and quiz sessions for the men in hospital, in collaboration with Padre Mathieson and Padre Cunningham. An issue of cheroots accompanied the answering of a question, the cheroots being obtained for the sick from our force funds.

The attitude of the men towards their sick mates was beyond praise. Time and time again, starving men made sacrifices of food that was worth more than any money, to give a pal strength to hang on in the hospital hut. In my diary for 30 September I wrote:

Was talking to Johnnie when his cobber Bert came in with four eggs for him. Johnnie didn't want to take them, but finally gave in when Bert said he had four more for himself. Later, walking round the lines I struck Bert eating his rice. No sign of eggs. When questioned, he said: "No, I only got two bucks pay for last month because I was down with fever most of the time. The b—— boong would only give me four eggs for that." "When did you last have an egg yourself?" I asked. Bert: "Oh, a couple of months ago—that day we all got two." I wonder if anybody at home could ever appreciate what it costs a man who's craving for food of any kind to give his all as Bert did tonight?

Our cook-house was so utterly destitute of all rations except rice, that it was impossible to do much for the sick. But of such sugar and other supplies as did occasionally filter into the camp, the hospital patients received the lion's share. We did not even have the luck to supplement the sick ration as they did one day at the 100-kilo camp. An 18-foot python was caught and killed by the camp cooks, on the hospital roof. Next day it was announced to the sick that the Japanese had made a present of fowls for the hospital. This was so remarkable an event that rumours of peace and of a cessation of hostilities immediately started. That day the wrecked men had chicken broth and juicy white meat for the first time. All declared that it was "wonderful". It was only on the following

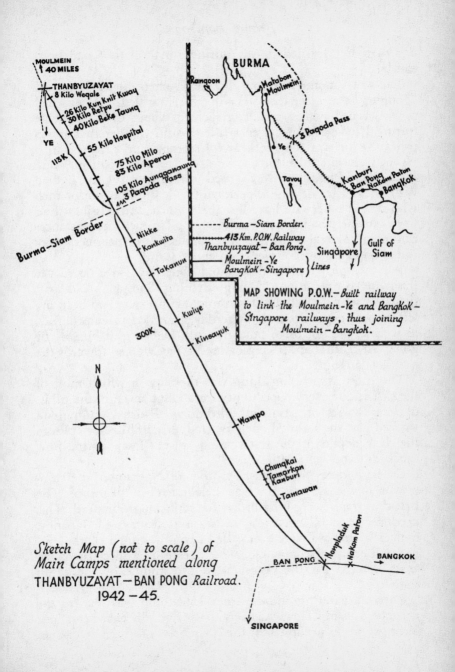

MOULMEIN
↑ 40 MILES

THANBYUZAYAT
8 Kilo Wegale
26 Kilo Kun Knit Kway
30 Kilo Retpu
40 Kilo Beke Taung
55 Kilo Hospital
75 Kilo Milo
83 Kilo Aperon
105 Kilo Aunggananung
113K
YE
3 Pagoda Pass

Burma–Siam Border

Nikke
KonKwita
TaKanun
300K
Kwiye
Kinsayuk

Wampo

Chungkai
Tamarkan
Kanburi
Tamawan

BURMA

Rangoon

Matabon
Moulmein
3 Pagoda Pass

Ye

Kanburi
Ban Pong
Nakom Paton
BangKoK
Tavoy

Singapore
Gulf of
Siam

––––– Burma–Siam Border.
═══ 413 Km. P.O.W. Railway
Thanbyuzayat – Ban Pong.
——— Moulmein – Ye
BangKoK – Singapore } Lines

MAP SHOWING P.O.W.– *Built railway
to link the Moulmein – Ye and BangKoK–
Singapore railways, thus joining
Moulmein – Bangkok.*

Nonpladuk
NaKom Paton
BAN PONG
BANGKOK

*Sketch Map (not to scale) of
Main Camps mentioned along*
THANBYUZAYAT – BAN PONG *Railroad.*
1942 – 45.

SINGAPORE

day that they learned it was Burmese python they had been eating.

The worst moments in our day came when the M.Os started "gouging" the ulcer cases. Having the raw flesh and exposed nerve scraped with a curetting spoon is about the most acute torture I have ever experienced. It was no wonder that sometimes the air was rent with awful screams and groans which escaped, despite all efforts at control, from the patients' lips. Poor John Higgin, our M.O., used to return to the hut bathed with sweat after having to perform this loathsome job for men who would otherwise have lost their limbs, and possibly their lives. No one who has not seen "gouging" in such circumstances can form any real picture of what thousands of prisoners were called on to endure for weeks on end.

But the spirit remained splendid. One day I overheard the following conversation: "Doing anything, Snowy?" "Not particularly, why?" "I thought you might come over and hold my leg while I get it gouged. Yesterday it needed three orderlies, as well as the doctor to hold me still. Didn't give him a fair go." "O.K., old man. It's a pleasure." They walked towards the hospital laughing.

The most astonishing thing was the way in which most of the sick seized every opportunity for a laugh, even in the midst of long weeks of pain and sordidness. Padre Cunningham walked past the hospital one day, clad only in his shorts. From the dark depths of the hut came a voice: "I say, padre, how much did you get for the shirt?"

On 20 and 21 November, by order of Nagatomo, the completion of the railway line was "celebrated" in all camps. The first day was reserved, by order, for mourning our dead. This produced one of the most nauseating displays of Japanese hypocrisy that we were ever called upon to witness.

At all camps the Japanese laid a wreath on a special wooden cross, erected for the occasion, in the middle of the camp cemetery.

Then an exulting address from Nagatomo was read to the assembled camp, in which, with a fine disregard for our feelings, he congratulated the prisoners on their work in building the railway. The whole thing was an insult; but so limited and obsessed is the Japanese mind that it was probably not intended as such. In his official reply to this address, Colonel George Ramsay, as our camp commander, pointed out that we could not feel the same enthusiasm for the celebration which served to remind us—if we needed a reminder—of our position. He emphasized that "even these remaining troops who are now classed as reasonably fit physically, would not be so regarded in normal circumstances, the present classification being made on a comparative basis only. There are really few who have left sufficient body resistance to fight the disease and infection which they would normally have a reasonable chance of avoiding." In an unofficial speech in English, Colonel Ramsay put the case far more strongly and expressed the feelings of the entire force.

At this stage a "Letter of Condolence" from Nagatomo to our dead was read out. The comments from the boys were colourful and blasphemous. As an illustration of the Japanese mentality it should be quoted:

LETTER OF CONDOLENCE ON THE OCCASION OF THE MEMORIAL SERVICE FOR DECEASED POWs

As this first stage of the railway construction has now been completed I have on this day of Commemoration, the honour of taking this opportunity of consoling the souls of the POWs of the 3rd Branch, numbering 655* who have died in this district during the past year. In my opinion it is a virtue since ancient times to pay homage to the souls who have died in war, even though they be enemies. Moreover you were under my command and have endeavoured to work diligently in obedience to my orders, while always longing for the final repatriation to your own country, once the war is over and peace is restored. I have always done to my utmost to discharge my duty conscientiously taking responsibility for all of you as your commander.

Now you have passed on to the other world, owing to the unavoidable prevailing diseases and indiscriminate bombing, I cannot see you in this world any more.

Visualising your situation and that of your relatives and families, I cannot help shedding tears sympathising with your unfortunate circumstances.

This tragedy is the result of war, however it is owing to fate that you are in this condition and I consider that God has called you here. However today I try to console your souls and pray for you in my capacity

* Actually nearly 1000 by 20 November.

of your commander, together with the other members of my staff by dedicating a cross and placing a wreath in your cemetery.

In the very near future your comrades will be leaving this district, consequently it may be impossible to offer prayers and lay a wreath in your cemetery for some time to come. But undoubtedly some of your comrades will come here again after the war to pay sincere homage to your memory.

Please accept my deepest sympathy and regards and may you sleep peacefully and eternally.

Given on the 20th day of November, in the 18th year of Showa.

YOSHITIDA NAGATOMO, Lieut-Col.
Chief of No. 3 Branch of Thai War
Prisoners' Camps.

The next day consisted of enforced "merrymaking". The Japanese began the day with a special parade, chanting some weird incantation. Then we had four hours and thirty-five items of Japanese concert, which was so awful that many of the troops arose and departed, despite the threat of Hochi's wrath. In the afternoon there was a race meeting, largely memorable for the fact that all the former winners at Kun Knit Kway acted like most real favourites and let their backers down. The bookies made a killing, but as someone said: "We didn't lose the seat out of our pants because most of us haven't got any pants."

In the evening there was another concert—P.O.W. this time —in which the concluding item was performed by no less distinguished a personality than Hochi himself. This consisted of a spirited dance in costume, symbolizing the struggle of good with evil. It was the only thing which Hochi did satisfactorily while we were under his command.

Just at this time, the officers of the camp, and Blackforce officers in particular, were constantly harassed by the guards in the hope that we would bring pressure to bear on one of our group, a flight-lieutenant whose beautiful watch was coveted by Hochi. But the watch's owner ignored all threats and blandishments and announced that, if he died for it, the watch would go into the earth with him. Another air force officer with less romantic ideas said, unkindly but realistically, "Don't kid yourself; it'd be off you before you were cold."

The struggle for existence left little room for sentiment at the 105, but Hochi did not get that watch.

Bad as was our own plight, more harrowing tales came from farther up the line where Andersonforce and Williamsforce had now crossed the border. The camps from 108-kilo onwards to Nikke, at the 133-kilo mark, were all incredibly bad, several of them being merely bogs through which the prisoners ploughed their way, sometimes knee-deep in mud. In several camps streams of water ran through the huts and you had to step straight into the water when getting off the bamboo platform where you slept. In fact, in one camp prisoners enjoyed what they described as "angling *de luxe*", sitting on their beds fishing in the stream which ran down the gangway at their feet. Even Izaak Walton was never quite so "compleat" as our "rod-in-bed" men.

Captain Fitzsimmons and his Americans found themselves in a camp in which Asiatic coolies were dying like flies, and where the starvation had reached a pitch at which the coolies dug up and ate the meagre slops thrown out by our own under-nourished troops. Facing such conditions after the wet season led to a further acceleration of the death rate and, by the end of December, less than a fifth of the P.O.Ws in Burma could possibly be classified as fit for work of any kind.

At the 105, the arrival of some extra rations for the "celebrations" marked the beginning of a long period of utter dearth. The extra rations did us little good, for, to men unaccustomed to any meat, the little pork which we obtained proved disastrous and the whole force spent the next forty-eight hours climbing up and down the hill to and from the latrines—open trenches exposed on the hill-side.

That was our last sight of anything except rice and inedible white radish in that camp. Our hunger was the more acute as the monsoon had once again seized us in its icy grip. On skeleton-like figures, which had lacked all proteins and fats for many months, it was like a blast from the Arctic Circle.

Now the decomposition of our bodies became almost universal. Hideous pellagra sores and swellings broke out on our faces, our genital organs and inside our mouths. Many of us began to croak. Nobody wanted to look at a mirror. Inevitably, malaria thrived in bodies which had lost all power of resistance. I was no worse than most, and much better off than many, but I was going down with fever every ten days with clock-like regularity, while the inside of my mouth and my throat were so sore that every mouthful of rice was a huge effort. In any case, when one is doped to the eyes with quinine to the tune of twenty-seven grains *per diem* for ten days, one's interest in food is largely academic. When breakfast consists of boiled rice, with hot water to drink, lunch of boiled rice, with a rich stew of hot water and pepper, and dinner of boiled rice and an exquisite dish of more peppered hot water with odd pieces of wood-like radish or bamboo root floating in it, few fever cases are capable of taking sufficient nourishment to feed a babe in arms.

The death rate swept up, not because of more disease but simply because the sick could not get enough vitamins to give nature a chance in its fight with the attacking poisons. One sad instance was the death of Driver Darcy McInerney, of Canberra, who was acting as batman for some of the officers. He slipped one day and ran a piece of pointed bamboo into his arm. After having it dressed and bandaged immediately he thought no more of it. Within two days his arm had swollen like a balloon, and within the week he was dead. The truth was that most of us had come to the limits of our resistance.

Absurd prices were paid for any kind of foodstuff to supplement the diet. Native shintagar brought anything from sixty to one hundred times its pre-war price. One Dutchman farther up the line gave 150 Dutch guilders (£A25) for one packet. Another gave a beautiful pair of leather shoes—beyond price at that stage—for the same amount of shintagar.

At the 105 men were paying ten cents and twenty cents for a little extra rice burnt on both sides over a fire and squeezed into the form of a rissole, although it contained nothing but rice and a bit of chili or jungle leaf. I was in a bay with Alec Davis, of Launceston, and Jim Sutherland, of Ivanhoe, Melbourne. We all had "our agents" in the lines scouting for anything offering on the black market or any other market, but the best thing we "organized" was a piece of dried fish, which Alec collected from the rail above the bed of a sleeping Japanese guard.

Jim had an enviable and invaluable capacity for rice. When Alec and I had fever, he used to eat not only his own but ours as well with every appearance of satisfaction. In fact he thrived on it and never had fever himself, but for most of us there were days when rice was the anathema of all anathemas.

Our diet was so monotonous that we even excused Alex Dobbie for his achievement in eating his tea with a spoon in the belief that it was the "stew" which went with the rice. The only difference between tea and stew was that the former usually had rather more dirt and rather less pepper.

On Christmas day the cook-house, without means of any kind, attempted to convert the rice, with the aid of various bits of jungle, into a Christmas pudding. Most of us had one bite and then hastily disposed of the rest in the slop bucket. Charlie Howitt, who was in charge of the cook-house for our force, is still hearing about that "pudding" today.

At the beginning of December we heard that, at long last, the mail which, since April, had been lying at Ban Pong, only 150 miles down the railway, had at last come up to Burma. At nightfall on 20 December it arrived at our camp. Amidst intense excitement, we gathered round to find if there was any word from our loved ones of whom we had heard nothing in twenty-two long and bitter months.

The mail was old—none of it later than November 1942— but how precious it was! For days thereafter, men sat re-reading the priceless scrap of paper that brought memories and images from a world that seemed as remote as that of Tutankhamen.

For some of us the mail brought rejoicing, to some it brought only news of deaths and unhappiness. To Jim Sutherland, my bay-mate, came news of his promotion to flight-lieutenant; others heard of additions to their families since departure; for myself it was a mixed boon. Since Batavia I had been dogged with a presentiment that tragedy had attended the birth of our first child. For a long time I thought my wife had died; I learned in the letters that my wife was well but that the child had died immediately after its birth, two months after I was taken prisoner.

With the co-operation of the whole camp, I managed to collect six typed pages of general news from home. As the Japanese would not have allowed us to post this on the notice board, I went round to each hut in turn, after dark and gave it out orally. All things considered, and particularly in the light of heavy censorship, it was surprising how much of general interest could be gleaned.

Only one copy of the "Aungganaung News" ever saw the light of day, but I am not sure that it did not arouse more interest among those who heard its contents than anything I am ever likely to write subsequently. A résumé of the bulletin was sent down to other camps and, later in Siam, when more letters came to hand, I brought out four or five more bulletins with the news from home. To men cut off in the limbo of the jungles, even race results two years old brought a nostalgic glow of warmth. The argument and speculation aroused by each bulletin helped to keep thousands of Aussies in conversation for weeks.

At long last, at the end of December, the Burma prisoners began to move down to the Kanburi area which, by all accounts, was a land of milk and honey after the long, grim dearth in the jungle. By the beginning of January all except a few hundred of the least unfit had left the 105. None of us left with any regret, but even today our minds sometimes go back to the lovely hill-side amid the tall trees where Hunger and Disease stalked untramelled and where several score of our finest and best rest for ever in the little cemetery which, today, the jungle will have reclaimed as its own.

PART FOUR

SIAM

CHAPTER XXVIII

THE LAND OF MILK AND HONEY

And I am come down to deliver them out of the hand of the Egyptians, and to bring them up out of that land unto a good land and a large, unto a land flowing with milk and honey. . . .
—Exodus, iii, 8

ON the first day of 1944, the dawn found us packing into cattle trucks for the journey into Siam. We had been mustered on the parade ground, and our gear had been searched by the light of bonfires and lanterns in the small hours of the morning. Now, with eight trucks instead of the twelve which we had been promised, we were crushed together as no cattle have ever been, until there were 47 of us under the corrugated iron roof of the truck. Beside me, Lieutenant Bennie Cook, of Coburg, Victoria, should have been travelling on a stretcher. Instead, he was forced to sit upright on an uncomfortable pile of gear for nearly three hours unable to move an inch; and, do what we might, we could not ease his pain. In such conditions it was easy to understand how one or more of the sick in each batch died on the way to our new camp.

We detrained at Nikke, twenty kilometres past Three Pagoda Pass, which marks the border. The three pagodas are very old, and nestle amidst high surrounding forests on a hill-side. Passing them since time immemorial, ox carts and carrier elephants, soldiers, merchants, Buddhist priests and migrating families, have crossed the jungle-covered slopes of the mountains which separate the fertile coastlands on either side.

After spending most of the day among the sidings at Nikke, we rattled on again, now thirty-seven to a truck, but still with three empty trucks attached, occupation of which was for-

bidden us. Until the light failed, we could see on either side
of the track the big camps where P.O.W.s and Asiatics had
been quartered while the line was being built. Here and there
we passed the perpendicular yellow posts covered with hiero-
glyphics which marked the grave of a Japanese. Only once
or twice did we catch glimpses of the little wooden crosses
which indicated a P.O.W. graveyard in the jungles. In these
camps cholera had swept men away so fast that some of them
were buried in mass graves, while the bodies of others had
been immolated on a great fire that was kept burning day
and night in the centre of the camp.

In the middle of the night we stopped for some hours and got
some sleep, lying on the pebbles and ballast between the tracks.

Breakfast consisted of dried fish, of unbelievable saltiness,
and of rice which had gone bad overnight. But after the
starvation at the 105, we did not complain about our food on
this trip.

In the afternoon we began to pass through some of the
most difficult country along the whole track. Deep clefts and
ravines gashed the mountain-side, and our train jolted precariously over flimsy wooden bridges, supported by long
wooden beams and poles embedded in the bottom of the clefts.
For much of the journey the line clung to the higher ridges,
and every now and then we had a glimpse of a deep valley at
our feet with a wide, pleasant river wandering through it.
We came unexpectedly on a plashing waterfall which cascaded
down over mossy rocks from a height sixty feet above the
track. Here were deep cuttings running through the rock,
cuttings which had each claimed a hungry toll in human
blood, sweat and tears.

For us this was no ordinary railway journey. We were running over sleepers laid at a terrible cost in the lives of our
fellow prisoners and the Asiatic workers. So the cuttings
through the steep rises and the bridges which spanned each
dizzy abyss had a personal message for each one of us.

Frequently we saw rolling-stock lying at the foot of steep
embankments, sometimes over a hundred feet below us. The
signs of wreckage were so numerous that we felt confident of

sabotage, even allowing for the rickety nature of the bridges and of some sections of the line.

Nature has rioted lavishly over this whole area. There are forests of tall hardwood trees whose lofty pinnacles form such a dense mass of leafy shade as to prevent the sunlight from ever reaching the ground below. There are intricate intertwining vines, impenetrable bamboo thickets, tall spear grasses and great stretches of low, dense scrub. Vegetation clings persistently to the rocky sides of even the sheerest slopes.

It is little wonder that it has taken over a century, since the invention of the steam train, for man to build a railway across this belt of country. Even now it remains primitive, savage, untrammelled and unconquerable. Man holds only a causeway a few feet wide across the virgin jungle. It will need merely a lapse of a few months and the jungle will again swallow up its preserve—inexorably; soon, only an expert guide will be able to find traces of man's invasion.

We passed the whole day—my wedding anniversary—in the cattle trucks and just before dark we seemed to free ourselves at last from the mountain ranges. Yet it was not until after midnight that we finally ground to a halt and formed up in the darkness to march into our new camp at Tamarkan, near the town of Kanburi. It had taken us forty-two hours to cover less than two hundred miles, but by Japanese standards on that railway we had had a particularly quick passage.

Arrival at Tamarkan was marred for me by the loss of my diary, carried in a small notebook that I had bought at Than-byuzayat. Believing that we were to be searched at the camp, I put the diary inside my shirt in the hope that our persons would not be inspected too closely. It turned out, contrary to all rumour, that there was no search, but I had the mortification to find that my diary had fallen to the ground somewhere between the railway and the camp. Four days later, when I had abandoned all hope, it was returned to me.

Our first information here was not reassuring. Bombers had been coming over with fair regularity in recent weeks; the camp was hard up against an ack-ack battery and less than two hundred yards from a major railway bridge. We crawled into the hut assigned to us, amidst assurances that the ack-ack opened up on the least provocation, that much of the flak fell in the camp, and that retaliation from our bombers was inevitable. I thought this rather a poor anniversary of one's wedding, but was so tired that I fell asleep instantly and knew nothing more until reveille.

Within a night or two we learned just what our position involved. Somewhere after midnight, a shattering roar penetrated my sleeping consciousness. With an amazing reflex action I went straight up in the air and then started burrowing my way through the bamboo slats as if seeking sanctuary on the ground. It must have been several seconds before I became sufficiently awake to realize that the noise was simply the roar of the guns blazing away at planes which could be heard droning past. One of my neighbours found himself out of his bed, out of the hut and in the ditch outside, before he realized what had happened.

Thereafter, particularly during the nights when the moon was full, our sleep was frequently broken in this fashion. Occasionally in the daytime also the guns opened up as Allied planes flew down the railway towards Bangkok. Fragments of shrapnel and, sometimes, the driving band off a shell crashed through the attap roofs of the camp. But it was not until eleven months had passed that the bombers took the retaliatory action we had expected.

Tamarkan was so much better than the jungle camps that for some time we were very content. In a single day we received more greens in the ration than we had seen in the jungle in the past six months. Vegetables in profusion poured into this camp. At different times we had sweet potatoes, ketchang iju, haricot beans, spinach, Chinese cabbage, pi melon, turnip, onion, shallots, khan kong, pumpkin, dahl, split peas, lentils, tamarin beans, soya beans, sword beans, egg-fruit and a type of lettuce. We did actually see some meat, fish or pieces of egg in our evening stew. But best of all was the canteen. We could get bananas for a cent each, and quantities of duck eggs —fried, boiled or omeletted for ten cents. In those palmy early days when our cooked foods canteen was functioning we could even buy a roast duck now and then. On my birthday, a fortnight after arrival, with eight of my cobbers I had a discussion with four roast ducklings, stuffed with onions and herbs—a discussion more profitable in our pellagra-ridden condition than the finest of the Socratic Dialogues.

To men who had come from the desolation and miseries of the border jungle camps, this *was* a land of milk and honey—even if there was no honey and if a tin of milk cost you two dollars fifty cents—or ten days' pay for a private. Many of us had Burma rupees, which had been quite worthless in the jungle, but which were slowly exchanged here for Thai *ticals* or *bhats* (the Siamese dollar) at one for one. In the early weeks, and occasionally later, it was possible to exchange English pounds or American dollars for Thai currency—the general rate being thirteen to seventeen ticals for a pound sterling.

By the middle of March almost all of our rearguard had been brought down from the jungle, and the majority of the prisoners in Thailand were concentrated around the Kanburi area. At Kanburi the two main arms of the Meklong River met. The Tamarkan camp lay on one arm, the Chungkai camp on the other. There were two more camps at Kanburi itself and another at Tamawan, seventeen kilometres nearer Bangkok. Before the end of January hospital staffs and workers had been dispatched from all camps to open up a P.O.W. hospital at the town of Nakom Paton, about twenty miles west of Bangkok.

In these camps the bulk of the prisoners who remained in Siam spent most of the last year and a half of their captivity. Rations did not remain at the same standard as when we first arrived: canteen supplies diminished and prices spiralled steeply as time went on; but we never starved in these camps. At worst they were far better than the Burma jungle.

Tamarkan was now the headquarters of No. 3 Group, with which the smaller No. 5 Group from Burma had been incorporated. Other ex-Burma prisoners were with Colonel Williams at Kanburi, or went to the hospital camp at Nakom Paton. Chungkai had been the base hospital of No. 2 Group, and more than 2000 P.O.W. dead lay in its garden cemetery, which was devotedly made and maintained by fellow-prisoners. Tamawan was the headquarters of No. 4 Group.

The following official Japanese figures reveal how the various groups and nationalities had fared prior to 1 March 1944:

Group	Total	Alive	Dead	Dead (Per cent)
H.Q. - - -	6,504	5,972	532	8·2
1 - - - -	9,491	8,129	1,362	15·3
2 - - - -	8,919	7,540	1,379	16·5
3 and 5 (Burma) -	11,686	9,776	1,910	16·5
4 - - - -	13,706	11,597	2,109	15·3
Totals - - -	50,306	43,014	7,292	14·5

Nationality	Total	Alive	Dead	Dead (Per cent)
British - - -	23,871	20,488	3,383	14·2
Australian - -	8,458	7,174	1,284	15·1
American - -	668	541	127	19·0
Dutch - - -	17,391	14,901	2,490	14·0

These figures, however, exclude the 10,000 prisoners of F Force and H Force of whom more than 4000 (approximately 3200 British and 800 Australians) were dead in Burma and Thailand before the remainder were withdrawn to Singapore at the end of 1943. This casualty rate of over 40 per cent was incurred in less than eight months. It raises the total deaths along the railway, during the construction period, to nearly 20 per cent of the 60,000 prisoners engaged.

After we were brought down to the base camps in Siam, the death rate dropped sharply; but hundreds of men who died in Siam, Malaya or in other parts of Japanese territory during the remaining months of captivity owed their deaths to what they underwent in the 1942-3 period on the railway.

Tamarkan camp was bounded on the south by the river-bank covered with wide, spreading mango- and tamarind-trees. Across the river was a plantation of kapok-trees, thin and gaunt with their branches at right angles to the trunk like so many gallows. To the west were the railway and the

Japanese ack-ack battery, with the camp cemetery beyond. To the north, disused padi fields stretched to the foot of a steep ridge some 1500 yards behind the camp. To the east, a banana grove, coco-nut palms and jungle extended down to the township of Kanburi.

The river was an immense boon; each afternoon hundreds of us endured an extra parade in order to enjoy a few minutes in the stream. At its lowest, it was not more than 50 yards wide and you could walk across it if you were tall enough. The rains converted it into a mighty flood, four hundred yards across, which at times threatened to overflow the last bank and inundate the camp of the Japanese guards, which stood between the P.O.W. camp and the river.

The worst feature of life at Tamarkan was the long tankos —usually two per day. Working conditions in the jungle had made tankos, in most cases, irregular and reasonably brief. At Tamarkan, for months at a stretch, we had two counts daily, men sometimes being held on parade for more than an hour.

On the dawn tankos, at times, it was possible to see the Southern Cross, low over the tops of the trees along the river's bank. Beyond the patrolling guards and the fence which marked our captivity, above the shabby huts which surrounded the parade ground, it was a constant reminder of home and of the days that yet might be.

The monotony and barrenness of the hours on tanko were partially broken by the antics of the wild squirrels which used to play in the tree-tops just outside the camp fence. A flock of vultures seemed to adopt the camp as their permanent headquarters. They were doubtless attracted by our slaughter pit. Obscene and repellent as they crouched like round-shouldered ghouls on the coco-nut palms which were their favourite vantage point, they exercised a certain fascination when they wheeled aloft and circled with pinions motionless, gliding and dipping over the area. Their soundless communication system seems to work through some sixth sense unknown to human beings. As soon as one bird zooms down towards an object of interest, hundreds of vultures, previously asleep on trees or scattered all over the ground, suddenly flap off in the same direction, even though most of them could not possibly have seen the departure of their scout.

The camp itself developed into something of a menagerie. Countless sparrows and miners nested along the apex of the roofs of living-huts and cook-houses. Several of them built their homes in the hollow ends of the bamboos which made up hut framework. Cats abounded from the first and soon we had several batches of kittens. A duck yard and pig pens were established in the eastern part of the camp. We were told that the livestock was to be fattened up for our own ration but, in fact, we never saw any of this meat, which all went to the guards.

The Japanese attitude to these animals was a constant source of amusement to us. The keeper of the ducks was instructed that he must hold a tanko of his flock every morning and evening. Anybody who has sought to count 2000 milling ducks will realize the difficulties which this task involved. The American sergeant who was placed in charge of the pig pen was sacked by the Japanese because the sow farrowed prematurely and all the piglets died. We were accustomed to the absurdities which the Japanese exacted from us, but even we were amazed at the disciplinary action which they took against their livestock.

On one occasion, when the camp was prepared for the inspection of some senior officer, the pig men had to wash all the pigs' faces, so that they would be presentable. One pig immediately went and got his snout dirty again. A furious Japanese ordered him to be re-washed and placed in a separate pen by himself. Unrepentantly, he dirtied his face again. After the inspection he was placed on half-rations for three days as a punishment.

In another camp a pet monkey committed lèse majesté by biting a Japanese officer. He was solemnly chained up in front of the guard-house for several days just as if he were a defaulting soldier. A prisoner, returning from work past the guard-house entered his hut with the announcement, "There's been a mutiny, I think. The Jap commandant is chained up in front of his own guard house."

Before the end of 1943 it had been announced in the jungle camps that 10,000 of the fittest prisoners along the line were to be sent to Japan. After many parades, medical inspections and the issuing of hats, shirts, shorts and boots, parties were sent away, the men being divided into groups of 150 with one officer to each group. Many men volunteered for the party because they believed that conditions and treatment would be better in Japan, or because their friends were going.

The parties began to leave the Kanburi area in March, and the last of them reached Saigon by May. However, it proved impossible to ship them from Saigon owing to the stranglehold established over this port, as over Bangkok, by Allied bombers. After working in Saigon for several months, the bulk of the party was sent by train down to Singapore, where some were put on ships, while others remained on the island until the Japanese capitulation.

In September one of the ships carrying Allied P.O.W.s, including many Australians, was torpedoed by an Allied submarine. After gruelling days on the water, 150 of the survivors were picked up and brought to an allied port. They brought to the Allied world the first full story of our sufferings along the railway. To thousands of anxious families scattered throughout Australia they gave news of men whose fate had been shrouded in an ominous silence for three years.

On arrival at Tamarkan we found a gang of British captives engaged in building a memorial to those who had died on the railway. The Japanese chose a point midway between the camp and the Tamarkan bridge across the river for this memorial, which had commemorative tablets at its four corners and a tall cenotaph in the centre.

On 21 March Brigadier Varley, together with a selected number of officers and men, was marched over to the memorial to witness the opening service. Representatives of the various native races and sects employed on the railroad work were present, while gold-braided officers of the Thai army, navy and air force sat with Japanese officers under a specially erected marquee. The Japanese, sublimely unconscious of the irony of things, decked out the whole memorial as if for a harvest festival, the cenotaph and the oblation stone before it being covered with many types of the fruit and vegetables for lack of which the prisoners had died.

While newsreel photographers filmed us from every angle, various Asiatic representatives delivered speeches which were received with absolute apathy by the natives present, who looked as if they had been shanghaied into attendance. The Japanese and Thai officers fidgeted and looked glum and bored throughout the whole ceremony. Finally, Brigadier Varley read out a statement emphasizing that the conditions under which prisoners had worked would be investigated after the war.

The entire ceremony was an insult to God and man, carried through with a blatant hypocrisy and a lack of sincerity which no Japanese took the trouble to conceal. At the end, they lined us all up, black, white, yellow and brown, and solemnly presented each person with a tin of biscuits—a gesture apparently meant to suggest that all was now forgiven and forgotten.

I have never been present at any function so patently meaningless to everybody concerned. Prisoners and Asiatics alike, knowing the Japanese by bitter experience, knew that this was merely a gesture required by the demands of face. The only real point of interest, was that on the memorial the Japanese admitted 76,000 deaths among the fellow Asiatics whom they were "redeeming from Anglo-Saxon bondage".

The bringing of prisoners to Kanburi, and the better rationing in the camps, suggested to many of us that someone in Tokyo had at last come to realize the possible effects of killing off so many Allied prisoners in Burma and Thailand. We had further evidence of this in the reports which came up from Nankom Paton, regarding the new base hospital being constructed there. When our "heavy sick" were sent down there in thousands in April, they had better quarters, far better canteen supplies and a more adequate provision of medical requirements than we had ever received during our captivity.

The Land of Milk and Honey

Now, in April, in all camps, prisoners were requested to write freely and frankly on forty-four subjects dealing with our life, work, conditions and treatment on the railway. An assurance was given that no measures would be taken against anybody, whatever the views expressed. The forty-four essays listed covered all the heads under which a report would have been made to the Allied governments, and we seized with avidity the chance to say our piece.

I was asked by Lieutenant-Colonel George Ramsay to handle the first two essays dealing with the main issues involved in our treatment along the line. In these I outlined our story since our arrival in Burma. Lieutenant-Colonel Anderson, who, as senior officer, controlled the essays, asked me to tone down my expressions of opinion, although he admitted that nothing in the essay was either inaccurate or unjust. I set out to modify it, but found that this was impossible, for I had put forth the whole case exactly as I saw it. I therefore told the colonel that I could alter nothing and was quite prepared to sign the essay and put it in on my own responsibility. This was refused. Brigadier Varley, however, told me that he felt the essay should be placed before the Australian Government as, in his opinion, it covered the whole story fully and fairly, and he asked for a copy of it to incorporate in his own report.

A number of us felt that this request for our opinions had come from high quarters in the Japanese Government, over the heads of the local P.O.W. administration. It seemed to us a time to speak our minds as clearly and bluntly as we would have done in a report to our own government. Our sole concern was for the future, and we felt that nothing was to be gained by being mealy-mouthed about the inhuman treatment which had killed so many of our comrades. A particularly fine essay was that written by the Perth barrister, Jim Lalor, dealing with the bombing of Thanbyuzayat and Japanese refusal to identify prison camps.

Towards the end of March many thousands of letters arrived in the camp. Their delivery to us was held up for weeks, in some cases for months, while some of the letters were not given to their addressees until the Japanese had capitulated. This was partly due to a gentleman named Motogima.

Interned in Singapore at the outbreak of war, he had been sent to Adelaide where, on his own admission, he was very well treated. Although it was only a few months before he was exchanged, he received letters from his wife. However, she did not receive his letters, and he now announced that he had every intention of seeing that we did not get ours. When it was pointed out to him that thousands of men had received no word from home during over two years of captivity, he said that prisoners of war had no right to expect letters anyway.

This was not one of the coolie-ignorant guards, but a man who had been making his living under the British flag, and who had already seen how differently we treated Japanese prisoners. The way he persecuted us by withholding mail, which could bring some comfort to men who had so little, was a measure of Japanese inconsistency and vindictiveness.

In most camps, the Japanese, as a means of tormenting their prisoners, used the excuse that they had to censor the letters. All Japanese censors knew perfectly well, after seeing some hundreds of them, that nothing of the smallest military value or significance to Japan was contained in letters, which were anything up to two years old and which had already been censored by the Allied authorities.

After September 1943 all letters to prisoners were restricted to twenty-five words but, even so, the Japanese censors seldom did more than a couple of hundred in a day. They took holidays at frequent intervals, and refused to allow senior P.O.W. officers to make themselves personally responsible for censorship of the twenty-five word letters. On one occasion at Nonpladuk, the British commander, Colonel Toosey, was allowed to censor the mail. He worked conscientiously, for his life was at stake. In five days he dealt with more letters than the Japanese censor had tackled in nine months.

All over Siam, P.O.W. letters accumulated, often remaining for many months in the same camp as the man to whom they were addressed, but being withheld from him. The whole handling of our mail gave opportunity for a refinement of cruelty which afforded great satisfaction to the Japanese.

From the first days of our arrival in Siam, we heard that the Swiss consul in Bangkok was coming to visit the camps, with a view to organizing Red Cross supplies for us. In fact, we were never allowed to see him.

Whereas in Burma there was a complete absence of Red Cross supplies, we did, in Siam, receive a thin trickle of native tobacco, cheap cigarette papers and poor quality soap, bought by the consul with Red Cross funds. The only parcels we saw were distributed throughout the Siam camps in May 1944, when we got one parcel for each six prisoners. A special card acknowledging this had to be sent home by selected personnel. In our forty-two months of captivity we received the grand total of one-sixth of one monthly parcel per head!

However, we had ample evidence that the Japanese made good use of Red Cross goods sent for their prisoners. Guards were frequently seen with Red Cross cigarettes and tins and, in one jungle camp near Aperon in the middle of 1944, the Japanese guards lived for a period of five months on the Red Cross tins and foodstuffs which should have gone to their prisoners.

Some Australians working along the railway one day saw three goods vans packed with American Red Cross boots going up to the Japanese forces in Burma. When a protest was made, the local Japanese officer admitted the fact, said it was very shocking and he was very sorry, but this was the order of the Japanese military authorities. Similar instances in many areas caused some of us to express the hope that no Red Cross goods were being sent from home, since most of such supplies were seized by the enemy for his own purposes.

After the capitulation we received many cases of Red Cross books, which would have been worth their weight in gold for recreation and study in the camps. These had been withheld by the Japanese, although they could not possibly have derived the smallest benefit from them.

It is doubtful whether any months during our captivity dragged so painfully as those at Tamarkan, when we were waiting for the establishment of the second front. Caswell had been forbidden to operate his radio set, in view of the risks involved, and we were without direct news, although a number of newspapers did make their way into the camp.

In the spring of 1944, with the long-awaited second front still unestablished, we could see no term to our captivity and were, inevitably, despondent.

In the middle of May strong rumours of a successful Allied landing across the Channel became current. As in Burma at the time of Mussolini's downfall, rumour outran events by some weeks, but foreshadowed them with curious fidelity. Then, in June, passing Thais began signalling to prisoners that Germany was beaten. From Chungkai, where the Webber brothers of the British Army were operating a set, we received confirmation of the landing, and followed step by step the violent struggle that ensued.

When Paris was seized, the German armies being in full retreat, a tremendous wave of optimism spread through the camp. The officer who brought the radio reports from Chungkai solemnly offered to allow himself to be kicked all round the parade ground if Germany did not surrender within a fortnight. One Australian major laid a bet of £100 sterling that we would be free by Christmas. The optimism and general gaiety throughout the camps at that period was never reproduced until the actual ending of the war twelve months later.

It was on arrival in Thailand that we first got word of the Thai Secret Service organization which was assisting prisoners in Siam.

First contact with the Thai organization known as "V" was made by British canteen officers in Ban Pong in December 1942. The officers were informed that an organization had been established in Bangkok to supply money, medical supplies, clothing, food and information to P.O.W. camps in Thailand. It intended to send out of Thailand to the Allies lists of names, lists of sick, lists of deaths and details of P.O.W. conditions. Money was to be supplied at the rate of 1500 ticals per month to each unit with representatives in Thailand. All

A camp concert party making up for a show.

officers with troops in Thailand had at all times free access
to supplies from this organization.

Letters requesting supplies were smuggled out of the camps
by many devious methods, such as in the framework of empty
baskets returned to native traders. They were written in English with statements regarding the regiments in the camp, and
the nature of Japanese treatment. Letters from the V organization concealed in match boxes and bamboos, were received
regularly by various British officers. They were always typewritten in English and signed with a V.

The main agent along the Meklong River, beside which
the camps and railway line lay, was a major in the Thai army
seconded for this special work. His name was Nai Boon Pong.
Through the V organization, contact was established between
British officers and Prince Chaluk, of the Thai Royal Family,
Minister for Youth, who had coxed the Oxford crew in 1932.

The Portuguese consul in Bangkok, Mr De Campos, and
the Swiss consul, Mr Salzman, did splendid work in raising
subscriptions from the European community in Bangkok,
including Germans.

The Thai Freedom Society, behind this V organization,
was connected with the pro-Allied section of the Thai army.
Its contact with the outside world lay by a route running north
of Chengmei into China and on to Chungking. Thai army
officers used this channel to send messages and lists of prisoners
to the Allies from April 1943 onwards.

At the Wan Yan camp, Nai Chom, a supply contractor and
a representative of the Thai Governent, kept in touch with
prisoners along the Kwai Noi branch of the river and reported
to his government all movements of Japanese troops and supplies to Burma, as well as furnishing reports on P.O.W. conditions. He carried on this work until October 1944, when he
was arrested in Bangkok by the Japanese, and imprisoned on
trumped-up charges of fraud.

Before arrest, he reported to senior P.O.W. officers that Thais
were actively sabotaging the Singapore-Bangkok railway, and
this was later confirmed. He also gave us first news that para-
chutists, with portable radios, had landed south of Bangkok,

and that Allied submarines operating in the Gulf of Siam were in active communication with the Thais. He stated that at the cessation of hostilities a Thai organization would take over the P.O.W.s. In fact, in August 1945, a number of Thais were working and drilling with the British paratroop organizations scattered throughout Thailand. These were preparing to seize prison camps and release prisoners before the end of August.

At several camps the secret radio sets were kept supplied with earphones, batteries and valves, thanks to the efforts of the V association in Bangkok. Many of the medical supplies smuggled into P.O.W. camps were War Department supplies from Malaya. They had apparently been stolen from secret caches, and from Japanese stores in Singapore and other towns. They were then forwarded by Chinese, Indians and Thais to the white prisoners 800 miles away in the Siamese jungle.

The courage and fearless devotion with which the V agents daily risked a horrible death to aid the prisoners should never be forgotten. The families of Allied P.O.W.s in Siam owe a tremendous debt to all those in this brilliantly organized underground society, which helped to save the lives of hundreds of British, Dutch and Australian prisoners.

CHAPTER XXIX

JOURS D'ATTENTE

And not by eastern windows only,
When daylight comes, comes in the light,
In front, the sun climbs slow, how slowly,
But westward, look, the land is bright.

(Lines from Clough's "Say Not, The Struggle Naught Availeth" recited from the Tamarkan stage when we got news of the rout of the German armies in the Battle of France.)

My Tamarkan diary contains some entries that suggest the easing of the tension we all felt after the struggle for existence in Burma:

January-February 1944. In building the memorial to the men murdered along the railway, Nippon is expending more energy than would have been necessary to save thousands of them. It is a comment on the basic hypocrisy of Japanese thought that all that matters is the observance of form and ceremonial. They seem to feel that the meanness and brutality of their system can be effaced by the erection of a monument to their victims. . .

Cigarette papers are available here quite cheaply, so some of us are hoping that the practice of cutting up precious books will come to an end. In the jungle it was common to hear: "Ten pages of *David Copperfield* for five cents" or "Smoke *Gone With the Wind*—fine quality paper." In spite of certain protests by some of the padres, prayer books and Bibles, their sheets being rice paper, have been the most popular smoking material. Overheard: "Have you seen a copy of *Merchant of Venice?*" "No, it's the only Shakespeare play I haven't smoked."

The Jap guards say that Thai agents must be in communication with the British, because the bombers come over within a few hours of the arrival of any convoy at Bangkok. One guard told the buppin workers that Burma and Thailand would be "presentoed" to the British inside two months. There is growing evidence that, for the first time, the rank and file of the I.J.A. are coming to realize that the war may be lost. However, no such qualms assail the writers of *Greater Asia* who, describing a sitting of the new Burma Assembly, state: "At this stage a perceptible expression of determination and desire for annihilation of the enemy was observed on the faces of the delegates." This is what I call really observant journalism.

(In code). Brigadier Varley has placed all his diaries, records and confidential papers in my hands, so that I may help him in preparing a report for the Australian Government on our conditions in Burma. Other precious records, duplicating most of this information, are buried in one of the graves at Thanbyuzayat. In view of the danger of Japanese searches, I am doing most of this work in the brigadier's cubicle at H.Q., where one can get fair warning of the approach of any guard. The brigadier has asked me to make as few notes as possible, but to try to commit the main details to memory in case the Japanese seize his papers. Therefore I spend every second day carefully rereading and digesting all that I tackled the day before. . . .

The pay officers have just come down from the 105 where conditions are as bad as when we left. The diet is rice and "white death" (melon) exclusively and they have had a death a day lately. However, it seems definite that they will all be brought down here to rejoin the rest of us next month. Harry Farmer reports a conversation with an English-speaking Indian on the train down. The Indian, who had just come up from Singapore, stated that inflation was fantastic and all food very short. Rice costs twenty-five times as much as it did two years ago and the textile ration is three metres (nine feet) of sarong cloth per family per year!

March-April 1944. The siding at the 105 has been machine-gunned by Allied aircraft. Some bullets came into the camp and one Dutchman was killed . . .

The camp is laughing at the story of a twenty-stone Dutchman, who has worked in the camp cook-houses ever since we left Java. The other night he was on hut picket when a guard came round. The fat Dutchman bowed low, this action forcing wind very audibly from his massive stomach. The guard growled angrily. The fat Dutchman, overcome with embarrassment, hastily bowed again and again, each time with the same sound effect. The guard, furious, but helpless before the blast, at last melted into the surrounding darkness. This seems to be the first anti-Jap gas attack on record.

Last night there was a sunset that drew us from our books, our beds and our talk to stand, open-mouthed and marvelling, gaping at the glory of the sky. The centrepiece, dominant and lighting the rest, was a banked mass of flaming orange. Above it, away from the horizon, were royal blue, cobalt, teal blue and ultramarine shot with greens and golds and darkened by fingers and slivers of dusky purple. The effect was of a foreshore with dark sandbanks amidst incredibly lovely pastel pools with a great bushfire behind. As the lights of the heavenly proscenium dimmed, a long line of flaming scarlet broke forth, but the delicate duck's egg blues lingered almost to the last. Never in Burma, in the Indian Ocean or in the Mediterranean have I seen anything quite equal to this. It would have brought to life a man of clay.

The diary entries from March onwards are full of the magnificent shows put on at our Tamarkan theatre by Norman Carter. Nearly every week the concert was worth seeing, but the shows which will linger in the memories of all P.O.W.s were "Ali Baba and the Forty Thieves", "The Wizard of Oz", "Snow White", "When Knights Were Bold", "Viennese Nights", "Pinnochio" and "The Dingbats Abroad". The finest show of all came in June when Norman put on "The Gay Nineties" with such old tunes as "Won't You Buy My Pretty Flowers?" "Dolly Gray" and "Waiting at the Church"—tunes so old that they were fresh to us and the whole camp whistled them for months afterwards.

Stars of these Tamarkan concerts were Teddy Weller, Kingaroy; Jim Anderson, Hampton; Dick Mory; Val Ballantyne (our singers); Les Atyeo, Colac; Wally MacQueen, Korrumburra (our comedians); Jim "Hole-in-the-road" Jacobs (manager and stage villain); Ron Wells (swing); Norman Whittaker, Ashfield (band); Arnold Westgarth (choral); "Busty" Badger and "Happy" Marshall (female impersonators); John Vance, Sunshine (secretary); and Joe Harris, Ivanhoe.

A hard working and immensely resourceful team backstage contributed tremendously to the success of Norman Carter's shows. As stage managers, Arthur Shakes, of the Sydney *Sun,* George Plunkett, of Glen Iris, Melbourne, and Norman Halliday, did yeoman work. The designing of costumes and artistic decoration fell to Rae Nixon, of Sydney, while amazing evening dresses and faultless dinner suits made out of hessian sacking, dyed black, constituted a triumph for the nimble fingers of Frank Purtell. The scenic designs and backgrounds of Frank Brydges, of the *Sydney Morning Herald*, evoked round after round of applause.

May-June 1944. The departure of the Nakom Paton party has broken up the best discussion group to which I've ever belonged. For the past three months it has been meat and drink to all of us. We have reached a degree of intimacy and frankness which would be impracticable at home, and have discussed freely experiences which went pretty close to the bone.

The main stimulant has possibly been the very different occupations and environments from which the group has been drawn. Members—Des Woodbridge, International Brigade and car salesman; Jack Fitzgerald, of the Myer Emporium, Melbourne; Flip Relf, artist; Joe MacConnell, a jockey who rode with success in Victoria; Jack Simpson, British Electric salesman, whom I would back to sell a refrigerator to an eskimo in the Arctic Circle; "Bluey" Fitcher, from one of the N.S.W. Government departments; and, occasionally, Keith Mathieson, representing the Kirk.

. . . For the past week I have been receiving condolences from all and sundry on losing many papers during the search on 10 May. As usual, I was warned of the search well in advance, but foolishly put some papers out under a pile of logs, instead of burying them under my bed. Some batman went and sat on the very log. A guard, who had nothing to do with the search, came across to speak to the batman and spotted my papers, which he duly handed over to the searchers. Rotten bad luck but, thanks to the co-operation of Peter Rossiter and half a dozen good friends, I have already copied up most of the lost documents and diary and will rewrite the short stories. . . . (Later) Motogima handed back the novel manuscript after vigorous argument by Arthur Hence, but burned everything else, including the passport. Thank goodness I'd hidden my main diary in another place. The search probably resulted from the seizure of the brigadier's papers, when he was moved out of the camp on the first stage of his journey to Formosa, three days ago. We understand that they got all his diary and records, but I have most of it in my head.

. . . On the night of 27 June there came into this camp the first Red Cross medical supplies we have seen as prisoners. Colonel Hamilton, who showed us the stuff today, computed that it is worth £4000 and some of it is in sufficient quantity to last us for two years. All other camps, particularly the hospital at Nakom Paton, have received similar supplies in proportion to their strength. The tragedy is that we did not get even the smallest fraction of these drugs and dressings a year ago. There are sulphanilamide, sulphapyradine, atebrin, digitalis, ether, vitamin tablets in many forms, syringes and instruments, and 36,000 bandages. Heguchi, the horse doctor, admitted to Colonel Hamilton that he was amazed and broken hearted to see that the Allies still had such things to send to the prisoners. It is, of course, quite contrary to all Japanese propaganda.

(In code) Traders are going out every night. Some of the coloured Dutchmen go into Kanburi where they have friends among the native population, and even go to the pictures there under the noses of the Japs.

One Eurasian, allegedly, has become engaged to a Siamese girl. The Thais outside the camp are offering 1000 ticals for a revolver—enough to keep a P.O.W. in comfort for years. I believe there were several weapons at Thanbyuzayat, but I doubt if there is more than one left in this camp now . . .

July-August 1944. (In code) There is tremendous optimism everywhere as a result of the news. Many seem to expect Jerry to fold up within a month and think the Nip will then throw in the towel. I only wish I could believe it. . . . The new guards are so casual that Thais are coming into the camp for trading. One man stepped out of the strides he was wearing and got ten ticals on the spot. Another parted with his false teeth and got twenty-five. I don't know how he's going to cope with the rice without them. . . .

August began well. Alec Davis announced confidently that this would be our last August in captivity, and then Dave Thompson, of Kogarah, killed a rat and a python in swift succession. He sighted the python under the hut, pulled out one of the bamboo slats and was out of the hut before anyone else had moved. Even so, the python was twenty yards from the hut and streaking for the jungle before Dave broke its back. Then the medical orderlies claimed it and I gather that fried python fillets are on the menu at the R.A.P. tonight.

. . . Some of the work parties that have been sent up-jungle from here seem to be faring reasonably well. . . . On the other hand, George Evans, adjutant at Major Hellyer's camp at 198-kilo mark, reports a grim situation there through lack of quinine. Of 327 men in the camp only nine are fit to go out to work on the job of maintaining five kilometres of railway. All the rest are down with fever and quinine has been lacking for three weeks. Don Cummings, M.O. at this camp, has only a little atebrin for the worst cases. Several of the men have cerebral malaria and are walking round uttering the usual nonsense. One man keeps butting at trees like a goat or a horse with walkabout disease. Others are not sure whether they are Jesus Christ or Mahatma Gandhi. This reminds me of one cerebral case we had at Retpu, who was always packing up his bedding and setting out for the jungle with the statement that Wavell had sent for him and a special plane was waiting at the back of the camp to fly him out.

We have now ceased to be No. 3 Branch and have become amalgamated with the British group at Chungkai as No. 2 Branch. We had an all-day tanko for everybody including the sick before we were handed over to the No. 2 Group administration.

Soft ball has become the game of the moment. Yesterday, the whole camp turned out to watch a tremendous struggle—Yanks *v.* Aussies. The Americans have had long experience at the game, whereas all our men are new to it, but we have far greater numbers to draw from, which evens things up. The Australians were nine runs behind at the end of the seventh innings, but a batting rally saved the day. Cheer leaders, bands and supporters in fancy dress made this a gala occasion. On the previous evening some of the medical staff, who have never played the game, were having a hit. ———, a Red Cross man and a Scot, pulled off a surprising catch. When the watchers gasped with amazement, someone said, "Oh, you know these Scots. They'd grab anything!"

(In code) After all the rumours, it is at last confirmed that we have reoccupied Paris and that the German armies are in full retreat. It is good to think that, after five years of bondage, Paris is free again. I'd like to organize a band with a lot of brass horns, drums and tin cans and march round the camp playing "The Marseillaise", but I hardly think that the Japs would approve. . . . Have persuaded Norman Carter to put Johnny Crook on the stage to recite Clough's lines.* . . . (Later) Great enthusiasm among the troops and, of course, the quotation went completely over the heads of the Japs.

September-October 1944. Two amazing illustrations of the Japanese mentality:

1. The Japanese have just announced that our canteen will be stopped from buying meat, sugar and salt. The reason given: "Under the Geneva Convention you should get these things from us. If you have to buy them it means we are not giving you enough. If we stop you from buying them, therefore, it means you are getting enough." This is Jap logic *par excellence*.

2. From Chungkai comes the story of Japanese generosity to a British P.O.W. who jumped into the river to rescue a Japanese who fell off a barge and was in danger of drowning in the current. The Japanese presented the rescuer with an illuminated address and an envelope containing "a sum of money". When he opened the envelope, he found in it 50 cents (about 3d. today). When his mates expressed their disgust, he merely shrugged saying, "Oh well, that's about all he was worth, after all."

General expectations are that things will become increasingly unpleasant from now until the end. A Japanese N.C.O. stated yesterday that if Japan faces certain annihilation, all prisoners will be driven into a compound and shelled or machine-gunned. . . .

October has seen a reaction to our previous optimism. (In code) The Allies seem bogged down before the Siegfried Line. These days of waiting, when the end seems at last clearly in sight, are the hardest thing of all. Everywhere you go you are asked how much longer you think it will be. Many of us are beginning to ask what part of our lives we must write off under the heading "the years that the locusts have eaten".

* See head of chapter.

CHAPTER XXX

BOMB HOSTAGES

I tell ye naught for your comfort,
Yea, naught for your desire,
Save that the sky grows darker yet
And the sea rises higher.
—G. K. CHESTERTON

IT was 6.30 p.m. on 29 November 1944. The entire camp,
except those sick in the huts was drawn up in closely packed
files on the Tamarkan parade ground, the officers' battalion in
front. Suddenly the Dutch colonel in front of the parade
pointed towards the west, crying out, "Look! Planes!" Then
we saw twenty-one four-engined bombers in close formation
sweeping in over the camp. They were very low, purposeful
and menacing. For a moment the entire parade gaped at them.
One misguided officer called out, "It's all right, they're Nips!
Stand firm." But no one had ever seen Japanese planes like
these. The order was reversed and, as one man, we dived for
the slit-trenches along the huts on either side of the parade
ground. It was a bad moment. The bombers could not have
failed to see that serried mass of men. Even as we reached
the trenches the ack-ack opened fire, and a second later the
bombs came tumbling down.

Virtually all the Australian officers were crushed into the
three feet drains at the end of No. 1 hut. We heard the whistle
of the falling projectiles, and then there was a series of
explosions just as the planes passed directly over our heads at
less than 5000 feet. At any instant we expected to hear the
machine-guns start chattering. But, to our immense relief the
planes droned past. We were just getting up from the trenches
when the whole formation began to turn, swinging north,
and we all thought, "Here they come again!"

Bomb Hostages

Most of us started to make towards the banana grove at the east end of the camp, where our boundaries had been extended a little to enable establishment of a dispersal area. The planes now turned eastwards but kept on their course and passed over beyond the ridge to the north of the camp, disappearing into the west.

Then, at last, we were able to take stock of the situation. A few bombs had fallen in the river, or near the bridge without damaging it. The majority had plastered the ack-ack battery, but three bombs had overcarried and fallen within the camp, demolishing the ends of No. 1 and No. 2 huts. There was a crater about forty feet deep and a hundred feet in diameter where two bombs had fallen together.

Getting what tools we could, we immediately set to work, trying to dig out the sick men who had been at the ends of the stricken huts. However, the Japanese called everybody on to parade and held a long, maddening tanko, regardless of our anxiety to excavate the buried men. At last, about fifty volunteers from the officers' battalion were released for the job and, with spades and chunkels, we set to work trying to penetrate the mountains of soggy mud and wrecked bamboo under which the missing men were entombed.

We worked frantically, seeking vainly to make fast progress through the heavy earth and tangled wreckage. At least sixty men, wounded by bomb splinters and flying debris, were treated at the R.A.P. Well after dark, we were relieved by another shift who took over our tools and carried on. A number of bodies were recovered and about two o'clock in the morning a man was dug out alive. A comrade, who had lived for a few hours after the bombing, lay dead across his knees. How he himself survived suffocation for eight hours is one of those inexplicable mercies which crop up in war.

When I got back to my bed, I found the bamboo shelf above it wrecked, my wife's picture and the others things on it scattered over the bed and floor; in the middle of the bed, among some cards from home that had arrived that evening, lay a long, jagged bomb fragment.

It was not until late on the second day after this that the

last of our seventeen corpses was recovered. It seemed fairly clear that the bombers had not sought to hit the camp, but that one bomb-aimer had overshot badly in his run on the ack-ack. Had he hesitated a fraction of a second more, his bombs must have wiped out most of the officers and N.C.Os in the camp. From where we lay it was only forty yards to the lip of the crater, and we had felt the blast which rushed up the trenches.

The only really surprising thing about the attack was that it had been delayed for so long. The camp was put in the closest possible proximity to the railway bridge and to the battery defending it and, as at Thanbyuzayat, P.O.W. casualties were inevitable the moment the obvious target was attacked. We knew that the raid on the battery was only a prelude to heavy bombing of the bridge and that we could look for more casualties.

The Japanese said that we received no alert because the planes had been thought to be Japanese. We had never seen a four-engined Japanese plane, or twenty-one Japanese planes together in this country. Allied Liberators and Fortresses droned over in dozens, so this was nonsense. A Japanese officer said to Lieutenant-Colonel Tom Hamilton, chief of our hospital, that he was very sorry and would do anything he could. The colonel immediately asked if he could be given a red cross to place on his hospital. The Japanese said no, as this would give protection to other prisoners who were not entitled to it. Colonel Hamilton then asked that the Allied authorities be given the location of the hospital. Again the Japanese demurred on the ground that international law was disregarded today. Finally the colonel asked for all possible steps to be taken to protect the sick P.O.W.s. The Jap officer said, "We have given you guns right beside the camp *to defend you against the planes.*"

For Tamarkan, the writing had been on the wall since 6 September, when the Nonpladuk camp, fifty-six kilometres away, at the junction of the new railway with the Singapore-Bangkok line, was bombed.

This camp lay in the middle of the main marshalling yards

and workshop centre west of Bangkok. The camp was bounded on one side by sidings, on another by workshops, and on the third by supply sheds and anti-aircraft batteries. All these major targets were within a few yards of the huts where prisoners were huddled together on top of each other.

The inevitable results of the situation had already been forcibly pointed out to the Japanese authorities by the British C.O., Colonel Toosey. But despite all protests, no identification marks were allowed and the prisoners were refused the right to dig slit trenches for their own protection. Strong, deep shelters had already been prepared for the Japanese guards, but the prisoners were told that they must remain in their huts.

On 6 September three Japanese ammunition trains lay in the sidings alongside the P.O.W. camp. Twenty-one Allied planes came over in the first wave. They bombed with deadly accuracy, destroying the three trains with a number of Japanese on board, and wrought great destruction in the workshop area; not a single bomb fell on the prison camp. The next wave of aircraft consisted of twelve planes, of which eleven dropped their bombs on the targets. The last plane released its bombs too soon, and the stick fell right across the camp. The prisoners, who had been herded into their huts at the point of the bayonet, were lying on the bamboo platforms a couple of feet above the ground. The bomb splinters simply tore apart the frail huts, killing, maiming or injuring 434 men, of whom 98 died.

Lieutenant-Colonel Sugasawa, who since August had been supreme commander of all Allied prisoners in Burma and Siam, visited the camp next day and listened impassively to a moving appeal from Colonel Toosey for the removal of personnel from this death-trap. Around Sugasawa, as he stood in the middle of the hospital, lay the maimed and shattered men. But with complete indifference to their suffering, he said: "This will happen many times again. You are soldiers. You must be prepared to die." He told the colonel to look after the slit-trenches which would now be allowed.

Yet the 3000 Allied prisoners were kept cooped up in "the

Nonpladuk death triangle" while night after night Allied planes bombed and strafed the workshops, sidings and supply sheds. More prisoners were killed and injured, and the Japanese at last ordered the evacuation of the camp. This was five weeks after Japanese headquarters had received a letter from Colonel Toosey couched in terms as blunt as if he had been reporting to the British Government. Of the senseless massacre of helpless prisoners in such circumstances Colonel Toosey wrote: "It is against all rules of humanity, all international law, and even against commonsense."

We now entered upon a period of constant alerts and anxiety. It is doubtful whether anything imposed so great a strain on the sick men, lying helplessly in the hospital huts, as this hourly apprehension of attack by their own planes. It was a refinement of mental torture.

The raid of 29 November ushered in a series of late afternoon attacks on the bridge at Tamarkan and the Kanburi area. On 2 December, and again on the eighth, tenth and thirteenth, Allied planes circled over the area for several hours. They dropped a number of bombs on the store sheds and Japanese supply dumps at the Kanburi station, but fortunately missed the hut in which P.O.W. mail was stored. Practically every shed in the area was razed to the ground. On 13 December there was a series of attacks on the bridge. One plane came down in a dive over the camp, just skimming the ridge behind us. He opened up with his machine-guns, spraying lead all over the camp area, killing one man in a slit-trench and seriously wounding the man beside him. It was a nerve-racking experience, for the planes came straight over the camp and we were never sure whether we were to be the target.

On 8 December came a mass onslaught on the whole line from the Burma border to Kanburi. At Brencasi, where sidings and the river-bank alongside were bombed and machine-gunned, seventeen prisoners were killed and fourteen were wounded. At Kwiye, two planes came over a train loaded with prisoners. Many of the men took off their hats and waved. The planes turned and ran back over the train, but still the men stayed waving. On their third run, a Dutchman added to the war's collection of "famous last words" by calling out: "Look, they're dropping pamphlets!" The bombs smashed up the trucks causing 111 casualties, of whom 41 were killed.

From then on, the whole railway line was attacked continually until the Japanese capitulation eight months later. All major bridges were repeatedly broken up, and much rolling-stock was destroyed. The railway, which had never been a great supply channel for the Japanese forces in Burma, became completely disrupted. In many cases trains had to be unloaded at the river-bank and the goods ferried across the stream in junks or barges to be loaded on to another train on the other side. Few trains moved at all in the daytime, and the confusion on the single-track line was appalling. It sometimes took a month for goods to travel the 350 miles from Bangkok to Moulmein.

Perhaps the worst raid at Tamarkan occurred on 5 February 1945, when Allied planes bombed the bridge and anti-aircraft post for over four hours. Only about fifteen men in the camp were injured, but great fragments of jagged shrapnel strewed the camp area, one huge piece of bomb casing falling into a slit-trench 300 yards from the bridge. One bomb fell at the end of No. 9 hut, which had been evacuated, and a splinter from another burned down the canteen and the adjacent hut.

Colonel Chris Black, wounded in the Thanbyuzayat raid, decided that he was our Jonah about bombing. He reached Tamarkan after ten months at Nakom Paton on 29 November, a few hours before the first raid. He returned to Tamarkan from Chungkai on 5 February, and once again the bombers appeared to celebrate the occasion.

Most men found these raids more terrifying than anything they had experienced during the war. The sense of being trapped, and of being ignorantly hammered by your own people after three years of Japanese maltreatment, produced a measure of fear and despondency out of proportion to our actual casualties, but very natural in the unhappy circumstances. There seemed to be a gigantic irony in the wiping out of men who had battled their way through the ordeal of the jungle by the very agents to whom they had looked for liberation.

For three years we had sung in the prison camps, to the tune of "She's a'coming round the mountain", the words—"They'll be flying Flying Fortress when they come" and "They'll be dropping thousand pounders when they come". After the long, long vigil of waiting "they" had come with their thousand pounders, but at times it seemed to us that their coming meant not liberation but annihilation.

Fortunately, most of us managed to preserve our sense of humour, even when things were stickiest. I remember a conscientious medical orderly running across to Commander Epstein, just after we had taken to the slit-trenches as a formation of bombers came heading towards the camp: "Sir," he panted, "so-and-so is definitely running a fever: his temperature is up." "Waal," drawled the commander, "I guess there's quite a few of us running a little fever right now."

On another day we had a very bad moment when we sighted over a score of B-29s, which altered course and ran straight in over the camp. They were by far the biggest planes any of us had seen. Just as their roar seemed to make the very air pulsate, I heard a Cockney voice from the next slit-trench exclaim: "Blimey Bill, there's a bloody flying town hall, clock tower and all."

Our guards were tremendously impressed with the size of the planes, and with the contempt they showed for the ack-ack fire. One Korean guard said: "No ——— good. Too many *skorki*.* Too much! Too big! All Nippon paradiso go!" The boys: "You bet!" A Korean's description of our reconnaissance aircraft, which came over every day about noon, was excellent: "Come-look-see-go-back-speakie-plane."

Many prisoners discovered that they could produce an unexpected burst of speed when the bombers were on their way. I heard one man say: "You should have seen X going through. I was left dizzy by his eddy." His mate, with disarming can-

* Japanese for plane.

dour: "That's nothing. He went past me too; but not half as fast as I went past him when I heard what he'd heard."

In August 1944 Allied planes had dropped pamphlets in English along the line, telling prisoners of the successes in France and of the general swing of the war. These pamphlets ended with the words: "Take heart, we are coming!" By the end of the year, as one wag said, the message should have been amended to read: "Take cover, we are here!"

Tamarkan camp was evacuated in February 1945, the officers being sent to Kanburi, while the other ranks were scattered over various camps. Before the evacuation was complete, on 13 February, there was another big raid on the bridge by over a score of Liberators. One bomb fell in the parade ground within a few yards of our bamboo theatre, but, fortunately, all personnel remaining in the camp were in slit-trenches a couple of hundred yards away. In the light of the tragedy at Nonpladuk, the staggering thing about the Tamarkan raids was that casualties were so low. It was no fault of the Japanese that many hundreds were not killed or maimed as our bombers battered the bridge and its defending battery.

From the Kanburi camp we witnessed half a dozen more major raids on the bridge, which was knocked down as fast as the Japanese repaired it. The main concrete railway bridge was finally put out of action altogether. Most of the traffic in the last months of the war passed over a wooden bridge, which prisoners had to maintain and rebuild after each attack. Working on this job was no sinecure, but the Japanese engineers, whose camp across the river was bombed and machine-gunned, were by this time as bomb-happy as anyone, and usually gave ample warning of the approach of bombers.

Farther up the line towards the border, several prison camps suffered casualties in attacks, but none had such frequent ordeals as Nonpladuk and Tamarkan.

At one siding a group of prisoners, under a Jap sentry, were pushing a truck along the rail when two planes came over. The guard refused to allow them to take cover as the planes swept down to attack. At the last minute the men jumped down the embankment to either side. Nine prisoners were killed on the side where the bombs fell. Unfortunately the guard had jumped the other way.

In another working camp up-jungle, the Japanese forced all prisoners on to a square in the centre of the camp and covered them with machine-guns and hand-grenades. As the planes approached, the Japanese stated that whoever got killed in the attack, the prisoners would die first. This was symbolic of the Japanese attitude. It was similar to their view about crowding prisoners into hellships without any identification mark. As one Jap officer said: "Enemy sink Japanese ship—very bad. Enemy sink own people too—not so bad."

In all, about 800 prisoners were killed or wounded by Allied bombing in Siam. The menace of attacks by our own planes on camps habitually placed against military objectives was the main shadow over our last year of captivity. Many felt that the Japs might, or might not, succeed in massacring us all before we were released. But they were at pains to give our own bombers every chance of exterminating us in the meantime.

CHAPTER XXXI

GENTLEMEN IN G-STRINGS

In idleness alone is there perpetual despair.
—CARLYLE

FROM the time of our arrival in Burma, a struggle raged between the Japanese and their prisoners as to whether officers should work. In Burma, thanks to the firm stand taken by the Australian officers, nobody with a commission did actual manual labour on the railway for the Japanese. It was felt that by this insistence on at least one point of international law officers might be able to retain some status which would enable them to intervene and act as a buffer between our captors and the men whom they wished to convert into coolies and slaves.

In Siam, where some hundreds of British officers, belonging to the Indian Army, were separated from their Indian troops, the large number of officers made it impossible for all to find jobs in charge of kumis or in the P.O.W. administration of the camps. There was a showdown at which all officers were herded into a square and told that they would be shot if they did not agree to work. A number were in favour of defying the Japanese to do their worst, but at a vote of lieutenant-colonels it was decided, by a narrow majority, that further resistance could lead only to massacre. Thenceforth, officers' kumis worked on the construction of embankments, cuttings and bridges, in the same way as kumis composed of other ranks. They drew no pay for this work, but received the normal thirty ticals a month allowed to officers in Siam. Lieutenant-colonels were the only officers exempt from this work, and several of these acted as kumi leaders.

After the completion of the railway, when the bulk of the prisoners were congregated in the Kanburi area, different policies regarding officers prevailed in each group, but all officers were called on to do a job whether administrative, in charge of working parties, or in manual work.

At Tamarkan in October 1944, after various crises, officers were faced with a choice of doing manual work under Japanese instructions, or watching sick men from the hospitals driven out to the job. In the circumstances there was no choice at all. All fit officers not on the headquarters staff or running kitchens, canteens or other departments were sent out on hut construction, gardening and other work. Some of us grumbled and hated it; most of us grumbled but rather liked it.

The Japanese adjutant at Tamarkan was a black-bearded officer, far better than the average run of Jap officers, who rejoiced in the nickname of "Bluebeard" or "Whiskers Blake". He and a small, fat warrant-officer, who waddled round in shorts with short socks held up by purple suspenders, procured some vegetable seeds, and announced that officers could lay out a vegetable garden on the river-bank, between the huts occupied by the Japanese administration and the river.

Captain Rex Salier, of Scottsdale, Tasmania, took charge of the garden, and officers formed syndicates to handle so many beds. Our syndicate of three started with two beds and ended up with eight, the last four of which were literally carved out of the jungle. In these, by the beginning of January, we had about 300 tomato plants as well as khan kong, beans, Chinese cabbage and lettuces.

The fierce tropical sun scorched the beds for twelve hours a day, and every drop of water had to be carried up the steep river bank, but we thrived on the work. I doubt whether, at the beginning, Thailand boasted three more inexperienced vegetable growers than Don Capron, John Crooke and myself. Don was O.C. of the tool shed, and Johnny Crooke had a battalion to worry about, whereas I handled the canteen for our hut, which left me free for part of the morning and afternoon; so I had to do most of the watering. If you really wish to appreciate the garden hose in your backyard at home, try carrying sixty to eighty pounds of water on twenty to thirty separate trips up a steep bank and then tipping the water over your plants. It gives you a much better idea of what the word "peasant" means.

The fierceness of the sun had its advantages, for the plants grew with gratifying rapidity. There was a certain primitive satisfaction in scrambling barefoot up and down the muddy bank with the tin cans. Socks were at a premium, and without socks boots blistered your feet. Clogs were impossible on the slippery bank, so it was easiest to work barefoot in the best Asiatic tradition. You could really experience a sense of something achieved when you had hacked your way through the jungle shrubs and grasses, dug out the clinging roots and produced a civilized looking garden bed where, a few days before, nature had seemed permanently triumphant.

The best hours of the day were early in the morning and in the late afternoon. I used to stand sometimes gazing across the river to the opposite bank where a Siamese family, probably forced out of Bangkok by bombing, was endeavouring to clear a patch for padi and vegetables. They had little more in the way of tools and equipment than ourselves and, being engaged in a similar job, one came to understand something of the Asiatic coolie's philosophy and patience.

The river was always interesting. Barges, on which whole families lived year after year, were often moored along the bank or on a sand-bar just opposite our plot. Sometimes they built fish traps in the water which were raided from time to time by both the Japanese and ourselves. The river contained some quite big fish and many little fellows, who made up for their lack of inches in ferocity. At one time, I was laid up for over a fortnight because of a very personal attack by one of these brutes, who had never heard of the Marquis of Queensberry's rules. Some men had their toes bitten through to the bone. When this befell one of the unpopular guards, a number of prisoners gathered round, with grave expressions. The guard, who could not understand a word of English, was quite satisfied that they were condoling with him. Actually, the boys were saying with considerable satisfaction: "Pity it didn't bite your toe right off!" and "That's only a joke compared with what's coming to you."

Bird life teemed on the river. The Indian shite-hawk and the ubiquitous vulture patrolled up and down the stream with nonchalant, graceful glides, quite incompatible with their ugly waddle when they alighted on the sand-banks. Then there was a black and white kingfisher which, with frantic beatings of its small wings, would hover motionless in one place for fifteen or twenty seconds before descending in a power dive on some unfortunate small fish or insect on the water's surface.

Cormorants, water hens and an occasional crane would appear from the reeds and vegetation on the bank, to make their sorties for food. A bevy of ducks belonging, I think, to our guards, used to tantalize hungry prisoners, drawing water for the gardens, until, just before Christmas, several of them came to an unpleasant end in the noble cause of our Christmas dinner.

Those days on the river-bank provided a blessed refuge. Frequently one did not see a Japanese or Korean all day. After three years with others always at your elbow, you were able to find a little privacy in the garden. You became familiar with the scores of beetles, spiders, ants and other insects that swarmed out of the jungle to inspect the cultivated earth. In the quiet of the evening, before you had to go back to camp for tanko, it was blissful to lie on the sand-bank in the subdued rays of the setting sun watching the river birds hunting their evening meal. Here, for the first time since I had left the little bamboo thicket at Kun Knit Kway, I did manage to forget at times the shabby huts, the bamboo stockades, the strutting guards and the interminable "kiwotski" and "kiri" of our existence.

Of course, just as our tomatoes were ripening in numbers, we were moved to Chungkai. Those officers who remained at Tamarkan were called on for hut building, trench digging and other jobs, and the garden languished sadly. Still, we had had those precious months.

At Chungkai, about three miles from Tamarkan, on the

Quai Noy branch of the Meklong, gang work was the order of the day for most of us. In November the Japanese had received orders to build bunds with deep moats and palisades around all prison camps. We were not quite sure of the reason for this step. Some felt it was a further precaution against attempts to escape, and against the activities of the traders who were going out from all camps to trade with the Siamese every night. The more pessimistic considered it a device to facilitate the "liquidation" of prisoners in the event of a paratroop landing or some other emergency.

At Chungkai the building of the bund involved the clearing of hundreds of dense bamboo thickets. The bamboo in Siam is not of the pleasant variety we know in Australia. It is covered with thousands of long, jagged thorns and is a more awkward obstacle than any tree. It is too green to burn and, even when the stems are separated from the root, each stick adheres to the clump with a thousand thorny branches and shoots. The Japanese solution to the problem was to harness teams of forty or fifty on a long rope to each stick and pull it by main force from the clutches of the rest of the clump. I worked on one of these bamboo rope-gangs throughout the weeks at Chungkai, except for a couple of days of water-carrying in the big communal garden, which stretched over eight or ten acres to the north of the camp.

Many officers complained continually that it was inconsistent with their dignity to work as coolies, clad only in shorts or loin cloths. Yet it seemed to many of us that the Japanese had already committed enormities which made such protests, at this stage, rather absurd. The food at Chungkai was quite good, by prison camp standards, and most of us put on weight. The grumbling came largely from the bone-lazy, for in comparison with working conditions along the railway, this was a very soft assignment.

The Chungkai camp was the best in Burma or Siam. The river formed one border of it and, even with bathing hours restricted, it made life more agreeable. Big trees offered shade and broke down the harshness of the prison camp. Gardens, long established, particularly those in and around the camp cemetery, offered the pleasantest environment we had encountered.

A gifted concert party, directed by Leo Britt, and including Charles Faulder, an excellent actor from Shanghai, put on Shaw's *Major Barbara* and other successful shows.

Unfortunately, at the beginning of February, 1945, following many rumours that we were all to be transferred to Malaya, to Japan and to Hanoi—to build another railway—we moved again. For the first time since they had captured us, the Japanese followed the accepted tenets of international law and separated all officers in Siam, except a handful of doctors and padres, from the men. We were moved from Chungkai via Tamarkan—where we were just in time for the hair-raising raid of 5 February—to the Kanburi camp. Over 3000 Allied officers—Australian, American, British and Dutch—were packed into the narrow confines of this bare, unpleasant camp which lay on the edge of a padang between the township of Kanburi and the railway line. Here many were to remain for the last six months of our captivity, although some of us had another move just before the atom bomb put an end to Japanese resistance.

Before we were moved from Chungkai to Kanburi, the Japanese arrested Captain William A. Parker, of the 131st U.S. Field Regiment, captured on Java. Captain Parker had been responsible for organizing a constant supply of *Bangkok Chronicles* at Tamarkan. This newspaper, edited by a German, and published in English, contained a reasonable amount of war news, although most of it was from the Domei Agency. It proved invaluable in enabling us to fill in the gaps in the résumés of the B.B.C. bulletins sent over from Chungkai. The Japanese had caught one of the Americans involved in obtaining this paper from the Thais, while watching the camp herd outside camp boundaries. Captain Parker's arrest followed. Here is his story of the way in which he was handled by the Japanese kempis:

On the afternoon of January 31, interpreter Takahatchi started the investigation. I was handcuffed, led from the cell and tied to a table leg. He asked me a number of questions about age, name, nationality, place of birth, etc., then announced that he wanted to know all about the *Bangkok Chronicles* that entered Tamarkan camp. He stated that I might as well tell the truth as he knew all about it in detail and had enough evidence to convict me. When I started getting *Bangkok Chronicles*, I had had an understanding with Seaman Gus Foresman, U.S. Navy, who was bringing in the papers from outside; if we were caught by the Nips we two were to deny nothing, take the punishment and leave all others out, if any others were implicated. Of course my idea of punishment was mild compared with what we received. Takahatchi asked me who brought the papers to me. I answered that I didn't know his name, but could identify him. I did this because I wanted to see what the Nips had on hand. Foresman was brought out and I promptly identified him as the one. Foresman was led back to his cell and Takahatchi continued his investigation.

At about this point he stated that up until now they had been treating me as a gentleman, but now they would treat me otherwise. He immediately started bashing me with a heavy rod (bamboo). He was soon joined by a Nip sergeant and another Nip, who had long hair and was quite handsome. These three carried out their so-called investigation, punctuated by asking questions, beating, questions, beating and so on. Each session lasted from two to four hours, the instrument used being a heavy rubber insulated wire loop. The long-haired Nip on the third session, broke this whip while beating me. Then he placed small bamboo sticks between my fingers, and with his hands started pressing with all his might on my fingers, which created a terrific pain upon the middle joints. After tiring of this he sat down. At this time (3 days of beating) my back and legs from my shoulders to my ankles were solid with bruises, cuts, abrasions, etc. The blood was streaming from the cuts in my back when a fourth Nip, not in the investigation group at all, passed by, picked up a double handful of sand and gravel and proceeded to rub it into my wounds. None of the three said a word to stop him. After this they threatened me with a very heavy rope, the strands centred with wire. They used a fan belt (automobile) this same session.

This third session was my worst, the first two being a grim experience but this third, and last (thank God!) was so severe that, on getting back to my cell, I gave Major Gerrsen (a cell mate) my wife's name and address and asked him if he made the grade to write her, as the Nips in my opinion, were going to beat me to death. The bruises were fifty-nine days in leaving my back and legs. This may be verified by Major W. H. Rogers, U.S. Army, who was in the same case, and when transferred to Bangkok, was in the same cell with me. All this time, while the investigation lasted, the food (passed through a small opening in the door) was a small bowl of rice covered with a sprinkling of vegetables, and it had to be passed to your mouth with your hands.

After the investigation my papers were sent to Bangkok about January 28, and a period of lightened treatment followed. We were allowed to eat our own food outside the cell, saw wood and go to the river for a bath. About 2 o'clock one morning I was brought out for investigation, but this time they did not beat me. On February 8, 16 men, tied with ropes (3 together) were transferred to Kempis H.Q., Bangkok. We slept on the porch, and on the morning of February 9, we were moved to a small gaol in the Nip Thai G.H.Q. We stayed here from February 9 to

March 2. 25 men in a cell for 10, a latrine that was stopped up usually, no ventilation, no mosquito net (mosquitoes in large numbers), only 3 small cups of tea a day—very hot and very trying. Here we started out routine that lasted until our release on August 15, viz., sitting at attention for 15 hours a day, arising at 8 a.m., allowed to go to sleep at 11 p.m. No rest, no talking. If a guard caught you at any time violating the above he usually came into the cell or ordered you outside for a bashing. . . .

At the court martial on 19 February 1945, prisoners from various camps charged with having received or seen *Bangkok Chronicles* were sentenced to from five to seven years each. Captain Parker and Foresman received six years apiece. It should be remembered that their sole offence was obtaining local papers, controlled by the Japanese, which any other country would have supplied daily to its officer prisoners. Captain Parker's story is representative of the experiences of a number of English and Dutch officers arrested at this time on charges of news dissemination and of obtaining ticals from Thais with cheques payable post war. It reveals the delight in the torture and degradation of white officers which was a feature of the Japanese treatment of prisoners in all theatres. Captain Parker's account concludes:

We European prisoners had to clean the latrine boxes for all prisoners with our hands, and many times were not allowed soap to wash our hands. . . . Food . . . we got what was left after the guards and Nip prisoners— usually half to a third of the amount the Nip prisoners received. Only one time did we receive fruit (2 bananas) in six months. Weak tea (nothing else to drink), no tobacco, never any bread. Generally the quality of the food was O.K., but the quantity was not enough.

. . . One Chinaman and two Thais were executed while we were here —one of these Thais was the bravest man I have ever heard of—for approximately three months he received beatings that brought him near death, but he walked out of the cell under his own steam. On one occasion I counted over 120 licks as they bashed him with stout bamboo, iron chains, etc. They tortured him at length, in several ways of which we had to use our imagination. The thuds, bangs and groans come from his cell sometimes every day.

. . . While working we moved large numbers of rice bags of 100 kilograms [220 pounds], 125 kilograms of peas, heavy logs, bags of wet clay. Standing working in the mud and rain, no headgear ever allowed to be worn while working outside. . . . [We were often] so hungry [that we] had to pick over Nip garbage baskets. . . .

CHAPTER XXXII

WE MEET THE POMMIES

For Allah created the English mad—the maddest of all mankind!
—RUDYARD KIPLING

WHAT were the relations of the Australians with their fellow captives in the prison camps?

Practically every one of the 12,000 Australians who worked in Burma and Siam made contacts with men of other countries, from the United States, the N.E.I., or from Great Britain. Many men, particularly those who had never left Australia before the war, acquired a new outlook on many things as a result of conversations with men from other lands with vastly different backgrounds, interests and points of view. Hundreds of friendships formed in these camps will remain, although the men concerned may never see each other again. By the end of our captivity most of us had at least one friend among each of the other nationalities. Any discussion of group relationships involves generalizations to which there were many exceptions.

It would be false to pretend that our relations with the Dutch were particularly cordial. On many occasions, officers and men of the other nationalities were left with the feeling that the Dutch had not acted up to our expectations. Collectively, both the Australians and the English disliked the Dutch, and it is very probable that the feeling was reciprocated.

It is pointless here to dig up the feuds and grievances which recurred in so many camps. In the battle for self-preservation it was natural that men should put their fellow countrymen first all the time. Inevitably, this led to charges and counter-charges of selfishness and discrimination.

The Dutchmen, doubtless, have their own grievances and resentments. However, the fact must be chronicled that the Dutch, collectively, lost a great opportunity of forging powerful links of friendship with the 12,000 officers and men from the land which is their nearest neighbour in the Pacific.

There were Dutchmen who were immensely popular with the men of other nations. A number of these were fine men —able, cultured and generous. Unfortunately, *en masse*, this was not the impression that they made on their fellow-captives. Rightly or wrongly, the verdict of almost all Australian and British prisoners was unanimous: "Yes, some of them are good fellows, but as a whole ———"

The Americans were a small phalanx of hundreds among the many thousands of other nationalities. Nearly all of them were from Texas, or surrounding States. Having similar home backgrounds, they pulled together and at all times displayed a splendid team spirit in looking after their sick.

There was a great deal of argument and chyacking between the Americans and ourselves but, in most instances, our relations were good. In those camps where team competitions, such as volley ball, soft ball and basket ball were allowed, the Americans more than held their own. Their star players evoked the warmest expressions of admiration from the sport-loving Australians.

At times the high-powered salesmanship of the Americans provoked retaliatory wisecracks from the rest of us. One United States ensign, who was particularly flamboyant in his championship of things American, seldom failed to snap at even the most obvious bait. One evening, an Australian officer said innocently: "I say Johnnie, when President Roosevelt declared war, how did he get King George's permission?" The air became sulphurous!

On American Independence Day, six weeks before our release, Galloway Stewart strode into the Americans' hut before breakfast. "Gentlemen," he announced in his great voice, "I have come to offer you my sincere condolences on the anniversary of your great mistake in breaking away from the British Empire!" For a moment there was a stunned silence and then, as Gall strode out, there was a roar. No one could say that the Yanks lacked a sense of humour.

Some of their best lie beside some of ours along the railway. They will be remembered with our own dead by all their Australian friends.

The Americans did not hit it off so well with the British as they did with us. The old school tie, always in evidence where you have large numbers of British regular officers, was a sore point with many of the Yanks. Whereas the Australian tended to laugh, derisively sometimes, but usually with tolerance, the American was apt to become exasperated. The supercilious attitude of some of the senior British officers did not help matters, but, all things considered, there was surprisingly little friction.

The Australians and Americans would leap the hurdles of varying slang, idiom and pronunciation with much banter and leg-pulling. Some of the British found the language barrier more difficult.

There was the instance of the British officer who discovered that his fellow occupant of the bathing platform was a Texan. Seeking to make conversation, he said: "I suppose you have a great many rahnches out there?" "Naw," said the Yank, "I can't say we have, but there are ranches." "Of course," murmured the Englishman apologetically, "how stupid of me!" When the American left the bath house, the Englishman turned to one of my friends, saying: "That's the trouble with us, you know. We will insist on talking English to foreigners!"

It was not until the last year of our captivity that the Australian officers who had been in Burma met many of the British. But at Tamarkan, Chungkai and Kanburi—the camp where all officers were congregated from February 1945 onwards— we had the opportunity of getting together with our closest kinsfolk. There is no doubt that this contact with men from all parts of the British Isles was enormously stimulating and instructive. Many of us feel that we learned a great deal from those from the United Kingdom—and perhaps we can hope that they learned something from us.

At Kanburi in July 1945, at the invitation of some of the

senior British officers, I organized a team of Australian speakers to go round to the British field officers' hut—irreverently known as the "Imperial War Museum"—to talk about Australia to those officers especially interested in the future of the British Commonwealth. Colonel Chris Black, of Australian Glass, spoke of the progress and future of Australian secondary industry; Major Hec Greiner, of Echuca, dealt with our primary production; Captain Bob Concannon, brother of the Sydney M.L.C., discussed the Dairy Farmers' Co-operative in Sydney, and outlined the history of our trade union movement; and I sketched some kind of picture of our Constitution and our political history.

Without any previous collaboration, all four of us stressed the widespread Australian belief that the future of the British Commonwealth depends largely on building up the population of the Dominions and on fuller development of their resources. Tremendous discussions ensued on the issue of mass emigration from Britain to the Dominions. Analysis of past blunders in migration policies was frank on both sides. The arguments adduced created great interest among scores of men in many different walks of life. If we did not all see eye to eye, we did gain a better appreciation of the other fellow's point of view.

We were warned, and expected, that regular army officers would be a stumbling block. As one English Liberal put it to me: "You know, the pukka sahibs still tend to regard all Australians and Canadians as rather temperamental children who may, at any moment, start throwing tea into the harbour!"

Certainly, one or two of the comments were a little difficult to cope with. One dear old colonel, with no intention to offend, said: "You know it's all very well for you chaps to talk about moving millions of English out to your countries, but it simply can't be done, y'know. The Empah couldn't stand it. You see, you simply couldn't breed the men!"

Another distinguished officer said: "Of course, the trouble about going out to Australia is that in two or three generations, with that sun of yours, half of you will be black and the other half brown."

Some of the members of the "Imperial War Museum" were a constant source of delight to other officers. For the first time, many of us met in the flesh the colonel who previously had existed only in the pages of *Punch*, or P. G. Wodehouse. Some people believe that the Poona pukka sahib and Colonel Blimp are moribund, if not defunct. At Kanburi, we had ample evidence that they are not only alive but vigorous. Many of them are undoubtedly magnificent soldiers, but perhaps their juniors, and many of the Australian officers, could be forgiven for taking great delight in some of their utterances. One amiable cavalry officer became very worried whenever he had to deal with the Japanese. On one occasion, when confronted with a difficult problem of negotiation with the Jap administration, he exclaimed petulantly, "It's no good coming to me. You know I can never think unless I'm on horseback!" One of the English majors, in exasperation, whispered *sotto voce*, "I've always thought so. For God's sake, someone, get the old —— a horse."

The same officer was very distressed by an account of our method of planting corn by machine. "But," he exclaimed, "you surely don't plant it in rows?" "Yes, of course," same the reply. "But—good heavens!—" he stammered, appalled, "Doesn't it spoil the shooting?"

At Chungkai one evening, a group of Indian Army colonels were discussing the amputation of the finger of a fellow colonel, thanks to an ulcer. Amidst the general commiseration, one of them raised his voice: "After all," he said, "he's rather lucky; it isn't his triggah fingah!"

But if we poked fun at some of the idiosyncrasies of the huntin', shootin', and fishin' fraternity, I daresay they had their amusement at our expense. One Englishman was heard to confide to another, "Amazin' fellows, these Australians. One of them just said he couldn't introduce an English visitor to a group of his friends because they had one of their politicians among 'em. Apparently (on the social scale) an Australian politician comes somewhere between a prostitute and an habitual criminal!"

Yet we found in the British officers' huts many of the outstanding personalities of the prison camps. One of these was Major Jack Marsh, of Austins, Birmingham. Tall, broad, fair-haired and blue-eyed, Jack combined an insatiable thirst for knowledge on all matters political, social and economic with a tremendous flair for organization. He was one of our political group, whose members were as diverse in political faith as any circle one could hope to organize without each meeting ending in open fisticuffs. All of us were constantly lecturing to groups throughout the camp on our own particular viewpoint. The coming together was sometimes electrical.

At this Kanburi camp, as at Tamarkan, a group of us who were interested in trying to write fiction formed a "Storyteller's Club". We tried out stories which we had written in the prison camps before pencil and paper were denied us by the Japanese, or which we hoped to write in the future. The thinking out and polishing of these stories, in the week before one's own turn came, provided a splendid escape during the last and most tedious months of our captivity.

One of the most popular figures at Kanburi was our sole French representative, Captain Willie Rosenthal, fifty-four-year-old veteran of two wars, who served with the French Army evacuated from Dunkirk, and afterwards was C.O. of the Salvage Corps of the Indian forces in Malaya. Winner of the Croix de Guerre, equally well known in India and in Paris, where he is a manufacturing jeweller, "Rosie" was the good-humoured butt of scores of enthusiastic young officers anxious to practise their rusty French. Rosie's experience of Australia was limited to six months in Broome but, in spite of this, he had a very soft spot for Australia and all things Australian (except perhaps our wine, about which he was very witty, very French, but not quite so polite). To hear Rosie in full rhetorical flood on the joys of motoring in the Midi, or on the gastronomic delights of certain beloved cafés, was a delightful avenue of escape from bamboo, boiled rice and Japanese persecution. With his massive, bristling moustache in the approved French tradition, his sparkling wit and genius as a raconteur, Rosie would have gone far towards converting most people into Francophiles.

In this camp, we also got to know such personalities in the sporting world as Major Pycock, British Olympic swimmer, Captain Riches, English tennis star, and Major E. W. Swanton, B.B.C. and *Evening Standard* cricket critic. Major Swanton conducted a weekly "cricketers' meeting", attended by several well-known County players and other cricket enthusiasts, at which discussion ranged from W. G. Grace to Len Hutton, and from the finer points of cricket lore to searching questions about obscure records gleaned from the two much-studied copies of *Wisden's Almanack*.

Despite the fierce discipline, and many searches at Kanburi, a secret radio set was operated by the Webber brothers, officers in the Malay Regiment, so that we received regular news bulletins. The Webber brothers first started operating in February 1943 at Chungkai. From that time they kept up a continuous service of bulletins, supplying their own and other camps with over 700 bulletins and commentaries from the B.B.C. and other Allied stations. After the radio discovery at Kanburi in August 1943, the operation of the sets was carried on under increasing difficulties and dangers. At one time in Chungkai the operators had to go outside the camp, at night, in order to work their radio, thus running an additional risk of shooting. The Webber brothers' set was carried from Chungkai to the Tamarkan camp in the legs of chairs, and in stools made of bamboo. From Tamarkan to Kanburi, the set was secreted in bamboo building poles. Max Webber carried six months' supply of batteries in his army pack from Chungkai to Tamarkan, under Japanese escort. Despite searches at both ends of the march, he came through successfully. These men deserve special recognition.

Thomas Douglas, an officer in the Royal Corps of Signals and, prior to the war, a B.B.C. technician, constructed no fewer than eight radio sets and continuously operated a "dickybird" in jungle working camps.

Nearly all the radio sets constructed in Thailand and Burma were made from small standard components. When built, these sets usually had two-valve or three-valve circuits; often they were so made as to fit into the bottom of an army water bottle. Power was supplied by torch batteries, about thirty being required to work a set. These, known in camp parlance as "birdseed", were usually obtained from Thai sources and from Japanese soldiers engaged in rackets.

All discussion of news given out in the secret bulletins was banned and, in any reference to this mainstay of our hopes, the word "news" was never employed. We spoke of the good oil, the doovah, swen, the dope, the jen, the good guts or the nightingale.

Our association with the English in Siam brought home to those Australians who might have doubted it previously the fact that we, as a people, remain closer to our kinsmen of the United Kingdom than to any other people. Differences of accent and pronunciation usually offered scope for that common sense of humour which provides perhaps the warmest bond between us.

Two stories, which went the rounds at Kanburi, delighted us all. In the latrine at night, it was impossible to see which cubicles were occupied, and one proceeded by questioning. "Is anyone there?" demanded a voice outside one cubicle. The occupant replied, "Yes," but to his indignation, the questioner proceeded to enter. "I said 'Yes,'" thundered the occupant. "Oh," said the intruder apologetically, "I thought you said 'No.'"

Then there was the senior British officer who was told about a bet. "A friend of mine," someone said, "will win a bottle of beer for every day we are released prior to 9 January 1946. He will lose a bottle of beer for every day we remain in captivity after that." The senior officer said he did not understand; so, very slowly and carefully, the statement was repeated. "Ah! I see," said the senior officer, with profound satisfaction. "Er—when does it begin?"

CHAPTER XXXIII

UNDER NEGUCHI

In the sixteenth century Montanus said: "They take delight in cruelty and bloodshed and the like." They still do. Their passion for blood is not confined to the admiration of political or patriotic murder. . . . The mentality of modern Japan . . . is the mentality of a primitive tribe that has been trained in modern warfare.

—TAID O'CONROY.

THE separation of officers from men in February 1945 flung a heavy burden on the shoulders of the senior N.C.Os who had to take over the entire internal administration, which had previously been controlled by officers. The segregation of those with commissions put an end to the constant supply of fresh funds for camp hospitals from officers' salaries. However, a considerable amount of money was left with the senior N.C.Os as force funds. The officers received no more because, at this stage, as a punishment arising from the disclosures about *Bangkok Chronicles,* the Japanese announced that no officer would receive more than twenty ticals a month. Owing to the sudden inflation of prices at the beginning of 1945, the tical was worth less than half its value twelve months before and our buying power in Australian money was less than sixpence a day.

Some thousands of P.O.W.s were now moved away from the railway to Petchaburi and Rathburi, where they were employed on aerodrome construction and other work.

The Kanburi camp into which the officers were crowded had been in use for three years. Latrines and rubbish dumps had been sown over the whole area not covered by the P.O.W. and Japanese huts. We were packed together far too closely, and when the rains came the latrines and drains flooded and the camp became a quagmire. We were constantly anxious about the contamination of our water supply, all water being drawn by hand-pumps from two wells in the camp area.

All fit officers had to work—some in the kitchen, bakehouse or canteen, others in pump teams or on wood carrying, while most of the remainder were usually engaged on what the Japanese called "levelling". This was a ludicrous and irritating procedure whereby one day you dug up and carried earth on tungas (consisting of a bag stretched over two bamboo poles) from point A to point B. A few days later you moved the earth again to point C whence, in due course, another work party moved it back to A again. Nobody was overworked, but everybody was exceedingly bored.

Intensive searches were carried out by the Japanese at frequent intervals in the attempt to enforce the innumerable restrictions imposed on us by the camp commandant, Neguchi. He was one of the worst specimens we met in any camp. His sole aim and interest was to persecute his prisoners by every interference with their liberty and amusements that his mind could conceive. His attitude was that prisoners were criminals. His inferiority complex produced a fierce delight in the infliction of every possible inconvenience and humiliation on the 3000-odd Allied officers under his command.

One day he sent round for a return concerning all degrees, diplomas, etc., held by his prisoners. A few days later he told our hard-working camp commander, Lieutenant-Colonel P. W. D. Toosey: "I know there are officers in this camp more travelled and educated than I am. But to me you are just a lot of prisoners—you can still be shot. There is no appeal beyond me." This officer refused to pass on our letters of protest against the absurd regulations enforced in his camp. He said that if he passed them on he would lose face and have to commit hara-kiri. Here are some of the niggling rules he enforced upon us. We were not allowed to:

1. Lie or lean back on our beds between 8 a.m. and 6 p.m. except at lunch-time.

2. Read at any time during the above hours.

3. Read during air alerts. (This was apparently Neguchi's idea of nerve warfare.)

4. Smoke outside huts except beside certain tins.
5. Play any card games, etc., between 8 a.m. and 6 p.m.
6. Have a knife, razor, tool or pair of scissors.
7. Speak from the stage during concerts—no applause, no laughter
8. Go ahead with our "backyard" cricket competition.
9. Visit huts other than our own.
10. Keep any tinned foods or private medicine.
11. Have any means of writing notes, or material for studying.

Many of the Koreans, including some who had been notorious along the railway, now gave evidence of fear as to their fate when Japan lost the war. Reports of the bombing of Japan and the collapse of Germany led several guards to some bitter self-questioning. One day, when Colonel Toosey had seen all his requests for amelioration of our condition refused by Neguchi, a Korean said to him: "Soon, in London, Captain Neguchi wear this" (touching the arm band which indicated Colonel Toosey was one of the "assistants" of the P.O.W. administration). "Then he come to you and you say, 'No! No! No!'" This, and many similar remarks by Koreans, indicated nothing less than a revolution in their thinking. When we had first come to Burma no one ever dreamed of hearing a Korean make derisive remarks about his officers.

The trend of the war had no softening effect on Sergeant Shimojo, a notorious bash-artist. He paraded through the camp seeking every opportunity to beat up Allied officers on any and every pretext. Shimojo was racked with secondary syphilis and delighted to vent his sufferings on us. If by some miracle he escapes shooting by the Allied authorities, he should be safe for a permanent job at Hollywood as an Oriental villain. He had the face of a cartoonist's ogre and would have been a howling success as the sinister henchman of Fu-Manchu.

An even more dangerous customer was "The Undertaker", a guard named Kanaishii. Towering about fourteen inches above his fellow Koreans, he was always bullying and fighting. When roused, he developed a sadistic mania and lost all self-control. He had earned his nick-name at Tamarkan in 1943 when he bayoneted to death two British Army officers who had escaped. One of these was an American in the Argyles, named Pomeroy, who had been a war correspondent in Shanghai.

The Undertaker's favourite sport was to beat up the sick with his rifle butt. On one occasion at Kanburi, when some members of our working gang shouted a protest against the brutal punishment he dealt out to an officer who had sought to stop him from torturing a goat, he drew his bayonet in an ungovernable rage, and bloodshed was averted only by a matter of inches.

Sometimes on parade at Kanburi our self-control was gravely endangered by the absurd costume in which our captors conducted the parade. Having no sense of the ridiculous, the Japanese saw nothing incongruous in appearing in full uniform, with sash of office and ceremonial sword; but, below, the legs were bare from the untied ends of their knicker-bockers down to a pair of down-at-heel rubber sneakers. Other Japanese delighted to wear short socks held up by parti-coloured suspenders below their knickerbockers or shorts. Wretched as we were in our rags, we were constantly amused at Japanese slovenliness.

The Japanese saw nothing odd in the way in which a pompous little lieutenant or W.O. strutted on to a parade and then mounted a table in order to take a prolonged salute from the prisoners; afterwards he would calmly walk across to the pet monkey chained to its tree and stand there in front of the parade while the monkey picked the lice out of his hair.

The Japanese Army has a penchant for arm bands. Bands of all kinds were worn by members of the forces and all civilian personnel attached to the I.J.A., whatever their office. At Changi, on one occasion, a prisoner found one of these armlets with various Chinese characters on it. He thought it might be useful to enable him to pass the guard-house so he put it on. Then he noticed that some of the guards seemed to be very amused; however, they let him through. On his way back he noticed more giggling. That night, he took the arm band to the camp interpreter and discovered that the characters on his arm announced to the world: "PROSTITUTE. I am a clean woman."

Mess Parade.

At the beginning of April all sick officers, regardless of their condition, were sent up to Kanburi from Nakom Paton hospital camp. They had a long and weary train journey, then they had to carry their own gear and their stretcher cases from the railway station to the camp. The fact that one or two of these men were on the point of death mattered not at all to the Japanese medical authorities at Nakom Paton.

Three officers were killed and six wounded at the Kanburi camp on 22 March, when Allied aircraft, in bombing a railway engine, missed rather badly and dropped three small bombs on and inside the camp fence. We had no adequate slit-trench accommodation for many officers because Neguchi would not allow us to dig the requisite trenches. During the regular raids on the Tamarkan bridge many bombers flew straight over the camp in making their run on the target; but on some occasions, despite the earlier casualties and the massacre at Nonpladuk, men in some huts were not allowed to take shelter in the trenches, although most of the guards and Japanese administration were huddling in strong underground shelters protected by heavy beams. Neguchi made mock of our protests.

After Germany's surrender, Neguchi was obviously a very worried man. One day he said to Colonel Toosey that the Allies might take Mandalay (we knew they already had done so), Burma, and even Kanburi, but Japan must win. The Vital Force was all that mattered and Japan was the Sun which was always rising. He forgot to add that it is always setting, too.

"The glorious first of June" lacked glory for us at Kanburi, since all officers were confined to barracks, following a dispute about menial work demanded of officers. For ten days we were cooped up in the packed huts unable to read, lie down or play games of any kind. An armed attack by Thais on the Japanese at Ban Pong, resulting in Japanese deaths and much damage to important stores and machinery, may have been a contributing factor. However, it had nothing to do with the treatment handed out by Neguchi to Captain Bill Drower.

Drower, who spoke perfect Japanese, had done a splendid

job all along the line and was particularly popular. From his great height he dwarfed the Japanese and, while always courteous, undoubtedly filled most of them with a sense of inferiority. It appears that Neguchi hated him.

The incident arose over the refusal of a British officer to fill a bucket of water for a Japanese medical orderly—a private. A phrase which Drower used in discussing the affair caused Neguchi to seize his heavy swordstick and strike Drower twice. In the words of Colonel Toosey, who watched the attack:

The first blow raised a lump the size of an egg on his right temple. The second blow split his left ear like a ripe tomato. Following this attack on Drower, Neguchi jumped at him and grappled with him on the floor of the Japanese office, kicking and fighting with him and using jiu-jitsu. Lieutenant Tagasaki, who was also present, struck Drower several times on the face with his hand. During the mêlée most of the Japanese office was wrecked.

After this, Captain Drower and three other officers concerned in the water bucket incident, were compelled to stand in front of the guard-house. After three days these other officers were released. Tagasaki apologized to Colonel Toosey for the fact that two Japanese officers had lost their tempers and struck a British officer. The British commander immediately asked for the release of Drower. This was refused.

For ten weeks Neguchi embarked on a deliberate attempt at slow murder. He refused to discuss the matter with the British commander, although six extremely strong protests were made on behalf of the whole camp.

After the first three days in front of the guard-room Drower was put in a hole in the ground, partially filled with water, where he was kept for six and a half weeks. For the first three days he received no food or water. After this treatment he received two rice balls a day and water twice a day to drink. He was not allowed to wash or shave. After seven weeks, when he was found to be on the point of dying, the Japanese agreed that he should receive proper nourishment from the British cook-house and he was placed in one of the Japanese detention cells behind the Japanese guard-room. Here he remained for a further three weeks up to the surrender of Japan. There was evidence that his mind was wandering, and he was in appalling physical condition.

The Drower persecution cast a gloom over the whole camp. The other Japanese officers and many of the guards indicated that it was entirely an affair of personal spite on the part of Neguchi, and some of them helped to smuggle a little sustaining food to Drower now and then. But the vindictiveness of the camp commandant was now shown to be without limits. It lent support to those who believed that the imminence of our release might lead to a manufactured incident and a massacre.

We now learned that all officers were to be moved to an area a hundred miles north-east of Bangkok. Koreans suggested that the move itself would be unpleasant and that, at the end of it, we should find ourselves in the middle of a Japanese perimeter containing 30,000 troops. This sounded like the site of Japan's last stand for the defence of Siam and, with our bombers becoming daily more numerous and an invasion imminent, it did not seem likely to be a health resort. Nevertheless, I could not feel sorry about leaving Kanburi.

A day or two before I was moved, I spent the last hour before dawn on picket at the end of our hut. In front of me, out of the darkness where the high bamboo stakes on the bund were faintly outlined, came the tramp of the changing guard. Behind, to the east, the first hint of dawn just coloured the horizon, cut off by the same grim palisade marking our captivity. It was one of those melancholy, reflective hours that came to all of us. Behind us stretched over 1200 days and nights of bondage. We had received no sign that the fanatical foe was contemplating anything but a fight to the bitter end.

Yet on that day a new and terrible portent descended from the sky on a Japanese town. Its appearance was probably to affect vitally the whole future of mankind. As the merest incidental, it determined the precarious fate of the 30,000 Allied prisoners remaining in the Japanese prison camps of Siam.

CHAPTER XXXIV

FINAL GLORY

The darkest hour comes just before the dawn.

At the end of June the advance party set out from the Kanburi officers' camp for the Nakomnayok area to carve a new camp out of the jungle. A month later in groups of four hundred, roughly at five-day intervals, the rest of us followed them.

After our experiences travelling under the aegis of Nippon, nobody contemplated the move with an easy mind. In the first place, there was the virtual certainty that we should be spending long periods in railway yards, sidings, godowns and other military objectives, and every month was increasing the tally of P.O.W. casualties along the line. Secondly, we were told there was a long march, carrying all our worldly gear, at the end of the journey. We had heard that this march was over a hundred kilometres, but later estimates reduced this by half. It was actually forty-eight kilometres. Finally, bitter experience suggested that a camp in the jungle in a new area would probably be very poorly supplied with both rations and canteen goods.

For weeks before the move, hundreds of us engaged in "training gallops", hardening feet and muscles for a long trek with packs up. Unfortunately, food was so poor at the end of July that it was dubious whether the training justified the probable weakening of one's reserves.

Radio news cut out at the beginning of July. The Webber brothers had been doing a splendid job operating their set in the bakehouse just after dark, often within a few yards of prowling sentries who were, of course, well watched by our outposts. On one occasion Neguchi himself passed within ten yards of the operators without causing them to remove the headphones. However, the reserve cache of batteries had been made unusable through seepage of water and for the first time in many months we found ourselves without "birdseed". So the "dicky-bird" did not whistle during the concluding six weeks of war.

This was offset by the bringing into camp, through various subterranean channels, of several pamphlets in Japanese and Thai, as well as some vernacular papers which gave us a fair picture of developments up to 20 July. Then the Koreans told us of the coming of a Labour Government in England. We heard nothing of the Potsdam ultimatum of 26 July and no hint of atom bombs up to the time when my party of four hundred left camp on 10 August. Consequently, despite the aerial and naval successes of the Americans, many of us felt that there was little cause for more optimism than we had felt on 9 May when Germany capitulated. Many felt that Japan was determined to fight on her own soil, regardless of cost.

Yet after at least a hundred disappointments, some of the "any day now" school still clung to their faith. A friend of mine who had been saying "I can't see how it can go on for more than a month or two" ever since the break-through in France, confessed that although he had never expected to leave Kanburi as a Japanese prisoner, it now seemed inevitable.

In retrospect I can see that the rumour that on 8 August there had been very bad news for the Japs in one of their papers, and that Neguchi had been seen reading it in great distress, was the first hint of the beginning of the end.

Our party was paraded on the eve of departure and instructed by the English C.O. that Neguchi "wished us to remember that we were officers and not beggars"—a gratuitous insult of a type so common that one just laughed or said "little yellow ———", and left it at that. Neguchi on this parade, as always, resembled nothing so much as the furtive snooper of a private detective agency. The man was incapable of looking like a soldier or of looking anyone straight in the eyes. To anyone watching the parades he would have appeared a hanger-on seeking to remain unobserved. It is very doubtful whether we ever struck any Japanese officer with so pronounced and exaggerated a sense of inferiority. Hence the constant barrage of threats, jibes and abuse, and his consuming desire to demonstrate his own omnipotence.

The story of our move was roughly the story of each party, so I shall transcribe it directly from the account in my diary. As an example of the gross inefficiency with which all Nippon moves of prisoners were conducted, and the needless misery inflicted on prisoners, it is in some ways comparable with the hellship journeys or our various moves in Burma.

On 10 August, after being messed about in the rain for three hours, we finally got into the train about five. We were all in open cattle trucks, about thirty-two to a truck. We moved five hundred yards to Kanburi station where we lay until after seven o'clock. This station saw the big Kanburi raid in December last year when all Jap supply huts, sheds and camp buildings in the area were completely destroyed. Instead of being a major railway centre and marshalling yards, it now resembled a derelict country station in the outback at home. Beyond Kanburi, the Jap engineers had been at great pains to disperse engines among the thickest jungle. Numerous spurs lay off the main line in all directions. It started to rain at nightfall, which made things unpleasant. After a prolonged wait at one station, a Bangkok train going up-jungle with about sixty cars (half of them empty) pulled in. With great shouting, gesticulating, arguments, and the aid of train guards, engineers and station officials, a skip into which seven pomelos and one roll of tobacco were solemnly counted was transferred to the station yard. Then, after at least fifteen minutes delay for this immense undertaking, the other train went off and we chugged along at an average of twenty-five m.p.h. to Non-pladuk, where we arrived in driving rain after midnight.

In pitch blackness, the total illumination in the huge marshalling yards being provided by two small hurricane lamps and one candle without a candlestick, after the usual tankos and confusion, the Nips succeeded in transferring the four hundred of us to roofed cattle trucks lying in the yard. We were only fifteen to a truck, so could stretch out, or at least you could have done so if you'd been prepared to lie on the floors which were indescribably filthy with native urine, refuse, mud, dust, oil and grease. I sat up and had a sleepless night, but a few of the others dozed for an hour.

At dawn we bundled out and ate most of the remnant of our haversack ration, consisting originally of a loaf of bread, six eggs and two patties. No one was very happy about the prospect of hanging around Nonpladuk in the middle of the yard—there were too many P.O.W. ghosts about the place, for well over a hundred had been killed here. But finally about 10 a.m., after much shunting, our train got under way for Bangkok.

An hour later we pulled in at a Thai village and for the next hour and a half had a fascinating close-up of Thai community life.

On the whole I like the Thais better than any boongs I've seen. The Malays, Sundanese and Javanese don't compare with them and they seem to have far more verve, independence and good looks than the Burmese, although none of us is ever likely to forget our good friends at Moulmein.

Some quite pretty Thai girls were selling fruit, egg dishes, dried fish, chicken giblets, and smokes, but of course they were not allowed to approach us and we were not allowed to buy. The village, like all Thai villages, swarmed with infants from weeks-old sucklings upwards. The Thai kiddies mature much faster than ours, and all seem to walk at eight or ten months. It's not unusual to see tots who can't be more than three or four carrying heavy trays of merchandise, and sometimes an even younger brother or sister on their hips. The boys wear nothing until they are six or seven years old except, occasionally, a little triangular protection on the loins made apparently of fine metal. Most of the girls wear a sarong, cloth or rag of some kind.

The women, like all other native women in the tropics, age rapidly and it is impossible to guess whether many of the old harridans, their teeth stained with betel juice and their hair prematurely grey are thirty, forty, or sixty. The men wear much better, although we saw here one mis-shapen old monster with two of the worst squinting eyes I've ever seen, a humped back, and a beard that was every colour from grey to orange.

Fun came from a Thai youth who, from a vantage point behind a truck, kept firing eggs into our truck whenever the numerous guards round us seemed to be looking elsewhere. These were caught with an efficiency and undemonstrativeness worthy of Bertie Oldfield in a test match. Neguchi had threatened the direst penalties for anyone accepting anything from the Thais, and we didn't know how strictly the guards would enforce his orders.

Mongrel dogs, hens, ducks, pigs, and innumerable children seemed inextricably mixed in the village street and in the houses themselves, into which we could peer through the open doorways. There certainly had been no food shortage in this part of the world and, outside the big cities, few people could have been so little affected by the years of war as the Siamese.

We finally rattled on through miles of padi fields, dotted with palm-trees, water buffalo and men and women knee-deep in water, transplanting the padi. In due course we came to Nakom Paton where the base hospital camp was. It seemed a large town and had a fine clock-tower and what appeared to be a city hall. As we were now on the main Singapore-Bangkok line, Thai officials were running the station. Apparently, it was only beyond Nonpladuk on the railway built by the prisoners that the Japs had taken over the Thai railways. The Thais here stood no nonsense from the guards, who treated them with more respect than I had yet seen Japanese display towards their fellow Asiatics.

A little farther on we detrucked, shouldered our packs and walked on to one of the big rivers which feed the Menam at Bangkok. Here the R.A.F. had done a magnificent job and the big steel and concrete bridge was smashed in every span. For some Nipponese and therefore obscure reason, an appallingly bad job had been made of constructing a footbridge over the wreckage of the main railway bridge. In an hour with a few planks and ropes fifty of us could have made a safe and solid causeway across that bridge. As it was, you crept gingerly along swaying bamboos, with gaps gaping at you everywhere and no holding rail. With the river a flood torrent fifty feet below, it was no pleasant experience and many of the Dutch spent up to five minutes in crossing.

On the other side of the bridge, Bertie Farr and I joined up with the other five Australians in the party: Harry Farmer, of the Bank of N.S.W., Sydney; John Carey, of Beckwith, Tamworth; Ron Greville, a vet. from Melbourne; Peter Campbell, accountant, of Sydney; and Vern Toose, of the Bank of Australasia, Sydney. We all had a wash in the water of a padi field, ate some food, and then, after about three hours, piled into another train. This time the thirty-two of us had to climb on to a mass of wood fuel which filled a closed truck to within three feet of the roof. We passed innumerable dwellings along the banks of the canals, apart from which unbroken padi fields seemed to extend to the horizon on all sides.

Gazing out at the Thais, their bare toes deep in the rich mud of their fields, I couldn't help thinking how much these simple Siamese peasants have which millions in Europe and other parts of Asia would have given their all to possess during the past terrible years.

At last the padi fields ended and we ran through thick banana and bamboo groves into the bomb-wrecked marshalling yards of the Bangkok station. The railway ends within a few yards of the Menam, and here we saw what some guff-filled commentator, who had seen no more of the Orient than its Grand Hotels, christened "the Venice of the East". For dirt, smells, numbers of river craft—junks, barges, prahus, sampans, daks, feluccas, skiffs, outriggers, lateen-rigged fishing vessels and motorboats—it probably is comparable to Venice: and having said that, let's say no more about it, because anything less like an Italian city than Bangkok could not be conceived.

We spent the next five hours on a piece of swampy ground between the crater-pitted railway yards and a corrugated iron fence covered with barbed wire, behind which seemed to be a hospital or asylum. It was a most unhealthy spot because, if the bombers came over, you were smack-centre in the main target area of Bangkok, with the river on one side, the marshalling yards on the other, and this fence on the third. After our experiences it needed little imagination to picture the panic of the guards and the general tumult in the event of a raid.

After it was fully dark, we had to load the twenty or thirty tons of camp gear and Jap baggage which we were taking with us, first of all from the train to a dump, and then from the dump into barges. When all this was done we stood around in our parties, with packs up, for an hour and a half having endless tankos and were then crammed into the barges —fifty or fifty-five men to a barge, nine-tenths of them on top of their gear inside a cabin space adequate for about ten.

Then, instead of moving to the godown, as the Nip warrant-officer commanding the party had promised, we spent a wretched night drifting about the centre of the river in the most acute physical discomfort and crowded misery that even a Jap guard could invent. This was the second successive sleepless night.

Dawn on 12 August came at last after hours that dragged with snail-like slowness, and about 8 a.m. a motorboat collected all the barges and towed us down-river for nearly three hours to the godown.

This godown did not exactly promise a rest-cure either. It was the biggest and only undestroyed shed of importance that we had seen and the roof and windows were scarred with bomb splinters. It had been the godown of a Dutch Borneo company and the whole enormous structure, extending for over a thousand yards, looked about the best bombing target Bangkok had still to offer· Barbed-wire blocks, which could be drawn across the godown doorways, showed that the Japs intended to keep us penned up there in any raid, while they of course took refuge in the big shelters regularly spaced along the wharf. Rail tracks, with odd rolling-stock scattered about, were on both sides of the godown, and a number of junks and sampans were being unloaded along the wharf. A lot of us prayed silently that no reconnaissance aircraft would come over on the old noon "reccy".

I was on the working party that had to unload the camp gear from the barges and then after lunch—a particularly vile meal—was on water fatigue. An hour's doze at five o'clock was the first sleep snatched in sixty hours.

The godown had several hundred cases of Thai Red Cross goods addressed to us, but they had been there many months and I felt there was no prospect of our seeing them out in the jungle.

Here it was rumoured that the Russians were in the war against Japan. This pleased me particularly, because I had been predicting for many months that the Russians would be in against the Nips as soon as possible after they'd finished with Jerry. Most people were very dubious about this, and I won a bet of £10 to £5 with five weeks to spare.

I saw 78-inch John Garran, of Canberra, son of Sir Robert Garran, ex-chief of the Attorney-General's Department, and an old friend, for a moment on a working party. There was a guard there and we were forbidden to speak to any other prisoners in the godown. I said out of the corner of my mouth, "Chin up, old man: It won't be much longer now." (I had no idea what a good prophet I was this time!)

The guards here were pretty jumpy and there were innumerable restrictions. All Jap N.C.Os had to be saluted. At night rain flooded the godown, but Bertie and I had bagged a spot on a wooden trap-door and the water drained down the cracks without touching us. So it was a good night's sleep despite the myriad mosquitoes.

We were very worried in the morning (13 August) about rumours of a kempi search, so I hid some papers at the back of the latrine, and others under piled sandbags in the corner of the godown where they were nearly ruined by water. Actually only the prisoners in the next section of the godown were searched.

In the afternoon we loaded Jap gear on to rolling-stock shunted in front of the godown. Between two and five most people were a little on edge, because this was the time when the bombers had usually been over in recent weeks.

In the evening I had a dip with the other Aussies in a pond

at the back of the godown. Bertie and I felt much more cheerful with the prospect of getting away on the morrow—Gwyth's birthday. Of her eight birthdays since we met we have had two together. For the others I've been on the Indian Ocean, in Moscow, in Batavia, in Burma, and now here. Not a very good record! Have had some uncongenial wedding anniversaries: last year I spent it hunched up with thirty-seven others in a cattle truck travelling between the Thai border and Tamarkan; this year about forty Super-Fortresses appeared and swung off-course to come straight in over us at Tamarkan.

We sat around all the morning yarning, drawing rations, and hearing optimistic furphies which I was in no mood to believe. Finally, we were packed into trucks—thirty-eight men in ours—and after interminable delays and shunting ran up-river a few miles to the main marshalling and service yards of the Thai railways. Practically every workshop and locomotive shed in the area had been gutted by bombs, only the outer husk of bomb-scarred wall remaining. Smashed rolling-stock littered the yards. Apart from one pagoda and a couple of houses on the edge of the yards which had been partially wrecked, there was every evidence of the deadly accuracy of our bombers.

The guards told us the train was late and that we should not get going until 10 p.m. Like their statement about the barges, this proved entirely false and from nine o'clock until dawn we were crowded into our cattle trucks, acutely uncomfortable and expecting to hear the drone of the big bombers at any moment.

Some Thai boys caused amusement by a determined onset with stones against the Jap guard. After the nine o'clock tanko, we were herded into the trucks, which were like furnaces. So tightly packed that it was impossible to move a foot without the co-operative movement of four or five others, we sat stewing through another sleepless night. It reminded me vividly of the hold of the *Mayebassi Maru* coming up Malacca Strait three years before, and it was just as hot. Finally, I joined another fellow hanging outside the truck on a projecting rail. I found that he had been at Trinity, Cambridge, while I was at Balliol and we improved that unpleasantly moonlit night in the Bangkok goods yards with a tremendous discussion of English politics and politicians from the days of Charles II to Churchill.

Finally, one of the guards had a merciful lapse and allowed us to crawl out and lie on the rubble between two sets of tracks. We were on the point of dozing off when there was a frightful outburst of yelling and screaming. Men, suddenly roused, leaped up expecting the familiar whistle of bombs, but the cause of the alarm was merely the arrival of a locomotive—the first we'd seen in hours, coming along the rail beside which we were lying.

We were all hounded inside again, and a Jap troop train drew up on one side of us and an ammunition train on the other, so that, as Bertie said to me, everything was teed up for a real picnic if the bombs started. So we sat stewing till daylight.

On 15 August (capitulation day!) we went off at last at a good bat at least eleven hours behind schedule and ran out for about an hour to a small wayside station in the midst of what the boys called "miles and miles of Fanny Adams"— translated here as padi fields. Here we passed a passenger train, crammed with Thais dressed Europeanwise, apparently bound for business or shopping in the big metropolis. They were cheek by jowl with a spattering of native huts which reached a new low in squalor and wretchedness.

At the next stop, about noon, I got a guard to bring a Thai vendor to the truck. The Thai had a basket with big bananas for which he wanted the extortionate price of two ticals per hand. The normal peace-time price being five cents, this meant 4000 per cent inflation. There were six hands and I offered him ten ticals. The bargaining was in full career, when the Thai took the ten tical bill and handed over five bunches. The guard was doing his best to get us the sixth when one of the Dutchmen in the truck leant out, put two dollars in the Thai's hand, and took the bunch. We were utterly staggered at this, particularly as the Dutchman immediately started to wolf them down. A dozen people pointed out to him forcibly in Dutch and in English, with a useful admixture of Australian adjectives that, with six bunches between thirty-seven men, this was a piece of effrontery and greed beyond the pale.

A big range of mountains loomed up to the north-east and we drew steadily nearer them. Finally, at Nakomnayok we detrained, unloaded gear once more, had a meal of fried rice which was all sour, and then, about four-thirty, shouldered our packs and set off on the 48-kilo march.

No one expected that on top of three sleepless nights out of five this would be a lingering memory of joy; but we did hope for a little better than what we actually experienced. The Japanese marched us for fifty minutes at snail's pace and then halted for ten. Then there was the usual inevitable tanko while we stood around with packs up. The controlled slow step, not much faster than a ceremonial funeral parade, strung the march out in heartbreaking fashion, when most of us had forty or fifty pounds on our shoulders and had had no chance of keeping fit in the previous months. Instead of covering about five kilometres an hour, we were lucky to do three, and so one carried one's pack half as long again as was necessary. We were all in a constant lather of sweat and soon started filling and draining our water bottles from the springs en route. The Jap issue of water in the thirty hours since leaving the godown had been three-quarters of a pint per man.

After the evening meal we stood on the road for an interminable tanko, improved by a slashing rain squall which in five minutes soaked all without waterproofs and then steadily added poundage to our packs and bedding rolls. Through almost constant rain we staggered on for about five hours, pausing irregularly to collapse on the saturated roadside. Finally, towards 3 a.m. the guards found an empty temple with about adequate floor space for a hundred men, into which the whole lot of us were packed somehow. I undressed, got into a dry sweater and, curled up somehow in about four square feet, fell sound asleep for three hours. Most of the party were not so lucky and had their fourth sleepless night.

On the morning of 16 August it was again wet, but a more serious problem was that the guards were now down to a mile and a half an hour, which made the whole effort twice as irksome. We tramped through a sizeable village and were told by prisoners on passing trucks that it was seven, eight, or ten kilometres more. Actually, it proved to be nearer fifteen. It got very hot after noon and we finally stopped for lunch, exhausted and with feet blistered to the point of agony; some men recently recovered from malaria, or just discharged from hospital, staggered drunkenly over the road, although their gear was being carried by loyal friends.

About four o'clock we at last turned off the main road along the two and a half kilometres of cleared track that led to the camp. Hundreds of officers from the four parties which had preceded us were working here on what was called "long bamboo carry"—which meant shouldering two or three heavy bamboos for twenty or thirty kilometres a day up to the camp for building purposes.

The rain now rounded things off effectively by coming down in an unbroken sheet for the last ten minutes of the march before we staggered under shelter in huts just outside the camp area. Sitting here, rather happy at the finish of things despite our filthy and soaking condition, we heard, for perhaps the hundredth time since we had been prisoners, that the war was over. And in loud and emphatic voices Bertie and I said: "B——s". We were told that Lieutenant-Colonel Toosey, the C.O., had said that in his opinion it was true, that a Japanese N.C.O. had given him the whole story. The Russians were in, there had been heavy bombing of Japan, the Allies had issued an ultimatum and Japan had surrendered. We felt it was just another jungle rumour provoked by the grim conditions at this new camp.

When we were finally over at our huts, the usual good Aussie friends turned up to look after us, to get us straw, water, etc. We found that the palatial quarters which the Japanese had promised us in this new officers' camp consisted of bays, nine metres by five, in which fifteen officers were jammed together sleeping on the mud floor. And we had thought we were badly off at Kanburi with seven sleeping in the same area on raised balis or bamboo platforms!

Now people surged around with more and more confirmation of Japanese surrender. The guards who had been driving the labour gangs up to the day before had lost all interest during this afternoon. Many had got drunk and some had come chattering to the boys saying "All finish" and "What happen Koreans when British come?"

The strongest evidence of all was the behaviour of our old friend Neguchi. He had arrived at the camp in his private car on the morning of the fourteenth and had immediately sentenced three officers to stand at attention at the guardhouse for the frightful crimes of having accepted in one case an egg, and in another case a tical, from Thais en route. One officer had been sentenced to stand at the guard-house "until the end of the war". This officer had begun his sentence before Neguchi's arrival and actually stood at attention for eighty-four hours, much of it in driving rain.

Neguchi had raved at Colonel Toosey, rejecting all his pleas for an alleviation of the shocking conditions prevailing in this camp, and had stated that officers were "beggars and criminals" and would henceforth be treated as such. Colonel Toosey returned to the camp, in his own words, "more dejected and pessimistic than in the past three years of setbacks and rebuffs". He told officers that obviously the Japanese had had very bad news, were out to create incidents, and were prepared to go to extremes. The colonel warned all officers that there was certainly a sticky time ahead.*

During the night of 15-16 August, Neguchi was taken down to Bangkok in a staff car. His return in the morning was so complete a reversal of form that it had paved the way for

* There unquestionably was. Friendly Koreans had warned prisoners that Neguchi was preparing to massacre us all. At the time many were sceptical, but Japanese documents and other evidence discovered since the capitulation indicate that all camp commanders had received orders to kill prisoners in the event of paratroop landings or invasion by Allied Forces. In the light of Allied plans, it seems certain that the attempt to massacre all prisoners in Siam would have begun within a few days. At Nakom Paton the date 28 August was already specified.

the growing belief in the camp that, after the long years of mirage and disillusionment, Der Tag had dawned at last.

Neguchi had stepped out of his staff car, walked up to the officers in front of the guard-house and said: "Gentlemen, we are all officers here together. You are serving your King as I am serving my Emperor. We must help each other. You may go." The leopard had changed his spots with a vengeance! Within forty-eight hours the bully of Kanburi was to prove himself more abject than the most craven of his Korean guards.

Next day Neguchi handed over tens of thousands of letters which had been withheld from us. I got a letter from my wife dated October 1942, which had been in Siam and even in the same camps with me for the past two and a half years. Within a few days of the Japanese capitulation I got more than half as many letters as I'd received in the past three and a half years; and thousands of others had a similar experience.

Neguchi handed over the keys of the Red Cross hut to Colonel Toosey and that night we had a British Red Cross parcel—the first we'd ever seen—between five of us. In the previous forty-two months our total parcels received had been one-sixth of one American parcel per head. Now we also got Red Cross clothing and cigarettes on a limited scale, which was still a vastly better issue than the Japs had ever allowed. Two days later the Japanese tried to persuade Colonel Toosey to back-date the receipts for the Red Cross goods to show that they had given them to us before capitulation. But we were not playing.

Late on the afternoon of the seventeenth, Neguchi, who had already admitted the end to one of our interpreters, sent for Colonel Toosey, sheepishly admitted the war was over, and told the Colonel that within the camp fence he was in command.

Five hours later, as the growing moon came up behind the forbidding ridge above our camp, every man who could walk assembled around a large bonfire at the back of the camp. And there, with the Union Jack fluttering at the top of the masthead, rather more moved than we dared to admit, we joined thankfully and exultantly in singing the National Anthem until the echoes rolled back from the frowning heights above. That moment will not be forgotten.

There was a great moment next day when the operators of the "dicky-bird" asked the Japs for batteries for the wireless set. "What wireless set?" said the Nips. "The one we've been operating for the past three years," was the reply. I believe Neguchi was almost speechless with baffled fury.

Most of the Koreans were now wholly on our side and intent only on saving their skins, trying to curry favour with any-one with whom they had had amicable contact before. About five days after capitulation, the Japanese gave each Korean in Thailand 200 ticals, told him he was discharged from the I.J.A. and that he must find his way home as best he could.

Neguchi now began to be very concerned about his per-sonal safety and particularly sought to win protection from those who had worked in the so-called "chemical" factory at the Kanburi camp. He said he was glad the war was over as he could now go back to his chemist's shop in Kobe. We felt this came under the heading of wishful thinking. Neguchi made several attempts to invite groups of men to dine with him but, courteously yet emphatically, he was told that after the way he had treated Drower and others at Kanburi this was impossible.

Sugasawa, who was now completely subservient to the senior Allied officers in Bangkok, had now investigated the Drower affair and immediately ordered Neguchi's arrest. We were told Neguchi had received a three years' jail sentence, but we were confident that this would not save his skin when the British took over.

Drower was suffering from blackwater fever when released, was appallingly emaciated and had a beard reaching down to his chest. However, with careful feeding and medical attention, he was out of danger by the end of the month.

I spent most of the next few days collating material from my notes, which I now unpacked from their secret hiding-places. On 24 August a group of us had a magnificent farewell supper with a huge rooster I bought from a Thai. Next day all Australian officers and men at Nakomnayok were taken down by truck to Bangkok.

The mood in which we travelled down to the capital was so different from that of a few days before that at times you caught your breath at the sudden realization that the nightmare was over.

All the way down through the villages, and particularly as we drove down the tree-lined avenues of Bangkok, the enthusiastic cordiality of the Siamese was tremendous. Close to Nakomnayok the roads were jammed with Japanese troops and mule trains and, as we drove gaily past in the A.S.C. trucks specially provided for us, one couldn't help an ironical comment when one saw Japanese staggering along the roadside carrying bamboos coolie-fashion for the construction of their quarters while waiting to surrender to our forces.

But the thing which surprised us most was the entire absence of any desire for revenge or for the humiliation of the wretches from whom we had suffered so much. Now in defeat they seemed as contemptible as ever but also infinitely pathetic. Dozens of men who had sworn that they would never be able to pass a Japanese without wanting to smash him in the face, found that when the chance came it just wasn't worth doing. Even after three and a half years of brutalities and degradation one just didn't feel interested in kicking the man who was now down.

I do not believe it matters very much whether most of the brutal guards in Burma and Thailand are punished or not. The men who must be got are the officers controlling P.O.W. administration and camps and the people in Tokyo who devised the whole gigantic project of mass murder.

CHAPTER XXXV

CHAPTER FROM THE ARABIAN NIGHTS

And it happened to him that he bore one day a heavy burden, and that day it was excessively hot; so he was wearied by the load and perspired profusely, the heat violently oppressing him. In this state he passed by the door of a merchant . . . he then advanced to that door, and found within the house a great garden, wherein he beheld pages and slaves and such things as existed not elsewhere save in the abodes of Kings and Sultans; and after that, there blew upon him the odour of delicious, exquisite viands, of all different kinds, and of delicious wine.

—From SINBAD.

On the night of 25 August most Australian officers in Bangkok were transferred to the Oriental Hotel and the adjacent building of the Hong Kong-Shanghai Bank. The latter had been Japanese kempi headquarters for Thailand, and next day I had the pleasure of sitting up drafting dispatches for the Press beside the dovecote on the Bank's roof where carrier pigeons had brought intelligence to the Nippon Gestapo.

Sitting in easy chairs on the lawn of the Oriental, watching the ever-changing river scene with its thousands of native craft of all sizes plying up and down stream, it seemed difficult to believe that less than two weeks before one had watched this same scene with the jaundiced eyes of the captive.

Norman Carter and I were most anxious to open up communications with London and Australia immediately. I had been sitting on what I felt was a tremendous story for three years and naturally was not anxious to be kept tied up in military red tape while scores of Allied correspondents poured in and picked up the story of the 60,000 Allied prisoners who had worked along the railway. Having been "in the bag" while dozens of other war correspondents were winning fame and fortune in many theatres, I had the journalist's craving to get my story out before it was scooped. The result was that the unfortunate senior officers were harassed by a series of urgent letters, as I sought to open up some line of communication.

On 27 August Dakota transport planes landed on the main Bangkok aerodrome with personnel and supplies for the "shadow" organization under Lieutenant-Colonel D. Cleagh, which had taken over effective control of the Thailand prisoners. These planes had orders not to return empty but to fly twenty or twenty-five prisoners back to Rangoon on each trip. Other planes landed on aerodromes in other parts of Thailand with similar instructions, so hundreds of P.O.W.s of all nationalities, regardless of rank, were rushed to the dromes to stand by against the arrival of transport.

On the morning of Wednesday the 29th Lieutenant-Colonel Ramsay, Australian C.O. at the Oriental, informed me that he had instructions to send me out to the aerodrome. Carter had already been notified the night before. Captain Gordon Fraser, a good friend of mine, stood down from the next party to let me go. The parties were being dispatched from the Bangkok godown, so we had to spend another night sleeping on the floor of that mosquito infested shed: but after many delays we were finally sent out to the aerodrome at noon next day. No more Dakotas arrived, however, until the following morning. Then, amidst the tremendous excitement of some 600 madly impatient P.O.W.s, including a number of Indians who had been in different camps in other parts of Siam, no fewer than twenty-seven planes swept in over the drome in rapid succession.

The night before we left we were entertained by Thai Air Force officers in their mess at the aerodrome. I was called away from this happy party by a message stating that a staff car was on its way to take Carter and me to Allied headquarters in Bangkok. We didn't like this at all, as it seemed that we were being recalled when just on the brink of release. However, the staff officer who arrived with the car soon reassured us, saying that Colonel Cleagh was anxious to put us in full possession of the facts about the take-over in Thailand before we flew out to contact the publicity authorities in India.

So that night, in the grotesquely roofed buildings which had been the Princes' Training College at Bangkok, we learned from Colonel Cleagh and his staff the full story of what had previously been merely hearsay and disconnected rumour.

The British authorities in Burma had been very worried by Japanese threats to massacre their prisoners if the Allied bombing of Japan continued. As a precautionary measure, Allied paratroops had been dropped in the vicinity of several of the camps in Thailand during July and early August. For some months the British had been in the closest touch with Thai agents and had a fairly accurate picture of the location of prisoners in Thailand. Unknown either to Japanese or to prisoners, paratroop officers had spent many hours within a few hundred yards of certain prison camps watching the comings and goings of guards and work parties.

These paratroop forces had been kept supplied from the air with food and with arms with which they equipped and trained a number of Thais. Plans were already complete for the seizure of certain camps at the first hint of a Japanese attempt to massacre prisoners.

The main gate and guard-house in each camp was to be attacked with hand-grenades, the guards tommy-gunned and the prisoners released. Zero hour had been fixed for a period between 18 and 28 August.

The paratroop forces were in constant communication with Allied headquarters through their field transmitting sets. Within a few days of the Japanese capitulation, Allied paratroop officers walked into a number of camps and calmly took over administration of the prisoners and control of the camps from the amazed Japanese. On 25 August Colonel Cleagh's "shadow" headquarters was established in Bangkok and, within a short time, was in wireless communication with British signallers in the fifteen main prison camps scattered throughout Thailand. British officers, accompanied by Japanese from Colonel Sugasawa's headquarters, were sent out from

Bangkok to all camps and, on Sugasawa's instructions, the local Japanese administrations accepted British orders without any trouble.

Immediately after the capitulation, Sugasawa, desperately anxious to save his own hide, had brought senior Allied P.O.W. officers to his own headquarters in Bangkok, and there had been little trouble since then. On one occasion some trucks which Colonel Cleagh had requested did not arrive on time. A note was immediately sent to Sugasawa asking if this was to be interpreted as a refusal to comply with Allied wishes. The Japanese trucks arrived within the next half-hour.

Up till the time when we left Bangkok there is no doubt that Japanese discipline in all matters concerning the hand-over had been faultless. Many Japanese officers and N.C.Os revealed in defeat a cringing servility only equalled by their arrogance and brutality while they had been on top.

The way in which the paratroop organization, designed for very different activities, suddenly took over the administration of the 30,000 prisoners in Thailand and began immediately to supply their needs of food, clothing, and medical supplies both by parachute from aircraft and by lorry from Bangkok, was one of the smoothest pieces of adaptation in this war.

At one camp, after capitulation, a body of prisoners was brought back to the camp by train. At the station one of the prisoners was struck in customary brutal fashion by a guard. A moment later a tall British paratroop strolled in with a tommy-gun. He beckoned the bewildered Japanese over to him saying, "Just a moment, little man", then stretched the bully on his back with a terrific left to the jaw. The Japanese made no attempt to seize his rifle or retaliate in any way.

Next morning we had breakfast in the European internees' mess in another part of the same grounds, and then were driven to the aerodrome by a paratroop major in his jeep, with which he had been landed at Bangkok a few days before.

About 2 o'clock that afternoon our Dakota, carrying twenty-five prisoners, took off from the aerodrome and a few minutes later we were flying back over the jungle where we had spent the past three years and where so many good friends and comrades now lie buried.

We came over the Irrawaddy about 4 o'clock and as we looked down at the docks where the *Mayebassi Maru* had lain three years before we could not help thinking what a much better place Rangoon was now than it had seemed after a fortnight in the hold of the Jap hellship.

The huge Rangoon aerodrome was covered with many hundreds of aircraft, ranging from great four-engined Liberators to tiny Moths. After tea at a reception centre we were speeded down to the 52nd I.G.H. where our particulars were taken and we were given beds in the hospital wards. So, tired but very happy, for the first time since leaving Singapore I put on a pair of pyjamas and crawled between clean sheets in a bed that seemed fantastically soft after forty-two months on bamboo slats or mother earth.

Next morning half a dozen friends whom I had not seen since the officers had been separated from other ranks came round to see me. I met Dave Manning and Bill Briscoe of *Perth* who had been with me in the Serang cinema and jail at the very beginning of it all. The transformation had come so rapidly that we couldn't quite take it in, and just sat on my bed sublimely happy, making remarks which were probably completely inane.

A few minutes later Group-Captain Bell, R.A.A.F., whom Colonel Cleagh had told me to contact, arrived. With him, to my amazement and delight, was my old friend Johnny from Singapore, now a full-blown major in charge of all broadcasting from Rangoon.

For the next three days Johnny was father, mother and fairy godmother to Norman and me. I'm afraid that we sadly interfered with his administration of the broadcasting unit. Although nominally on the roll of the hospital, we were never there between breakfast and bedtime, but divided our time between Johnny's headquarters and mess.

That afternoon I wrote a broadcast to be picked up by New Delhi for transmission to the B.B.C. and Australia. This was duly sent off and transcribed in New Delhi next afternoon.

Portions of it appeared in the London, Indian and Australian Press and on the night of 12 September I broadcast a similar script over the National Network in Australia.

I wanted some souvenirs of Burma and on the last afternoon we went shopping in a native village on the outskirts of the city. All textiles were fantastically dear, an ordinary lungyi or sarong costing 100 rupees or nearly £A10. I managed to get what Kipling calls "a whacking great cheroot", similar to those we had seen men, women, and even toddlers smoking in the Thanbyuzayat area, in exchange for an English Players' cigarette.

One of the biggest satisfactions was to sit down at Johnny's baby portable typewriter, a twin to the one I had been forced to abandon on the Singapore docks.

On the morning of the fourth, we were up and dressing before four o'clock and Johnny ran us out in his car to the aerodrome, where a Dakota was waiting to take us to Calcutta.

There was nearly a murder at the hospital before we left. Norman's early morning cup of tea means more to him than to anybody else I know, and on the preceding night he had been at infinite pains to arrange for a cup at four ack-emma. Unfortunately, the orderly took it to the wrong bed and aroused an English major who immediately gulped it down. Norman came up to me quite incoherent with fury damning and blasting the unfortunate major in no uncertain fashion. This gentleman then showed what seemed to me a strong tendency towards hara-kiri by invading our room with a flood of polite small talk, while I tried to keep all lethal weapons out of Norman's reach.

At the airfield we sat on the bonnet of Johnny's jeep eating R.A.F. iron rations and watching the pale Burmese dawn creep across the eastern sky, in a far happier frame of mind than I remember during hundreds of similar dawns.

Then we were soaring away again across the interminable expanse of padi field which seems to stretch with few breaks from Indo-China across to Bombay. Six hours after leaving Rangoon we came down at the Dum-dum airfield in Calcutta.

At Hungerford Street, headquarters of British Propaganda

in Calcutta, we were very kindly received and Major Seagrue called Government House and New Delhi on the phone in connexion with letters of introduction I was carrying from Group-Captain "Josh" Bell.

Then the major said, "There's someone here who's anxious to see you"—and who should walk in the door but Mavis Gully, of the Ministry of Economic Warfare, whom I had last seen at a party on the top of the Cathay during one of the big night air raids on Singapore at the end of January 1942. There and then Mavis took over the role which Johnny had laid down a few hours before.

At first she was so surprised to see us, whom she had long thought dead, that it gave me a first-hand insight into the reaction I can expect if I ever achieve resurrection. It was indeed an amazing coincidence that the first persons we met in Rangoon and Calcutta should have been ex-members of the staff in the Cathay.

After a long session of inquiries about mutual friends, we went off to a café where Norman and I filled ourselves with ice cream and chocolate cream cakes in complete disregard of all the medical advice that had been pumped into us. The nature of my weaning off rice should either kill me in the near future or cause our P.O.W. M.Os to eat their hats.

When we returned to Hungerford Street, we were told that the Governor of Bengal (the Right Honourable R. G. Casey) wished to see us at six-fifteen. R. G. Casey seemed to have altered little since I fought him across a tennis net at a Canberra tournament in January 1938, although in the meantime he had been Commonwealth Treasurer, first Australian Minister at Washington and U.K. Minister of State in the Middle East for the British Government. His onerous responsibilities during these hectic years may have added a powdering of grey to his hair, but he still has the finest presence of any representative the Commonwealth has sent abroad for many years.

"H.E." was most charming, but got a shock when he opened Bell's letter and found out that I was a son of one of his oldest friends. We were there and then told to move our gear into Government House forthwith. We protested that we had no presentable clothes, apart from what we stood up in, but the answer to that was that Sir Shenton Thomas, who had just been released from Singapore, had looked far worse, and anyhow clothes didn't matter at all.

So half an hour later the hall servants and khitmatgars of the House were appalled to find themselves confronted with old packs and bedrolls which would have been no advertisement for a swaggie. Shades of ambassadorial wardrobe trunks and the lavish baggage of our pukka sahib predecessors!

As I lay in the bath prepared by red turbaned servants in spotless robes so dazzlingly white as to hurt a P.O.W.'s eyes, I thought of all the baths I'd had out of buckets and bamboo containers, in jails, in filthy huts and on the edge of padi fields since I last lay in comfort in such a bathroom in Singapore.

Before dinner we met Sir Shenton Thomas, Captain Hughes, Private Secretary, and Pat Jarrett, Private Secretary to Mrs Casey, and formerly of the Melbourne *Herald*.

Sir Shenton Thomas had had a pretty thin time but as he said, "nothing like as bad as you fellows in Burma". At one stage, he told me he had bathed under a dock hose on the Singapore wharf while waiting shipment to Manchuria on one of the Japanese hellships. He must be the first Governor of the Straits Settlements who can lay claim to such a performance.

Mrs Casey sent us to bed early with strict injunctions about staying there for twelve hours. But when I got into the huge bed in the middle of the Wellesley suite, I was so comfortable that I didn't sleep at all well and was up writing at the crack of dawn.

I doubt whether many in their lifetimes ever pass with such rapidity from the squalor of the floor of a coolie hut to the magnificence and luxury of a Government House suite. Cinderella may have understood our feelings. At times Norman and I wanted to rub our eyes to make sure that we were not acting in some lavish drama based on the Arabian Nights.

Next day, thanks to the good offices of my friend, Ted Sayers, now Director-General of Information in New Delhi,

Norman and I received two months' pay, and of course with real money in our pockets for the first time in forty-three months we went out with Mavis on a shopping expedition, on which I bought everything from silver beer mugs to diaphanous female underwear.

That afternoon I had the pleasure of giving Mrs Emerson, wife of one of the Calcutta *Statesman's* sub-editors, first news of her husband, a friend of mine, at Kanburi. In the evening, after a wonderful dinner, the cup was filled to overflowing by the arrival of one of my father's C.S.I.R. men, Mr S. A. Clarke of the Forest Products Division, who had left Melbourne only a few days before and who brought news of my family.

Then I lay in bed reading Melbourne papers only a few weeks old with a delight which only fellow journalists will understand.

Norman and I got down to the main entrance by ten to eight next morning and at eight o'clock H.E. and Mrs Casey appeared. We then drove off through the streets in procession. After driving through Java, Singapore, Burma and Thailand packed like a sardine among fellow sardines in the back of Jap army trucks, Norman and I found ourselves in a huge saloon car preceded first by the Governor's car then by a carful of police with tommy-guns and revolvers, and followed by other cars carrying officials and pressmen. The occasion was a distribution of rice and cloth to some 18,000 of Calcutta's very poor. This had been arranged and made possible by the unsparing efforts of H.E. himself·

We stopped at four centres, at each of which thousands of Mohammedans and Hindus were waiting in long queues to receive their issue. This was a pound of rice and a *dhoti* for the men, or a *sari* for the women—consisting of five yards of cloth, or rather more than an entire family in Singapore received as its textile ration from the Japs for an eighteen months' period.

The women, who were in the great majority, proved a fascinating study—child-wives, toothless old harridans, widows and unmarried girls registering every phase of human expression; but the predominant note in the faces of all was an Oriental and almost unworldly patience and resignation. Some of them revealed delight at the gifts. Others would have skinned Al Capone at poker.

After Mrs Casey had fitted us out with shoes and other things which had been given to her for distribution to P.O.W.s and internees, we went off to Simpsons, a jeweller recommended by Mrs Casey, where Norman and I threw rupees around like confetti.

It is impossible to exaggerate the kindness with which we were overwhelmed by everybody in Calcutta. Pat Jarrett arranged air transport for us to Colombo through the High Commissioner's department in New Delhi and both she and Captain Hughes must have breathed a tremendous sigh of relief when we were finally safely on board the Colombo plane at dawn on 7 September.

All over the world I have found that Australians stick together, but I doubt whether any Australians have ever received as much kindness as Norman and I were met with by the Caseys, Pat, and Mavis of Calcutta.

We arrived at Colombo about five o'clock in the evening after an uneventful flight "over India's sunny plains". Personally, I felt that flight in a Dakota at 200 miles per hour was a vastly better method of travelling through India than the foot-slogging of Privates Mulvaney, Ortheris and Learoyd, but of course they had not been the guests of the Mikado for nearly four years and were probably never half so impatient to get home.

At Colombo we got a room in the annexe of the Galle Face Hotel and next day were booked to fly by Skymaster to Perth on the tenth. If there is anything better, after being cooped up in jungle prison camps, than the evening breeze and the sight of the big breakers rolling in from the Indian Ocean to crash on the foreshore by the Galle Face, I can not imagine it.

We had flown 4000 miles in the past week and now had every prospect of being in Melbourne in a matter of days. Things had happened so rapidly since we slept on the concrete floor of the godown at Bangkok on 29 August that I found myself battling hard to see things in perspective.

At Colombo we were kindly looked after by Sir John and Lady Talbot who fitted us out with Red Cross goods. We also met another member of the skeleton staff who carried on to the end with Singapore radio. This was Aubrey Herbert, now director of the Colombo Station. We had a delightful time with Aubrey and his wife on our last night before leaving for Australia. Norman and I had been intensely amused to find that another member of the M.B.C. staff had written a book called "Singapore Goes Off the Air" in which we featured prominently, if not always accurately. The publishers claimed on the cover that "the author reported the day-by-day advance of the Japanese army down the Malayan Peninsula". As I saw the script of all news bulletins and commentaries that went on the air in the last five weeks from Singapore, this statement surprised me considerably.

Our Skymaster, the biggest plane I have ever seen, took off and headed south-eastwards for the Cocos at 9 a.m. Monday, 10 September. We struck one bad storm which buffeted us about badly for perhaps ten minutes and recalled the hammering we had taken over the Timor Sea on our way to Singapore in a Qantas flying-boat. But this time we were not worried about being shot down on the flight as the Qantas boat ahead of us and another one behind had been shot down in January 1942.

My previous recollection of the Cocos was that sometimes when you went past in a mail-boat, you dropped a waterproof bag over the side a mile or so from the shore and watched a small rowing-boat put out to collect it. Now the place has become a major airport linking Australia to Asia and Europe. One of our fellow passengers had left London four days before, reaching Colombo only sixty hours after leaving Croydon.

We had dinner and a few drinks in a mess tent close to the magnificent wire strips laid down across the island. These strips can accommodate even the largest planes. Clearing for them has involved the cutting down of many hundreds of palm-trees for which, we were told, a royalty of £1 per tree is paid to the Clunies Ross family, who own the Cocos. At 9 o'clock that night the huge plane took off once more and we were on the last lap of our journey to Australia.

Just after daybreak next morning we began to come down and, as the sun rose, we caught our first glimpse of the Australian coastline through the clouds beneath us. Norman and I pummelled each other in the ribs like a couple of schoolboys. Walter Scott wasted his fulminations in "Breathes there a man . . ." as far as we were concerned.

We got into Perth about ten o'clock after Norman and I had had a bad scare when a uniformed woman doctor entered the plane at the aerodrome, closed the door firmly and proceeded to spray us with disinfectant. We thought this might be the first step to the quarantine station, and sat quiet as mice while she asked questions about papers. However, it all blew over and, tremendously relieved, we found ourselves once again in the streets of Perth thinking, "Thank God, not a blanky thing has changed at all."

From the post-office, with the kind co-operation of the trunk-lines people, I got a call through to my father's office in Melbourne in something under six minutes. That was one of the moments that one won't forget.

After we had wired and phoned for an hour we went down to the Esplanade Hotel. There they looked after us as if we were members of the family and when we left in the evening refused absolutely to offer us any bill. During the day we got in touch with the wives and mothers of a number of fellow P.O.W.s and passed on news of their safety and health. I also saw Mr C. P. Smith, managing editor of the *West Australian* and dictated a 1700 word interview which was published next day throughout the Commonwealth. I had a few minutes with an old friend, Professor Walter Murdoch, Chancellor of the University and author of my grandfather's biography, and as usual received some very sound advice.

Soon after dark we were climbing aloft again in the same Skymaster but with a different crew, heading this time for Sydney. We came down at Mascot just after six next morning and the first person I saw was my aunt, Elsie Rivett. Thanks to the good offices of certain Air Force personnel, Norman and I were put aboard a Dakota which should have left an hour before. Before we left Sydney I had time to ring the mother of my pal Don Capron and give her last-minute news of him. Then, after thrusting a few scribbled messages and addresses into my aunt's hand, we were off again on the last stage. My aunt rushed to the Sydney post-office and wired the family that I was already heading for Melbourne, hours ahead of schedule.

It was just after ten o'clock when we saw the sprawling mass of Melbourne's roofs through the plane window, and then the door was opened and I tumbled down the ladder and across the drome towards the sheds. As I did so a man came out of the reception office and I recognized my father. Then mother and Gwyth came running out of the office and I realized that it hadn't really been a dream from the Arabian Nights after all.

GOOD-BYE TO ALL THAT

Most of us will try to forget as quickly as possible.

Remembering the thousands of our comrades who will never return from Japanese captivity, and knowing the intentions and mentality of our captors, there is no doubt that we have been immensely fortunate to come out alive.

When our minds go back to these years which stretch like a deep abyss across the plateau of our lives, we will tend to think of the brighter side. The heavy pall of uncertainty and oppression has been rent aside. Yet, now and then, a word, a sound or a meeting with old friends will arouse memories.

Again the great yellow Burma moon will drench the jungle with its light; the midday sun after tropic rain will make the matted vegetation steam like a Turkish bath; again we will feel the icy fingers of the November monsoon clutching at our thin half-starved bodies clad in rags, the sweeping, sighing rustle as the rains drove across the jungles towards us; we will catch the throbbing of the drums and tom-toms and the high howling of the dogs from some native village, the confused hammering of the rains on attap roofs, the protesting creak of ox-cart wheels lurching along the rutted road; and once more we will hear the poignant notes of "The Last Post" as it rang out across the little jungle cemeteries each time one of our mates was laid to rest.

These things have been a part of our lives.

We will never quite forget.

APPENDIX

APPENDIX

P.O.W. GLOSSARY

In every camp throughout the world, slang and service jargon played a big part in nearly all conversations. But in the P.O.W. camps we had a fusion of army, navy and air force slang from representatives of Australia, Britain, the United States and the N.E.I. Superimposed on this were all the words we acquired from the local vernaculars of Java, Malaya, India, the Middle East, Burma and Siam. Then we had to learn certain words in Japanese, and we adopted a number of pidgin English or dog-English expressions used by our guards. In one sentence it was not uncommon to hear a man use a Hindu word acquired in service in India, a Malay word picked up in Singapore, a Jap P.O.W. term and some service slang. Many of the terms will perish with the ending of our captivity; others will produce only an uncomprehending stare when we come out with them at home. But for three and a half years they were in our ears daily. Here is a collection of a few of them. It does not pretend to be complete. I have left out many hundreds of slang words widely used during the war in the English-speaking communities. But most of these expressions acquired almost an international flavour in the prison camps. They might serve as a basis for compilation of a guide to "P.O.W.-ese"—the lingua franca of the Jap prison camps.

If a word were largely confined to one area or service before we became prisoners, I have in some instances indicated that source. The Japanese and other Asiatic words as well as the Dutch are mainly anglicized and phonetic versions. Some words taken from Asiatic tongues were doubtless completely misused in camp parlance.

J=Japanese (P.O.W. version) or word used by the Japanese; D= Dutch; M=Malay; A=Army; N=Navy; H=Hindu; B=Burmese; S=Siamese.

Adge, adjutant.

Agents (I have my —), there are ways of getting things.

Air raid red (N), Jap guards in hut.

Air raid yellow (N), Jap guards approaching.

All mens (J), everybody.

Ananas (M), pineapple.

Antreger! (D), on parade! (Corruption of *aan het 't regel*)

Arigato (J), thank you.

Arimasen (J), all right.

Ayah (M), water.

Ayah Minim (M), drinking water.

backup, second helping.

Backup king, man always chasing second helpings.

Bad house, cell, prison.

Bagus (M), good.

Baht, Thai dollar.

Bali (Java), bamboo platform.

Bamboo-and-attap, Japanese aircraft.

Bamboo rattler, man who disturbs neighbours by his movements on the bali.

Banga, bag and poles for carrying dirt.

Banjo, (J), latrine.

Banjo bottle, Dutch toilet necessity.

Banya Bagus (M), very good.

Bash artist, guard always beating up P.O.W.s.

Beat it up, make whoopee.

Beokee (J), sick, sick man.

Beokee house, hospital.

Besar (M), big, important.

Bible basher, padre, priest.

Big fellows, Liberators or other 4-engined Allied bombers.

Bimbo, batman.

Birdie, secret radio.

Bite, ask for, borrow.

Blazer rade, razor blade.

Blue, a row, trouble.

Blue (the), show, fight, battle.

Blue Danube, P.O.W. "stew" with ketju ichang.

Blue Orchids (A), army chaffing for air force.

Bomb happy, especially nervous about bombing.

Boof head, one with a big head.

Boong, any Asiatic or coloured person.

Boong brandy, native spirit.

Boongs with boots on, Japs.

Boxing presento, Jap term for a punch or beating.

Braid (to pull —) (R.A.A.F.), to invoke superior rank.

Brig, prison, cell.

Bronze gods, A.I.F. 8th Division. Term was used by a woman journalist visiting Malaya, and subsequently derisively.

Bronzie, member of the 8th Division. Used by officers to indicate other ranks, by British to indicate Australians.

Brothel of a place, poor place.

Browned off, fed up, weary.

Bug (the), fever.

Buggero! (J), swearword.

Bullshartist, great talker of nonsense, a garrulous person.

Bumf, paper of any kind.

Bumfluff, a small or poorly grown moustache.

Buppin (J), works department.

Buppin kakari (J), works officer.

Burma apple, vegetable somewhere between a potato and an apple.

Burma bowler, bamboo hat, bowler-shaped.

Burma spinach, native vegetable.

Burned out, finished, without reserves.

Burnt off, fed-up, furious.

Cafe panas (M), hot coffee.

Cart, (in the —), in trouble, facing trouble.

Cat house, brothel.

Cattie (M), about 1¼ lb.

Chai (H), tea.

Changey changey (J), exchange.

Changi major, someone promoted to field rank on or after 15/2/42.

Chapattie, native pancake.

Chat, (to —), to delouse.

Chat happy, weary of delousing clothes, etc.

Chee chee (J), interpreter.

Cheese eater, Dutchman.

Cheesed off, browned off.

Chicken feed, weed served in stew.

Chicky, girl.

Chiefs, (N), chief petty officers.

Chinese cabbage, a native vegetable (Siam).

Chips (N), carpenter.

Chui (J), lieutenant.

Chunkel (D), native hoe, mattock.
Chusa (J), colonel.
Chotapeg (H), whisky and soda.
Clomper, wooden clog, typical P.O.W. footwear.
Coco-nut oiler, Jap aircraft.
Coffee king, man with large business, probably employing other P.O.W.s making and selling hot coffee—often "ersatz".
College of colonels, senior officers' gathering.
Conyero (J), swearword.
Crabs, *(draw the—)*, attract bombers and bombs.

Daffodils (A), air force personnel.
Dahl, native peas.
Death house, dysentery or other hospital hut with high mortality.
Deknackered, emasculated.
Dhobie (M), washing.
Dicky-bird, secret radio.
Do, *(to —)*, to punish.
Dog's disease, malaria.
Doings, news, secret radio bulletins.
Doovah, a rice cake or "extra", radio news.
Dope, radio news.

Ear basher, one who talks too much.
Ear bashing, a long harangue.
Eat-a-harlot! Australian corruption of Dutch mess call *Ete(n) hale(n)*. Come and get it!
Eechee (J), one.
Eechee, nee, san (J), one, two, three.
Ejo Arimasen (J), everything correct.
E Joe 'Arry Mason, Australian version of above.
Extra, a cake, rissole or other addition to a meal apart from rice and soup.

F.A. *(sweet —)*, nothing at all, nil.
Face fungus, beard.
Fanny Adams, nothing at all, nil.
Few shin bones, Australian version of *foo she bun*.

Flap, anxiety, confusion.
Flog, sell, exchange for food (usually gear, clothing).
Fly spot, officer's pip.
Foo she bun (J), sentry, picket.
Form, news, situation, position.
For the high jump, sentenced to death.
Funk hole, slit-trench, shell slit.

Gash, extra, second helping.
Gink, term of abuse.
Go (J), five.
Go bush, take to the jungle.
Gold braid, rank.
Good guts, news, information, secret radio news.
Go through, leave.
Go through on, take something away from, steal.
Gott verdikke! (D), exclamation.
Gott verdommer! (D) oath.
Grass, jungle leaves put into soup.
Greveller, a try-on.
Griff, news, radio news.
Growter *(on the—)*, putting something over.
G-string, loin cloth.
Gula (M), sugar.
Gunso (J), sergeant.
Gurr (B), liquid molasses.

Had it, finished, ruined.
Hag's bush, tobacco.
Haku (J), hundred.
Hank, cattie, roll, section of native tobacco.
Hathi, elephant.
Heads (N), latrine.
Heat, light for a smoke.
Hen fruit, eggs.
Hot cock, nonsense, boasting, vain talk.
How is it possible? expression overused by Dutch and used by other P.O.W.s to signify Dutch.
Hurry hurry (J), hasten! be quick!
Hut 4, see "Imperial War Museum".

Ignition, a light for a cigarette.

Ikan (M), fish.

Imperial War Museum, Hut 4, Kanburi camp, occupied by senior British officers.

Impi (J) tool.

Impi house, tool house.

Impi shoko, O.C. toolshed.

Insert the plunger (bridge), to double.

In the red, credit.

Itch, tinea and other forms of dermatitis.

Ivories, dice.

Jalan (M), far, farther, a distance.

Jap happy, somebody unduly afraid of or subservient to the Japanese.

Jappy, as above.

Jen (R.A.F.), news, information.

Jiggy jig (J), sexual intercourse.

Jumped (to be —) (R.A.A.F.), to be attacked.

Jungle leaves, any herb or leaf added to stew.

Jungle spinach, type of jungle leaf.

Kakaricho (J), commander, C.O.

Kampong (M), hut, group of huts.

Kang Kong (S), vegetable which grows like a creeper, leaves edible.

Kasira Hidari (J), eyes left!

Kasira Migi (J), eyes right!

Kasira Nakka (J), eyes on officer taking salute.

Kempi (J), military police, Gestapo.

Ketchang iju, small peas like peppercorn.

Kipper, Englishman.

Kiri (J), salute! bow! hail!

Kitchi (M), small, little.

Kiwotski (J), attention.

Ku (J), nine.

Kumicho (J), officer in charge of a kumi.

Kurra (J), stop! what! come here! I say! now then!

Kwali (M), cooking dish, often shaped like a bowler hat.

Lagi (M), more, further.

Lalang, long grass, scrub.

Lampang, a measure of quantity in grain or tobacco—about a cattie.

Lao, native wine or toddy.

Latrine buzz, any wild improbable rumour.

Lats, latrines.

Lily root, Burma root which proved poisonous.

Limey (U.S.), Englishman.

Little yellow b——s, the normal term for Japanese.

Lungyi (B), sarong, main feature of Burmese costume.

Mac mac (Java), sexual intercourse.

Macan (M), food, mealtime, provisions.

Macan up! Come and eat!

Mad as a maggot, particularly crazy.

Mad mick, pick.

Mae (J), men.

Mafeesh, it doesn't matter (from Middle East).

Marrstar (S), small candy made of peanuts and native sugar.

Matelot (N), sailor.

Mazuma (J), money, cash, dollars.

Means (the —), the material for making a cigarette.

Millipede, Burmese worm-like creature with innumerable legs.

Mind your backs please! get out of the way, clear a path.

Mishi (J), food, meal.

Mishi boo (B), finished, all over, none left, disappeared.

Monty, a certainty, safe thing.

Mooblah, pancake made from rice flour.

Mulga, the surrounding jungle.

Mutta mutta birds, aircraft, Allied bombers.

Nanda? (J), what goes on? how? what's that?

Natter (N), to converse, chatter.

Nauri (J), as you were.

Nasi goreng (M), fried rice.

Nasi Tim (M), mess of rice, with minced vegetables, liver, kidney, brain, well boiled for sick, particularly dysentery cases.

Nee (J), two.

Nightingale, radio news, secret radio.

Nogoodenah (J), not good, bad, very bad.

No good house, prison, cell.

No good kah? no good? is it useless?

No second prizes, you are only copying.

Number 1 (J), very good, the best.

Offal eater, Dutchman.

Oil, news, information.

Olds and bolds, older officers, usually in cushioned jobs.

On the nose, ill-smelling, unsavoury, suggestive of dishonesty.

Ooloo, jungle, scrub.

Op de plaats! (D), on the spot!

Orderly dog, orderly officer.

Organize (A), obtain, steal, scrounge, acquire.

Over the fence, outside the camp. Particularly of sales of clothing, trading.

Over the wire, as above.

Padang (M), open field.

Padi (M), rice.

Panas, hot.

Pango! number, count off!

Pap, soft, mushy boiled rice.

Papahler! Australian corruption of Dutch mess call.

Pap Halen, Hale(n) (D), come and get your pap. Mess call.

Parang (M), heavy knife.

Peanut basher, one who pounded peanuts in a mortar to make "peanut butter" for canteen.

Peanut coffee, drink made with burnt peanut kernels.

Peanut star, peanuts set in congealed sugar.

Peter, cell, prison.

Pigi (M), go, get out, scram!

Pinhead, one with a small head.

Pips (to pull the —), to make use of superior rank outside normal routine.

Pisang (M), bananas.

Pisang goreng, fried bananas.

Pissaphone, bamboo urinal.

Prang (R.A.A.F.), to destroy, ruin, bomb, attack.

P.R.I. (British), canteen.

Puff puff macan (J), wood cut for use as locomotive fuel.

Racketeer, one engaged in buying, exchanging or dealing inside or outside the camp, particularly salesmen of various food and drink.

Rackets, ways of making money without working.

Radish water, "stew" made of hot water, white radish and pepper (perhaps).

Rank (to pull —), to use one's rank to get something.

Raw prawn, something far-fetched, difficult to swallow, absurd.

Rechts Rusten (D), right dress!

Rice coffee, cooked or uncooked rice burnt on dry pan produced a drink when hot water was poured over it; but it was very "ersatz" coffee.

Rice happy, one who has had too much rice.

Roku, (J), six.

Rock, shake, surprise, amaze.

Rotate, as above.

Rupes, Thai dollars, rupees, etc.

Ryoshu kakari (J), kitchen department.

Salaamat (M), hail, good-bye.

Sambal (D), condiment usually made with chilis and sharp-tasting vegetable to help consumption of rice.

Sambal badjak, variety of sambal.

Sambal deler, as above.